Restless Empire

A HISTORICAL ATLAS OF RUSSIA

IAN BARNES

With an Introduction by

DOMINIC LIEVEN

THE BELKNAP PRESS *of* HARVARD UNIVERSITY PRESS

Cambridge, Massachusetts, and London, England

2015

Library of Congress Cataloging-in-Publication Data

Barnes, Ian, 1946 – author.
Restless Empire : a historical atlas of Russia. / Ian Barnes; with an introduction by
Dominic Lieven.
pages cm
"Copyright © 2015 Historia Publishing Limited."

Includes bibliographical references and index.
ISBN 978-0-674-50467-7 (alk. paper)
    1. Russia—Historical geography—Maps. 2. Soviet Union—Historical geography—
Maps. 3. Russia—History—Maps. 4. Soviet Union—History—Maps.
    I. Lieven, D. C. B. , writer of introduction. II. Title. III. Title: Historical atlas of
Russia

G2111.S1B3 2015
911'.47—dc23
2014039894

Contents

PREFACE

When assessing Russian history, a historian must come to terms with the sheer size and diversity of this huge country—diversity in land-type, resources, peoples, and problems. Subjected to much stereotyping and derogatory comment, Russia needs to be understood in its own terms. This Preface seeks to examine some key themes and issues that have constrained Russia's inhabitants to behave in certain ways.

One historian, B. H. Sumner, likens Russian expansionism to America's move westward. The Slavs seem to originate from the Vistula and Pripet marsh regions and the upper reaches of the Bug and Dniester rivers. Expanding in every direction, they divided by the sixth century into: the Western Slavs (Poles, Czechs, Slovaks, Moravians); the Southern Slavs (Bulgarians, Serbs, Croats, Slovenes); and the Eastern Slavs (Great Russians, White Russians, Ukrainians). Over time, the Russians have settled along rivers and river portages, and agriculture tended to follow the hunters and adventurers. The advancing Slav tide was always meeting new peoples, conquering them or being halted, as was the case with the steppe peoples. Following Sumner's analogy, the Russian and the American agriculturalists moved forward fighting the forest-living hunter-gatherers and the plains and steppe nomads. Americans conquered their grasslands and turned the land over to the plough with a furious pace of exploitation, which ultimately caused severe erosion, such as in the Oklahoma dust bowl. The Russians surged at a slower pace and used little agricultural machinery and the land was less damaged. It was not until much later, during Stalin's collectivization of agriculture and Khrushchev's Virgin Lands Campaign (1950s) that the soil was exploited and destroyed.

The American historian Frederick Jackson Turner suggests that the expansion and development of frontier and settler societies impact upon economics, politics, and people's characters. One must remember that whereas America is approximately 2,500 miles wide, Russia is nearly 6,000 miles with an area two and a half times the size of the United States. The size and the difficulty in controlling and administering such vast tracts of land at a much earlier period of Russian history, compared to the later period of American expansion, might explain Russian political development and its harshness; authoritarian, despotic, and autocratic characteristics grew well before Britain and America created liberal democracies. Before territorial expansion really began under Ivan III and Ivan IV, the Slavs were confined to forest lands by well organized nomads such as the Scythians, Khazars, Polovtsy, and Tatars. Political and social survival depended upon certain political formations of a feudal, warrior band mentality designed to combat the enemy. In this environment, the Principality of Muscovy grew and finally burst out of its forest constraints and moved into the steppe in the sixteenth century.

The condition of the Russian peoples has been affected by major communication problems that have driven Russian leaders into a continuous search for the development of trade links and defensible frontiers. The Russian land mass is surrounded by five seas—the Baltic, the Black, the Arctic, the Caspian, and the Pacific. The interior is drained by several river systems: the Ob-Irtysh in western Siberia; the Onon–Shilka–Amur, which flows into the Pacific and forms part of the Russo-Chinese border; the Volga; the Yenesei; and the Lena. All of these are wholly or partially icebound in winter, as are the seas. Access to the latter has been fought over by many other people: Turks, Poles, Danes, Swedes, Germans, Tatars, Chinese, and Japanese. A major theme in Russian history has been pushing the frontier ever onwards. The waterways linking the Baltic to the Black and Caspian Seas, such as the Dnieper, Volga, Dvina, and Oka, were especially important during the Kievan and medieval periods, as they included trading posts and towns. The founding of the White Sea port, Archangel, in 1584, was prompted by the desire for a Baltic port, which was blocked by Russia's enemies. Western weapons, skilled artisans, and military technical aid were essential. Ivan IV commenced the search for a Baltic outlet in the Livonian War (1558–83), a policy successfully completed by Peter the Great in 1721. The construction of St. Petersburg as a gateway to the Baltic introduced a new security issue for Russia. Whoever controls the southern coast of Finland and the coast of Estonia threatens the sea lanes to the capital. Finland became independent in 1917 and Estonia in 1991—a potentially ominous state of affairs.

The Black Sea frontier was achieved between 1676 and 1812 during thirty years of intermittent warfare between these dates. The final defeat of Turkey meant that Russia could dominate the Black Sea steppes and build naval bases in the Crimea. Freedom to navigate the Straits of Constantinople was essential for access to the Mediterranean in order to trade and to project naval power, as Russia did during the Napoleonic wars. Russia also became geographically nearer to fellow Orthodox Christians in the Balkans and Russia occasionally took their interests to heart, especially in Serbia, Montenegro, and Bulgaria. Murder in Sarajevo brought Russia into the First World War, and, later, conflict in Bosnia produced a conundrum for Yeltsin's foreign policy. Would an alliance with the West take precedence over Russia's traditional great power policy in the Balkans, which is based upon ideas of pan-Slavism and a common perception of religion and ethnicity? Ultimately, American diplomatic power resulted in the Dayton Peace Accords in November 1995, which over-shadowed and diminished the role of all European powers and Russia too.

The Russian Pacific frontier was reached rapidly during the sixteenth and seventeenth centuries after the Cossack leader Yermak initiated the eastward movement. Fuelled by flight from the excesses of Ivan IV, farmers and Cossacks moved into the Yenesei, Lena, and Amur River valleys in a constant search for land and minerals and sites for settlement such as Okhotsk on the coast, founded in 1649. Swift eastwards conquest was aided by the fragmented tribal nature of the indigenous Siberian peoples, their small numbers, and superior Russian weapons technology. Despite early Pacific settlements, Russia was confined by China to icebound coasts. After Britain and France opened up China by war in the 1840s, Russia feared their expansion throughout the Orient. Accordingly, Governor-General Nicholas Muraviev of Siberia prevented this scenario by seizing all Chinese territory north of the Amur River in 1858, then grabbed lands east of the Ussuri and founded the warm-water port of Vladivostok, which soon became the Russian Pacific naval base. When the Trans-Siberian railway was built, eastern Siberia and Vladivostok could be fully developed.

The Caspian Sea was essential for the Russian conquest and control of the Caucasus, finally achieved in 1878. These wars introduced Russia to the internecine strife between its inhabitants and to the important Baku oilfields. The acquisition of independence by Georgia, Armenia, and Azerbaijan in 1991 carried on old traditions of fighting between the last two states over the issue of Nagorno-Karabakh. This Caucasian dispute in the "near abroad" has drawn in Russian troops as part of the Commonwealth of Independent States peacekeeping forces. Also, the bloodbath of the Chechen war mirrors the difficulties Russia had with Shamil in the nineteenth century.

The growth of Russia meant that the settlers confronted more and more peoples. Nevertheless, non-Russians are a small minority in Russia. Traditionally, non-Russians have been assimilated, dispossessed, or surrounded, creating islands of linguistic difference. Only two areas have been, and remain, strongly non-Russian: the Caucasus, whose peoples, Armenians, Azeris, and Georgians amongst others, were finally defeated in 1878; and central Asia, where various mainly Turkic speaking peoples, such as Uzbeks and Kazaks, continued the traditions of their Tatar predecessors. Elsewhere, Finns and Poles have comprised solid linguistic blocs under Russian control. Under Soviet rule, the USSR comprised the Russian Soviet Federated Socialist Republic plus 14 other republics: Estonia, Latvia, Lithuania, Belorussia, the Ukraine, Moldavia, Georgia, Armenia, Azerbaijan, and the Turkmen, Uzbek, Tadzhik, Kirgiz, and Kazakh republics. Within these republics lived other ethnic groups with autonomous status. Their numbers determined whether they were granted an Autonomous Soviet Socialist Republic (ASSR), an

Autonomous Oblast (AO), or National Okrug (NO). To confuse matters further, the Yakut ASSR in Siberia has a majority of Russians while the Dagestan ASSR is inhabited by at least twenty nationalities. Complexity bedevilled the system, and some nationalities, such as Koreans, Poles, Bulgarians, Greeks, and Gypsies, had no ethnic area and hence no administrative status. In sum, about 75 percent of the population spoke a Slav language followed by one-eighth speaking a Turkic tongue. However, all ethnic groups needed to speak Russian before the USSR collapsed to help pursue career opportunities and to communicate widely. The breakdown of the Soviet Union and the creation of the Commonwealth of Independent States (CIS) has seen some ethnic minorities, such as the Tatars, Bashkirs, and Chechens, demanding fully independent states.

Other reversals of fortune are taking place. Russia's birth and fertility rates are decreasing at an accelerating rate. The birth rate has nearly halved, and the total fertility rate has fallen from 2.1 children born per woman in the late 1980s to 1.4 in 1996. To compound demographic problems the death rate was increased by 55 percent during the same period and life expectancy declined from 63 to 60 years overall. With men the decline was from 64 to 56 years, and for women, 73 to 70 years. This means that between 1989 and 1995 the country's population decreased; migration exacerbated this trend. According to some analysts, men are affected by smoking and alcohol consumption and stress occasioned by changes in the economy with marketization and increasing unemployment rates. The problem particularly affects the poor, who are the least able to use the "black economy." This social situation has worsened; people are subject to pollution, cutbacks in state medical services and resources, a deficient diet, and growth in preventable diseases such as diphtheria and tuberculosis as well as bronchial asthma and other respiratory diseases, dysentery, and typhoid.

Russia possesses the greatest reserves of mineral resources in the world. Energy supplies are vast, with extensive coal fields (second largest in the world) throughout Russia with the largest in the Donbass and huge quantities east of the Yenesei River in Siberia and also in the Lena River basin. Oil is found in western Siberia and the Volga-Ural region, giving Russia the eighth largest reserves in the world; other reserves exist near the Black Sea and in the Bashkir Republic, which is also plentiful in natural gas. The world's largest gas reserves are in Russia and are situated near Kazakhstan, Turkmenistan, and in the Komi Republic, part of the Russian Federation. Metals are abundant and extensive gold reserves exist in the Sakha (Yakutia) Republic.

Russia has always found it hard to develop economically and in an appropriate fashion. Hence, Russia has been concerned with its resources and their extraction, but whenever Russia builds industry it has shown scant interest in environmental implications. Despite the collapse of the Soviet Union from imperial overstretch when its resources failed to match its interests, Russia remains a potentially powerful state with huge resources. Furthermore, the problems of a new market economy with unemployment, low wages, and declining social welfare will never detract from the fact that eventually appropriate planning and investment should release the enormous latent energy in the Russian economy.

The environment is an issue that is mirrored in the West, but Russia is having to contend with the political process of mediating numerous green lobbying organizations. Despite Russia possessing vast quantities of untouched tundra and forest, in Soviet times the country constantly suffered from depredation caused by Five-Year Plans concerned with heavy and defense industries and with agricultural problems stemming from Stalinist collectivization and Khrushchev's Virgin Lands Campaign. Other dangers emanate from general air, water, and soil pollution, badly constructed nuclear power plants, and decommissioned nuclear submarines such as those sunk in shallow sea waters around Novaya Zemlya.

Agricultural techniques with thoughtless use of fertilizers and pesticides have contaminated rivers and catchment areas. Together with industrial effluent and poorly treated sewage, many rivers are in a critical condition with rising levels of infections, such as typhoid caused by foul drinking water supplies. The Black Sea's marine life is dying while the Caspian Sea is polluted by sewage and oil spills. Recently, it has been noticed that irrigation for the cotton industry in Turkmenistan has raised water levels so high that the archaeological sites of the ancient cities of Merv on the Silk Road are having their walls undermined. Fortunately, Lake Baikal, the world's largest fresh water lake, has been protected to some extent, with controls on the Baikalsk pulp and paper plant, and was made into a national park in 1992 and a World Heritage site in 1996. In 1989, despite pressures from Greenpeace and other environmental lobbyists, there remains a tension between income generation and employment and conservation. Wildlife is under threat with the destruction of habitats, the over-fishing of sturgeon, hunting, and poaching. Some animal products reach the Chinese market to make traditional medicines. Some hope lies in the opening of two more World Heritage sites in the virgin Komi Forest (Urals) and the Kamchatka peninsula. Environmental awareness is increasing, but the Russian state faces the financing of conservation areas, and the need to respond to Russian environmentalists on one hand while facing powerful business interests on the other.

Russia is faced with the necessity of transforming the highly specialized economic regionalism of the USSR. The breakup of the Soviet Union means that each successor republic has an unbalanced economy; for example, the Donbass coalminers used pit props grown in the Baltic state forests and the major truck factories are in Belarus. Such fragmentation requires rationalization. Reform takes place slowly in a society constrained by the legacy of communist economic conservatism. The shock therapy of the market has generated opposition from those convinced that Russia lacked an infrastructure suitable for workable reform and was paralyzed by monopolistic economic practices. However, partial success has shown that the command economy is forever relegated to the past as is the history of mismanagement, maladministration, failed modernization, and inadequate investment. Yet economic downturns can occur; the outcome of the devaluation of the rouble in August 1998 saw stability and stagnation. Some degree of stabilization occurred in the first decade of the twenty-first century, and it seems likely that Russia can stumble into the future, assuming the avoidance of foreign wars or more violence, such as the Chechen fiasco, or the further escalation of the conflict in Urkraine. Substantial Russian minorities in independent former USSR states are also proving challenging. In March 2014, when President Yanukovych of Ukraine was deposed following popular protests, Russia annexed the Crimean region, which has a large population of Russian-speakers, following a referendum, and unrest in eastern Ukraine continues.

Ian Barnes
England, August 2014

It is with great regret that we announce the death of the author, Dr. Ian Barnes, in November 2014, shortly before the completion of this work. With the encouragement and approval of his family and the publisher, the production team, working under the guidance of Professor Dominic Lieven, completed the work.

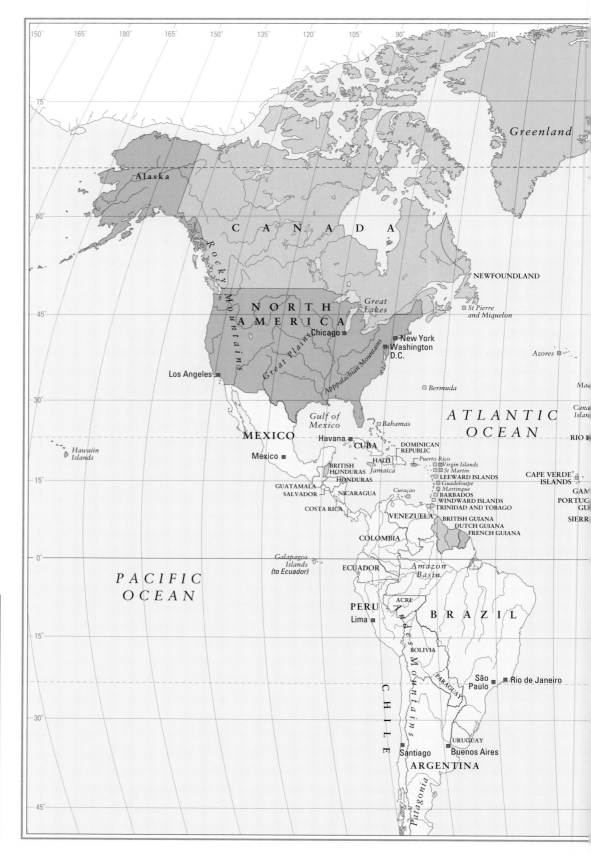

The World in 1900

■   Major city

    Russian possessions

    British possessions

    French possessions

    German possessions

    Italian possessions

    Portuguese possessions

    Spanish possessions

    United States possessions

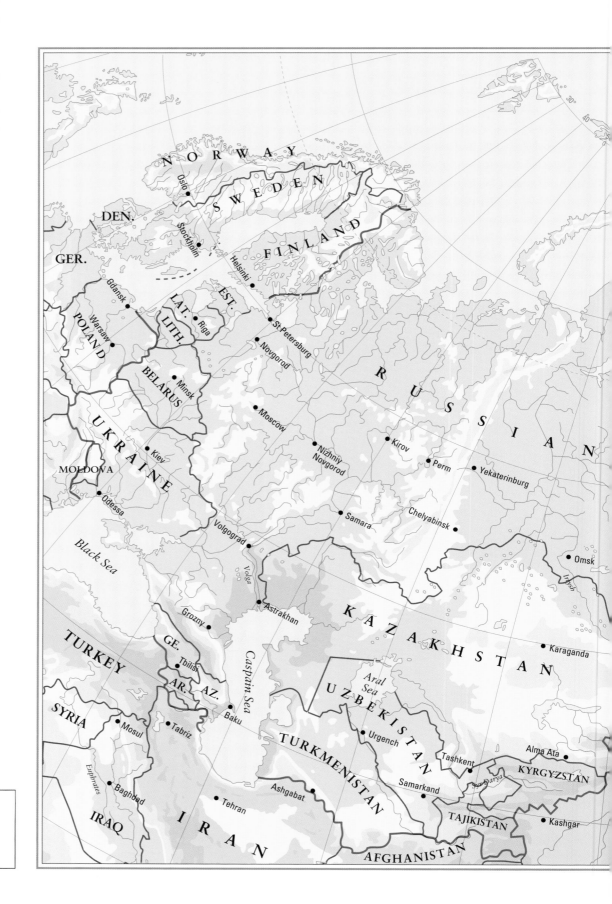

**Russian Federation
—Physical**

Former boundary of
USSR to 1991

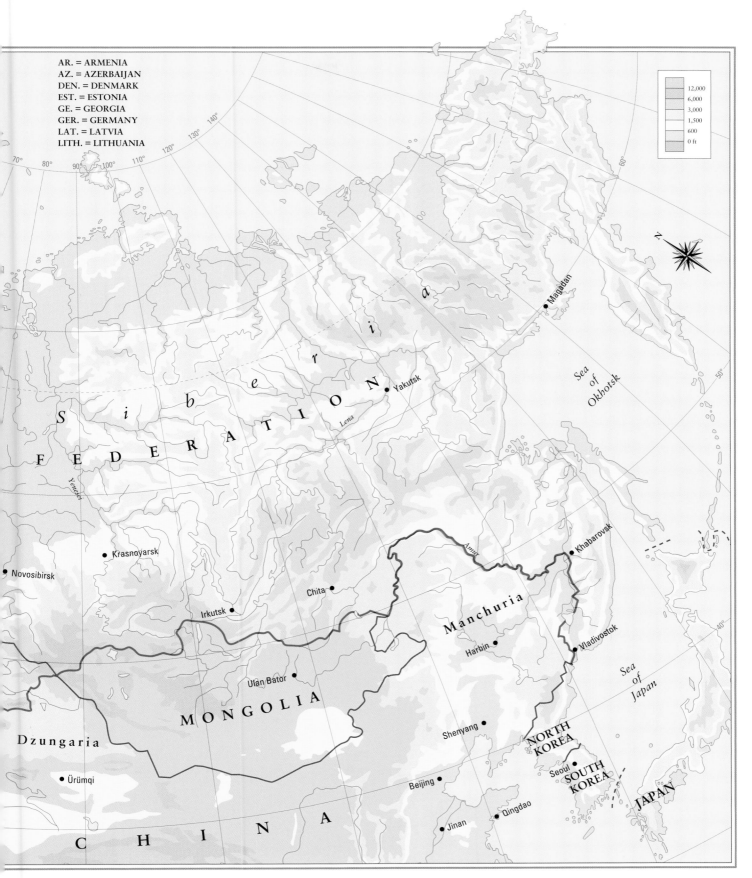

AR. = ARMENIA
AZ. = AZERBAIJAN
DEN. = DENMARK
EST. = ESTONIA
GE. = GEORGIA
GER. = GERMANY
LAT. = LATVIA
LITH. = LITHUANIA

12,000
6,000
3,000
1,500
600
0 ft

Siberia

FEDERATION

Yakutsk

Lena

Yenisei

Magadan

Sea of Okhotsk

Krasnoyarsk

Novosibirsk

Chita

Irkutsk

Amur

Khabarovsk

Manchuria

Harbin

Vladivostok

Ulan Bator

MONGOLIA

Sea of Japan

Dzungaria

Shenyang

NORTH KOREA

Ürümqi

Beijing

Seoul

SOUTH KOREA

JAPAN

CHINA

Jinan

Qingdao

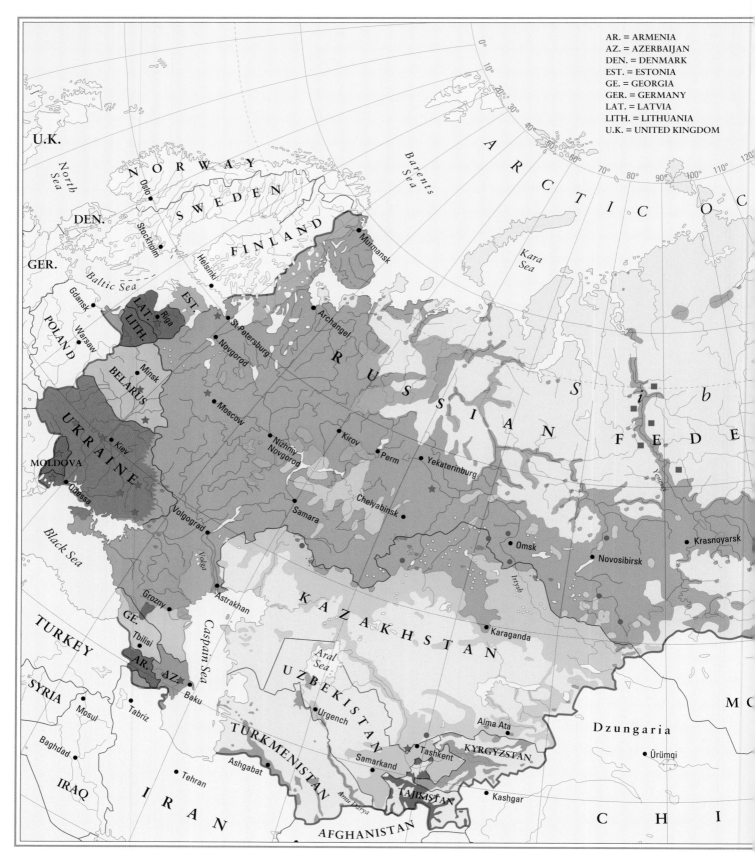

AR. = ARMENIA
AZ. = AZERBAIJAN
DEN. = DENMARK
EST. = ESTONIA
GE. = GEORGIA
GER. = GERMANY
LAT. = LATVIA
LITH. = LITHUANIA
U.K. = UNITED KINGDOM

U.K.

North Sea

DEN.

GER.

NORWAY

SWEDEN

FINLAND

Oslo

Stockholm

Helsinki

Baltic Sea

Gdansk

Warsaw

POLAND

LAT.
LITH.
EST.

Riga

Minsk

BELARUS

UKRAINE

Kiev

MOLDOVA

Odessa

Black Sea

St. Petersburg

Novgorod

Moscow

Volgograd

Volga

Grozny

Astrakhan

GE.

Tbilisi

AR.
AZ.

Baku

TURKEY

SYRIA

Mosul

Tabriz

Caspian Sea

Baghdad

IRAQ

IRAN

Tehran

Ashgabat

TURKMENISTAN

Amu Darya

AFGHANISTAN

Barents Sea

ARCTIC

Murmansk

Archangel

Kara Sea

OC

RUSSIAN

Nizhniy Novgorod

Kirov

Perm

Yekaterinburg

Chelyabinsk

Samara

Omsk

Novosibirsk

Irtysh

Krasnoyarsk

Yenisey

S

FEDE

E

i

b

KAZAKHSTAN

Karaganda

Aral Sea

UZBEKISTAN

Urgench

Samarkand

Tashkent

KYRGYZSTAN

Alma Ata

Kashgar

TAJIKISTAN

Dzungaria

Ürümqi

MO

CHI

xvi

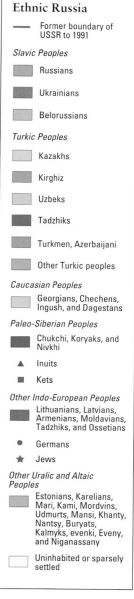

Ethnic Russia

— Former boundary of USSR to 1991

Slavic Peoples

Russians

Ukrainians

Belorussians

Turkic Peoples

Kazakhs

Kirghiz

Uzbeks

Tadzhiks

Turkmen, Azerbaijani

Other Turkic peoples

Caucasian Peoples

Georgians, Chechens, Ingush, and Dagestans

Paleo-Siberian Peoples

Chukchi, Koryaks, and Nivkhi

▲ Inuits

■ Kets

Other Indo-European Peoples

Lithuanians, Latvians, Armenians, Moldavians, Tadzhiks, and Ossetians

● Germans

★ Jews

Other Uralic and Altaic Peoples

Estonians, Karelians, Mari, Kami, Mordvins, Udmurts, Mansi, Khanty, Nantsy, Buryats, Kalmyks, evenki, Eveny, and Niganassany

Uninhabited or sparsely settled

INTRODUCTION

This atlas is a fine introduction to Russian history for anyone coming to the subject afresh. Even people like myself who know something about Russian history will enjoy the splendid maps and benefit from the insights they provide.

Of course the history of all countries is rooted in their geography. In England's case, for example, the fact that it is an island off the northwestern coast of Europe, very close to the continent but protected by the sea, and with open access to the Atlantic trade routes, was of huge importance for the country's fate. Geography was, if anything, an even more crucial factor in Russian history.

Probably the most basic fact about Russia since the sixteenth century is its huge size. It is much bigger than any other country today. If you count the whole British Empire as a single state then it was bigger at its zenith than Russia. So too was the Mongol Empire in the few decades before it broke up into separate states. But as a single consolidated state, which survived for centuries, Russia's size makes it unique. As the historian looks in detail at specific issues in Russian history it is easy to note Russia's size and then forget it, but in reality there were few aspects of Russian life on which the country's enormous size did not have a major impact. Of course the arrival of the railway and telegraph, followed by the aeroplane, to some extent "shrank" Russia, facilitated administration, and linked raw materials, sources of energy, producers and markets, but the problem of size far from disappeared. When a modern intrusive state began to develop in Russia by the turn of the twentieth century, for example, it faced the problem of bringing schools, hospitals, and communications to the more than half a million settlements scattered across European Russia, an area vastly larger than any other European country. The immense spaces of Russian Asia presented an even more awesome challenge to the modernizing state. After the collapse of communism economists and political scientists busied themselves debating theories of how to transform command economies and authoritarian regimes into democratic polities and capitalist economies. These theories were useful, but those who created them would often have benefited from looking at a map. There is a world of difference between implementing such changes in the small states of eastern Europe and in Russia, whose enormous distances had greatly multiplied the effects of the planned economy's 'irrational' (in the capitalist sense) distribution of factories and cities.

Second only to Russia's size as a key element in its history comes Russia's location. Only Canada matches Russia in latitude but, unlike Russia, the great majority of Canadians live in its southern borderlands. Contemporary Russia is unique in possessing many cities in the far north, where the state placed them partly for military reasons and partly because in Stalin's USSR the population's well-being or wishes were of no concern to the government. If the location of so many of its population in the far north was a problem for Russia after 1991, the extreme Russian climate has had a major impact on all of Russian history. Foreigners get some insight into this in the context of spectacular events such as the destruction of Napoleon's army in the retreat from Moscow. But in reality the climate imposed a hefty value added tax on almost all administrative and economic activity in Russia. In the Russian heartland agricultural seasons were compressed, with work in sowing and harvesting crops necessarily very intensive. The climate imposed heavy heating costs through the long winters, while communications disappeared beneath spring and autumn muds.

Among history's great Eurasian empires Russia was uniquely far from the centers of world trade and civilization. This means both the Atlantic trade routes, around which so much of modern world history revolved, and the more ancient trade routes and civilizations that grew up in Persia, around the Mediterranean and the Indian Ocean, and on the Yellow and Yangtse rivers in China. Trade and cities meant liquid wealth, the rise of the middle classes, and widespread education. Russia was weak in all three respects, which was, for instance, why the tsarist state imported so many professionals and artisans from Europe to support the modernization of government, economy, and society in the eighteenth and nineteenth centuries. Weak as regards trade and cities, Russia was a quintessential agrarian empire, forced to squeeze the resources on which imperial splendor and power rested out of farmers. Agrarian empires usually exploited their own subjects more ruthlessly than mercantile empires, but once again the Russian case was exceptional. The peasant populations at the core of most agrarian empires were usually densely concentrated around a number of rivers: for example the Nile, the Yellow River, the Tigris and Euphrates. But the Moscow region, core of the Russian Empire, is an area of forests and infertile soils in which the peasant population was initially widely dispersed. The Russian system of serfdom above all existed so that the country's scarcest resource—its people—should be fixed to the land and thereby forced to support both the landowning nobility and the state's administrative and military machine.

In the modern Western imagination Russia is a country with an immense population. This perception colored European thinking about Russia for generations. Panic at the future power of the ever-multiplying Russian "hordes" was a major factor in persuading the German government to launch what it perceived as a pre-emptive war in 1914 before Russian hegemony in Europe became an established fact. But, in reality, for most of Russian history the problem has been that there were far too few people to fill the country's space. Russia's population only overtook that of France in the mid-eighteenth century. It then grew rapidly for two centuries, coming to dwarf the population of any other

European country. But from the 1960s a process of ever-steepening decline in birthrates set in. One of contemporary Russia's greatest problems is declining population. If the same is true in many other countries of the First World, these countries are a fraction of Russia's size. Population decline has grave economic and cultural side-effects, especially in the Russian provinces. In the vast and empty regions of Russian Asia, bordering on powerful and populous China, it also raises strategic dangers and anxieties.

This atlas traces the history of Russian demography as well as the colonization by Russians of most of northern Eurasia from the sixteenth to the twentieth centuries. The expansion of Russia was part of the expansion of Europe. It entailed—as for instance in North America—expropriating the land of (often nomadic) natives and putting it under the plough. Khrushchev's Virgin Lands Scheme of the 1950s was in many ways the last gasp of European territorial expansion at the expense of the Asian and Islamic world, in this case the Kazaks. "New Russia," in other words the lands between Muscovy and the Black Sea which the tsars conquered and colonized in the eighteenth century, was Russia's equivalent of the grasslands settled by British colonists in North America and Australasia. In 1913, as a result of developing New Russia, the Russians were competing with the United States to be the world's greatest exporter of grain. Odessa, founded in the 1790s, had something of the feel of Chicago or Sydney. West Siberian dairy produce was beginning to out-compete Danish butter in the British market. But the colonial societies created in New Russia and Siberia were different. New Russia was a bit like the plantation south in the USA. It was a world mostly dominated by noble landowners, an extension of the society of core Russia. Siberia was different: here there were no nobles or big estates, but by 1914 there were increasing numbers of rich peasant farmers, whom the Soviet regime called "kulaks."

Empires' enormous size makes their communication systems a near obsession of their rulers. Roman roads remain a feature of the European landscape. River systems also had a great impact on the history of states and regions. They often determined whether a state could be built and sustained, where its key population and political centers lay, and some at least of its key strategic objectives. Without the many navigable rivers that wind their way through European Russia it would have been difficult to build an imperial state across European Russia. Once such a state did exist in the sixteenth century it was almost certain to advance down the rivers in order to control the riverheads and thereby guarantee its access to the outside world. This does much to explain Russian expansion down to the Caspian, Black, and Baltic seas, which dominated much of Russian diplomacy and warfare between 1500 and 1800. Success greatly eased Russia's involvement in the global economy, which grew exponentially in the century before 1914 and became ever more closely entwined.

Successful expansion to the riverheads only increased the concern of Russia's rulers about the fact that all the seas through which Russia's trade flowed were closed. By blockading the Danish Sound and the Straits at Constantinople a superior naval power could close down Russian sea trade at will, thereby doing vast damage to the Russian economy. Between 1815 and 1914 the main target for Russian fears was Britain, the world's leading naval power and Russia's rival in the so-called Great Game, the struggle for supremacy in Asia. Whereas the Russians saw themselves as threatened by British maritime power, in London's eyes most of the advantages in the Great Game were on the side of the huge continental power whose unceasing expansion brought it ever closer to Britain's Indian empire. A key element in British paranoia was Russia's expanding railway network, well-documented in this atlas. Few other countries had so much to gain from the railway in terms of both military power and economic development as huge and continental Russia, deep in whose landlocked provinces were found not just immense agricultural potential but also the world's richest treasure trove of minerals, sources of energy, and precious metals. At the beginning of the twentieth century the father of British geopolitics, Halford MacKinder, saw the railway as the key factor dividing the three previous centuries, which had been dominated by seapowers, and a future world order dominated by land empires, with Russia probably in the lead.

To mention geopolitics is to turn attention to the state. Though this atlas covers geography, demography, the economy, and Russian culture, its focus is on politics and government. Given the crucial role played by the state in Russian history this focus makes sense. So we have maps illustrating Russia's territorial growth, its internal administrative boundaries and centers, and some key events in Russian political history. Above all, the atlas provides graphic illustration of the wars fought by imperial and Soviet Russia. In the Russian case the old adage that "war made the state and the state made war" fits well. For most of Russian history it is pointless to ask whether these wars were forced on Russia or were the product of its own expansionist tendencies. In this world of dog eat dog, aggression was the same thing as survival. The tsarist state was dominated by a military and landowning nobility. The interests and the values of the monarchy and the nobles were focused on military glory and the rich pickings it brought as regards territorial expansion. But it is also true that Russia's geopolitical position made formidable military power essential to survival.

Russia bordered on the greatest grasslands in the world, which stretched from Hungary to Mongolia. These grasslands were populated by the world's most formidable military nomads, of whom Genghis Khan is only the most famous. For a millennium or more before 1500 in military terms nomads had all the advantages with regard to neighboring sedentary communities. Subsequently the balance of power turned in favor of settled societies and the firepower generated by their professional armies. As a result Russia conquered and colonized the steppe, hugely increasing its population, economic strength, and military power as a result. But as one threat waned, another grew. From 1500 until 1945 the huge expansion of European and then Western power was the single most important fact in global history. Russia was half in and half out of Europe in both cultural and political terms. The struggle to become and remain a European great power determined much of the history of tsarist Russia. The tsars enjoyed great success in this struggle but were brought down by the strains of the First World War. Though the Bolshevik regime that replaced them was based on very different ideological foundations it too became sucked into a geopolitical struggle with its Western rivals, though in this case geopolitics was reinforced by ideological rivalry. In the twentieth century tsarist and Soviet Russia smashed itself to pieces by competing first with the Germanic bloc in central Europe and then with the Anglo-Americans. The limited recovery of Russian power under Vladimir Putin cannot hide the fact that Russia faces the great challenges of the twenty-first century weaker than it has been at almost any time in the last three hundred years.

Dominic Lieven
England, November 2014

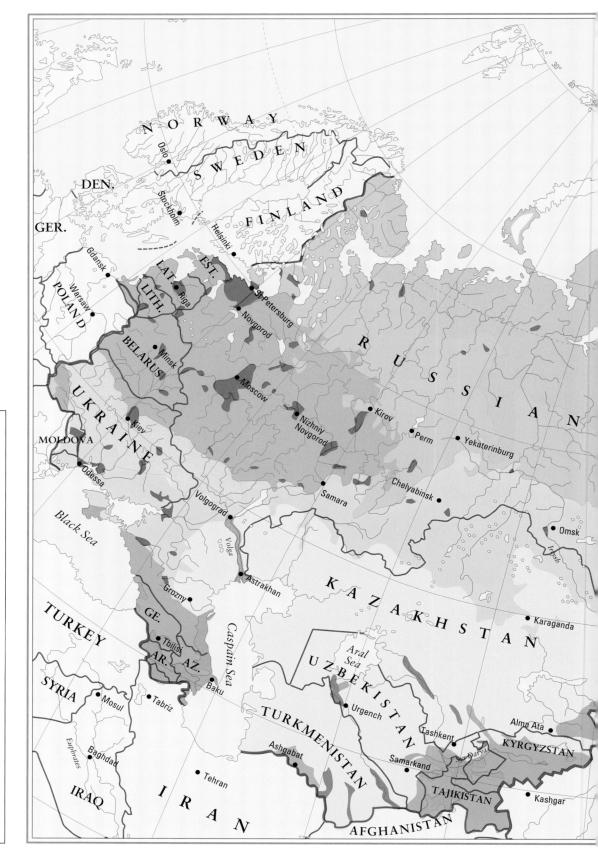

Russian Federation —Land Use

— Former boundary of USSR to 1991

Primary Agricultural Land

Grain, livestock. potatoes, vegetables, industrial crops

Livestock (dairy and meat), industrial crops, potatoes, vegetables

Sugar beet, grain, livestock (dairy and meat)

Cotton, orchards, vineyards. silk culture

Fruits, vegetables, vineyards

Market gardening, vegetables, fruits, dairy cattle

Marginal Agricultural Land

Desert pasture (sheep and goats)

Mountain pasture (sheep, goats,cattle)

Non-Agricultural Land

Forestry, hunting, livestock

Reindeer herding

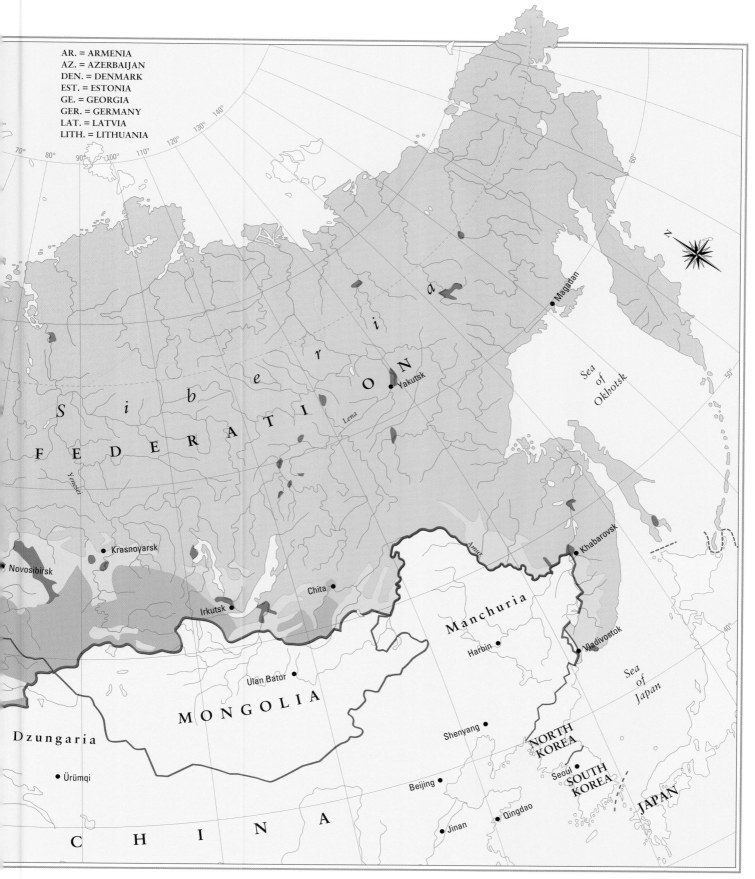

AR. = ARMENIA
AZ. = AZERBAIJAN
DEN. = DENMARK
EST. = ESTONIA
GE. = GEORGIA
GER. = GERMANY
LAT. = LATVIA
LITH. = LITHUANIA

70°   80°   90°   100°   110°   120°   130°   140°   60°   50°

Magadan

S i b e r i a

Sea of Okhotsk

S
F E D E R A T I O N

Yakutsk

Lena

Yenesei

Krasnoyarsk

Novosibirsk

Khabarovsk

Chita

Amur

M a n c h u r i a

Irkutsk

Harbin

Vladivostok

Sea of Japan

40°

Ulan Bator

M O N G O L I A

Shenyang

NORTH KOREA

D z u n g a r i a

Seoul **SOUTH KOREA**

Ürümqi

JAPAN

Beijing

Qingdao

C H I N A

Jinan

The Coming of the Slavs and the Origins of Russia

The territories from which the Russian state would emerge were uniquely unpromising— mostly birch and pine forests, unfertile soils, and a short growing season.

The Slavs, speaking an Indo-European language, are thought to have originated in the lands between the Baltic Sea and the Danube River. Some Eastern Slavs claim to have always lived in the Dnieper River valley and archaeology shows that a well-developed agricultural society certainly existed as early as the fourth century BCE before the Slavs were first mentioned in written history. The Greek historian Herodotus (c. 484–25 BCE) did not mention them in his Histories but that does not mean that they were not there. Waves of nomads swept through the region, placing it under their control. One group, the Central Asian Scythians, who ruled from the seventh to third century BCE, were followed by the Iranic Sarmatian tribes, one of which, the Alans, still survives as an ethnic ingredient in North and South Ossetia today. Next came the Goths, defeated by the Huns (370 CE), who in turn were overthrown by the Bulgars and the Avars. The Khazars succeeded these groups and created a state in the seventh century CE.

Slav society coexisted with the invaders; indeed, trade between them was mutually beneficial and the Slavs learned to use the horse and the recurved version of the bow, which was favored by the nomads. The Slavs lived in village settlements but, realizing the value of trade, they constructed fortified towns where they supplied honey, wax, and grain to other peoples; sometimes these goods were purchased with Arab coins. Some fortified towns, strategically located on rivers, grew into cities such as Ladoga, Novgorod, Suzdal, Chernigov, and the mighty Kiev. The different Slav tribes never created a unified state but still managed to levy men for defense against invaders and were considered a threat by Byzantium from 500 CE. Rus sources of the mid-800s enumerate several East Slav tribes. These included the Dulebians of western Ukraine, the Polyanians around Kiev, the Severians and Vyatichans east of the Dnieper, and the Krivichians and Slovenians further north.

In time, traders and raiders voyaged along

Indo-European Migrations
5000–900 BCE

- Settled urban culture
- Probable Indo-European homeland
- Other major movement
- Indo-European movement, 3000–2000 BCE
- Indo-European movement, 1000 BCE
- *SLAVS* Indo-European peoples
- *HYKSOS* Other peoples

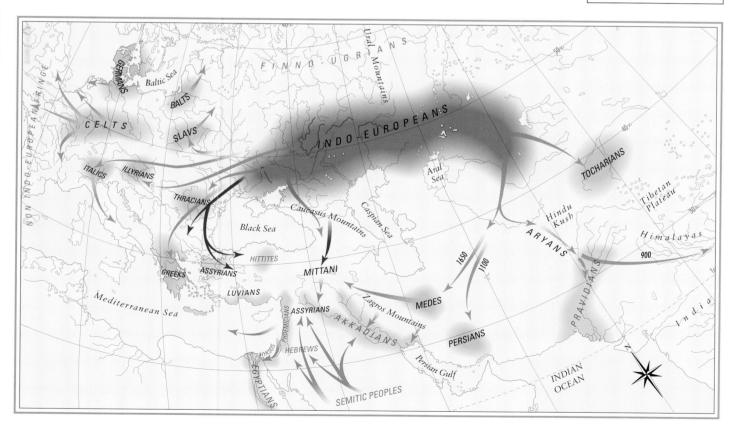

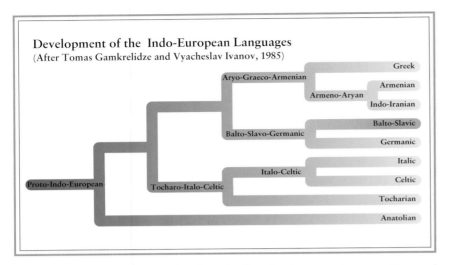

Development of the Indo-European Languages
(After Tomas Gamkrelidze and Vyacheslav Ivanov, 1985)

Proto-Indo-European

Aryo-Graeco-Armenian
- Greek
- Armeno-Aryan
  - Armenian
  - Indo-Iranian

Balto-Slavo-Germanic
- Balto-Slavic
- Germanic

Tocharo-Italo-Celtic

Italo-Celtic
- Italic
- Celtic
- Tocharian
- Anatolian

the rivers in Slav lands, sometimes trading and sometimes exacting tribute. These men are called the Rus in history but neither historians nor philologists can agree on the word's origin. The Rus were probably not an ethnic group but just groups who traded and raided and therefore the term refers to an occupation and not a people. The traders are thought to include Vikings, especially from Sweden, but the crews probably included people the traders had met elsewhere—Sami, Finns, Balts, and other Baltic peoples. The Rus sailed the rivers from Lake Ladoga, down the Volkhov and Dnieper to the Black Sea to Constantinople, called Miklagarð by Norse folk. There, many joined the Varangian Guard of Byzantium. The Rus preyed on the Slavs but transformed themselves from rapacious adventurers into state builders who moderated their demands while stitching a state together, peopled by the various Slav tribes.

In the twelfth century, Christian Slav monks wrote the *Primary Chronicle*, which purported to explain the story of the Rus. It relates how the Slavic tribes were continuously at war with one another and, to end this state of affairs, they invited the "Varangian Rus" to rule over them and restore law and order. One of the Varangians, Ryurik, settled in Novgorod with his two brothers. This Ryurik is the legendary hero and father of all grand princes and tsars until 1598. In 882, after Ryurik had died, a relative, Oleg, led a Rus-Slav army down the

Dnieper and captured Kiev and exacted tribute from the local Slav tribes. Oleg then mounted an assault on Constantinople but failed to conquer the city. Instead, he managed to obtain favorable trading terms and gifts. Kiev was passed to Igor, Ryurik's son, who was succeeded by Sviatoslav. Igor had to lay siege to Constantinople again to keep his trading rights and to extract money in return for peace. He also had to reconquer the Slav tribes to ensure the payment of tribute. One tribe, the Derevlians, resisted Igor and killed him when he came to exact tribute in 945. Sviatoslav wanted to control the east-west trade coming from Central Asia and waged war against the Volga Bulgars and the Khazars, and later, against a new wave of nomads, the Pechenegs. Sviatoslav's death (972) at their hands caused a fratricidal war, won by Vladimir in 978.

Vladimir seemed content to rule a sedentary agricultural population but still managed to expand his lands. In 981, he conquered the area of Poland known as Red Ruthenia, and in 981–82 he re-conquered the Vyatichi and defeated the Yatvingians, a Baltic people. In 984, he subdued the rebellious Radimichis and, in 985, he fought and defeated the Volga Bulgars, but did not incorporate their lands. Instead, he signed a peace treaty with them, thereby obtaining a friendly buffer country against the East.

Vladimir attempted to reorient trade towards Byzantium rather than Central Asia, converted to Christianity, and married Anna Porphyrogenita, the daughter of the Byzantine Emperor, a payment for the armed aid he had given to Byzantium against an uprising. Greek Orthodox monks were imported to Kiev to forcibly convert the Slavs but more importantly they brought a written language and literature and linked Kiev to Byzantine civilization. Slav and Rus united to form a Slav state and nation, together with a fairer taxation system and administration. Vladimir was also recognized as the legitimate ruler by the emperor of Byzantium, which gave him diplomatic standing with his neighbors in Hungary and Poland.

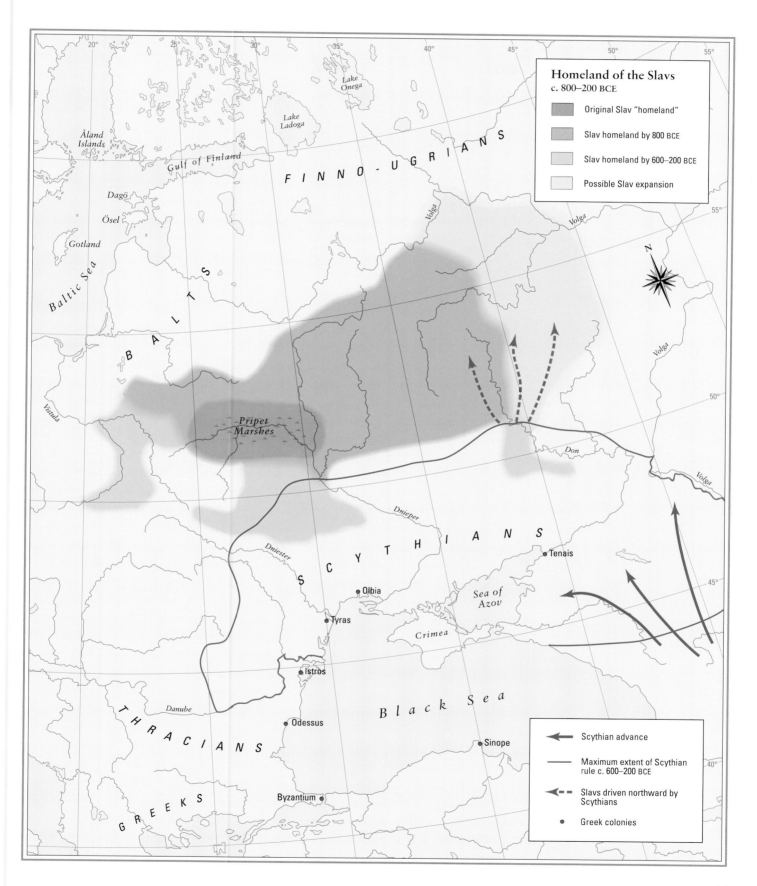

Homeland of the Slavs
c. 800–200 BCE

Original Slav "homeland"

Slav homeland by 800 BCE

Slav homeland by 600–200 BCE

Possible Slav expansion

Åland
Islands

Gulf of Finland

Lake
Onega

Lake
Ladoga

FINNO-UGRIANS

Dagö

Ösel

Gotland

Baltic Sea

B A L T S

Vistula

Volga

Volga

Volga

N

Pripet
Marshes

Dnieper

Don

Volga

Dniester

S C Y T H I A N S

Tenais

Olbia

Sea of
Azov

Tyras

Crimea

Istros

Danube

Black Sea

T H R A C I A N S

Odessus

Sinope

G R E E K S

Byzantium

Scythian advance

Maximum extent of Scythian
rule c. 600–200 BCE

Slavs driven northward by
Scythians

Greek colonies

From the Arrival of Christianity to the Golden Age of Kiev

Under Vladimir, who ruled from 980 to 1015, Rus became a virtual federation of city-states glued together by family bonds amongst the ruling princes, the descendants of Ryurik, the Rurikovichi. Rus developed in ways that were entirely different to western Europe, where kings sought to create centralized national states, albeit feudal, and the monarch was the source of law. Vladimir, however, failed to develop a bureaucratic structure to execute his will and rule. Rus was not regarded as a unified entity but became something different. Vladimir ruled the city of Kiev while he placed twelve of his sons as princes of the twelve largest cities of Kievan Rus. Neither did Vladimir build a unified national army under his sole command. Instead, neighboring princes combined their retinues against any common threat. Rus sources affirm that Christian Varangians possessed their own church in Kiev by 944. Sometime between 945 and 957, Princess Olga (890–969), wife of Igor, converted to Christianity, but it was her grandson Vladimir who ordered the mass conversion of Kievan Rus to Christianity. The Orthodox patriarch in Constantinople appointed a Metropolitan bishop in Kiev and he, in turn, appointed a bishop to each of the principalities in Rus. The principalities became dioceses and their bishops looked after priests, churches, and religious affairs within them.

Bishops possessed jurisdiction over contraventions of religious law, crimes committed by church personnel, and crimes against Church property. Fines obtained from these violations helped finance the Church. Bishops, who were responsible for all religious rituals, could also pronounce upon family life and outlawed certain aspects of sexual behavior. Christianity also brought the practice of monasticism to Rus, which created a sense of cultural unity. It was a group of hermits living in caves overlooking the Dnieper River who formed the first monastery in Rus, and their second abbot, Theodosius, created a model for future monasteries, which combined Christian asceticism, discipline and communal living, and Christian social services. The monks cared for prisoners, provided food and medical treatment for the poor and physically disabled, and gave beds to travelers.

Orthodox Christianity did not take root immediately and had to coexist with paganism for a long while, although it was wholeheartedly resented by Finno-Ugric shamans. Eventually people began to create icon corners and shrines in their homes, even though they feared household spirits. Nature was venerated in prayers and Mother Earth was an object of reverence. A "model" Christian was Vladimir Monomakh (1053–1125), who waged incessant war against a Cuman-Kipchak confederacy of the steppe. He was pleased to relate how he butchered captured Kipchak princes before throwing their bodies into a river, as if he were making some type of ritual sacrifice.

The Church became a breeding ground for religious writings with many gifted priests and monks transcribing and translating Byzantine texts and religious works, such as books of sermons and prayers. City-states commissioned histories and chronicles of their dynasties and cities, such as the *Primary Chronicle*, or *Tale of Bygone Years and the Chronicle of Novgorod*. Accounts of pilgrimages were also popular, as exemplified by Abbot Daniil of Chernigov, who recounted his visit to the Near East in 1106–07 and described the holy places.

The sense of identity forged amongst the peoples of Kiev by this outpouring of religious writing was particularly important. Some writings were political sermons, saints' lives (hagiographies), and general history. Metropolitan Hilarion was the first native Kievan to achieve that position, which was normally held by a Greek appointed by the Patriarch in Constantinople. He wrote the *Sermon on Law and Grace*, *Confession of Faith*, and the *Sermon*

The Viking River Road
to Constantinople

→ Viking trade routes

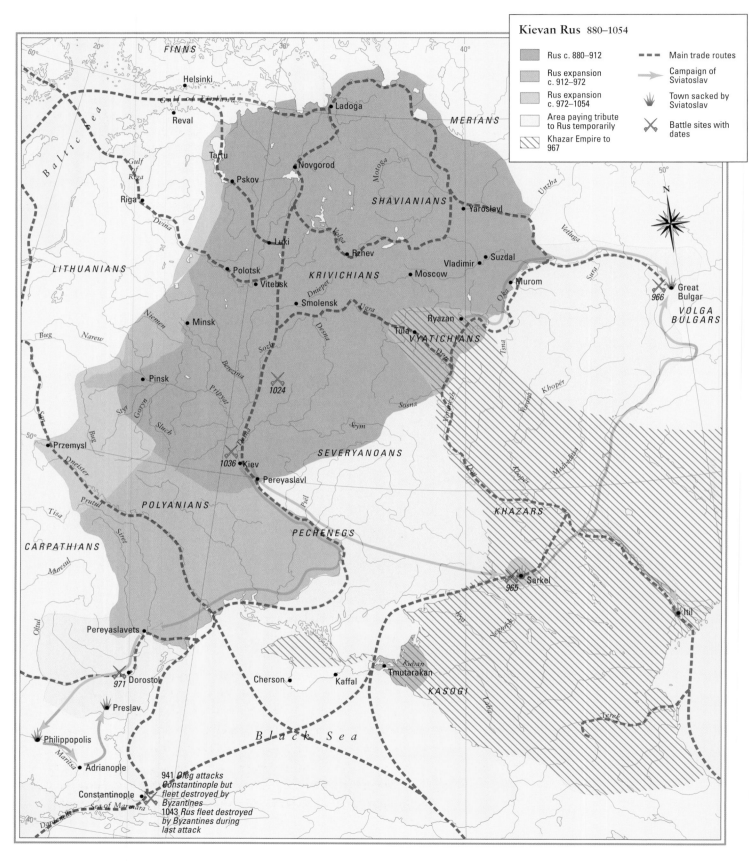

FINNS

Helsinki

Reval

Tartu

Riga

Pskov

Novgorod

Ladoga

MERIANS

SHAVIANIANS

Yaroslavl

Mologa

Luki

Rzhev

Volga

Polotsk

Vitebsk

KRIVICHIANS

Vladimir

Suzdal

Moscow

Murom

Oka

Dvina

Niemen

Minsk

Smolensk

Dnieper

Ugra

Ryazan

Sura

Unzha

Vetluga

Great
Bulgar

966

VOLGA
BULGARS

LITHUANIANS

Bug

Narew

Pinsk

Styr

Goryn

Sluch

Berezina

Pripyat

Sozh

Desna

Tula

VYATICHIANS

Don

Tsna

Voronezh

Khopër

1024

SEVERYANOANS

Seym

Sosna

Psël

Vorona

Khopër

Medvedista

Przemysl

San

Bug

Dneister

1036 Kiev

Pereyaslavl

POLYANIANS

Prut

Siret

CARPATHIANS

Maresul

Tisa

PECHENEGS

Don

KHAZARS

965 Sarkel

Iera

Negorlyk

Itil

Olu

Pereyaslavets

971 Dorostol

Preslav

Cherson

Kaffal

Tmutarakan

Kuban

KASOGI

Laba

Terek

Philippopolis

Maritsa

Adrianople

Black   Sea

Constantinople
Sea of Marmara

Dardanelles

941 Oleg attacks
Constantinople but
fleet destroyed by
Byzantines
1043 Rus fleet destroyed
by Byzantines during
last attack

N

Kievan Rus 880–1054

- Rus c. 880–912
- Rus expansion c. 912–972
- Rus expansion c. 972–1054
- Area paying tribute to Rus temporarily
- Khazar Empire to 967

- - - - Main trade routes
→ Campaign of Sviatoslav
Town sacked by Sviatoslav
✗ Battle sites with dates

Baltic Sea

Gulf of Finland

Gulf of Riga

14

on Spiritual Benefit to All Christians. Many Kievans were stirred by the hagiography entitled *Lesson on the Life and Murder of the Blessed Passion-Sufferered Boris and Gleb* (c. 1070s). These princes, who were murdered by their older half-brother Sviatopolk in 1015, were canonized by the Church, and were the first Kievan saints to be created since the arrival of Christianity. The two princes, designated as royal martyrs who had died for Kiev, were buried in Vyshhorod Cathedral and a cult grew up around them.

Thus historical writings glorified Kiev and its dynasty. These narratives were read and spoken about throughout Rus and helped to demonstrate how Kiev had a united Christian destiny. The construction of new religious buildings was also instrumental in creating a sense of unity for Kiev. Similarly designed wooden, then stone, churches all followed the dictates of Byzantine architecture, such as the St. Dmitrii Cathedral in Northern Vladimir and the Cathedral of St. Sophia in Kiev.

The princes held key positions, both judicially and administratively, yet it was also essential that they accommodated existing structures of local government, especially in towns. The rise of the boyar duma, which developed in consultation with the prince, reflected the rise of the boyar class, which was composed of the prince's retainers and local nobility, as well as the increasing prominence of higher clergy. While its powers were limited, the duma governed in collaboration with the prince, and he heeded its advice. The cities, ruled as principalities, became administrative centers rather than merely tribute collection points. The prince of Kiev held a special status, with the title of grand prince. This set him apart from all the other principalities.

Each city possessed an assembly of all free males who became part of the prince's retinue, or druzhina. This assembly, or veche, never objected in principle to rule by a Rurikovichi prince, but sometimes refused to accept a particular prince or chose to curtail the prince's policies. In reality, only the upper ranks of the assembly wielded power, but this institution gave the ordinary people a feeling that they were participating in the power structure. A major problem with the structure of princely rule was that when Vladimir died, he left no direction as to his heir. If Rus customs worked properly, his eldest son, Iaroslav, would become grand prince of Kiev, each brother by age would move up the ladder to the next most prestigious city and so on within the generation, and when the last brother died, the grand Principality of Kiev would pass to the most senior son of Iaroslav. In reality, chaos, fraternal strife, and violence ensued until one brother emerged as victor and moved to Kiev.

In the military sphere, Vladimir attacked and defeated Lithuanian tribes in the north and reconquered Przemysl and Cherven in Galicia (981) from the Poles, allowing the Kievan state to stretch from the Baltic Sea into the deep south. Around 983 he seized the lands between the middle River Nieman and the western Bug River. Vladimir also acquired Tmutarakan on the Taman Peninsula, just east of the Crimea. The actual events that led up to this territorial gain are unknown but it became a Kievan principality under one of Vladimir's sons. Iaroslav the Wise (1019–94) continued a western advance against the Poles, Lithuanians, and Finns, founded the town of Yurev (Dorpat) in the northwest, and made further gains in the region, which gave Novgorod sovereignty over the southeastern coast of the Gulf of Finland.

Agriculture, based on the growth of peasant communities, underpinned economic expansion. Agricultural production attracted increased taxation, which funded the growth of cities. State revenues were also swelled by judicial fines (in the comparatively mild Kievan justice system fines were frequently preferred to the death penalty) and to trade tariffs and duties. Kiev acted as an entrepôt for the other cities and directed trade to Constantinople, while Novgorod linked Kiev to northern Europe and via the Volga to the Muslim Near East.

The Decline and Fall of Kievan Rus

Iaroslav the Wise divided his Kievan domain amongst his five sons, a move that initiated succession problems for several generations with bout after bout of internecine strife. Civil war ensued during the reigns of Iziaslav (1054–77), Sviatoslav (1073), and Vsevelod (1078–1132). Eventually, there was a period of peace and stability during the reigns of Vladimir II Monomakh (1113–25) and his son Mstislav (1125–32). But a century of conflict ensued and the state of Kievan Rus fragmented under the assaults of nomadic Polovtsy (Cumans), Poles, Lithuanians, Swedes, Hungarians, and the crusading Teutonic Knights.

The Polovtsy appeared out of the steppe during the 1060s, displacing the Pechenegs. Known for their relentless, ferocious raiding, they repeatedly tore through the Russian principalities and disrupted trade along the Water Road between Lake Ladoga and the Black Sea. Kievan trade with Byzantium diminished and this contributed to Kiev's decline. Some principalities were so weakened that they were forced to employ mercenary Pechenegs in civil wars and to defend against the Polovtsy; these warriors were valuable because they used the same nomadic feigned retreat tactics as their enemies.

Succession disputes were a major cause of Kiev's decline despite the stable interlude introduced by Vladimir II Monomakh. He managed to mediate the disputes between various princes and then he defended Kiev against incursions by the Polovtsy. He led raids against them and won a resounding victory at Salnitsa in 1111. This redeemed the Rus as compensation for their previous defeat at the Battle of the Stugma River in 1093. Intent on rebuilding the fortunes of Kiev, Vladimir fought against Livonia, the Finns, the Volga Bulgars, the Poles, and the Hungarians and occasionally raided the Danube basin.

Monomakh's son, Mstislav, succeeded to the throne without incurring any rivalry and he continued the military exploits of his father by fighting in the Baltic regions. He fought the Lithuanians in 1131 and his son, Vsevelod of Novgorod, continued this policy, achieving victory over his enemies in eastern Estonia. However, family dissension recurred and Vsevelod was obliged to use the services of the Polovtsy to hold his principality (1135). The death of the next grand prince, Iaropolk (1132–39) was followed by a civil war between uncles and nephews who were fighting for succession to Kiev. Kiev was fatally weakened by dynastic rivalry and the sheer size of the state with its poor communication inevitably led to the disintegration of Kievan Rus into a collection of very loosely federated principalities and cities.

Kiev was further weakened by a new set of rivals. Prince Andrew Boguliubsky of Suzdal sacked Kiev in 1169 and made his court at Vladimir (1157–74), not Kiev. Kiev was sacked again in 1203 and nearly wiped out by the Mongols in 1240. A number of other factors contributed to the decline of Kiev. In 1204 a Crusade captured Byzantium and the empire was partitioned leaving two rump Byzantine states, the Empire of Nicaea and the Despotate of Epirus. The Genoese and Venetians seized many Greek islands in the Mediterranean and controlled sea trade.

The economic power of Kiev declined as the center of economic activity moved north to Novgorod, which had achieved independence in 1136. This well-fortified city had a mercantile heritage that extended from early Varangian times. Being the northern outpost of the Water Road, it linked Russia to the Baltic and was a bastion against the Teutonic Kinghts, Swedes, and Lithuanians. The Teutonic Knights were especially dangerous and had seized Dorpat (Yurev) and threatened Pskov and Polotsk. Elsewhere, Novgorod expanded into the far north, which provided rich pickings in the fur trade and could provide livings for refugees from Kiev. Another expanding center was the principality of Vladimir-Suzdal, which was home to the commercial center of Moscow, strategically situated on the River Oka.

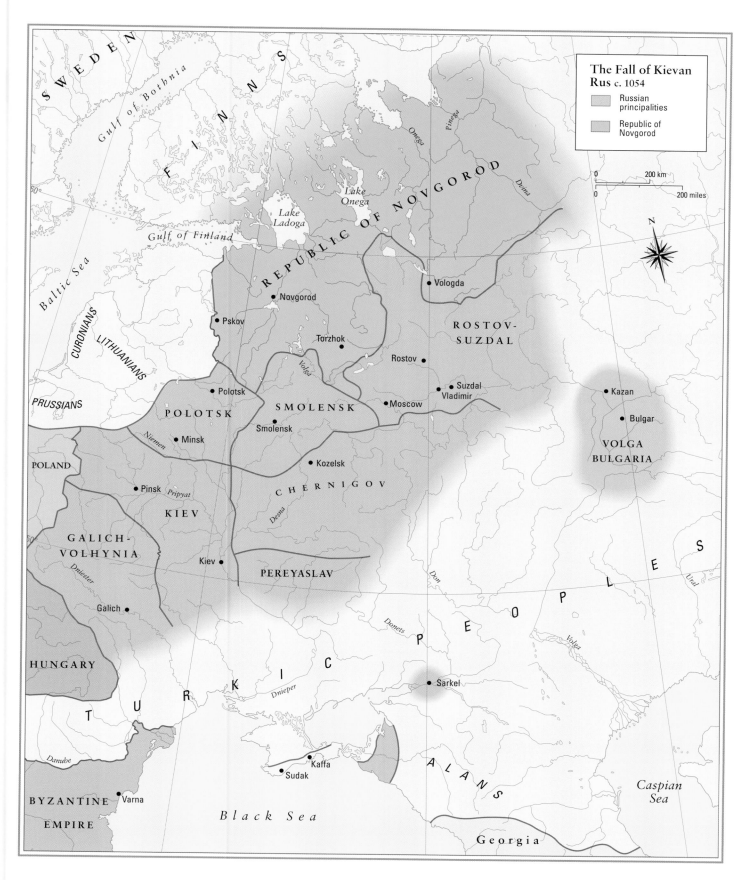

The Fall of Kievan Rus c. 1054

Russian principalities

Republic of Novgorod

0   200 km
0   200 miles

N

SWEDEN

Gulf of Bothnia

F I N N S

Lake Onega

Lake Ladoga

Omega

Pinega

Dvina

Gulf of Finland

REPUBLIC OF NOVGOROD

Baltic Sea

CURONIANS

LITHUANIANS

PRUSSIANS

POLAND

Vologda

• Novgorod

• Pskov

Torzhok

ROSTOV-
SUZDAL

Rostov

• Kazan

• Bulgar

• Moscow

• Suzdal
Vladimir

VOLGA
BULGARIA

Volga

• Polotsk

POLOTSK

SMOLENSK

Smolensk

Niemen

• Minsk

Kozelsk

• Pinsk

Pripyat

C H E R N I G O V

KIEV

Desna

GALICH-
VOLHYNIA

Dniester

Kiev •

PEREYASLAV

Don

Galich •

HUNGARY

T U R K I C

P E O P L E S

Ural

Volga

Donets

• Sarkel

Dnieper

A L A N S

Danube

BYZANTINE

Varna

Kaffa

Sudak

Caspian
Sea

EMPIRE

B l a c k S e a

G e o r g i a

17

The Tatar Invasions and the Mongol Yoke

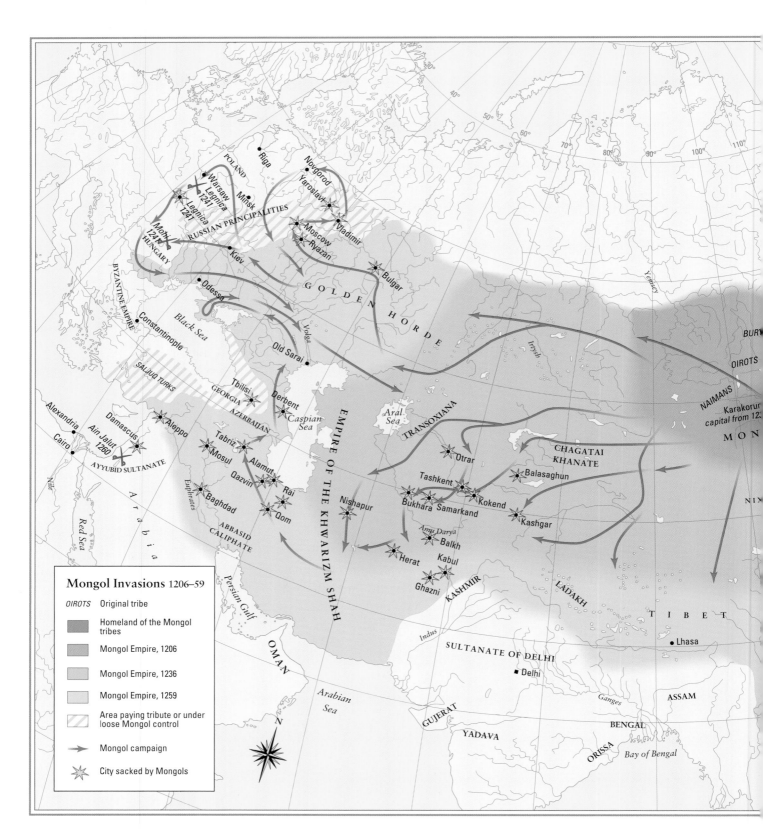

Riga
POLAND
Novgorod
Warsaw
Legnica 1241
Legnica 1241
Minsk
Yaroslavl
Legnica 1241
RUSSIAN PRINCIPALITIES
Moscow
Vladimir
Moh. 1241
HUNGARY
Ryazan
Kiev
Bulgar
BYZANTINE EMPIRE
Odessa
GOLDEN HORDE
Constantinople
Black Sea
Volga
Old Sarai
Irtysh
Yenisey
BURY
OIROTS
SALJUQ TURKS
Tbilisi
Derbent
NAIMANS
GEORGIA
Caspian Sea
Aral Sea
TRANSOXIANA
Karakorum capital from 123
Alexandria
Damascus
AZERBAIJAN
MON
Cairo
Aleppo
Ain Jalut 1260
Tabriz
EMPIRE OF THE KHWARIZM SHAH
Otrar
CHAGATAI KHANATE
AYYUBID SULTANATE
Mosul
Alamut
Tashkent
Balasaghun
NIX
Qazvin
Rai
Bukhara
Kokend
Samarkand
Baghdad
Qom
Nishapur
Kashgar
Euphrates
ABBASID CALIPHATE
Amu Darya
Balkh
Arabia
Herat
Kabul
LADAKH
Red Sea
Nile
Ghazni
KASHMIR
TIBET
Persian Gulf
Indus
Lhasa
OMAN
SULTANATE OF DELHI
Delhi
Arabian Sea
ASSAM
N
GUJERAT
Ganges
BENGAL
YADAVA
ORISSA
Bay of Bengal

Mongol Invasions 1206–59

OIROTS   Original tribe

Homeland of the Mongol tribes

Mongol Empire, 1206

Mongol Empire, 1236

Mongol Empire, 1259

Area paying tribute or under loose Mongol control

Mongol campaign

City sacked by Mongols

The nomadic Mongols (or Tatars) originated in the area of today's Mongolia. These various Turkic tribes were united by Temujin, better known as Genghis Khan, an outstanding military leader, with impressive diplomatic and administrative abilities. The first Mongol onslaught against Europe came in 1221 when their armies passed northwards through the mountains between the Black and Caspian Seas. The Mongol generals Subedai and Jebe Noyon rode westwards with their warriors on reconnaissance to spy out the steppes of southern Russia. The Polovtsy, dwelling in an area north of the Black Sea, were defeated and forced into Russian lands. Some Russian princes—from Kiev, Galicia-Volhynia, Chernigov, and Smolensk—joined forces with the Polovtsy against the Mongols, but they were crushed at the Battle of the Kalka River in 1223, losing an estimated 75,000 soldiers. After further raids, the Mongols retreated to the steppe to join Genghis Khan, leaving behind spies. The Mongol leader died in 1227, dividing his empire between his four sons.

Genghis Khan's grandson, Batu, with Subedai, attacked the Volga Bulgars at the junction of the Volga and Kama Rivers in 1236, then crossed the Volga in late 1237. Vladimir-Suzdal was ravaged as was Riazan, with numerous towns being destroyed. In 1239, owing to internal dissension between the various principalities, the lack of a united front against the Mongols meant that the nomads could overrun southwest Rus. In 1240, the Mongols advanced deep into the heart of Russia, destroying Kiev. They wintered near Przemsyl near the current border between Ukraine and Poland. Rus resistance was over and the princes surrendered to the Mongols. Novgorod, which had not been attacked, also submitted. Batu went on to invade Poland and Hungary, returning to Russia in 1241 after he heard that the Great Khan Ogadei had died, which meant that the Mongol princes would leave for an assembly in Mongolia. Novgorod was spared pillage because its prince, Alexander, accepted Batu as his overlord.

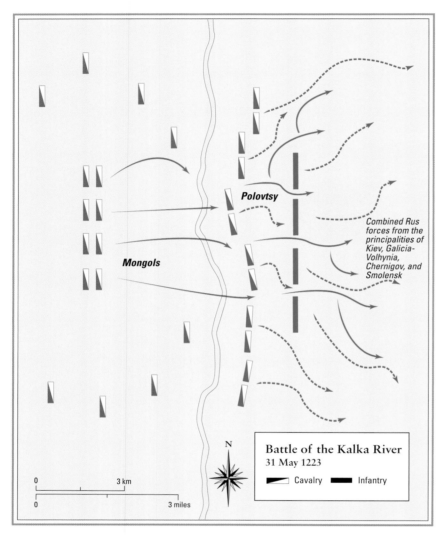

Polovtsy

Mongols

Combined Rus forces from the principalities of Kiev, Galicia-Volhynia, Chernigov, and Smolensk

N

Battle of the Kalka River
31 May 1223

◣ Cavalry   ▬ Infantry

0   3 km

0   3 miles

The Mongols achieved success in Russia for a number of reasons. The disunited princes were one reason, but the major factor lay in Mongol organization and discipline. Organized into *tumen* of 10,000 men, the Mongol army invading Rus numbered some 100,000 warriors. Their cavalry was well trained and used to obeying signals; flags were used during the day and colored lanterns at night. The Mongols could ride a hundred miles a day and during winter used frozen rivers as roads. The troops comprised 60 percent light horse archers armed with a composite bow, the rest of the troops were heavily armored lancers, used to press home a charge. The Mongols also used Chinese siege engineers against Russian cities and spread terror and panic when they massacred all the inhabitants of a town or city to encourage others to surrender. The use of prisoners and captive peoples as human shields was another tactic when mounting a siege.

The Mongols controlled Rus for some two hundred years from their capital city at Sarai. Batu's Khanate of the Golden Horde made about 48 military expeditions into Russian lands between 1326 and 1462 to quell rebellions and to aid various Russian factions against others. All princes had to travel to Sarai to be confirmed by the khan in their princely position. One prince, Alexander Nevsky, was made grand prince of Vladimir, the supreme Russian ruler, and he was successful in persuading the khan not to use Russian men in the Mongol armies. Nevsky's heirs became princes of Moscow. The Russian princes had to provide taxes or tribute to their Mongol overlords and were eventually given the task of collecting it themselves, often promising the Mongols higher tax returns in return for princely promotions.

Rich living and succession struggles eventually weakened the Golden Horde, which lost its fighting edge and suffered the destruction of Sarai at the hands of Tamerlane the Lame in 1395, after which it was split into the Kazan, Astrakhan, and Crimean khanates.

Batu's khanate was mainly pastoral and Turks, Kipchaks, Mordvins and others joined his Mongol soldiers. Regiments were raised and assigned pastureland on the steppes. The khan had no interest in occupying Russia or directly ruling the sedentary and agricultural Slavs. Here he differed from the Yuan dynasty ruling China and the Il khans ruling Persia and Mesopotamia. He preferred to recognize the authority of the Rurikid family, allowing them to govern, proving that they served his interests. The Rus princes were expected to give tribute to Batu at his capital, Sarai, and to provide armies to fight on his behalf. The prince of each principality was expected to travel to Sarai to swear loyalty to the khan when he first became prince and later if a new khan succeeded to the throne at Sarai.

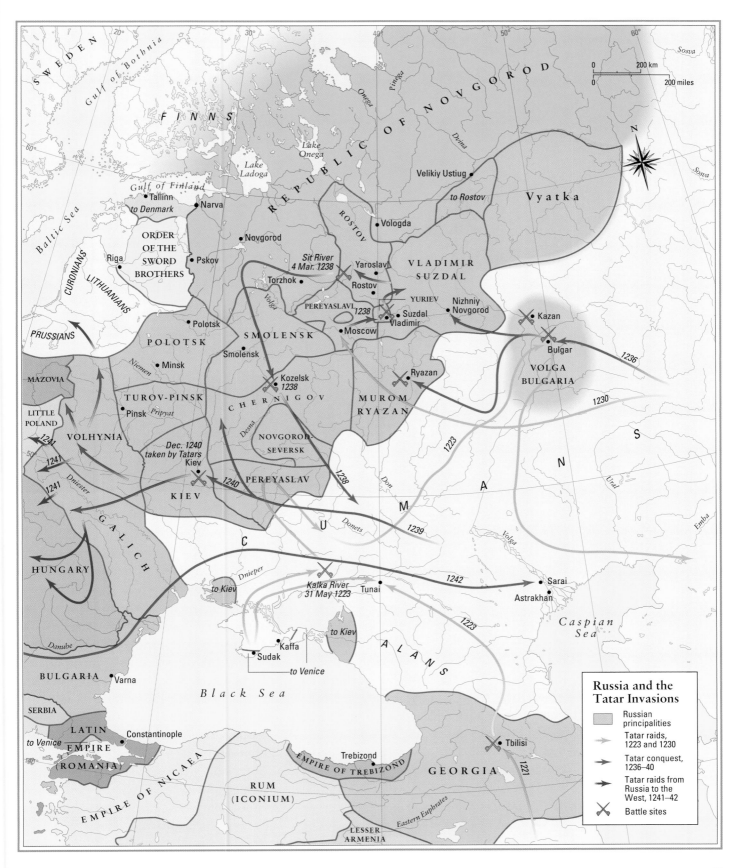

SWEDEN

Gulf of Bothnia

FINNS

Lake
Onega

Lake
Ladoga

Baltic Sea

Gulf of Finland

Tallinn
to Denmark

Narva

Riga

ORDER
OF THE
SWORD
BROTHERS

CURONIANS

LITHUANIANS

PRUSSIANS

MAZOVIA

LITTLE
POLAND

VOLHYNIA

GALICH

HUNGARY

BULGARIA

SERBIA

LATIN
EMPIRE
(ROMANIA)

to Venice

Constantinople

EMPIRE OF NICAEA

RUM
(ICONIUM)

LESSER
ARMENIA

Black Sea

Varna

Kaffa
Sudak
to Venice

to Kiev

to Kiev

Dnieper

Kalka River
31 May 1223

Tunai

ALANS

Trebizond

EMPIRE OF TREBIZOND

Eastern Euphrates

GEORGIA

Tbilisi

Caspian
Sea

Sarai

Astrakhan

1242

1223

1221

Volga

Ural

Embra

S A N

REPUBLIC

OF NOVGOROD

Velikiy Ustiug

Vyatka

to Rostov

Sosva

Sosva

Onega

Pinega

Dvina

Novgorod

Pskov

Polotsk

Minsk

POLOTSK

TUROV-PINSK

Pinsk

Pripyat

Niemen

SMOLENSK

Smolensk

CHERNIGOV

NOVGOROD-
SEVERSK

Desna

Torzhok

Sit River
4 Mar. 1238

ROSTOV

Vologda

Yaroslavl

Rostov

PEREYASLAVL 1238

Suzdal
Vladimir

Moscow

YURIEV

VLADIMIR
SUZDAL

Nizhniy
Novgorod

Kazan

Bulgar

VOLGA
BULGARIA

1236

1230

MUROM
RYAZAN

Ryazan

Kozelsk
1238

Dec. 1240
taken by Tatars
Kiev

KIEV

1240

PEREYASLAV

Don

Donets

1238

1239

1223

M

U

C

1241
1241
1241

Dniester

Danube

Volga

RYAZAN

Russia and the
Tatar Invasions

Russian
principalities

Tatar raids,
1223 and 1230

Tatar conquest,
1236–40

Tatar raids from
Russia to the
West, 1241–42

Battle sites

21

The Rise of Muscovy

This picture, by Apollinary Vasnetsov, portrays Khan Tokhtamysh's invasion and sacking of Moscow in 1382. Moscow's rise to power was by no means straightforward.

Moscow was first mentioned in Russian chronicles in 1147 but it did not become a principality until the mid-1280s when Alexander Nevsky made his youngest son, Daniel, its prince. This ruler annexed cities and lands and by his death Moscow was a viable economic unit and controlled the main waterways between Suzdal and Novgorod. Rivers were the major mode of communication at that time and Moscow was located on the River Moskva, lying at the center of a large, intricate river system between the Oka and the Volga, which in turn tied Moscow to the significant river systems of northern and western Russia. Moscow was connected to the Western Dvina and Dnieper, to the Volga, and also with the Baltic and Caspian Seas. A portage between the Oka and Don linked Moscow to the Sea of Azov and the Black Sea. Thus, Moscow was tied into the trade routes between northeast Europe, Astrakhan, and Persia.

Confronting Moscow were its more powerful neighbors, Tver, Novgorod, and Riazan. Daniel's son, Iurii (1319–22), fought Tver for the title of grand prince of Vladimir and was helped by the Mongols after marrying a sister of the khan. His younger brother Ivan I Kalita (1328–41) likewise was aided by the Mongols and was awarded the title of Vladimir and it remained in his family after he was succeeded by Simeon (1341–53) and Ivan II (1353–59). These princes continued to acquire more lands by annexation, marriage, and diplomacy. Ivan Kalita bought territory from Novgorod, Vladimir, and Rostov while Simeon bought territories in Pereyaslavl, Vladimir, Kostroma, and other principalities.

Moscow benefitted from its location in

other ways. Protected by the northern forest from steppe nomads, it became a sanctuary for refugees fleeing from the devastation caused by the Mongols. This swelled the population and also the size of Moscow's army. During the reign of Dmitrii Donskoi (1359–89), the area ruled by Moscow was doubled and became so powerful that most other northeastern princes were willing to follow his lead, meaning he could command a large

army. He became more authoritarian and forbade any of his lords from switching their allegiance, punishing disobedience by death and land confiscation. The tradition of primogeniture was introduced so a father did not split up his lands amongst his sons but bequeathed the totality to his eldest son. Dynastic strife was endemic in rival principalities, which broke up into ever-smaller polities. Nevertheless, the accession of Basil II

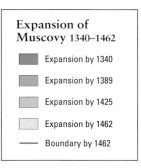

Expansion of Muscovy 1340–1462

- Expansion by 1340
- Expansion by 1389
- Expansion by 1425
- Expansion by 1462
- —— Boundary by 1462

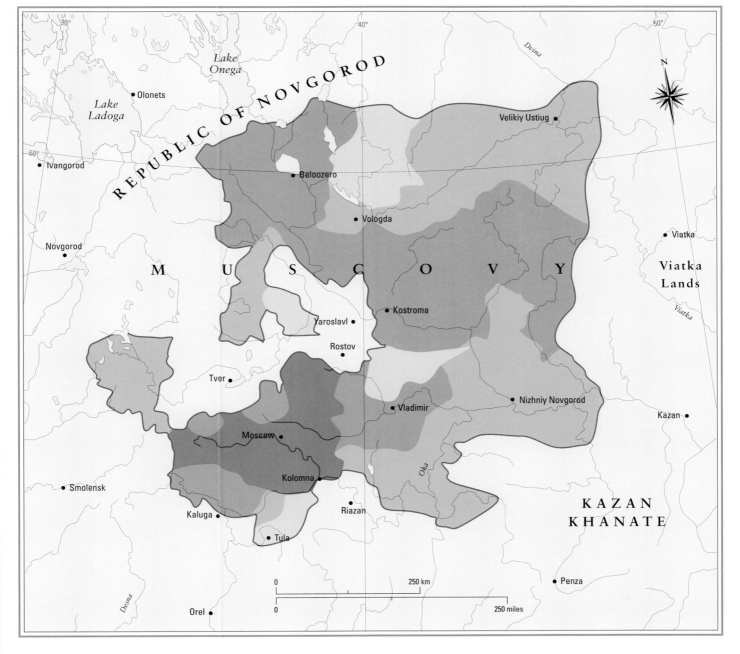

(1425–62), who was only aged ten when his father Basil I (1389–1425) died, soon descended into a bloody conflict. Young Basil's uncle Prince Iurii began to advance his claims to the throne, stirring up a violent family conflict. When he died in 1434 his two sons, resentful of the growing power of the grand prince of Moscow, took up the struggle. Basil II was ousted from Moscow on several occasions and blinded by his enemies (he was known as Basil the Blind), but eventually he prevailed, suppressing the rebellion in 1450.

The Mongols were still capable of causing trouble to the Muscovite princes. During the reign of Dmitrii Donskoi, Khan Mamai had made an alliance with Grand Duke Odgerd of Lithuania, intending to march on Moscow to attack Dmitrii for having bullied Mikhail of Tver. Before the Lithuanians and Mongols could come together, Dmitrii assaulted the Mongols, defeating them at Kulikovo on the upper Don River (1380). Although this proved the Mongols were not invincible, it did not end Mongol domination, and Dmitrii still had to pay homage to the new khan, Tokhtamysh, even though he was confirmed as grand prince and leader of all the Russias. He had also gained the right to rule Vladimir and fought his enemies in Riazan, Tver, and Rostov.

Dmitrii's son Basil I had continued to enlarge the principality, by gradually acquiring several new towns and their surrounding areas. He was engaged in a continuous struggle with Lithuania for the western Russian lands, and managed to keep his powerful father-in-law the Grand Duke Vytautas of Lithuania at bay for much of his reign: in fact a number of princes along the western border switched allegiance form Lithuania to Moscow.

Threats also came from the east. In 1395 Moscow narrowly escaped invasion by Tamerlane, one of the world's greatest conquerors, who had swept the Middle East and Caucasus and destroyed Riazan, before turning back to the steppes. In 1408 the Golden Horde subjected Moscow to a violent attack, to punish Basil for not paying his tribute or respecting his overlord. Much of the principality was devastated though the city of Moscow was spared. Troubled relations with the Mongols continued into the reign of Basil's son, Basil II. In 1445 Basil II was captured in battle and forced to pay a large ransom for his freedom. But the Golden Horde was breaking up, its territories divided, and the khanates of Crimea, Kazan, and Astrakhan were establishing separate identities. As the Golden Horde struggled to maintain its sovereignty, Moscow came under attack in a series of campaigns in 1451, 1452, and 1465. But by the end of the 1450s Moscow was effectively free of the Mongol yoke, though the formal cutting of ties did not occur until 1480.

Moscow's growing power was supported by the Russian Orthodox Church. During the reign of Ivan Kalita, in 1326, the Metropolitan moved from Kiev and took up residence in Moscow. This boosted the prestige of Moscow, and the Metropolitan claimed religious leadership over all territories previously ruled by Kiev. Moscow eventually became the religious successor to Kievan Rus. The Orthodox Church identified with the Muscovite state, which used the Church to bind the Russian principalities together under the religious leadership of Moscow, with the Metropolitan excommunicating those who failed to back Dmitrii in his policies. Moscow was firmly established as the spiritual capital of Russia.

When, in 1439, the Russian Metropolitan Isidore attended the Council of Florence, he supported an agreement that had been made there between the Greek Orthodox Church and the pope. His report of the Church union, made during a religious service in Moscow, was firmly rejected, and he was imprisoned in a monastery. A council of Russian bishops condemned the union and deposed Isidore, bringing the Russian Church's dependence on Byzantium to an end. In 1453 the Turks conquered Constantinople, cementing Russia's religious isolation.

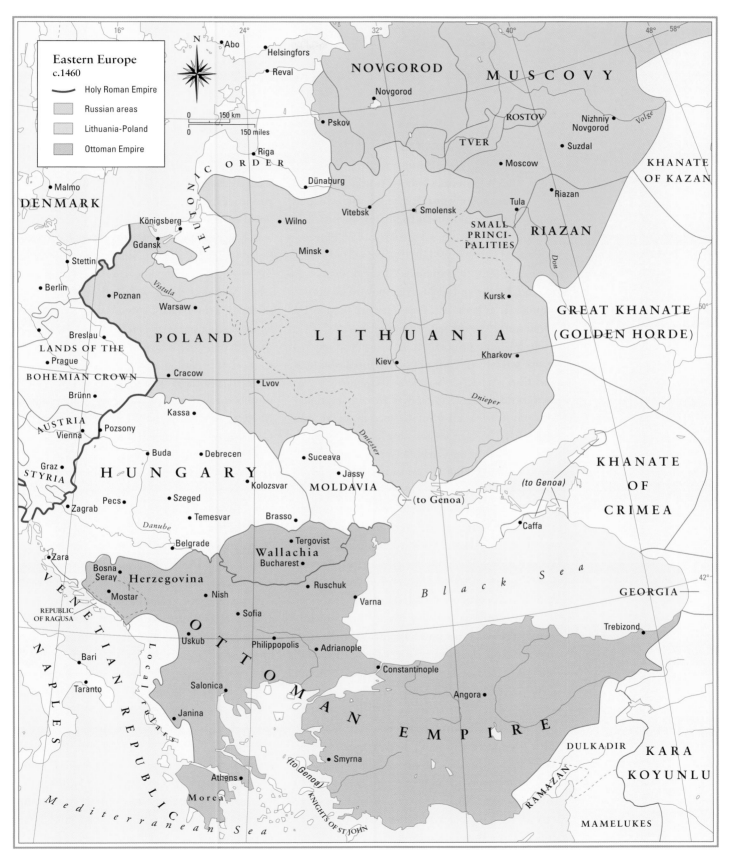

Eastern Europe
c.1460

— Holy Roman Empire
Russian areas
Lithuania-Poland
Ottoman Empire

0   150 km
0   150 miles

N

Abo
Helsingfors
Reval

NOVGOROD
MUSCOVY
Novgorod
Pskov
ROSTOV
Riga
TVER
Nizhniy Novgorod
Suzdal
KHANATE OF KAZAN
Moscow
Dünaburg
Vitebsk
Smolensk
Tula
Riazan
Wilno
SMALL PRINCI-PALITIES
RIAZAN
Minsk
DENMARK
Königsberg
TEUTONIC ORDER
Gdansk
Malmo
Stettin
Berlin
Poznan
Vistula
Warsaw
POLAND
LITHUANIA
Kursk
GREAT KHANATE (GOLDEN HORDE)
Don
Breslau
LANDS OF THE
Prague
BOHEMIAN CROWN
Cracow
Kiev
Kharkov
Lvov
Dnieper
Brünn
Kassa
AUSTRIA
Vienna
Pozsony
Buda
Debrecen
Suceava
Dniester
KHANATE OF CRIMEA
Graz
STYRIA
HUNGARY
Kolozsvar
Jassy
(to Genoa)
Pecs
Szeged
MOLDAVIA
(to Genoa)
Zagrab
Temesvar
Brasso
Caffa
Danube
Belgrade
Tergovist
Wallachia
Bucharest
Zara
Bosna Seray
Herzegovina
Ruschuk
Black   Sea
GEORGIA
VENETIAN
Mostar
Nish
Varna
REPUBLIC OF RAGUSA
Sofia
Trebizond
OTTOMAN
Uskub
Philippopolis
Adrianople
NAPLES
Bari
Salonica
Constantinople
Angora
Taranto
EMPIRE
DULKADIR
KARA KOYUNLU
Janina
Local rulers
Smyrna
RAMAZAN
(to Genoa)
Athens
KNIGHTS OF ST JOHN
Morea
MAMELUKES
Mediterranean   Sea

Volge
42°
50°
16°   24°   32°   40°   48°   58°

Ivan the Great

Ivan III (1462–1505) was the first of three reforming rulers of Moscow who transformed Moscow into an empire by expanding the principality and turning the many cities and lands into a centralized and relatively well-administered polity. The other two important rulers were Basil III (1505–33), and Ivan IV the Terrible (1533–1584). Territorially, Ivan III subordinated many Rurikovichi princes to his rule by purchasing land, forcing some to submit and conquering others. He annexed Iaroslavl (1463), bought Rostov (1474), and annexed Tver and half of Riazan. By the end of his rule the size of his domains was at least four times greater than at his accession to the throne.

In 1471 the principality of Novgorod made a treaty with King Casimir of Poland-Lithuania, and Ivan reacted decisively, leading his army to Novgorod, forcing its leaders to end the treaty and pay Ivan a substantial fine. In 1478, Ivan returned to Novgorod, accusing its leaders of dallying with Roman Catholicism and being disloyal, and placed the city under his direct rule. All the city's institutions were destroyed, its northern territories, with their rich fur trade, were seized, and the properties of the great landowners were confiscated. In 1491, Ivan forced Lithuania to sign a treaty recognizing him as "Sovereign of all the Rus" and, in 1502, he defeated Lithuania in war and seized one-third of its territory.

Ivan built a national army by drawing together, standardizing, and centralizing the various forces of the former northeastern principalities. All landowners were liable for military service and he seized the lands of anyone serving a foreign ruler. Ivan's father, Basil II (1425–62), had devised an institution known as "pomestie," land granted conditionally in exchange for service. This was used in the new Novgorod territories, which were divided among 2,000 military servitors. Such pomestie estates were also used to sustain soldiers located on the southern borders of Muscovy. Ivan began to standardize the legal system and reorganize Moscow's government. The administration was centralized, creating a basic bureaucracy in which state secretaries could register land, monitor servitors, and keep court and tax records.

Meanwhile, Mongol rule over the Rus was so weakened that Ivan made a declaration of independence in 1462. Twenty years later, in alliance with Lithuania, a Mongol army faced Russian armies at a tributary of the Oka. The Lithuanians failed to appear and the Mongols retreated without engaging the Russians. Now a fully sovereign state, Muscovy engaged in full diplomatic relations with the Papacy, some Italian states, some Scandinavian states, the Holy Roman Empire and the Khanates of Kazan, Crimea, Sibir, and Astrakhan, and the Ottoman Empire. Ivan adopted the title of "'tsar" and used the Byzantine double-headed eagle as his seal, suggesting that Moscow was the rightful heir of Byzantium after Constantinople had fallen to the Ottomans in 1453. He reinforced the message by marrying a niece of the last emperor of Byzantium. To provide more substance to his new imperial stature, a new Moscow Kremlin was built, with a new Cathedral of the Dormitian of the Virgin, thereby suggesting that Moscow was the political and religious capital of all the Rus.

Basil III continued his father's work. In 1509, Russian forces captured the Republic of Pskov and in 1520 he annexed the remaining half of Riazan. He whittled away at the Lithuanian frontiers and captured Smolensk and the east bank of the Dnieper. The Holy Roman Emperor acknowledged Basil as Tsar of all Rus. Nevertheless, Muscovy suffered Mongol attacks from the Crimea, some of them devastating. When Basil died in 1533, his oldest son, Ivan, was just three years old. Basil's wife, Helena, acted as regent, engaged in diplomacy, and built fortified settlements to defend the south against nomad and Cossack raids. But in 1538 Helena died and chaos ensued.

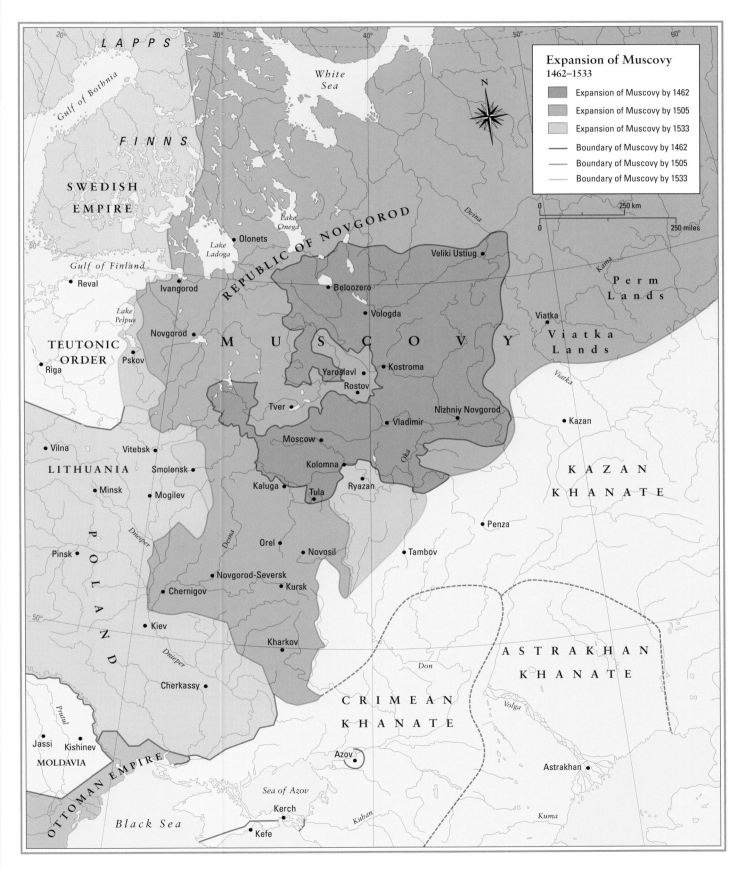

Expansion of Muscovy
1462–1533

- Expansion of Muscovy by 1462
- Expansion of Muscovy by 1505
- Expansion of Muscovy by 1533
- Boundary of Muscovy by 1462
- Boundary of Muscovy by 1505
- Boundary of Muscovy by 1533

0   250 km
0   250 miles

LAPPS

FINNS

SWEDISH
EMPIRE

Gulf of Bothnia

*White
Sea*

*Lake
Onega*

*Lake
Ladoga*

• Olonets

Gulf of Finland

• Reval

*Lake
Peipus*

• Ivangorod

REPUBLIC OF NOVGOROD

• Veliki Ustiug

Dvina

P e r m
L a n d s

Kama

TEUTONIC
ORDER

• Riga

• Pskov

• Novgorod

• Beloozero

• Vologda

M   U   S   C   O   V   Y

• Viatka

V i a t k a
L a n d s

Viatka

• Yaroslavl
• Rostov

• Kostroma

• Tver

• Vladimir

• Nizhniy Novgorod

• Kazan

• Vilna

• Vitebsk

LITHUANIA

• Minsk

• Smolensk

• Mogilev

• Moscow

• Kolomna

• Kaluga

• Tula

• Ryazan

Deona

Oka

K A Z A N
K H A N A T E

• Penza

Dnieper

P
O
L
A
N
D

• Pinsk

• Orel

• Novosil

• Tambov

• Kiev

• Novgorod-Seversk

• Kursk

• Chernigov

Dnieper

• Kharkov

Don

A S T R A K H A N
K H A N A T E

• Cherkassy

C R I M E A N

Volga

Prutul

• Jassi   • Kishinev

MOLDAVIA

OTTOMAN EMPIRE

K H A N A T E

• Azov

• Astrakhan

Kuma

Sea of Azov

• Kerch

Black Sea

• Kefe

Kuban

Ivan the Terrible

A portrait of Tsar Ivan IV, known as "Ivan the Terrible." In 1547 he became the first Russian ruler to be formally crowned as "Tsar of all Russia."

Ivan IV Grozny, known in English as Ivan the Terrible (meaning formidable), was born in 1530 and became Grand Prince of Moscow at the age of three on the death of his father, Basil III. As usual when a young ruler commenced a reign, the powerful boyars sought to control him and hence rule Muscovy. Initially, his mother Helena ruled in his name but when she died in 1538, possibly poisoned, court plots and intrigue ensued for several years, with the boyar Shuisky and Belsky families forming a virtually impenetrable oligarchy.

On his assumption of power, Ivan established the "Chosen Council," comprising personally selected advisers to act as a makeweight against the council of boyars (duma). Amongst the most influenial were the priest Sylvester, and a military commander named Daniel Adashev. In 1549, Ivan convoked the first national assembly, the Zemski Sobor, in order to develop and strengthen support for the crown. Over time the duma contained boyars of all ranks, senior administrators, and technical experts and by a 1550 Code of Law, the duma's assent was established as essential for promulgating laws. In reality, decisions remained in the hands of the tsar, who wished to expand tsarist autocracy in an attempt to administer his ever-increasing domain, following the acquisition of Kazan and Astrakhan. The Zemski Sobor, however, could provide a forum for boyar opposition.

In 1551, at the Council of a Hundred Chapters, decrees were put in place to consolidate the position of the Church in relation to society and to regulate ecclesiastical affairs. The Church forfeited the right to acquire land without the consent of the tsar. Local government reforms were presented to the Council. These were aimed at eliminating corruption, and devolved more power to locally elected officials. In some cases, localities were given permission to elect their own judicial authorities. The 1550s were also a period when Ivan reformed the army, establishing the first permanent regiments, and concentrating on artillery and engineering.

In 1553 Ivan ordered the establishment of the Moscow Print Yard, which housed Russia's first printing press. Several religious books were published here over the next decade, as well as books on behaviour and duty for the boyars, before the Print Yard was destroyed in an arson attack. Nevertheless, the Print Yard was rebuilt and printing resumed from 1568 onwards.

In 1553, Ivan became seriously ill and asked his Council of Boyars to swear an oath of loyalty to his young son, Dmitrii. Ivan's cousin, Prince Vladimir of Staritsa, who sought the throne, spearheaded opposition to the tsar. He was one of several boyars who did not want to see another young tsar with a regency. Even Sylvester, who was Ivan's spiritual father, and Daniel Adashev, key members of the Chosen Council, took Vladimir's part. Eventually, all decided to obey the tsar, though Ivan never forgot their opposition.

Throughout this period, Russia was beset by Tatar invasions, as the people of the steppes invaded Russian territory in search of slaves and booty. In 1552 Russia began a concerted campaign against the khanate of Kazan. After a six-week siege and bitter conflict, the Russians broke into the city of Kazan, razed its fortifications and massacred much of its population. It would take the Russians a further five years to establish control over the whole khanate. In Moscow, Ivan celebrated the conquest of Kazan by ordering the con-

struction of St. Basil's Cathedral. The Russians then turned their attention to Astrakhan, which they seized in 1554. Initially their own candidate was installed as khan, but by 1556 the Russians had annexed the khanate to the Muscovite state. Only the Crimean state remained; Crimean forces invaded Russian territory in 1554, 1557 and 1558, but were successfully driven back.

In 1557 the Livonian War broke out, directed against the Livonian Order and their Baltic strongholds. When Sylvester and Adashev opposed the Livonian War, arguing that the Crimean Tatars

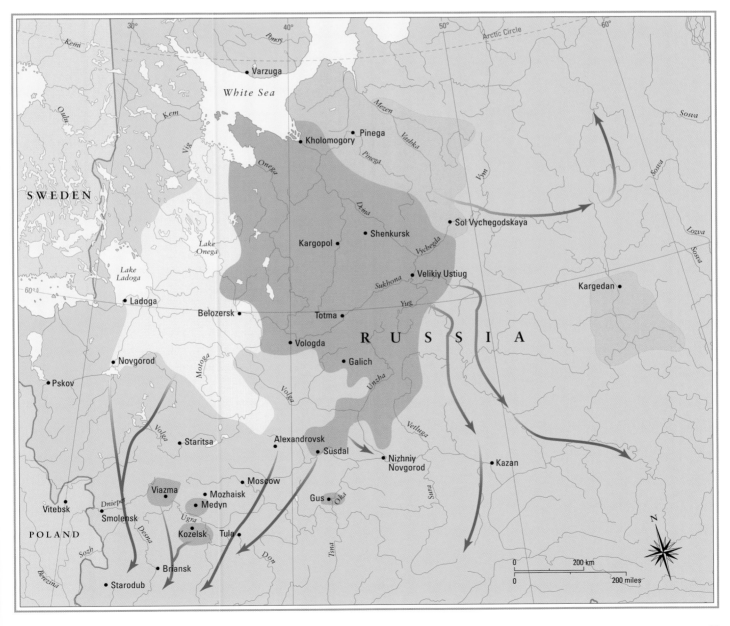

The Expropriation of Land by Ivan IV
1565–71

- Lands seized by Ivan IV in 1565
- Lands seized from 1566–68
- Lands seized from 1569–71
- Flight of dispossessed

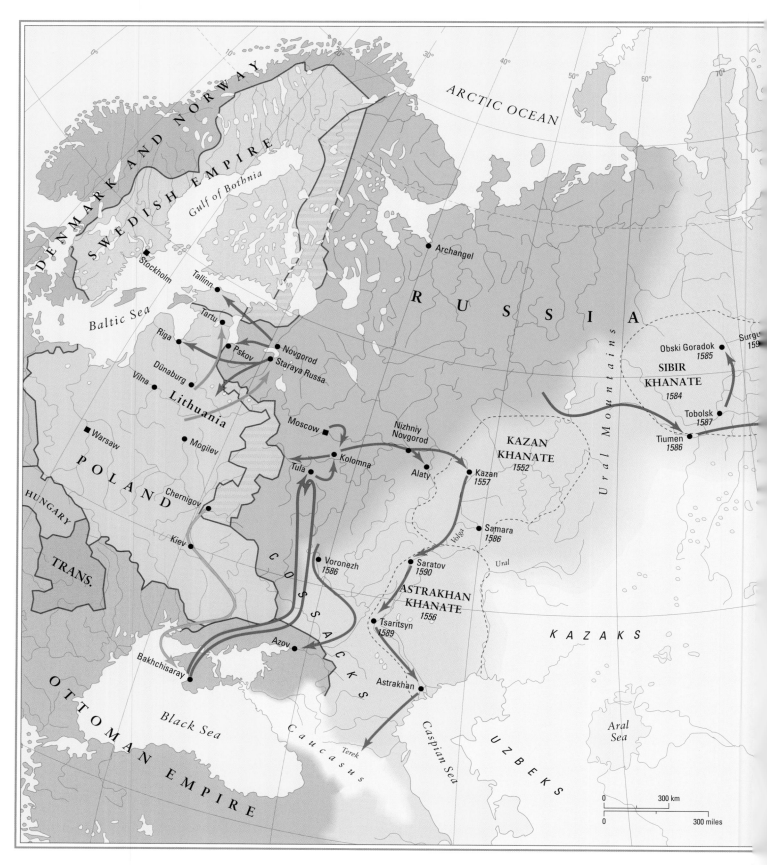

ARCTIC OCEAN

DENMARK AND NORWAY

SWEDISH EMPIRE

Gulf of Bothnia

Stockholm

Tallinn

Tartu

Riga

Dünaburg

Vilna

Pskov

Novgorod

Staraya Russa

Baltic Sea

Lithuania

Warsaw

Mogilev

POLAND

HUNGARY

Chernigov

Kiev

TRANS.

Moscow

Nizhniy
Novgorod

Alaty

Tula

Kolomna

C O S S A C K S

Voronezh
1586

Azov

Bakhchisaray

Black Sea

OTTOMAN EMPIRE

Caucasus

Terek

Archangel

R U S S I A

Ural Mountains

SIBIR
KHANATE
1584

Obski Goradok
1585

Surgu 159

Tobolsk
1587

Tiumen
1586

KAZAN
KHANATE
1552

Kazan
1557

Samara
1586

Volga

Saratov
1590

Ural

ASTRAKHAN
KHANATE
1556

Tsaritsyn
1589

Astrakhan

Caspian Sea

K A Z A K S

U Z B E K S

Aral
Sea

0   300 km

0   300 miles

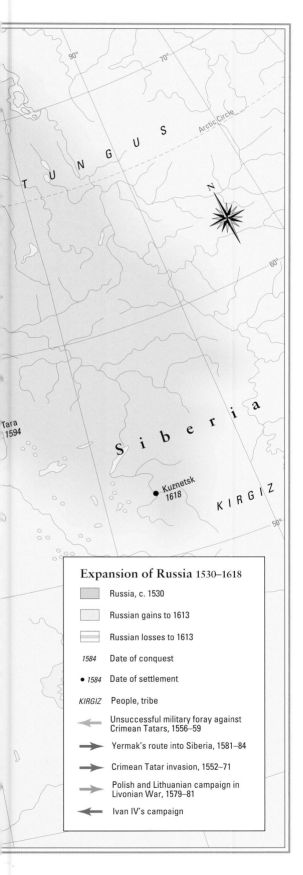

Expansion of Russia 1530–1618

Russia, c. 1530

Russian gains to 1613

Russian losses to 1613

1584   Date of conquest

● *1584*   Date of settlement

KIRGIZ   People, tribe

Unsuccessful military foray against Crimean Tatars, 1556–59

Yermak's route into Siberia, 1581–84

Crimean Tatar invasion, 1552–71

Polish and Lithuanian campaign in Livonian War, 1579–81

Ivan IV's campaign

should be attacked instead, Ivan's outright feelings of hostility led to an open rift. When Ivan's beloved first wife, Anastasia, died of suspected poisoning in 1560 Ivan became convinced that his old allies were involved in a plot to kill her. He initiated extraordinary judicial proceedings, during which they were not allowed to defend themselves, and they were condemned. Sylvester was banished to a monastery on the White Sea and Adashev sent to a post in Livonia. This state of affairs provoked the boyars, who refused to accept their friends' dismissal, and several were executed for publicizing their views.

Feeling that he was surrounded by hostile and untrustworthy boyars, Ivan secretly left Moscow (1564) for the Alexandrovskoe monastery. He wrote open letters to the Metropolitan, asking the people for their support, telling them that the boyars and priests were attempting to reduce his power and that he would not be able to defend them as their friend. The letters received popular acclaim and the people begged Ivan to return to Moscow where he could rule as he wished. Ivan travelled back to his capital and at this point initiated a reign of terror that would erase all actual or imagined opposition.

The aristocratic class became the target of a personally driven purge by Ivan. Their lands were confiscated and anyone who opposed him was killed or forced to flee the country. Ivan felt that the old boyar class was an obstacle to his divine right to unlimited power, and must therefore be destroyed. In their place would be set a "service" nobility, which could be paid with seized estates. Simultaneously, Ivan established the oprichnina, a personally ruled area located in northern and central Russia, including certain streets and suburbs of Moscow and Novgorod. Over seven years 12,000 landowners were dispossessed, while 6,000 personally loyal guards and supporters were settled in their place. His supporters, the "oprichniki," were generally members of the lesser nobility and foreigners. The oprichnina possessed its own special courts, ministers of state, and armed regiments. Its police wore black uniforms and rode on black horses. The tsar himself sometimes lived in a fortified Moscow suburb but also at the Alexandrovskoe monastery, where he existed in a state of self-abasement, pretending to be a priest, engaging in drunken orgies, or swallowing quack potions for a painful bone disease.

As the violence escalated, so did Ivan's feeling of paranoia and persecution. Ivan's cousin Prince Vladimir of Staritsa, his family and associates, perished in the purges, and an ever-widening circle of boyars were eliminated, their estates confiscated by the state. Opposition arose in Novgorod, where local businessmen resented Muscovite power, and Ivan accused its inhabitants of having pro-Polish sympathies during the Livonian war. In 1570, the city was attacked and a five-week orgy of murder, rape, and pillage ensued, the population being butchered to death or forcibly drowned.

In 1572, the oprichnina army proved totally incompetent in defending Moscow from an attack by the Crimean Tatars. The oprichnina was disbanded and its regiments reintegrated into the old army. Although the oprichnina only lasted seven years, Ivan's use of loyal sycophants gradually weakened the quality of the administration and government of Russia. The destruction of the old boyar class, which had built Muscovy, tore Russia apart and left many harboring great resentment and hatred towards tsarism that would fuel the later Time of Troubles.

This early police state was a manifestation of Ivan's innate violence, which was personal and pathological, as evidenced by the torture of prisoners in the Alexandrovskoe monastery and the murder of Prince Vladimir in 1581. The tsar was beset by feelings of persecution and prone to outbreaks of uncontrolled rage and violence. He even terrorized his own family: in 1581, he struck his son and heir, who was protesting against his father's treatment of his wife, with a stick, mortally wounding him. His daughter-in-law subsequently suffered a miscarriage.

Ivan's foreign policy can be assessed as both a success and a disaster. He annexed a considerable amount of territory but engaged in a long, very expensive, and ultimately lost, Livonian war with Sweden and Poland. At the same time, he could not prevent the Crimean Tatar raids. The buildup of Russian military power was essential given geopo-

litical threats but its cost was the oppression of the Russian peoples, over-centralization, exhaustion, autocracy, and backwardness. Between 1552 and 1556, Ivan conquered the khanates of Kazan and Astrakhan. Russia had now acquired the entire Volga region, reaching from the Caspian Sea to the Urals. This region could now be colonized and fortified and would act as an added bastion against the Crimean Tatars and their patron, the Turkish sultan. This victory over the remnants of the Golden Horde was a major step towards the creation of a great multinational empire dominated by the Russians.

Ivan opened up Russia to foreign trade and technical assistance, and his policies of expansion and conquest were typically Russian in a continuous search for secure borders, the acquisition of fertile land to settle, and control over trade routes. He controlled routes to Persia, Turkestan, India, and China via Astrakhan, the Caspian Sea, and the Silk Road. Russia was now a magnet for northwestern European traders, who were able to bypass the Ottoman Empire. Should Russia ever seize a Baltic port then trade could be developed to enrich the state. Also, more foreign technicians could be employed, such as the Dutch engineer whose skills in siegecraft were responsible for defeating Kazan.

This eastward and southward expansion formed the early part of a general eastward thrust. Russians progressed through the Urals, eventually arriving at Lake Baikal. With the tsar's approval, the wealthy merchant Stroganov family began to exploit these regions, trading fish and furs, and extracting salt on an industrial scale. The local native tribes resisted these incursions, encouraged by their suzerain, the khan of Sibir. In 1582, the Stroganovs, supported by hired Cossacks with Yermak Timofeyevich as their elected leader, captured the khan of Sibir's capital. This success brought the Ob-Tobol river systems under Russian control, providing Muscovy with the wealth generated by the region's fur trade. Private territorial acquisitions, such as those won by the Stroganovs, were taken over by the government in 1582. This was the beginning of Russian control of western Siberia: the fortified towns of Tiumen and Tobolsk, built in

1586 and 1576 respectively, both became important administrative centers.

If the start and end of Ivan's reign were crowned by successful expansion, then the middle years, 1557–83, were marred by the fruitless Livonian war. The tsar resented the blockade by Livonian towns, which cut off Russia from not only normal trade but also supplies of weapons, war materials, technicians, and mercenaries. The bishopric of Dorpat (Iurev) owed him tribute for which the knights were responsible, but payments had not been received.

With such a causus belli, Ivan declared war and initially had great successes in 1558. Narva was captured in May, Dorpat in July, and Reval placed under siege. Russia now had its window on the Baltic and Dutch, German, and English traders could trade with Russia direct. Ivan's victories led to the dissolution of the Livonian Knights (1561), who gave Livonia proper to Lithuanian rule, Courland to Poland, Estonia to Sweden, and the island of Oesel to Denmark. Ivan then fought Sweden and Lithuania to secure his conquests, capturing Polotsk (1563) from the latter and seizing Lithuanian territories as far as Vilna. A four-state struggle ensued; in 1566, the Lithuanians proposed peace but the Russian Zemski Sobor refused. As the war continued, Russia's position grew weaker and a number of factors, such as severe political disturbances, economic difficulties, tsar-boyar conflict, and the Novgorod massacres, exacerbated the growing fragility of Muscovy. In 1571 Crimean Tatars raided and sacked Moscow, burning much of the city, taking 10,000 prisoners, and capturing huge quantities of booty. Simultaneously, Lithuania became stronger.

In July 1569, the Union of Lublin merged Poland with Lithuania and in 1575 elected a new king, Stephen Bathory. He launched three successful campaigns against Ivan, strengthening his army with Cossacks and peasant infantrymen raised on crown estates. Bathory gained the co-operation of Sweden, which still held on to Reval. In 1578, a combined army inflicted a severe defeat upon Russia at Wenden, ushering a series of Russian disasters, despite the end of Swedish-Polish co-oper-ation. Faced with too many enemies, the Russians were forced to disperse their troops. Taking advantage of this situation, Bathory marched upon Pskov and Novgorod, taking Polotsk (1579), Velike Luki and Cholm (1580), and in 1581, he laid siege to Pskov, but failed to take the fortress. In 1583, Russia made peace with Sweden, giving up several towns and thereby losing access to the Baltic, which allowed Sweden to further its aim of controlling all trade routes between Russia and the West. This dream of commercial monopoly was not achieved until Gustavus Adolphus conquered Livonia in 1621. Meanwhile Russian trade moved to Dorpat and then to Riga or Pernau with the active co-operation of Bathory.

As far back as 1553, the English, led by Richard Chancellor, had reached Moscow by the White Sea and Archangel, opening up a new trade route. By 1555, the English had been given trading rights, thereby outflanking hostile Sweden and Lithuania. The English exported woollen cloth, metals and southern European goods, while the Russians sent out hemp, wax, tallow, cordage, timber, furs, and flax, much of this being essential for English shipping. England and Russia enjoyed cordial relations.

Ivan was certainly well-educated, literate, interested in domestic reform, and with the foresight in foreign policy to see that gaining a Baltic coastline was crucial. He made Russia a larger, potentially more dangerous state, a player on the European stage and a threat to Polish and Swedish ambitions. He opened up Russia to foreign trade, cementing a strong mercantile alliance with the English Muscovy Company. He diminished the powers of the boyars, suppressing the aristocracy that had failed to support him, and elevating members of the gentry, and created a centralized, autocratic government structure. Yet the mass movement of thousands of peasants to southern borderlands to escape the excesses of taxation during his reign led to ominous and long-lasting consequences. To prevent the weakening of the economic and military power of the state caused by this population movement, the government limited the peasants' legal right to move, thereby setting Russia on the road towards serfdom.

The Time of Troubles

In 1584 Ivan died, leaving the throne to his son, Theodore I (1584–98), whose power was exercised by his wife Irina and her brother Boris Godunov. Ivan IV's policies were continued with further penetration of Siberia and a war against Sweden that regained some lands lost in the Livonian War. When Theodore died in 1598, Godunov summoned a Zemski Sobor of boyars who elected him tsar (1598–1605).

Boris commenced a persecution of boyar families considered to be his enemies. Widespread frosts and crop failures caused famine, while a major rebellion was led by a man posing as Tsar Dmitrii, a child who was born of Ivan IV's seventh wife and died in 1591. This False Dmitrii, a Romanov peasant, created an army of Cossacks, peasants, and servitors from pomestie lands. Supported by the Poles, he marched on Moscow and was held at bay by Boris, who died in 1605, beginning the Time of Troubles.

Boris's son was named as Tsar Theodore II (1605), but was not accepted by the boyars, who had him strangled. The False Dmitrii was welcomed in Moscow as tsar but soon alienated the boyars. Dmitrii was murdered by Prince Basil Shuisky, who ruled from 1606–10. Elsewhere, a Cossack, Ivan Bolotnikov, recruited an army including pomestie servitors, boyars, fugitive slaves, and peasants. This socially mixed force marched on Moscow but achieved nothing after Bolotnikov turned revolutionary and ordered peasants to kill their masters and the poor to kill the rich. The boyars and servitors quit Ivan and joined Shuisky, who expelled the rebel army from around Moscow, defeating them in 1607 and killing Bolotnikov.

A new pretender emerged, the Second False Dmitrii, supported by a Polish army that reached the environs of Moscow at Tushino in 1608. Shuisky struck a deal with Charles IX of Sweden (1604–11), withdrawing Russian claims in Livonia in return for the assistance of the Swedish army in defeating the forces of the Second False Dmitrii. Sigismund III of Poland (1587–1632), concerned by Swedish military activity, invaded Russia in 1609. In this chaos, the Second False Dmitrii fled while the boyars, led by Filaret Romanov, welcomed Sigismund and his delegation, offering the Pole's son, Wladyslaw, the position of tsar of Russia. Meanwhile, the Poles pushed the Swedes aside while boyars, led by several Romanovs, arrested Shuisky and forced him to become a monk. The coup leaders let the Poles into Moscow and a Zemski Sobor elected Wladyslaw tsar of Russia (1610–12). Sigismund claimed that he would become the next tsar, although he refused to renounce Roman Catholicism.

By the summer of 1611, a Polish regiment was deployed in Moscow, an invading Polish army had captured Smolensk, while the Swedish army occupied Novgorod, whose population had accepted Charles IX as king. Furthermore, a rebel army of peasants and Cossacks was poised on the outskirts of Moscow with another pretender. In response the merchants, landowners, and clergy of the north Volga region began to gather funds and recruit a patriotic army of boyars and servitors from all over Russia. This army subjugated roaming Cossack bands, drove the Poles out of Moscow, and arranged a ceasefire with Swedish troops in Novgorod. A Zemski Sobor was held and sixteen-year-old Michael Romanov (1613–45) was elected tsar.

Negotiations with Gustavus Adolphus of Sweden (1611–32) culminated in the Treaty of Stolbovo (1617). The tsar relinquished rights to Ivangorod, Jama, Kopore, and Nöteborg and ratified the loss of Kexholm. Sweden returned Novgorod and other towns and Russia was cut off from the Baltic again. The 1618 Peace of Deulino ceded swathes of western Russia to Poland, including the cities of Smolensk and Chernigov. None of these settlements was considered final, however, and the lands would be fought over again.

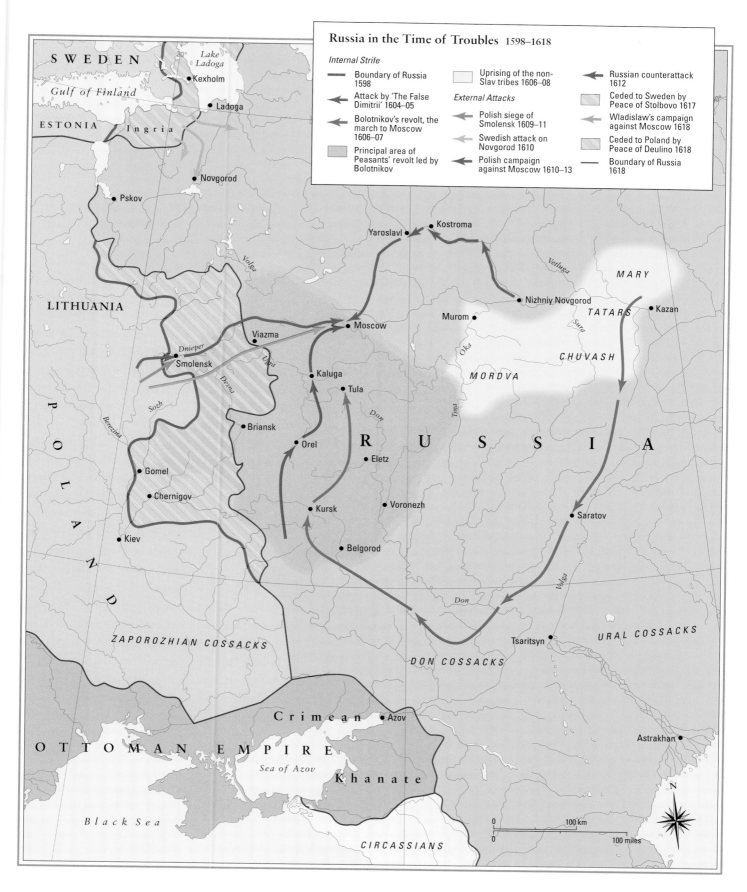

Russia in the Time of Troubles 1598–1618

Internal Strife

— Boundary of Russia 1598

→ Attack by 'The False Dimitrii' 1604–05

→ Bolotnikov's revolt, the march to Moscow 1606–07

Principal area of Peasants' revolt led by Bolotnikov

Uprising of the non-Slav tribes 1606–08

External Attacks

→ Polish siege of Smolensk 1609–11

→ Swedish attack on Novgorod 1610

→ Polish campaign against Moscow 1610–13

→ Russian counterattack 1612

Ceded to Sweden by Peace of Stolbovo 1617

→ Wladislaw's campaign against Moscow 1618

Ceded to Poland by Peace of Deulino 1618

— Boundary of Russia 1618

SWEDEN

Lake Ladoga

Gulf of Finland

Kexholm

Ladoga

ESTONIA

Ingria

Novgorod

Pskov

LITHUANIA

Volga

Viazma

Dnieper

Smolensk

Ugra

Desna

Sozh

Berezina

POLAND

Gomel

Chernigov

Kiev

Yaroslavl

Kostroma

Vetluga

MARY

Nizhniy Novgorod

Murom

TATARS

Kazan

Sura

CHUVASH

Moscow

MORDVA

Oka

Tsna

Kaluga

Tula

Briansk

Don

R U S S I A

Orel

Eletz

Kursk

Voronezh

Belgorod

Saratov

Volga

ZAPOROZHIAN COSSACKS

Don

URAL COSSACKS

DON COSSACKS

Tsaritsyn

Crimean

Azov

OTTOMAN EMPIRE

Sea of Azov

Khanate

Astrakhan

Black Sea

CIRCASSIANS

0   100 km
0   100 miles

N

The Development of Christianity in Russia

The golden domes of the Kremlin from a painting in the Hertiage Collection c. 1790.

Between the fourteenth and seventeenth centuries the Orthodox Church grew greatly in wealth and power. The Mongols not only tolerated but even in some ways favored the religions of the peoples they conquered: the Russian Church, for example, went largely untaxed under the "Mongol yoke" and partly as a result built up enormous landholdings. Together with the Kremlin (built by Italian architects) the buildings and icons created for the Church are the greatest memorials to a pre-modern Russia, which was Orthodox to the core. Before the end of the seventeenth century there was no such thing as a secular high culture in Russia.

From the fourteenth century Orthodox monastic life was especially vibrant, with monasteries in far-flung border regions sometimes also playing a missionary role. The most famous of all Russian saints, Saint Sergius of Radonezh, founded the still existing Trinity Monastery eighteen miles (30 km) north of Moscow in 1337, and both he and his foundation were a model to later monastic leaders. In the sixteenth century the wealth and power of the monasteries sparked a debate within the Church about the proper role of monks in the affairs of the world, which at times also included the proper relationship between the Church and the tsar. This issue resurfaced during the dispute between Tsar Alexis and Patriarch Nikon in the mid-seventeenth century.

A crucial point about Orthodoxy in these centuries was that it became wholly entwined with conceptions of Russian identity and uniqueness.

This process came from above and below. The fall of Byzantium and, even more, the Byzantines' attempt to save themselves by subordinating Orthodoxy to Roman Catholic doctrines and leadership, resulted in Russian Orthodoxy not only proclaiming its independence but also in future seeing itself as uniquely faithful to Christ's word. The destruction of Byzantium and the flourishing of the Russian tsardom confirmed Russia's status as God's chosen people. The tsar himself was seen as the protector of this people and the fusion of monarchy, church, and people was strengthened by the fact that Russia was wholly surrounded by hostile peoples of other religions—Catholics, Protestants, Muslims, and pagans. Between the fourteenth and seventeenth centuries the beliefs, rituals, and values of Orthodox Christianity penetrated deep into the lives even of the peasantry.

In 1654 Ukraine came under the tsar's suzerainty and over time Moscow's control over Ukraine tightened. The acquisition of Ukraine had enormous consequences not only for Russian power but also for Russian culture and religion. It was partly under the influence of ideas flowing from Kiev, a more European and cosmopolitan city than seventeenth-century Moscow, that Patriarch Nikon sought in the 1650s to introduce changes in the Orthodox liturgy and devotional practices to bring Russia into line with Greek and (as he saw it) Biblical tradition. This was met with furious resistance from some clergymen, led by Archpriest Avvakum, and followed by many Russians of all classes. This led to the secession from the Orthodox Church of what came by the nineteenth century to amount to millions of so-called "Old Believers," who held to their faith despite periodic waves of persecution. The fact that many of the most fervent and pious Russians thereby came to see both the official Church and the tsar as illegitimate remained even to 1917 a major weakness in the relationship between state and society.

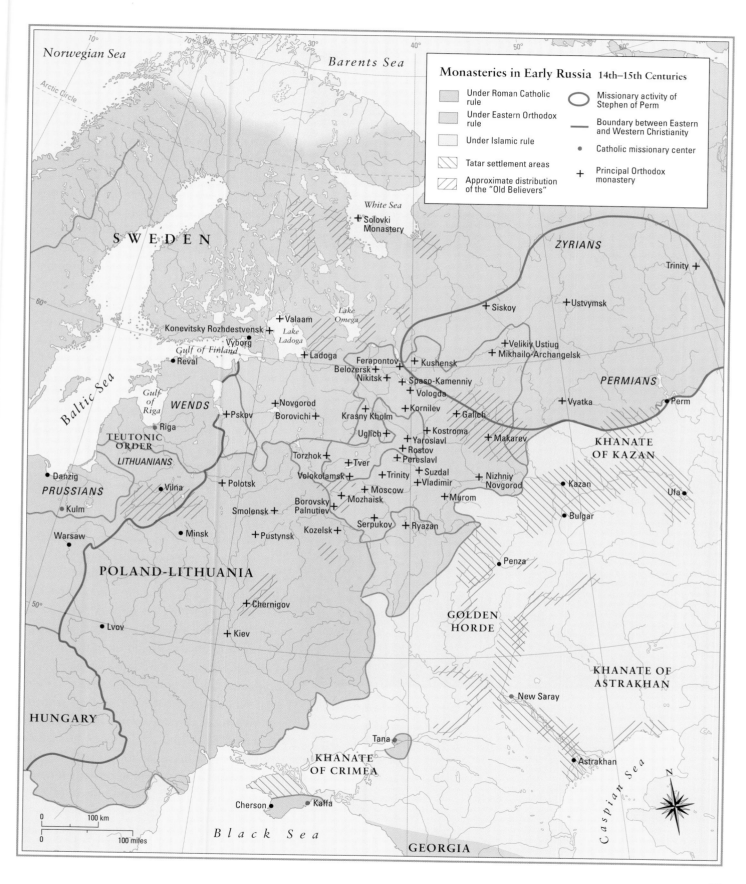

Monasteries in Early Russia 14th–15th Centuries

- Under Roman Catholic rule
- Under Eastern Orthodox rule
- Under Islamic rule
- Tatar settlement areas
- Approximate distribution of the "Old Believers"
- ⬭ Missionary activity of Stephen of Perm
- — Boundary between Eastern and Western Christianity
- • Catholic missionary center
- + Principal Orthodox monastery

Norwegian Sea

Barents Sea

Arctic Circle

SWEDEN

White Sea

+ Solovki Monastery

ZYRIANS

Trinity +

+ Siskoy   + Ustvymsk

+ Valaam
Konevitsky Rozhdestvensk +   *Lake Omega*   *Lake Ladoga*
Vyborg
Gulf of Finland
+ Ladoga   + Velikiy Ustiug   + Mikhailo-Archangelsk
+ Reval   Ferapontov   + Kushensk
Belozersk +   PERMIANS
Nikitsk +   + Spaso-Kamenniy
Baltic Sea   + Vologda   + Vyatka   • Perm
Gulf of Riga   WENDS   + Novgorod   + Kornilev
+ Pskov   Borovichi +   + Galich
• Riga   Krasny Kholm +   + Kostroma   KHANATE OF KAZAN
TEUTONIC ORDER   Uglich +   + Yaroslavl   + Makarev
LITHUANIANS   + Rostov
Torzhok +   + Pereslavl
• Danzig   + Tver   + Suzdal   + Nizhniy Novgorod   • Kazan   Ufa •
PRUSSIANS   • Vilna   + Polotsk   Volokolamsk +   + Trinity   + Vladimir
• Kulm   + Moscow   + Murom   • Bulgar
Smolensk +   Borovsky Palnutiev +   Mozhaisk +
Warsaw •   • Minsk   Kozelsk +   Serpukov +   + Ryazan
+ Pustynsk
Penza •

POLAND-LITHUANIA

+ Chernigov

GOLDEN HORDE

• Lvov

+ Kiev

KHANATE OF ASTRAKHAN

• New Saray

HUNGARY

Tana •
KHANATE OF CRIMEA
• Astrakhan

Cherson •   • Kaffa

0   100 km
0   100 miles

Black Sea

GEORGIA

Caspian Sea

N

The Rise of the Romanovs

Michael Fyodorovich Romanov ascended the throne on 21 February 1613, and reigned until his death on 12 July 1645. His life and reign was dramatized in an opera, The Life for the Tsar, *with an epilogue by Mikhail Glinka, which premiered in 1836.*

Michael Romanov was unanimously elected tsar, the first of the House of Romanov, in 1613. The gentle and self-effacing sixteen-year-old, confronted with the desperate aftermath of the Time of Troubles, asked the Zemski Sobor to remain in Moscow and to help him rule. His first priority was to make peace with the Swedes and Poles, although Polish-Russian relations were soured by Wladyslaw's refusal to give up any claim to the Russian throne. In 1632, when the Peace of Deulino expired, the Poles attacked Russia in the Smolensk War. A Russian siege of Smolensk failed but the subsequent Treaty of Polianov (1634), to last fourteen and a half years, included the Polish king's renunciation of his claim to the Russian throne. Elsewhere, in 1637, Don and Dnieper Cossacks attacked and took the fortress of Azov from the Crimean Tatars, offering it to Michael, who refused it in 1642. The tsar and the Zemski Sobor wished to avoid war with Turkey, Crimea's overlord, and Azov was returned. Nevertheless, territorial expansion did occur in Siberia, with Russian expeditions reaching the Pacific in 1639.

Before Michael died in 1645, Russia was transforming itself under foreign influence. English and Dutch traders, accessing Russia via the White Sea, were introducing new goods. By 1630, Russia had a standing army of 60,000 men, many of whose key officers were Swedish and Scots. In 1632, the Dutchman Andrew Vinius established a cannon-founding factory at Tula, while Saxons were prospecting copper in Solikamsk and Yeneseisk in Siberia. All industrial innovations were focused on the military requirements of the state, while foreign textiles, carriages, glass, and other luxury goods were traded. Nevertheless, at the end of Michael's reign state finances were in a desperate situation, despite a series of draconian taxes and levies, mainly because the Muscovite government's ambitions and obligations far outstripped the economic potential of the Russian people.

Russian Expansion in the West
1640–67

Advance by Russian and Ukrainian forces

Cossack revolts in 1648

Towns where Jews were attacked by Cossacks and Poles in 1648

Polish territory ceded to Russia by the Armistice of Andrusovo in 1667

SWEDISH EMPIRE

Baltic Sea

Gulf of Finland

Gulf of Riga

Tallinn

Novgorod

Riga

Königsberg

PRUSSIA

LITHUANIA

Kovno

Vilna

Grodno

Niemen

Narew

POLAND

Nevel

Polotsk

Vitebsk

RUSSIA

Volga

Dnieper

Viazma

Smolensk

Ugra

Borisov

Orsha

Andrusovo

Minsk

Mogilev

Desna

Berezina

Sozh

Byelorussia

Brest-Litovsk

Pinsk

Pripyat

Turov

Mozyr

Gomel

Starodub

Orel

Lublin

Kovel

Zamosc

Bug

Goryn

Western Ukraine

Lutsk

Rovno

Zhitomir

Desna

Chernigov

Eastern Ukraine

Kiev

Kursk

Seym

Kharkov

Belz

Berestechke

Przemysl

Lvov

Zbarazh

Pereyaslavl

Psël

Poltava

HUNGARY

Kamenets

Bar

Vinnitsa

Korsun

Donets

Siret

Prut

ZAPOROZHIAN COSSACKS

OTTOMAN EMPIRE

Sech

Khanate of Crimea

0   100 km
0   100 miles

Michael's son Alexis became the next tsar (1645–76), ascending the throne aged sixteen years. A sensitive and considerate man, Alexis was a dedicated and devout churchgoer, who was interested in Western culture, in particular architecture and theatre. At the beginning of his reign, Alexis came under the influence of his boyar tutor, Boris Morozov, and his father-in-law, Prince Miloslavsky. New taxes were introduced, which generated disturbances in various towns, including Moscow. Serfdom was tightened with peasant movement banned, and as a result increasing numbers of peasants fled to Cossack lands, providing an enlarged reservoir of the discontented to fuel further revolts. In 1650, the urban and rural poor rebelled, notably in Pskov and Novgorod. Discontent in Pskov was enhanced when grain was shipped to Sweden during times of poor harvests, raising prices in a non-grain producing area. Another problem occurred when the coinage was debased and copper coins were minted, which were regarded as worthless. The ensuing Copper Revolt in Moscow was crushed by troops.

The most dangerous challenge to Alexis occurred between 1667 and 1671 when the Cossack Stenka Razin raised a buccaneering army in the Volga valley. Razin captured a tsarist flotilla and was joined by runaway serfs, Cossacks, and members of national minorities. Everywhere he went he proclaimed the freedom of his followers from officials and landlords. In towns along the banks of the Volga members of the upper classes were massacred, while workers and soldiers welcomed Razin enthusiastically. He sailed the Caspian Sea, causing havoc, and captured Astrakhan. In 1670, he captured Tsaritsyn, Saratov, and Samara. Yet his forces were disorganized and undisciplined, and when Western-trained tsarist troops confronted Razin at Simbirsk, he was defeated and captured. He was executed in 1671 and thousands of his supporters were then hunted and executed. A few months later Astrakhan, which had been the center of his rebellion, surrendered.

Alexis's main claim to fame was his acquisition of territory at the expense of Poland. He supported Bogdan Khmelnitsky, a Cossack, against Polish rule, thereby winning Ukrainian Cossack allegiance. Alexis invaded Poland, capturing Smolensk and many Lithuanian towns. Simultaneously, Charles X of Sweden (1654–60) attacked Poland, taking much of Livonia and Estonia together with Poznan, Warsaw, and Cracow. Alexis immediately froze his Polish campaign and marched on Sweden, invading Livonia and capturing Iurev (Dorpat). The war dragged on until 1659 when mutual exhaustion ended the conflict, and the 1661 Treaty of Kardis restored the pre-war status quo. Another Polish war lasted from 1654 to 1667 with the combatants making peace with the Treaty of Andrusovo, which gave Russia Smolensk and Ukraine east of the Dnieper, including Kiev. The acquisition of east Ukraine brought difficulties because its Cossacks under Peter Doroshenko placed themselves and their land under the protection of the Ottomans.

Despite losing several battles, the Russian army had proved itself, laying the basis for military successes under Peter the Great (1682–1721) and Catherine the Great (1762–96).

In the latter part of Alexis's reign major reforms to the Russian Orthodox Church were undertaken by Patriarch Nikon. This intelligent and domineering cleric exercised strong influence over the more pliable monarch and was determined to exert his authority over that of the tsar. He was much resented by the boyars, who felt disempowered because the tsar invariably followed his advice. He initiated major religious reforms—to update Church practices and revise the translations of religious literature from Greek originals—that were to lead to a major division between the faithful, a decade of religious conflict, and ultimately to the defection of the "Old Believers." Eventually, his power became overweening and at an ecclesiastical council of 1666–67 he was deposed and defrocked, and exiled to a distant monastery.

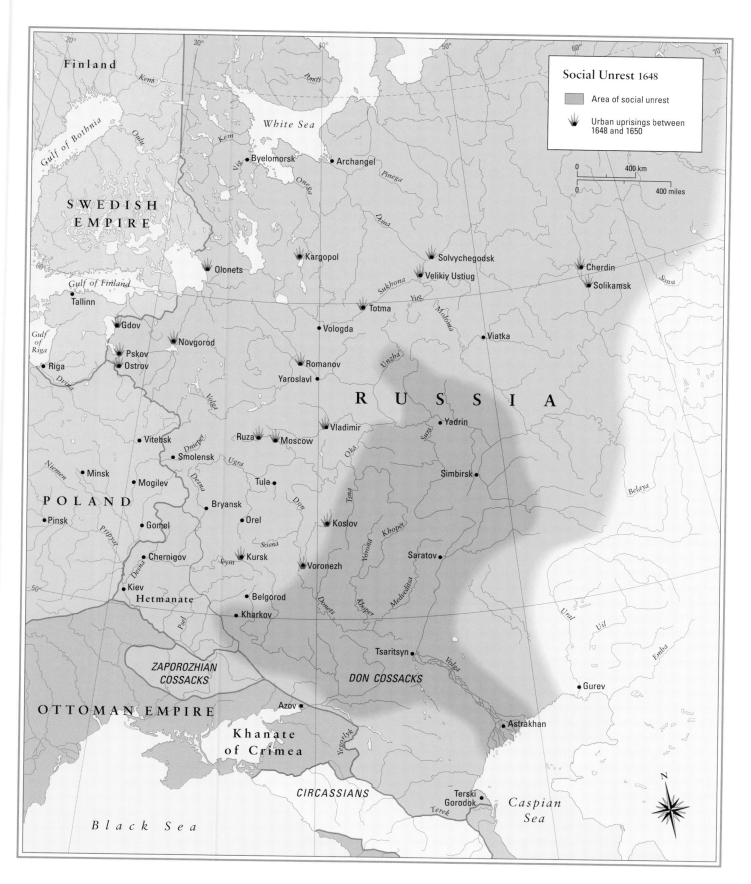

Finland

Kem

White Sea

Penoy

Gulf of Bothnia

Oulu

Kem

● Byelomorsk

● Archangel

Pinega

SWEDISH
EMPIRE

Vig

Onega

Dvina

Social Unrest 1648

Area of social unrest

Urban uprisings between
1648 and 1650

0   400 km
0   400 miles

● Kargopol

⚶ Solvychegodsk

⚶ Cherdin

Sova

Gulf of Finland

⚶ Olonets

⚶ Velikiy Ustiug

● Solikamsk

60°

Sukhona

Yug

● Tallinn

⚶ Totma

Molona

Gulf of
Riga

● Gdov

● Vologda

● Viatka

⚶ Novgorod

Unzha

● Riga

⚶ Pskov
⚶ Ostrov

⚶ Romanov

Dvina

Yaroslavl ●

R U S S I A

Volga

● Vitebsk

⚶ Vladimir

● Yadrin

Dnieper

⚶ Ruza ⚶ Moscow

Sura

● Smolensk

Ugra

Oka

● Simbirsk

● Minsk

Belaya

● Mogilev

Tula ●

Don

Tsna

Niemen

P O L A N D

Desna

● Bryansk

Khoper

● Pinsk

● Orel

⚶ Koslov

● Gomel

Sosna

Vorond

● Saratov

Medveditsa

● Chernigov

Seym

⚶ Kursk

Khoper

⚶ Voronezh

50°

● Kiev

Hetmanate

Psel

● Belgorod

Donets

Ural

Uil

● Kharkov

Embla

ZAPOROZHIAN
COSSACKS

● Tsaritsyn

Volga

DON COSSACKS

● Gurev

OTTOMAN EMPIRE

● Azov

Yegorlyk

● Astrakhan

Khanate
of Crimea

CIRCASSIANS

● Terski
Gorodok

Terek

Caspian
Sea

Black Sea

N

41

Petrine Russia—Centralization and Westernization

The accession of Peter I to the throne in 1682 inaugurated a period of transformation in Russia during which elements of west European technology, administration, and military techniques were introduced in a process of limited modernization.

Peter's father Alexis had died in 1676, and was succeeded by his son, Theodore III. On Theodore's demise in 1682, a battle for the control of Russia took place between the families of Alexis's two wives. The Miloslavskys supported Theodore and his brother Ivan (V) while the Naryshkins backed Peter, half-brother of both Theodore and Ivan. Peter was forced to watch the murder of various relatives and supporters by the palace guard (streltsy), leaving a deep impression on him and an abiding distrust of the streltsy, which acted as a kind of Praetorian Guard. Finally, Ivan and Peter assumed joint rule in 1682, with Peter's half-sister, Sophia, acting as regent until 1689. During this interlude Peter lived outside Moscow at Preobrazhenskoye. Here, he was free to develop his interests by acquiring an informal and alternative education. He developed knowledge of military and naval affairs, including siege-craft, together with a love of mathematics, instilled by a Dutch merchant named Timmerman, and became intensely concerned with the military and security needs of the state. In 1689, at the age of seventeen, Peter married Evdokiya Lopukhina who bore him a son, named Alexis. In 1689, she sympathized with a streltsy revolt, and Peter banished her to a convent; a similar fate befell his sister Sophia, who was closely involved with the revolt. On Ivan's death in 1696, Peter became sole ruler.

Peter was faced by a number of external problems. The Ottoman Empire, after immense expansion in Eastern Europe during the fifteenth and sixteenth centuries, was eventually beaten back by an Austrian offensive. Peter later joined Austria, constructing a naval flotilla at Voronezh on the Don with the intention of capturing Azov as an outlet into the Black Sea. In 1696 the Peace of Karlowitz ratified this acquisition, which was lost in Peter's second Turkish campaign. Peter focused most of his attention on the acquisition of ports on the Baltic coastline to such an extent that all reforms, internal restructuring of the state, and modernization would be focused on that sole obsessive aim.

In 1697, Peter traveled incognito through the Baltic states to study gunnery at Königsberg, then moved onward to Hanover and Amsterdam. Here, he worked in the shipyards of the Dutch East India Company. Ostensibly, this so-called Grand Embassy was designed to augment the anti-Turkish coalition but in reality Peter sought knowledge, especially in naval architecture, that could be used in Russia. After meeting the Prince of Orange (William III of England), this "artisan tsar" journeyed to England under his auspices. The 26-year-old tsar labored in the Deptford dockyards but also visited the Tower of London, Parliament, the Mint, the Woolwich Arsenal, Oxford University, the Royal Observatory, and Windsor Castle. Peter returned to Russia with a large number of recruited sailors, shipwrights, and various craftsmen. He recruited foreigners to teach at the new Mathematics and Navigation School and eventually transformed it into the Naval Academy. Peter's return to Russia was marked by another revolt of the streltsy. In 1698 hundreds of streltsy were executed and tortured on the wheel, and then the remnants were disbanded. Some 200 were hanged on the gallows outside Sophia's windows at the Novodevichy Convent as a warning.

Peter's desire for maritime access led him into another project. Through the efforts of King Gustavus Adolphus, Sweden had eventually become the dominant Baltic state with an empire controlling various river mouths in northern Europe, which cut off Russia from the sea. The Baltic was important internationally for its supplies of naval stores and

Russia Under Peter the Great
1689–1725

—— Russian border c. 1725

Azov Provinces established by Peter the Great

▢ Area ceded to Russia by Sweden 1721

Norwegian Sea

Arctic Circle

Barents Sea

SWEDEN

White Sea

• Archangel

Mezen

Onega

Dvina

Pinega

Archangel

Sukhona

Gulf of Bothnia

Baltic Sea

Gulf of Finland

• Tallinn

• St Petersburg (founded 1703)

• Vologda

Yug

Siberia

Sosva

• Viatka

Gulf of Riga

• Novgorod

Motoga

St Petersburg

R U S S I A

• Riga

Volga

Unzha

Vetluga

LITHUANIA

Dnieper

• Vilna

Moscow •

Nizhniy Novgorod •

• Kazan

Kazan

Oka

Sura

Belaya

• Minsk

Niemen

• Smolensk

Moscow

Don

Tsna

Narew

Sozh

Desna

POLAND

Berezina

Pripyat

• Orel

Voronezh

Tambov •

• Penza

• Samara

Sosna

• Orenburg

Goryn

Bug

Kursk •

Seym

Azov

Don

Khoper

C O S S A C K S

Ural

Uil

50°

Kiev

Psel

Kharkov •

Donets

Medveditsa

Embal

• Kiev

Poltava •

• Tsaritsyn

Volga

Stryi

Prutul

Danube

Azov

Khanate of Crimea

• Astrakhan

Caspian Sea

C O S S A C K S

Great Kabardia

Terek

CIRCASSIANS

Dagestan

Black Sea

O T T O M A N   E M P I R E

PERSIA

N

to Russia 1723–32

40°

| 0 | 300 km |
| 0 | 300 miles |

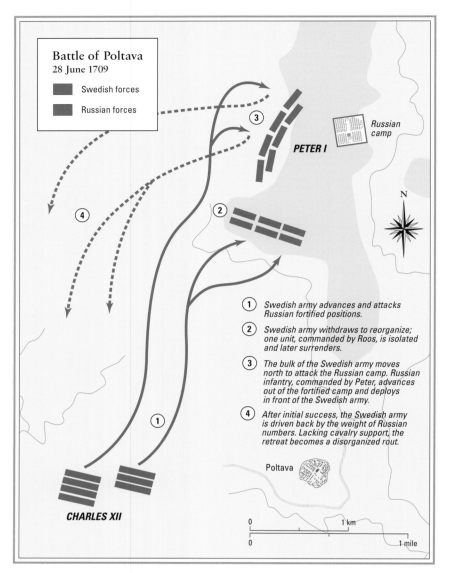

Battle of Poltava
28 June 1709

Swedish forces

Russian forces

Russian camp

PETER I

N

① Swedish army advances and attacks Russian fortified positions.

② Swedish army withdraws to reorganize; one unit, commanded by Roos, is isolated and later surrenders.

③ The bulk of the Swedish army moves north to attack the Russian camp. Russian infantry, commanded by Peter, advances out of the fortified camp and deploys in front of the Swedish army.

④ After initial success, the Swedish army is driven back by the weight of Russian numbers. Lacking cavalry support, the retreat becomes a disorganized rout.

Poltava

CHARLES XII

0   1 km

0   1 mile

forced Peter to hasten the retraining and rearming of his army, to develop a new, modernized artillery arm, and to focus all state resources on obtaining a Baltic coastline.

Rather than following up his victory, Charles decided that Saxony-Poland was his most dangerous enemy, and he became embroiled in a long, fruitless Polish campaign. Peter was, therefore, allowed time to rearm, invade, and capture some Swedish Baltic provinces. A Swedish counter-campaign against Russia in the Ukraine resulted in a disaster for Charles at Poltava (1709) and the remaining years of the war saw a Russian naval victory at Hangö (1714) and the occupation of Finland. The 1721 Treaty of Nystadt parcelled out most of the Swedish empire with Russia gaining Livonia, Estonia, Ingria, Karelia, and Kexholm in Finland. Russia now emerged as the dominant Baltic power.

Peter's final war took place against Safavid Persia (1722–23). Despite being preoccupied by the Swedish war, Peter had sent missions into central Asia and the Caspian region, excited by the prospect of trade, expansion, and Persian weakness. Taking advantage of a Turkish threat to Persia, Peter won the western and southern shores of the Caspian Sea, including Derbent, Baku, and Resht. Additionally, the 1724 Treaty of Constantinople gave Russia a sphere of influence in the Persian Caucasus.

The reign of Peter has been acclaimed for a range of internal reforms, which resulted in a more modern state. Peter wished to end Russian backwardness to facilitate his foreign policy, and to this end he introduced administrative changes in commerce, education, industry, technology, and culture. However, some historians believe that Peter did not plan his early reforms but merely responded to the exigencies of war and its demands. Such early improvisation later changed to a more rational, and prepared, set of policies. Thus, the pace of war dictated the nature of reform.

In 1711, Peter abolished the old boyar council, a hindrance to absolutist rule, and inaugurated the Senate to act on behalf of the tsar by

materials, while access to the wider world through the Baltic provided a means of expanding Russian exports to augment economic development. Peter attempted to create an anti-Swedish alliance comprising Russia, Denmark, and Saxony to combat Sweden in the Great Northern War. Learning of this threat, Charles XII of Sweden immediately attacked Denmark and, with the benefit of an Anglo-Dutch squadron as well as his own fleet, landed troops in Zealand, threatened Copenhagen, and forced Denmark to capitulate. The Swedes fought off a Saxon threat to Riga, but meanwhile Peter was pouring troops into Ingria and besieging Swedish-held Narva. Failure there

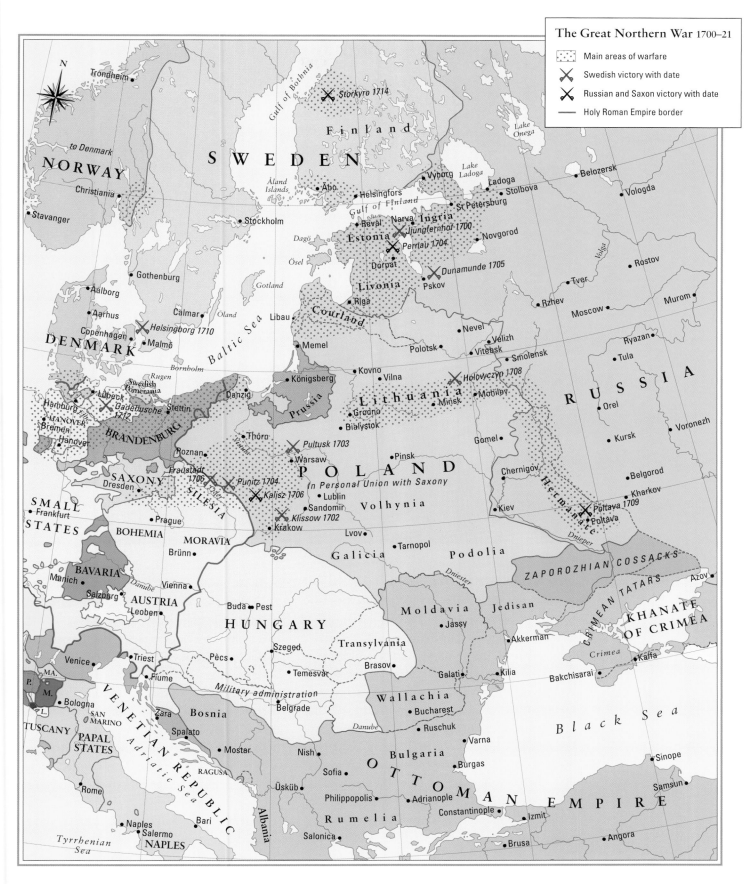

The Great Northern War 1700–21

- ⋮⋮⋮ Main areas of warfare
- ✗ Swedish victory with date
- ⤬ Russian and Saxon victory with date
- — Holy Roman Empire border

Trondheim

N

to Denmark

NORWAY

Christiania

Stavanger

SWEDEN

Finland

Åland Islands

Storkyro 1714

Gulf of Bothnia

Lake Onega

Belozersk

Vyborg Ladoga

Stolbova

Vologda

Åbo

Helsingfors

Gulf of Finland

St Petersburg

Stockholm

Reval

Narva Ingria

Novgorod

Ljungfernhof 1700

Estonia

Dagö

Pernau 1704

Rostov

Gothenburg

Dorpat

Dunamunde 1705

Livonia

Pskov

Tver

Murom

Aalborg

Gotland

Öland

Riga

Nevel

Rzhev

Moscow

Aarhus

Calmar

Libau

Courland

Velizh

Ryazan

Copenhagen

Helsingborg 1710

Malmö

Memel

Polotsk

Vitebsk

Smolensk

Tula

DENMARK

Baltic Sea

Bornholm

Kovno

Vilna

Holowczyn 1708

Orel

Kursk

Rugen

Swedish Pomerania

Königsberg

Lithuania

Minsk

Mobilev

RUSSIA

Voronezh

Lübeck

Gadebusche 1712

Danzig

Prussia

Grodno

Hamburg

HANOVER

Stettin

Bialystok

Gomel

Belgorod

Bremen

BRANDENBURG

Thorn

Poznan

Pultusk 1703

Pinsk

Chernigov

Kharkov

Hanover

Warsaw

Fraustadt 1706

Punitz 1704

SAXONY

SILESIA

Kalisz 1706

Lublin

Kiev

Poltava 1709

Poltava

SMALL

Dresden

Sandomir

Volhynia

STATES

Frankfurt

Prague

Klissow 1702

POLAND

In Personal Union with Saxony

Hetmanate

Krakow

Lvov

Dnieper

BOHEMIA

MORAVIA

Galicia

Tarnopol

Podolia

Brünn

BAVARIA

Munich

Vienna

Danube

ZAPOROZHIAN COSSACKS

Azov

Salzburg

AUSTRIA

Buda

Pest

Jedisan

CRIMEAN TATARS

KHANATE

Leoben

HUNGARY

Moldavia

OF CRIMEA

Venice

Triest

Szeged

Transylvania

Jassy

Crimea

Kaffa

Fiume

Temesvár

Brasov

Akkerman

Bakchisarai

Bologna

VENETIAN REPUBLIC

Zara

Bosnia

Pècs

Galati

Kilia

TUSCANY

SAN MARINO

Spalato

Wallachia

Black Sea

PAPAL STATES

Adriatic Sea

RAGUSA

Mostar

Nish

Bucharest

Ruschuk

Varna

Rome

Sofia

Bulgaria

Burgas

Sinope

Naples

Salermo

NAPLES

Tyrrhenian Sea

Albania

Bari

Üsküb

OTTOMAN

Rumelia

Philippopolis

Adrianople

Constantinople

Izmit

EMPIRE

Izmir

Samsun

Salonica

Brusa

Angora

Military administration

Belgrade

Danube

Peter I, who ascended the throne in 1682, was later known as Peter the Great for his modernizing policies.

overseeing other organs of state and controlling the budget. In 1718, Peter realized that the various chancelleries needed simplifying, with careful demarcation of tasks. Following Danish and Swedish models, he inaugurated nine colleges or ministries. Their number was eventually increased to thirteen, with responsibilities for policy areas such as foreign affairs, state revenues, justice, state expenditure, and mining and manufacture. This bureaucratized state administration was carefully regulated and encouraged to develop Russian resources to meet state needs.

Prior to the reign of Peter the lands of the nobility were either lands granted for state service or patrimonial lands. An edict of 1714 introduced primogeniture and all property became hereditary. The nobility became richer under Peter, acquiring more land and serfs, which gave them an increased stake in the new state. In 1722, Peter's Table of Ranks maintained that promotion in the state would be for services rendered, not ancient lineage. The boyars were gradually overtaken by new blood, which allowed people in the army, navy, and civil life to rise up the fourteen ranks to the first level, with hereditary nobility being conferred on reaching the eighth level in the civil service and fourteenth in the military. As well as the Naval Academy and the School of Mines, schools for mathematics were established in each province, and diocesan schools were opened.

Peter's reforms had such a devastating impact on Russia that opposition was not unusual, indeed there was a continuous murmur of discontent. Many were concerned by the attacks upon traditional aspects of life. The Old Believers, who had rejected various Church reforms (for example the new sign of the cross) were persecuted, while the Orthodox Church objected to the abolition of the patriarchate of Moscow, after which the Church was placed under the authority of the Holy Synod, a state institution. The tax on beards, intended to westernize Russian appearances, was an assault on Orthodoxy and stimulated a deep-seated conservatism and xenophobia. Peter also made harsh and excessive demands upon the population, with the growth of serfdom, the soul tax (a new unit of taxation based on a male of working age), conscription into the army for life or to work on building St Petersburg. Concern was sometimes expressed at the brutal, uninhibited manner of implementing reform with the use of coercion and military force. Peter's ruthlessness was an aspect of his energetic but flawed personality, which may be traced back to ill-treatment in childhood.

Opposition took many forms, with people drifting to the frontiers in Siberia to escape the new Petrine state. Some fled or ignored labor drafts, while the "Old Believers" deemed Peter the anti-Christ. After a Cossack rebellion on the Don led by Conrad Bulavin, the new leader Nikita Golyi protested that the Cossacks had rebelled to defend the Church and monks. Outright rebellion was common, as was demonstrated by the streltsy revolts. In addition, there was virtual colonial war in the Urals (1705–11) against the Turkic Bashkirs who tried to prevent Russian seizure of their lands. In 1709–10 there were also peasant revolts along the Volga.

Peter's relations with his son, Alexis, symbolize the problems of modernizing in an innately conservative country. Peter was worried that if Alexis succeeded him, then his modernizing achievements might be discarded. Alexis fled to Austria and upon his return, renounced his rights to the succession in 1718 and gave them to Peter's other son by Catherine. Peter's Secret Chancellery conducted a political investigation of opposition leaders and assessed whether Alexis was implicated in any plot. Although evidence of Alexis' hostility was found, that of organized opposition was not. Nevertheless, under prolonged torture, Alexis admitted treason and was condemned to death. He died in 1718 before the sentence could be carried out.

Peter was exceptional in the sheer, frenetic energy applied to every aspect of Russian life. With his urge to expand territorially, and gain an outlet to the sea, he transformed the military, political, economic, social, and educational dimensions of Russia. Peter's acquisition of a Baltic coastline was essential for Russia in becoming a European power and accelerated trade and economic development. Peter's personal character was unlike most monarchs'. He was coarse and lacked courtly gentility. As a military leader, Peter lacked genius but survived various vicissitudes and made the best of terrain and climate to eventually win the Great Northern War.

Peter introduced conscription to the army, and large numbers of Russians, with the exception of members of the clergy and the unfit, fell under the draft. Peter modernized his army, introducing a new military manual, and insisting that advancement—for aristocrats and peasants alike—was based on merit. Elite regiments of guards were created, and they were Peter's most loyal and dedicated supporters. Peter can also be credited with creating a modern navy, establishing a shipbuilding industry, and commissioning 48 major warships.

In conclusion, Peter inherited a backward and lethargic state and through sheer determination initiated some monumental reforms which his successors would need to refine and temper. He constructed an autocracy, which consolidated the state in alliance with the noble elite. Russia now had an institutionalized caste system, underpinned by an enserfed peasantry whose condition steadily deteriorated in ensuing years. Although Peter's policies had many opponents and imposed great sacrifices upon Russian society, they were mostly successful and were continued by his successors with the support of most of the Russian elite.

Russia after Peter: The Rule of the Empresses

After Peter's death in 1725, the succession was determined by a series of coups d'état carried out by aristocratic families who supported one member of the ruling house or another. Peter's widow and second wife, Catherine I (1725–27) succeeded to the throne, but her death re-opened the vexed question of succession. Prince Alexander Menshikov, with the support of the Guards regiments, managed to get his royal candidate Peter II (1727–30) accepted, but he died of smallpox aged fourteen years. Political intrigue followed, with Anne, Duchess of Courland (1730–40) being chosen. She was a daughter of Ivan V, Peter I's co-ruler. She refused to place limits on her power and, proclaiming herself an officer of the Guards, used those regiments to exile those families behind succession plots while she moved Baltic Germans into positions of influence. Anne hoped to ensure a smooth succession and chose as her heir Ivan VI (1740–41), great-grandson of Ivan V, as the next tsar, but he was overthrown by Peter the Great's daughter, Elizabeth (1741–62). Elizabeth chose her nephew, Peter III (1762) as her successor but he was overthrown and killed, and was succeeded by his wife, Catherine II the Great.

This tumultuous period benefitted from a number of reforms. Elizabeth returned the Senate to its previous function as a major policy-making and supervising body. The state's government could only operate with an educated and cultured nobility and gradually French influences entered Russia and were inculcated into a Corps of Cadets from 1731. Moscow University and the Academy of Arts in St. Petersburg were opened in 1757. Elizabeth's court was lavish and luxurious, but the court's vulgarity can be contrasted with notable architectural developments in St. Petersburg, such as the Winter Palace and the Peterhof, which introduced the Baroque into the capital.

Peter I's early industrialization drive was continued, based upon the mining, smelting, and processing of iron and copper. Ironworks at Tula, Lake Ladoga, and in the Urals produced so much that Russia became self-supporting in the munitions industry. Successful manufacturers and merchants were often ennobled: the most famous were the Stroganovs and Demidovs, who controlled mineral manufacturing, distilleries, woollen mills, paper, glass, and potash. Anne established 25 ironworks and Elizabeth a further 57. Russia became the largest pig-iron producer in Europe and an exporter of weapons of war. The Baltic and Caspian ports linked Russia to the West and the Caspian connected Russia to Persia and India. British and Dutch ships carried most seaborne trade, and Russia enjoyed a favorable balance of trade. Internal trade was developed with large trade fairs at Irbit, Tikhvin, Gzhatsk, Briansk, Chernigov, Kursk, Belgorod, Poltava, Nizhni Novgorod, and St. Macarius on the Volga.

In foreign policy, Russia entered the War of Polish Succession (1733–35) and supported the successful claimant, Augustus III of Saxony (1734–63), thereby acquiring influence in Polish domestic politics. Russia declared war on Turkey in 1736 but only acquired Azov, with its fortifications having to be razed as stipulated by the 1739 Treaty of Belgrade. A Russo-Swedish war lasting from 1741–43 was ended by the Treaty of Åbo (1743), which gave Russia Vilmanstrand and Fredrikshamn. These acquisitions provided an extra defensive cordon sanitaire for St. Petersburg. In 1746, Russia joined Austria in the War of Austrian Succession (1740–48) but the 1748 Treaty of Aix-la-Chapelle brought no benefits to Russia. In 1756, Russia joined with France and Austria to fight Prussia. Inconclusive campaigns followed and in 1762 Empress Elizabeth died and was succeeded by her Prussophile nephew, Peter III, who immediately withdrew Russia from the war. Nevertheless, the potential danger of Russia and the formidable quality of the Russian army were recognized throughout Europe after its performance in the Seven Years' War (1756–63).

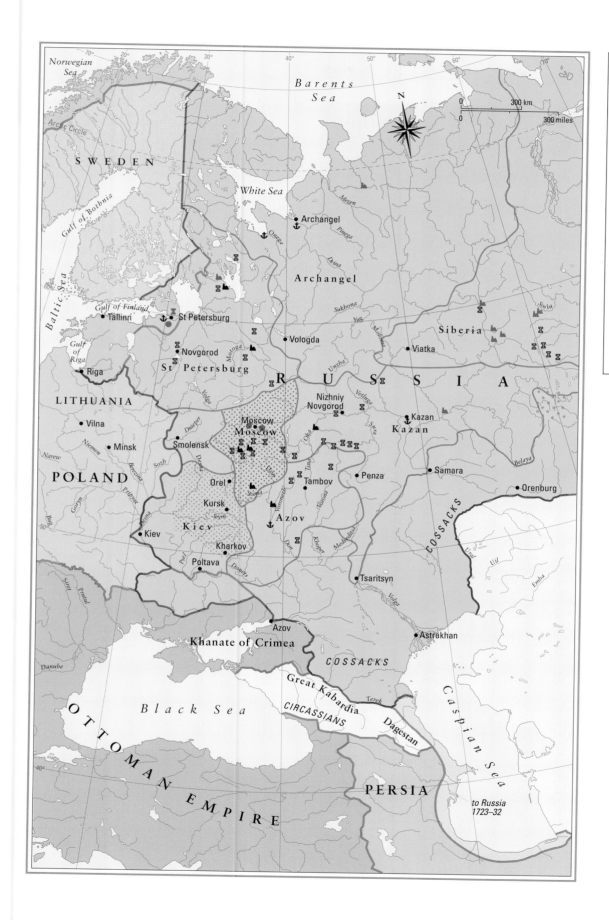

Industry Under Peter the Great
1689–1725

——	Russian border c. 1725
Azov	Provinces established by Peter the Great
	Area with over 20 inhabitants per square verst (1 verst = 2/3 mile/ c.1km)
	Area with between 10–20 inhabitants per square verst

Industry c. 1725

Iron foundries and smelters

Iron manufacturing

Major dockyards

Copper smelters and workshops

Copper manufacturing

Powder works

Catherine the Great

This painting, by Dmitry Levitsky, portrays Catherine the Great, ruler of Russia from 1762 until 1796.

ciously, graduating from novels to serious works on constitutional law by the English judge and politician Sir William Blackstone (1723–80), especially *The Commentaries on the Laws of England*. She wrote many stories, plays and music by herself. She communicated with Voltaire (François-Marie Arouet, 1694–1778), a leading French Enlightenment figure and philosopher, and Denis Diderot (1713–84), a major contributor to the *Encyclopédie*. She was also aware of Cesare Beccaria's (1738–94) works on criminal justice, notably his *On Crimes and Punishment*. Her financial aid to Diderot elicited a letter from Voltaire in December 1767 in which he praised her as "the brightest star of the North," who had saved his friend from hunger.

A highly intelligent woman, she imbibed new ideas of the Enlightenment and was a patron of literature. She founded schools, which were not always successful, but should be remembered for inaugurating the Smolny Institute for Noble Girls in St Petersburg. Her court was lavish, exciting and she gave her name to an "age," turning her capital into the "Venice of the North." Yet Catherine was a realistic, ruthless woman who immersed herself in raison d'état and manipulated the European balance of power to her advantage. She used her boundless energy and intellect to confront key problems in a relatively backward and conservative state. Like Peter, Catherine managed to modernize the state by educating a narrow elite whose ideas eventually percolated downwards into other social strata. This modernization came at the expense of sacrificing liberal reforms to territorial expansion and consolidating serfdom. These aspects were noted in Alexander Radishchev's (1749–1802) book, *A Journey from St. Petersburg to Moscow*, which was considered a threat to the state. The author was exiled to Siberia for ten years and the book was not seen unabridged until 1905.

Catherine's character was forged in adversity. In 1744, at age fifteen, she left her German home to marry the mentally-unstable Peter. Bullied and humiliated by her mother-in-law, who prevented her from seeing her son, she managed to survive and led a coup that overthrew her husband in 1762. Once she became tsarina, she resolved to rule Russia herself or through trusted advisers.

She spent her early years reading vora-

Russian Expansion to 1795

- Russian Empire c. 1725
- Bashkir Rising 1735–40
- Pugachev's Rebellion 1773–74
- ● Town captured by Pugachev
- Territory acquired 1730–95
- Russian border c. 1795

Norwegian Sea

Barents Sea

SWEDISH EMPIRE

White Sea

Gulf of Bothnia

● Archangel

Mezen

Pinega

Onega

Dvina

Archangel

Baltic Sea

Gulf of Finland

● Tallinn
Estonia
● St Petersburg

RUSSIAN

Novgorod

Sukhona

Yug

Sosva

Gulf of Riga

Livonia
● Riga

● Novgorod

● Vologda

Msta

Mologa

● Viatka

Molonia

Unzha

EMPIRE

LITHUANIA

Moscow

Volga

Vetluga

Kazan

Sura

● Kazan

Ufa
Zlatoust ●

● Vilna

1772

● Smolensk

● Moscow

Nizhniy
Novgorod

Oka

● Alatyr

Belaya

1795

Narew

Niemen

● Minsk

Dnieper

Berezina

Sozh

Desna

Don

● Orel

Tsna

● Tambov

Izh

● Penza

Moksha

● Samara

Tatishchevo ●
● Orenburg

POLAND

Bug

Goryn

Pripyat

● Kursk

Sosna

Voronezh

Belgorod

Voronezh

● Saratov

● Yaitsk

1731
Ilinskaya ●

1793

Kiev

Psel

● Kharkov

Don

Khoper

Medvedits

● Kamyshin

LITTLE HORDE
(Russian Vassal from 1731)

Ural

Uil

● Kiev

Vorskla

● Poltava

Donets

Zaporozhe
1774

Astrakhan

● Tsaritsyn

Volga

● Guryev

Emba

1791
● Odessa

1783

● Azov

1783

Danube

Black Sea

Kabardia

Terek

CIRCASSIANS

● Astrakhan

Turkestan
(Persian Vassal)

Caspian Sea

1786
● Tarki

Dagestan

GEORGIA

Prut

OTTOMAN EMPIRE

PERSIA

N

0   100 km
0   100 miles

Another criticism levelled at Catherine was her penchant for lovers such as Gregory Orlov (1734–83), Gregory Potemkin (1739–91), Peter Zavadovsky (1739–1812). and Platon Zubov (1767–1822). This predilection appears not to have affected her critical abilities, her focus on issues, or her capacity to rule. In fact, some lovers were Catherine's talented allies and played a key role in her success, as did other figures such as Count Nikita Panin (political mentor to Catherine), and leading military men such as Alexander Suvorov, Count Peter Rumiantsev, and Admiral Samuel Greig.

Catherine's reign was dominated by wars with Turkey, Sweden, and Persia and the destruction of Poland as a state. In foreign policy, Catherine II was Peter I's true heir. Driven by the desire to expand Russia's borders, to gain Black Sea ports and to influence European affairs, to acquire both territory and people, Catherine sought empire as a manifestation of Russian power. Catherine rejected her husband's military alliance with Prussia. In 1763, the king of Poland, Augustus III died, which left Poland's elective kingship up for auction. Stanislaw Poniatowski, Catherine's former lover, was elected king of Poland, protected by a Russian army of 15,000 men. A vicious war ensued between Russians and Polish nationalists, and when a contingent of Poles crossed into the Ottoman Empire, followed by Russian troops, the Ottomans declared war in October 1768.

The Russian campaign against the Ottomans was immediately successful, with troops seizing Taganrog and Azov on the Don, occupying Moldavia and capturing Bucharest. The Russian Baltic fleet deployed a squadron to the Mediterranean. In November 1769, Orlov led a British-officered Russian fleet from the Baltic to the Mediterranean to defeat the Turks at Chesme, destroying 70 enemy ships—a mixture of ships of the line, frigates, xebecs, galleys, and other small craft. Control of the Aegean encouraged minority groups in the Balkans to rise up and help the Russians and the victory aided the seizure of the Crimea.

Meanwhile, Rumiantsev beat Ottomans and Crimean Tatars at Larga and later at the Kagul where 27,000 Russians defeated 150,000 enemy troops; various forces on the River Pruth were also taken. Before the balance of power was totally overturned in Russia's favor, Frederick the Great of Prussia (1712–86) planned the first partition of Poland, so Prussia and especially Austria could seek recompense there for Russia's Turkish gains. By this partition Russia acquired White Russia and lands up to the Dvina and Dnieper, some 35,521 square miles (92,000 sq.kms.) with 1.3 million, mostly Greek Orthodox, inhabitants.

Success in Poland paved the way for an accommodation with Turkey. The Treaty of Kuchuk-Kainarji was signed in 1774. Russia made a number of gains including new lands adjacent to the Black Sea. Free passage for its merchant ships through the Dardanelles and Bosphorus was guaranteed and it was permitted to build fortresses at Kerch, which guarded the entrance to the Sea of Azov and Yenikale. Moldavia and Wallachia were granted autonomy, with a Russian right to intervene to protect the population, and Crimean independence was recognized. The Russians claimed that the terms of the treaty gave them the right to protect Orthodox Christians in the Ottoman Empire. This diplomatic success helped shape Russian foreign policy during the nineteenth century and led to plans to break out of the Black Sea into the Mediterranean. Russia now had springboards for future adventures on its borders. In the Crimea, a new khan came to power, Devlet Giray. Catherine thought her candidate, Shahin Giray, was more appropriate to Russian aims and he was supported by Russian troops in a successful bid to supplant Devlet.

In 1780, during America's struggle for independence, Russia promoted an idea of armed neutrality at sea to protect commerce. This notion received the support of Denmark, Sweden, Prussia, Austria, and Portugal, with France and Spain recognizing the principle. Russia argued that merchant vessels of nations not party to the American conflict had a right to trade freely with all nations, even belligerents, without interference and to carry enemy goods, excepting contraband. They also had a right to break a blockade if it was not enforced properly. This League of Armed Neutrality was anti-British in intent and to the extent that it limited Britain's freedom of action, assisted America.

Meanwhile, the Crimean khan gave his territories to Catherine in 1783. Russia was supported by Austria in this act and the annexation

was completed by the defeat of a Nogai Tatar rebellion in the Kuban. Generalissimo Prince Alexander Suvorov rendered the coup de grace at the battle of the Laba River. As a prelude to more Russo-Turkish hostility and warfare in the Caucasus, Catherine concluded the Treaty of Georgievsk (1783) with Hercules II (1720–98) of Kartalinia-Kakhetia (eastern Georgia). Russia would defend Georgia's territorial integrity and the continuation of the Bagratian dynasty in return for virtually controlling her

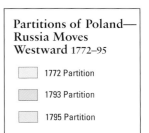

Partitions of Poland—Russia Moves Westward 1772–95

	1772 Partition
	1793 Partition
	1795 Partition

Emilian Pugachev, a disaffected ex-soldier, and leader of the Cossack rebellion. He assumed the leadership of an alternative government in the name of Tsar Peter III, attracting wide support proclaiming an end to serfdom.

a boundary along the Dniester River, while returning Moldavia and Bessarabia, which Russia had overrun. Turkey acknowledged Russia's acquisition of the Crimea.

In the years following the first partition of Poland, the Polish parliament (Sejm) implemented a series of governmental reforms and in 1791 introduced a new constitution that changed the elective into a hereditary monarchy, with the Elector of Saxony and his dynasty to succeed Poniatowski. Additionally, executive power was granted to the king and a council of state, a two-chamber legislature was constructed, and the old liberum veto was ended and replaced by majority voting. Catherine sat and watched, waiting for the Turkish war to end. After Jassy, troops were withdrawn from the south and Catherine and some Polish magnates signed the Confederation of Targowitz (1792) in defense of the old constitution or rather, Russian interests. This group was aided by 90,000 Russian troops who could fight without fear of Prussian or Austrian intervention since these two states were at war with revolutionary France. Eventually, Catherine struck a deal with Frederick William II of Prussia, who promptly invaded Poland to help partition that country a second time. Russia gained Lithuania, much of the western Ukraine and Podolia, acquiring an extra three million inhabitants and providing Catherine with a rich granary and borders on the Pripet marshes. A Polish national uprising followed, led by Tadeusz Kosciusko (1745–1817). This national hero fought until captured in October 1794, while Warsaw held out until November. Poland was then finally dismembered in a third partition in 1795. Russia acquired Courland, Samogitia, Volhynia, and the remnants of Lithuania with the city of Vilnius, some 46,332 square miles (120,000 sq.kms.) and one million inhabitants. Catherine had now pushed Russia into central Europe, making her a vitally important factor in a Europe that was confronting an expanding revolutionary France.

foreign policy, with Georgia promising not to be dependent upon any other power. Secret clauses allowed Russian troops to be stationed at the capital, Tbilisi.

In 1787, the Ottoman Empire, startled and apprehensive at Russian adventures in the Crimea and Caucasus, went to war against Russia, which was joined by Austria as in the terms of the 1781 treaty. The war failed to provide the immediate successes of the war of 1768–74. Nevertheless, Suvorov's victories helped force the Ottomans to an armistice after Admiral Theodore Ushakov (1744–1817) defeated the Turkish fleet at Cape Kaliakra. The 1792 Treaty of Jassy gave Russia Ochakov and

However, Catherine never had to face the difficult decision to fight revolutionary France because she died in November 1796. Catherine has been criticised for being tricked by Frederick the Great in 1772. Poland was already a Russian puppet, and Russia gained less by partition than by continuing the presence and life of a puppet regime. However, partition provided a permanent solution to Poland.

Although historians often focus on the impressive territorial gains made by Catherine, her domestic policies were instrumental in creating a specific type of despotic or autocratic state. Catherine was inspired by the thoughts and values of the Enlightenment. This suggests that Catherine was exposed to new philosophical ideas and that they were used to create a new, more rational, society based upon social contract theories, natural law, and concern with the welfare of their subjects. However, although Catherine was a natural reformer, she had to work within the constraints of custom, noble privilege, and within the context of rebellion and war. She read Montesquieu's *L'Esprit des Lois* and envisaged a society of estates, each possessing a specific function within the state. Thus, nobles, urban dwellers, and peasants were given certain freedoms and an increased role in local adminstration by the reforms of her reign.

The most important symbol of Catherine's reforming nature was her convocation of a legislative commission in Moscow to codify laws. The commission comprised members of all estates, even some classes of peasants. They received Catherine's Instruction (Nakaz) comprising several hundred articles, over half based upon Montesquieu's philosophy. Unfortunately, class differences and a lack of experience meant that little emerged from the Commission. She also learned that the nobility would never accept loss of their privileges, including their monopoly right to own serfs. Being a realist, Catherine realized that the monarchy could not rule Russia without noble support.

In 1773 the Cossack Emilian Pugachev (1740–75) led a serious revolt, an insurrection comprising Yaik Cossacks, traders, artisans, Volga boatmen, Ural miners, clergymen, exiled Poles, and Bashkirs. This rebellion reflected the anger of groups losing freedom as central government increasingly touched upon their lives. Pugachev promised the restoration of hunting and fishing rights to the Yaik Cossacks, an end to Old Believer religious grievances and freedom for oppressed nationalities. He decreed the abolition of serfdom and led his supporters against Orenburg in the Urals. Landowners fled and the rebellion was so serious that Catherine sent an army against him. Despite repeated defeats, Pugachev always managed to slip away and gather more followers. In 1774, Pugachev was finally defeated at Tsaritsyn by Suvorov and executed in Moscow in January 1775.

Catherine's reign failed to benefit 95 percent of the population but the aristocracy regarded it as a golden age. Catherine gradually changed over the course of her reign, moving from a liberal reform position to a more conservatively realistic stance after Pugachev's revolt. Catherine never interfered with French affairs, even after the king and queen were guillotined in 1793, preferring other countries to confront France with counter-revolutionary armies while Russia digested more Polish territory.

To survive as a foreign "usurper" on the Russian throne, Catherine needed to be unscrupulous and ruthless where necessary, but also very skilful as a politician; she was also vainglorious, domineering, and eager for power and territorial aggrandizement. However, she knew how to win over skilful associates such as Orlov and Potemkin, who served her with devotion and loyalty. Catherine considered Russia to be part of Europe and to that end she encouraged the further spread of European thought and civilization into her court and to the nobility, in the process consolidating the alienation of the nobility from the masses.

Russia as a Great Power, 1800

Catherine II's death was followed by the accession of her son Paul I (1796–1801), who sought to undo many of his mother's liberal reforms, thereby eradicating some early seeds of civil society by destroying autonomous local government institutions and the Charter of Nobles. He loved all matters Prussian, especially military drill and uniforms, and even decreed a courtly dress and behavior code, including a ban on dancing the waltz. Russia rapidly became a police state, which eroded the more enlightened aspects of Catherine's work and caused disquiet among elite groups who favored the previous regime.

Hating the French Revolution, Paul I played a major role in establishing the Second Coalition (1798) against France. This alliance with Great Britain, Austria, Naples, Portugal, and the Ottoman Empire had an ingenious if ambitious campaign plan. An Anglo-Russian army led by the British Duke of York was to clear out the French from the Batavian Republic (the Netherlands). Meanwhile, another Austrian army was to liberate Germany and Switzerland. The Russian contribution, in conjunction with Austria, led to a victory at the Battle of Cassano (April 1799), which freed Milan and destroyed the French client state, the Cisalpine Republic. General Suvorov went on to occupy Turin and clear the French from most of north Italy. He then crossed the Alps into Switzerland via the St. Gotthard pass to link up with a Russian force under General Korsakov which was liberating Switzerland with the Austrians. After Korsakov was defeated at Zürich, the Russians withdrew from Switzerland. Elsewhere, Britain and Russia had not co-operated very well and the Dutch campaign fizzled out. However, the Russians did enjoy some naval success; a squadron from Sevastopol seized the Ionian islands in the Adriatic from French control and occupied them until 1807.

At this point, Paul suddenly changed his views, a not unusual occurrence. Britain had attacked Denmark to prevent its fleet coming under French control. Owing to a Russo-Danish treaty, Paul established the League of Armed Neutrality of the major Baltic states against Britain, modelling it upon a similar league during the American War of Independence (1775–83). The League fell apart after the assassination of Paul in March 1801 and Admiral Nelson's destruction of the Danish fleet at Copenhagen in April 1801. Simultaneously, Paul had allied with Napoleon, planning a joint attack on India—Britain's imperial gem.

Paul's wilful and autocratic outlook combined with his arbitrary foreign and domestic policies drove a group of nobles to murder him. Alexander, his son, knew of the plot but presumably believed that Paul would be merely forced to abdicate in a coup d'état. Alexander became tsar the day following the assassination. To secure his immediate future, he granted amnesties to his father's political enemies and to those exiled by Paul.

Alexander (1801–25) has proved an enigma to historians. He received an enlightened education and did much during his reign to develop education in Russia and improve the effectiveness of the central government. But he was unwilling, or unable, fundamentally to change the authoritarian nature of his regime. He presided over a military machine, which saw Russia moving through Poland and into the Ottoman Empire. In Scandinavia, Finland was seized from Sweden in 1809 and war with Persia saw the annexation of Georgia and parts of Dagestan and Shemakha. In the Americas, Russia had established a settlement at Old Kodiak in Alaska in 1784 and founded New Archangel (Sitka) in 1804. In 1811 Fort Ross, just north of San Francisco in California, was founded to counter Spanish moves northward. A Russo-Turkish War (1806–12) gained Bessarabia by the Treaty of Bucharest.

Alexander's struggle against French hegemony in the Napoleonic wars would ultimately make him the arbiter of Europe's destiny. Russia was a world power, a prime factor in European affairs, instrumental in the inauguration of the Congress System ("government by conference"), which became a formalized method of resolving international disputes and policing the continent of Europe.

Russian Expansion in Europe 1800–09

- Russian Empire 1800
- Russian acquisitions 1800–09
- Russian dependencies
- French Empire or dependency
- Allied to France

SWEDEN

Finland
to Russia 1809

Åland Islands • Åbo
• Helsingfors • Vyborg
Gulf of Finland
• Stockholm • St Petersburg
Dagö • Reval • Narva
Lake Ladoga
Lake Onega
• Belozersk
• Novgorod
Ösel
• Dorpat
• Pskov
Gotland
• Tver
• Riga
• Rzhev
Calmar *Öland*
• Libau
• Moscow
Baltic Sea
• Memel
• Polotsk
Bornholm
• Vitebsk • Smolensk
• Tilsit • Kovno
• Tula
• Vilna
PRUSSIA • Danzig • Königsberg
• Minsk • Mogilev
• Orel
• Grodno
GRAND DUCHY OF WARSAW
• Bialystok *to Russia 1807*
• Kursk
• Poznan
Thorn
• Warsaw
• Pinsk
• Gomel
Oder
• Chernigov
• Belgorod
• Sandomir
• Kharkov
• Crakow
• Kiev
Lvov
Moravia
Galicia
• Brünn
• Tarnopol *to Russia 1809*
• Vinnitsa
• Poltava
Dnieper
AUSTRIAN EMPIRE
• Ekaterinoslav
RUSSIAN EMPIRE
• Vienna
Dniester
• Debrecen
• Buda • Pest
• Jassy
• Odessa
Hungary
Transylvania
Moldavia
• Akkerman
Crimea
• Pecs
• Szeged
• Brasov
Occupied by Russia
• Kilia
Russian
• Temesvar
• Bakchisarai
Dependencies
Military Frontier
Wallachia
• Bucharest
Bosnia
• Belgrade
1804
• Mostar
Danube
• Ruschuk
1803
Black Sea
• Nish
• Varna
RAGUSA *Occupied by Russia*
MONTENEGRO
Bulgaria
• Sofia
• Burgas
Adriatic Sea
• Üsküb
OTTOMAN
• Philippopolis
• Adrianople
• Bari
Rumelia
• Constantinople
• Izmit
• Taranto
Albania
• Salonica
• Brusa
• Ankara
Ionian Sea
• Janina
Aegean Sea
EMPIRE
N

57

The Napoleonic Wars

When Alexander I became tsar, he depended upon the nobility for support and the nobles depended upon peasant labor for their wealth. Russia's military machine, officered by nobles and filled by conscripted peasants who served for 25 years, also rested on serfdom. Alexander initially toyed with the notion of a constitution but this would antagonize the nobility and destabilize the state, so reform was forgotten. Russia lagged a century behind much of western Europe in terms of intellectual, social, and economic development. Russia's large peasant pop-

Tsar Alexander I striking a military pose in this portrait by Franz Krüger.

ulation was burdened by every state requirement in terms of taxes, soldiers, agricultural workers, and industry. The demands of foreign policy contributed to inertia and a lack of reform. The exigencies of many different wars made vast demands on time, energy, and resources, the major war being that against Napoleon.

Alexander's struggle against French hegemony ultimately made him the arbiter of Europe's destiny. In 1805 the Third Coalition was formed against France and Spain, comprising Great Britain, Russia, Prussia, Austria, and Sweden. Napoleon marched east from France and encountered a Russian army led by Alexander and Michael Kutuzov (1745–1813), which had joined an Austrian army at Austerlitz on 2 December. Napoleon achieved a decisive victory, which crushed Austria while the

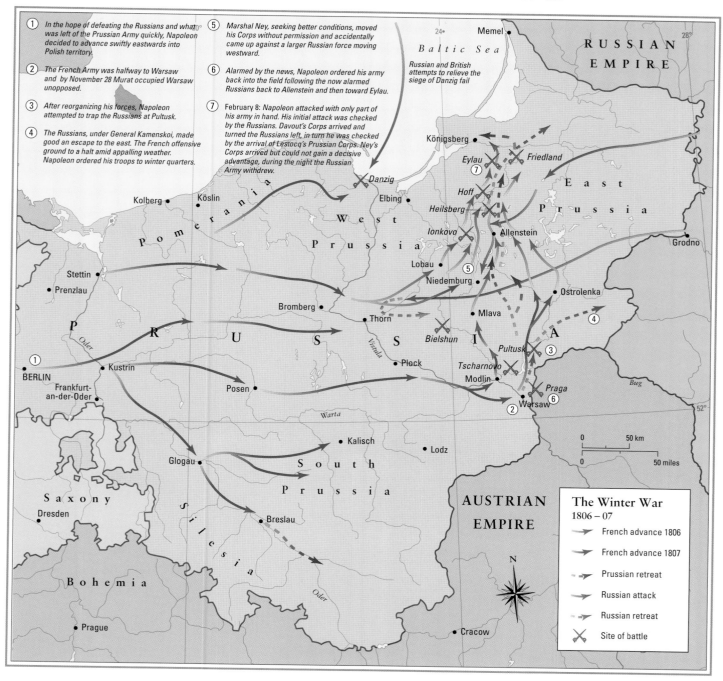

① In the hope of defeating the Russians and what was left of the Prussian Army quickly, Napoleon decided to advance swiftly eastwards into Polish territory.

② The French Army was halfway to Warsaw and by November 28 Murat occupied Warsaw unopposed.

③ After reorganizing his forces, Napoleon attempted to trap the Russians at Pultusk.

④ The Russians, under General Kamenskoi, made good an escape to the east. The French offensive ground to a halt amid appalling weather. Napoleon ordered his troops to winter quarters.

⑤ Marshal Ney, seeking better conditions, moved his Corps without permission and accidentally came up against a larger Russian force moving westward.

⑥ Alarmed by the news, Napoleon ordered his army back into the field following the now alarmed Russians back to Allenstein and then toward Eylau.

⑦ February 8: Napoleon attacked with only part of his army in hand. His initial attack was checked by the Russians. Davout's Corps arrived and turned the Russians left, in turn he was checked by the arrival of Lestocq's Prussian Corps. Ney's Corps arrived but could not gain a decisive advantage, during the night the Russian Army withdrew.

Russian and British attempts to relieve the siege of Danzig fail

The Winter War
1806 – 07

→ French advance 1806
→ French advance 1807
⇢ Prussian retreat
→ Russian attack
⇢ Russian retreat
✕ Site of battle

Russians retreated through Hungary and Poland. Prussia joined the fray but was routed at Jena and Auerstadt (October 1806). Russia rushed to aid Prussia and together they fought Napoleon at Eylau (February 1807) in an indecisive engagement. Napoleon then defeated the Russians at Friedland (June 1807) and the treaty of Tilsit compelled Alexander to join a formal alliance with France. Russia agreed to enforce a blockade of British goods while being allowed to expand into Turkish and Swedish lands.

The years between Tilsit and the French invasion of Russia in 1812 saw Russia wage war against Turkey, winning Bessarabia, and in February 1808 Russia occupied Swedish Finland making that country a Grand Duchy under the Romanov dynasty. A war with Persia (1804–13) and the subsequent Treaty of Gulistan meant that Russia gained territory in Georgia and

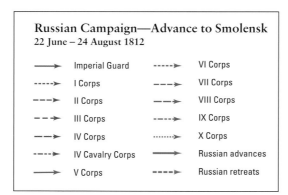

Russian Campaign—Advance to Smolensk
22 June – 24 August 1812

⟶	Imperial Guard	┈┈⟶	VI Corps
┈┈⟶	I Corps	┄┄⟶	VII Corps
╌╌⟶	II Corps	╌╌⟶	VIII Corps
╍ ╍⟶	III Corps	╍ ╍⟶	IX Corps
━ ━⟶	IV Corps	┈┈⟶	X Corps
┄┄⟶	IV Cavalry Corps	⟶	Russian advances
⟶	V Corps	╍╍╍⟶	Russian retreats

① June 24: Napoleon's Grande Armée crosses into Russian territory planning to destroy the two main Russian armies in succession.

② MacDonald's Tenth Corps, advancing through the provinces of Kovno and Courland, guarded Napoleon's northern flank.

③ Schwarzenberg, later helped by Reynier's Seventh Corps, protected the southern flank and faced Tormassov's Third Russian Army.

④ Jerôme failed to carry out Napoleon's instructions allowing the Russians to maneuvre out of danger. He was replaced by Davout.

⑤ Davout blocked Bagration's attempt to join Barclay by his intervention and victory near Mogilev.

⑥ Barclay intended to fight at Smolensk but faulty Russian staff work confused the Russian plan. But the errors stalled a turning movement by Napoleon which would have destroyed both Russian armies.

⑦ Napoleon pursued the Russians eastward again trying to turn their flank by crossing the Dnieper River. After a hard fought but unsuccessful battle, Barclay retreated to the east of Smolensk escaping Napoleon's intended trap.

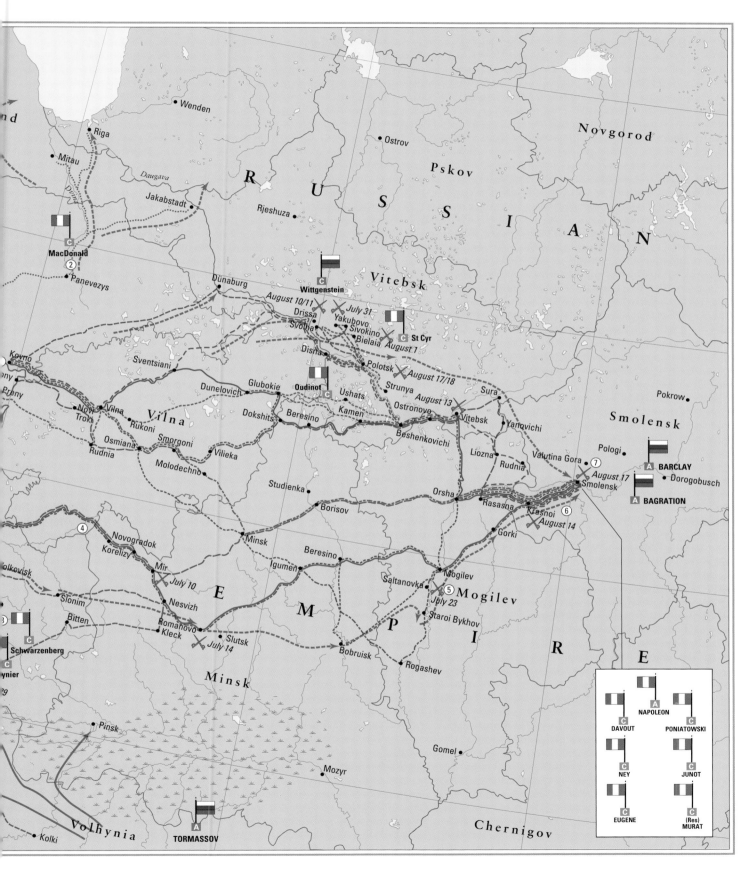

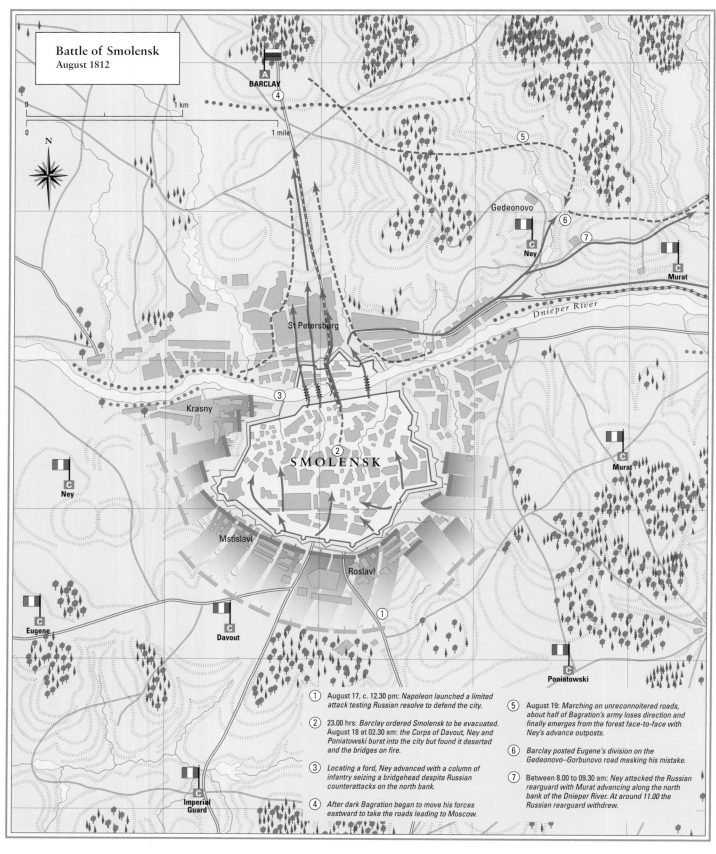

Battle of Smolensk
August 1812

0   1 km

0   1 mile

N

BARCLAY
④

⑤

Gedeonovo

Ney
⑥

⑦

Murat

Dnieper River

St Petersburg

③

Krasny

②

SMOLENSK

Ney

Mstislavl

Murat

Roslavl

①

Eugene

Davout

Poniatowski

Imperial
Guard

① August 17, c. 12.30 pm: Napoleon launched a limited
attack testing Russian resolve to defend the city.

② 23.00 hrs: Barclay ordered Smolensk to be evacuated.
August 18 at 02.30 am: the Corps of Davout, Ney and
Poniatowski burst into the city but found it deserted
and the bridges on fire.

③ Locating a ford, Ney advanced with a column of
infantry seizing a bridgehead despite Russian
counterattacks on the north bank.

④ After dark Bagration began to move his forces
eastward to take the roads leading to Moscow.

⑤ August 19: Marching on unreconnoitered roads,
about half of Bagration's army loses direction and
finally emerges from the forest face-to-face with
Ney's advance outposts.

⑥ Barclay posted Eugene's division on the
Gedeonovo–Gorbunovo road masking his mistake.

⑦ Between 8.00 to 09.30 am: Ney attacked the Russian
rearguard with Murat advancing along the north
bank of the Dnieper River. At around 11.00 the
Russian rearguard withdrew.

other parts of the Caucasus, while Persia was forbidden to have a navy in the Caspian Sea. Elsewhere, Alexander failed to enforce the blockade against British trade while Napoleon seized the Duchy of Oldenburg whose duke was Alexander's brother-in-law.

In June 1812 Napoleon invaded Russia with his Grande Armée of some 600,000 men. The Russians, led by Michael Barclay de Tolly (1761–1818), retreated, drawing Napoleon deeper into Russia. The French supply lines became extended and troops were lost along the route. A Russian scorched earth policy meant there was no forage and when Smolensk was reached, the city was burnt down to destroy Russian military supplies. Meanwhile, the Cossacks, commanded by Ataman Matvei Platov (1751–1818), were moving around Napoleon's advancing armies attacking isolated units and picking off any unfortunate stragglers. Napoleon pushed forward and eventually faced Kutuzov's army at Borodino. Napoleon never expected a full-scale battle with the Russians, thinking that just to invade Holy Mother Russia would lead to Russian capitulation. Kutuzov had decided to fight Napoleon's army before they reached Moscow. Accordingly he deployed his army of 114,000 near the village of Borodino where they faced a force of 130,000, Napoleon disregarded advice to turn the Russian left flank, and he insisted on a series of infantry attacks against the heavily-defended field fortifications. The fight was intense—the Russians hung onto their positions and counterattacked in dense formations. By around 4:00pm a desperate combined cavalry/infantry attack captured the Great Redoubt in the center of the Russian lines. At this point Napoleon could have exploited the breach and destroyed the Russian army; however, he refused to commit his Imperial Guard. As a consequence, the Russian army was able to disengage and slip away during the night leaving some 22,000 dead on the battlefield. The Russian army, now around 90,000 including the wounded, retreated southeast of Moscow. For Napoleon the road to Moscow lay open at the cost of 30,000 casualties.

Napoleon straggled into Moscow a week later and was surprised to find that the Russians had not sent a delegation to negotiate an armistice. Instead, the city's governor, Count Theodore Rostopchin, had evacuated the city, opened the prisons, and left a small squad to light fires throughout the city. Napoleon had imagined that Alexander would give in with the fall of Moscow but Alexander was made of sterner stuff, or the tsar was simply more afraid that his own advisors and courtiers, who were increasingly inflamed with anti-French nationalism, might assassinate him as had happened to his father. Napoleon stayed in Moscow for a month but winter was fast approaching and a military solution had to be found fast. On 19 October Napoleon marched southwest toward Kaluga, where Kutuzov was encamped with his army.

Napoleon hoped to take a more southern route than his invasion path but was stopped at the Battle of Maloiaroslavets. This town changed hands eight times during the course of the battle, leaving the French in control, thanks to the bravery of Italian troops. Kutuzov retreated to prepared defensive lines at Kaluga. Napoleon did not wish to face another Borodino and was forced to retreat along his line of advance. Harassed by skirmishers, Cossacks, hunger, and winter, the French finally reached the River Berezina to find the bridges burnt. French horses died during the retreat, thereby destroying the French cavalry and logistic train, while various battles along the way, especially at Vyazma, Krasnoi, and Polotsk, drained the French army of men. A battle to cross the river ensued and the river was finally crossed, thanks to lack of coordination among Russian generals and the courage of the French troops. About 25,000 men were left to reach Germany at the end of 1812.

A Sixth Coalition was constructed comprising Prussia, Russia, Great Britain, Portugal, Sweden, and some German states, and eventually Austria. Napoleon returned to France to rebuild his army and determined to defeat the various Sixth Coalition armies in detail. Kutuzov was declared Supreme Commander of the Allied armies; unfortunately he died soon after, in April 1813. Tsar Alexander I assumed command with General Wittgenstein, who took over command of the Russian army. On 2 May, Napoleon tricked the Prussians and Russians into a trap at Lützen, each side suffering severe losses. The French troops were so exhausted from marching all day that Alexander was lucky enough to extricate his troops. He was pursued but made a stand at Bautzen where each side suffered some 20,000 casualties. The Coalition decided on a new plan at the Convention of Trachenberg (July 1813). Its leaders had determined that they would not fight Napoleon directly but would at-

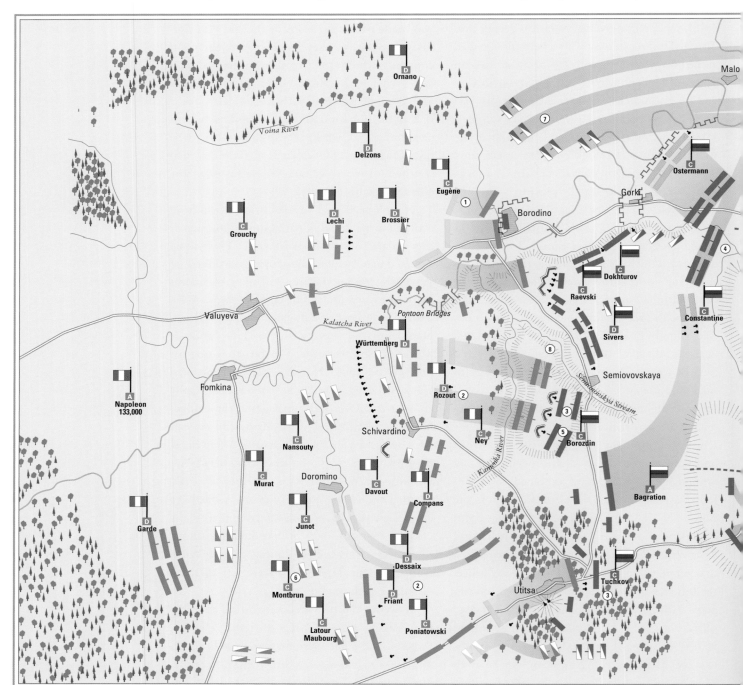

tack his subordinate marshals and so weaken his forces. Accordingly, Crown Prince Charles of Sweden (1763–1844), formerly French Marshal Bernadotte, defeated Marshal Oudinot at Grossbeeren while Prussian Marshal Blücher beat Marshal Macdonald at the Katzbach. On 26–27 August 1813, Austrian and Russian troops fought Napoleon at the Battle of Dresden, losing some 38,000 men.

Nevertheless, the Coalition gradually sapped Napoleon's resources and pushed him back. The turning point occurred at the Battle of Leipzig in October. This was the largest battle of the Napoleonic Wars, with 225,000 troops on the French side and 375,000 Austrians, Russians, Swedes, and Prussians on the other. Napoleon fought a series of desperate battles as the Allied armies marched on Leipzig, but he was fighting against growing odds and failed to defeat the converging forces. His German allies defected.

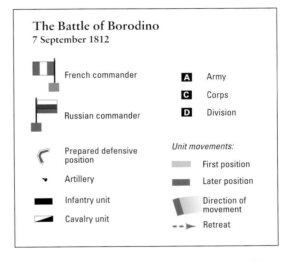

The Battle of Borodino
7 September 1812

French commander

Russian commander

Prepared defensive position

Artillery

Infantry unit

Cavalry unit

A Army

C Corps

D Division

Unit movements:

First position

Later position

Direction of movement

Retreat

(1) 6.00 am: *A preliminary bombardment by 120 guns is followed by an exploratory advance by Eugene against Borodino.*

(2) *Simultaneously Poniatowski advanced on Utitsa and Davout made ground in the center.*

(3) *Initial French advances are driven off in the center and checked near Utitsa.*

(4) *Kutuzov moves troops from his right to support his hard-pressed center and left.*

(5) 8.00 am: *The struggle for the flèches rose to a peak as Ney and Friant joined Davout in renewed assaults. The battle swung to and fro, the Russians held their ground, as French casualties mounted.*

(6) 10.00 am: *Napoleon had committed everything to the battle but persistantly refused to commit the Guard.*

(7) 12.15 pm: *Kutuzov launches a cavalry attack on the French left flank, they are eventually driven off by Grouchy's cavalry.*

(8) 2.00 pm: *A renewed attack on the Russian center, delayed by the cavalry action, was now launched. After another bloodbath, the Russians eventually gave way. Kutuzov manages to withdraw his battered army in reasonably good order.*

Baggovut

Platov

Uvarov

Korf

arclay de Tolly

etz River

Moscova River

Kutuzov
120,800

Moscow Militia

Old Post Road

N

0   1 km

0   1 mile

On 19 October he ordered a phased retreat, his army crossed the only bridge over the River Elster. However, the bridge was destroyed before the rear guard could cross. The battle cost each side tens of thousands of casualties but the Coalition was able to replenish its forces while Napoleon took back to France some 70,000 soldiers still under command, while 30–40,000 stragglers slowly followed on behind. In addition, there were still 90,000 soldiers holding fortresses east of the River Rhine and another 100,000 soldiers faced General Wellington's invading army in the southwest of France.

In January 1814, Prussian troops crossed the Rhine into France. Since Blücher's forces were widely dispersed, Napoleon launched a series of successful attacks at Champaubert, Montmirail, and Vauchamps. He then turned on the Austrians at Mormant, Montereau, and Méry. Blücher joined forces with the Swedes and al-

though their advance guard was beaten at Craonne they defeated Napoleon at Laon, forcing him to retreat towards Rheims. On 20 March, Napoleon faced his enemies at Arcis-sur-

1. Winter 1812–13: *Russian army deploys into Prussia and the Grand Duchy of Warsaw.*

2. 22 January: *Frederick William, King of Prussia, leaves Berlin for Breslau.*

3. Spring 1813: *Russian army launches a series of raids deep behind French lines. Berlin is occupied 4 March.*

4. April: *Napoleon concentrates his army to face Allied forces.*

5. May: *driving the Allied forces eastwards, Napoleon is victorious at Lützen and Dresden.*

6. 4 June–16 August: *armistice, Napoleon uses the time to train his inexperienced army.*

7. 12 August: *Austria declares war.*

8. 26–27 August: *Battle of Dresden.*

9. September–October: *after suffering defeats, ending with the Battle of Leipzig, the French army withdraws to the Rhine.*

10. 30–31 October: *Bavarian-Austrian army attacks the retreating French but is beaten off.*

Leipzig Campaign
1813

→ French advance

-→ French retreat

→ Allied advance

-→ Allied retreat

✕ Battle site

⌂ Major fortress held by French

▨ French Empire

▨ Territory under French control until Oct. 1813

▨ Allies 1813

▨ Joined Allies by August 1813

▢ Neutral

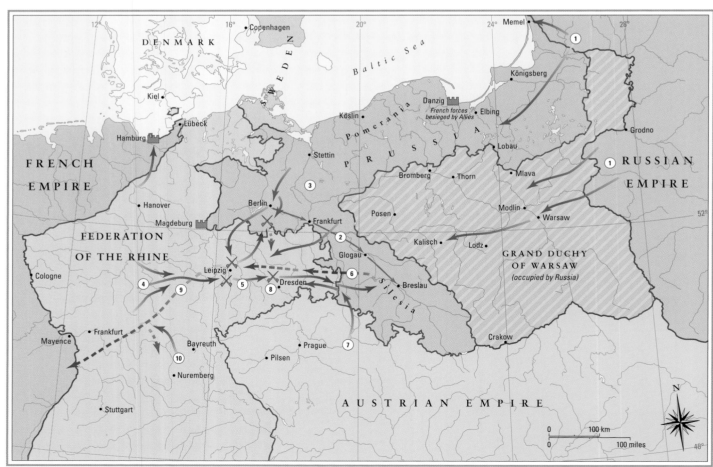

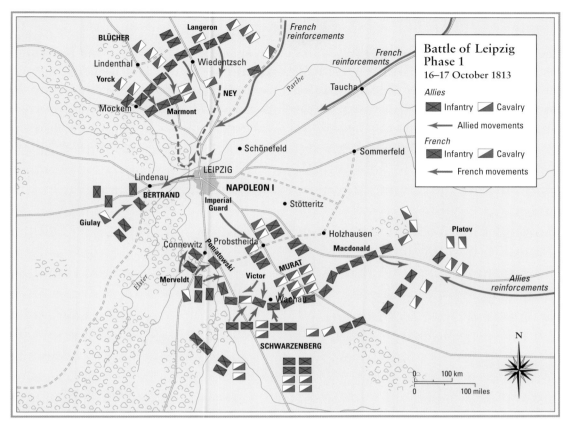

Battle of Leipzig
Phase 1
16–17 October 1813

Allies

Infantry   Cavalry

Allied movements

French

Infantry   Cavalry

French movements

French reinforcements

French reinforcements

BLÜCHER

Langeron

Lindenthal

Wiedentzsch

Yorck

NEY

Taucha

Mockem

Marmont

Parthe

Schönefeld

Sommerfeld

LEIPZIG

Lindenau

NAPOLEON I

BERTRAND

Imperial Guard

Stötteritz

Giulay

Probstheida

Holzhausen

Platov

Connewitz

Poniatowski

Macdonald

Elster

Merveldt

Victor

MURAT

Allies reinforcements

Wachau

SCHWARZENBERG

N

0   100 km

0   100 miles

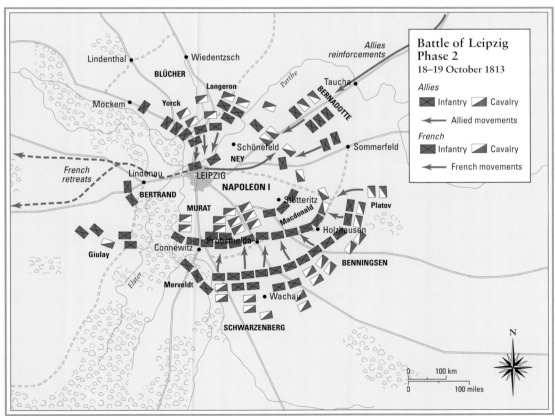

Battle of Leipzig
Phase 2
18–19 October 1813

Allies

Infantry   Cavalry

Allied movements

French

Infantry   Cavalry

French movements

Allies reinforcements

Lindenthal

Wiedentzsch

BLÜCHER

Langeron

Mockem

Yorck

BERNADOTTE

Parthe

Taucha

Schönefeld

NEY

Sommerfeld

French retreats

Lindenau

LEIPZIG

BERTRAND

NAPOLEON I

MURAT

Stötteritz

Platov

Macdonald

Connewitz

Probstheida

Holzhausen

Giulay

BENNINGSEN

Elster

Merveldt

Wachau

SCHWARZENBERG

N

0   100 km

0   100 miles

Aube but retreated in the face of huge numbers. Elsewhere, on 25 March, cavalry of Austria, Russia, and Württemberg routed a French force under Marshal Auguste Marmont at the Battle of Fère-Champenoise. On 26 March the final battle of the Napoleonic Wars between Russian and French forces took place at Saint Dizier. Although the Russians were beaten, Napoleon—unsure as to the precise location of the enemy—wasted three entire days, during which his capital was under threat. Meanwhile, Marshals Marmont, Édouard Mortier, and Bon-Adrien Moncey, seeing that prolonging the war was pointless, surrendered their troops to the Coalition at Montmartre. The French Sénat then deposed Napoleon and when his marshals mutinied he offered his unconditional abdication, ending the wars.

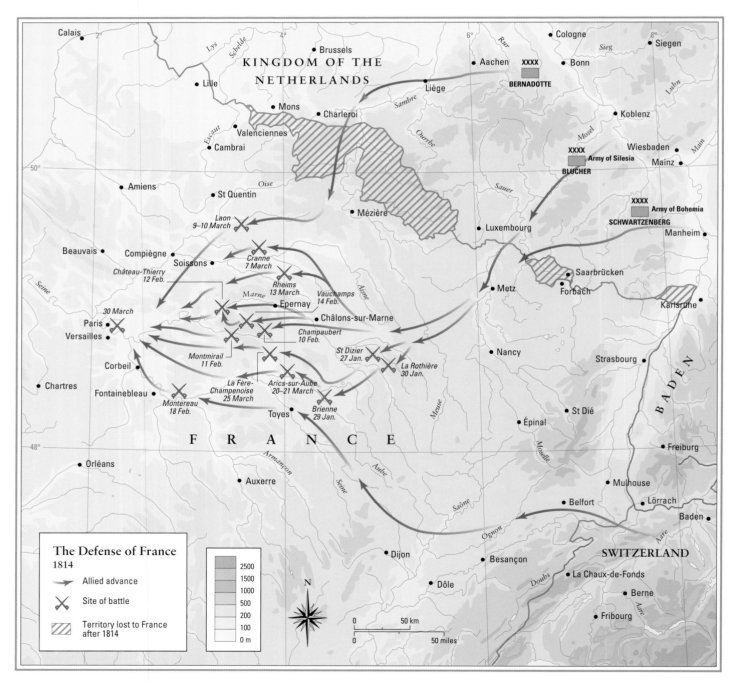

The Defense of France
1814

→ Allied advance

✗ Site of battle

▨ Territory lost to France after 1814

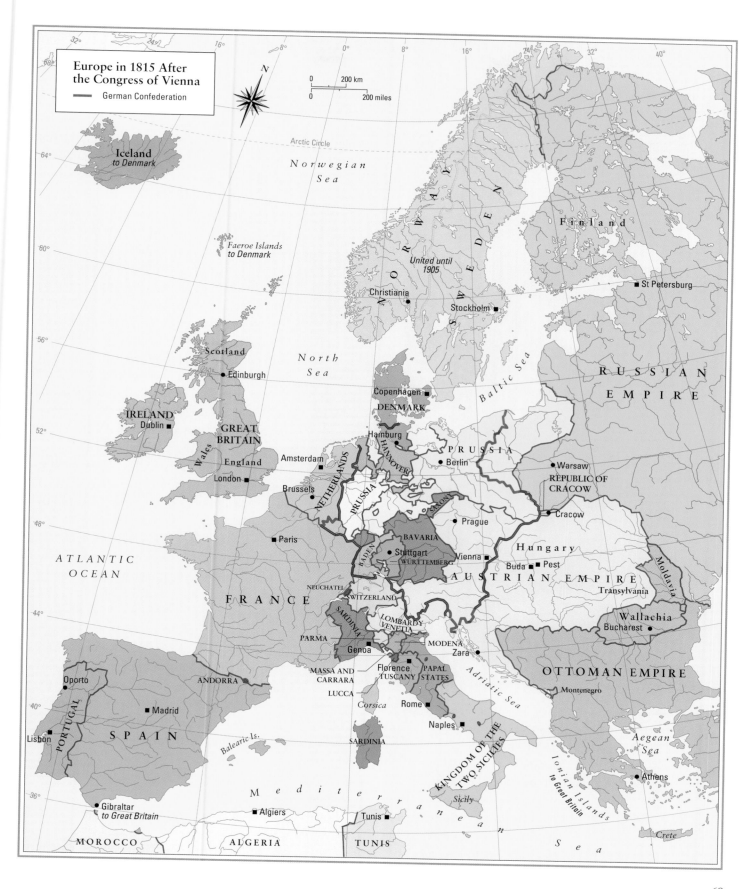

Europe in 1815 After
the Congress of Vienna
—— German Confederation

0   200 km
0   200 miles

N

Iceland
to Denmark

*Norwegian
Sea*

Faeroe Islands
to Denmark

Arctic Circle

United until
1905

Christiania

Stockholm

■ St Petersburg

F i n l a n d

Baltic Sea

RUSSIAN
EMPIRE

Scotland

● Edinburgh

*North
Sea*

Copenhagen ■

DENMARK

IRELAND
Dublin ■

GREAT
BRITAIN

Wales

England

London ●

Amsterdam ■

Brussels ●

NETHERLANDS

Hamburg

HANNOVER

PRUSSIA

PRUSSIA

● Berlin

Warsaw ●

REPUBLIC OF
CRACOW

SAXONY

Prague ●

Cracow ●

● Warsaw

ATLANTIC
OCEAN

■ Paris

F R A N C E

NEUCHATEL

SWITZERLAND

BADEN

BAVARIA

Stuttgart ●
WÜRTTEMBERG

Vienna ■

H u n g a r y

Buda ■ ● Pest

AUSTRIAN EMPIRE

Transylvania

Moldavia

SARDINIA

PARMA

LOMBARDY
VENETIA

Genoa ●

MODENA

Zara ●

Wallachia

Bucharest ●

MASSA AND
CARRARA

Florence
TUSCANY

PAPAL
STATES

Adriatic Sea

OTTOMAN EMPIRE

LUCCA

Oporto ●

ANDORRA

Corsica

Rome ●

Montenegro

Madrid ■

S P A I N

PORTUGAL

Lisbon ●

Balearic Is.

SARDINIA

Naples ■

KINGDOM OF THE
TWO SICILIES

*Aegean
Sea*

*Ionian Islands
to Great Britain*

● Athens

Gibraltar
to Great Britain

Algiers ■

Sicily

M e d i t e r r a n e a n

Tunis ■

S e a

Crete

MOROCCO

ALGERIA

TUNIS

Nicholas I and the Crimean War

Nicholas I of Russia inspects his troops deployed in Bessarabia.

Decembrists were noble army officers. In Petersburg the "Northern Society" demanded a liberal-constitutional political order. The more radical "Southern Society," headquartered in Chernigov, was in favor of a republic and emancipation of the serfs. The movement was crushed in December 1825. A few Decembrist leaders were executed, though most were banished to Siberia, becoming martyrs in the eyes of later Russian liberals and radicals.

The Decembrist revolt confirmed Nicholas I's belief that only the autocracy could save Russia from revolution and anarchy. But in the first two decades of his reign he introduced reforms that did much to improve the educational system, the quality of the bureaucracy, and the lives of the huge numbers of peasants who belonged not to private landlords but to the state.

A new ideological concept was introduced by Nicholas, that of "Official Nationality," based upon the three precepts of Orthodoxy, Autocracy, and Nationality. The peoples of Russia were to demonstrate loyalty to the unrestricted authority of the tsar, to the traditions of the Russian Orthodox Church, and to the Russian language. This conceptual social cement would lead ultimately to pressure on non-Russian peoples' languages, institutions, and even culture.

Internal opposition took various distinct forms. Peasant revolts occurred every year during 1828–54. Disturbances also took place in White Russia. More importantly, the Polish people and army joined together to rally to the nationalist cause, rebelling in 1831. Russian troops were poured into Poland to crush the rebels; Roman Catholics were persecuted and the universities of Warsaw and Vilnius were closed. Nicholas's hostility towards revolt is perhaps best seen when the Russian army marched into Hungary to break the 1848–49 Magyar revolution.

When Alexander I died in 1825, confusion over the succession occasioned a revolt by various revolutionary societies. The natural heir was Alexander's brother, Constantine, who had renounced his claims in 1822 in favor of his younger brother Nicholas (1825–55), although the wider public had not been informed of this decision. In the resulting chaos, there ensued the so-called Decembrist revolt; most

In foreign policy, Nicholas helped Greece

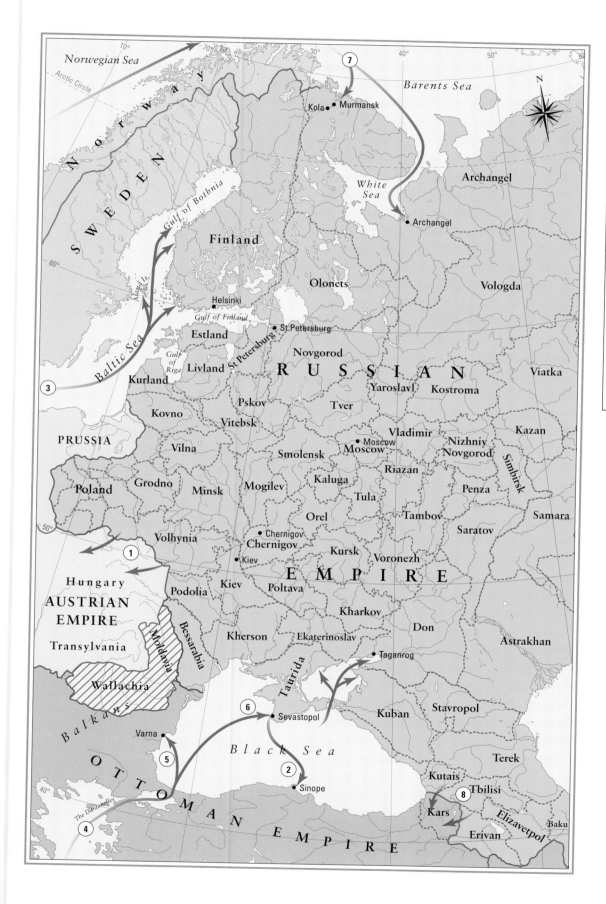

The Russian War
1853–56

1 Russian intervention in Hungarian Revolution 1848–49

Russian troops deployed in Wallachia and Moldavia in June 1853 until 1854, after which Austrian forces occupied the principalities

2 Russian destruction of Ottoman fleet at Sinople 30 November 1853

3 Allied fleet operated in the Baltic from April 1854

4 Allied attacks end of 1854

5 Allied Expeditionary Force lands at Varna July 1854

6 Allied land on Crimea September 1854— operations continued to 1856

7 Allied Naval operations April to November 1856

8 Caucasus—operations by Ottomans and Russian forces 1853–56

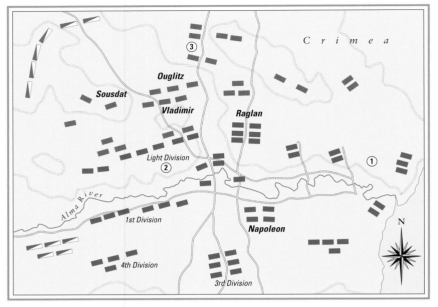

Battle of Alma 1854

(1) The French on the right scale the cliffs and assault the Russian left. Unable to bring up support the assault slows.

(2) An attack by the Allied center and left cause the Russians to begin to panic.

(3) The first battle of the Crimean war goes to the Allies as the Russians break and fall back on Sevastopol.

Russian

Infantry

Cavalry

Allies

Infantry

Cavalry

achieve a degree of independence and conducted a war with Turkey (1828–29). In the 1830s Russia enjoyed paramount influence in Constantinople. Following a conflict with Persia (1826–28). Russia gained Armenia, Azerbaijan, Nakhichevan, Nagorno-Karabakh, and Akhaltsikhe. Russia continued to expand in Central Asia and the subjugation of the Khazaks was achieved when the Elder Horde was defeated around 1847.

In 1833 the Treaty of Unkiar Skelessi was signed, which obliged Russia and the Ottoman Empire to come to each other's aid in the event that either was attacked. However, a resumption of warfare between Egypt and its nominal overlords, the Ottomans, annulled this agreement. It was replaced by the London Treaty in 1840, and the Straits Convention of 1841. Nicholas I proved a willing participant, and in 1844 he traveled to Britain, meeting with members of the British government, after which a memorandum was produced in Russia and accepted by both parties.

Nicholas I found himself confronted by an attempt after 1850 by the new French Emperor Napoleon III to challenge Russia's position in relation to the Ottoman Empire. The dispute initially centered on rival Catholic and Orthodox rights in Palestine. Negotiations col-

lapsed and, on 4 October 1853, the Ottoman Empire declared war on Russia. The Russian army had occupied Wallachia and Moldavia at the end of June 1853. Ottoman forces then concentrated along the River Danube. Concerned by these moves, Austria massed an army in Transylvania. Russian hopes of encouraging an Orthodox Christian rising in Serbia and Bulgaria came to nought. On 29 May 1854, under Austrian pressure, Nicholas I signed a protocol and withdrew his army from the Danubian provinces of Wallachia and Moldavia—largely ending the battle front with the Ottomans along the Danube. Austrian forces then occupied these provinces. Meanwhile, at sea on 30 November 1853, a Russian fleet, sailing from Sevastopol, had destroyed a Turkish fleet at the port of Sinope. Fearful of Russian intentions, Britain and France had deployed warships, initially to the Dardanelles and then into the Black Sea, in support of the Ottomans. Outraged by the Russian naval attack on Sinope, Britain and France declared war on Russia. In June 1854, a combined Allied Expeditionary Force was landed at Varna on the Black Sea coast of Bulgaria. From there, Britain and France landed troops in the Crimea, where they turned their attention to the Black Sea Crimean naval base at Sevastopol. A war of mutual attrition began with heavy losses on each side, mainly from disease. The battles of the Alma (September 1854), Balaclava (October 1854), Inkerman (November 1854), and Tchernaya (August 1855) followed before Sevastopol fell in September 1855. At Balaclava the British cavalry Light Brigade charged into the face of Russian artillery fire, leaving 40 percent of the cavalrymen dead or wounded, and inspiring Alfred, Lord Tennyson, British poet laureate (1809–92), to commemorate the event in verse.

The war was fought out over a much wider front than that of the Crimea. In the Baltic, a large amphibious operation was undertaken, designed to attack Russian trade and the important naval base at Kronstadt, adjacent to St

Petersburg, in April 1864, and again in August. The Russian fleet stayed close to the guns of the great naval base—the Allies withdrew. Successful attacks were carried out along the Finnish coast and in the Öland islands. In the fall of 1854, a squadron of warships sailed for the White Sea, they bombarded and destroyed the town of Kola and, after a day-long attack, their attempt to storm the port of Archangel failed.

In the Far East, an Anglo-French naval force carried out a series of bombardments and raids on Russian trade around Kamchatka and the Sakhalin islands.

In 1853 there were a number of clashes along the mountainous border of the Caucasus, a region that was already an area of tension between Russia and the Ottoman Empire. Russian forces in the area were mostly deployed in controlling rebellious mountain tribes. However, after reinforcement and reorganization,

Russian forces drove back initial attacks and advances. In 1854, Russia won further victories. By 1855, the Russians eventually captured the important town of Kars. Operations on both sides continued until the Peace of Paris in March 1856.

Nicholas died in February 1855, leaving his successor to make peace. After 1848 he attempted to insulate Russia from outside influences through repression and censorship. His policies to stabilize Europe in 1848 led to more repression at home. His foreign policy became increasingly aggressive over the "Eastern Question," dissipating Russian resources and exposing Russia's technological inferiority. The growth of intellectual dissent called into question the very edifice of tsarism and this early experiment in building a civil society led to demands for reform, which was to be attempted under the next tsar, Alexander II.

73

The Alexanders—Reform and Reaction

Alexander II (1855–81) ascended the throne during the Crimean debacle, which had shown up the weaknesses in Russia's political, social, and economic institutions. Consequently, he implemented a number of reforms by emancipating the serfs (1861), instituting elected local councils (zemstva) in 1864, revising the judicial system, (1864), and creating municipal government (1870). These reforms did not satisfy radicals, while alienating conservatives. As a result, political polarization increased and was manifested in the growth of revolutionary movements and a Polish revolt (1863). This in turn frightened Alexander II away from further liberal measures toward repression. In 1881 he was assassinated by a revolutionary socialist.

Peasant emancipation was the most significant reform. Some 50 million serfs, both state and privately owned, paid most of the state's taxes, provided landlords with a living, and underpinned the entire country. After protracted consultation and consideration by "gentry committees," established in all the provinces, Alexander signed an emancipation manifesto in 1861. The Emancipation Statute contained the principle that serfs should have enough land to support themselves, while at the same time honoring financial obligations to former masters and the state. The state paid the bulk of the "redemption" price, for land the serfs had acquired, to the landlords in interest-bearing bonds and would recover the cost from the peasants in redemption annuities spread over 59 years. The price paid was generally in excess of average land values.

Alexander II expanded Russia's imperial borders by finally conquering the peoples of the Caucasus, digesting all Siberia, acquiring land from China, and building Vladivostok on the Pacific. In Central Asia, Russia pushed into the khanates, thereby approaching British possessions in India and causing international friction. In foreign policy, Alexander wanted to restore Russia to the international position it held before the Crimean War.

Under the terms of the Treaty of Paris, which ended the Crimean conflict, Russia lost some territory and could not build forts nor possess a fleet in the Black Sea. This was a great blow, not just to Russian pride but also to its security.

When the Franco-Prussian War broke out in 1870, Alexander abrogated the Black Sea clauses of the Paris Treaty and subsequently joined the Three Emperors' League. Starting with a rebellion by the inhabitants of Bosnia-Herzegovina, followed by the Bulgars, Serbia, and Montenegro, Russia declared war on Turkey (1877–78) and won. The subsequent Treaty of San Stefano was modified by a congress of the Great Powers at Berlin. Russia gained the Turkish province of Ardahan with its cities of Kars and Batumi, and part of Bessarabia from Romania. At his death at the hands of terrorists of the Narodnaya Volya (People's Will) in 1881, Alexander had achieved vast eastward expansion and laid down the foundations of a modern state.

Alexander III (1881–94) reintroduced harsh rule with the reaffirmation of an autocratic police state. He persecuted non-Orthodox religions and national minorities faced persecution, discrimination, and Russification, especially in Poland, but also in many other regions. Anti-Jewish pogroms flared in the western borderlands in 1881–82.

The German-Russian Reinsurance Treaty replaced the League of Three Emperors in 1887 but this was not renewed and Russia sought a new ally in France. Elsewhere, in Central Asia, Russia acquired Merv and and Turkmen territories, reaching the borders of Afghanistan. Russian troops skirmished with the Afghans at Penjdeh in 1885 and killed many. Britain felt threatened, and only skilful diplomacy averted conflict. An Anglo-Russian Boundary Commission was established to define the border between Russia and Afghanistan, turning the latter into a buffer state between Russia and British India. The southward expansion of Russia was now halted.

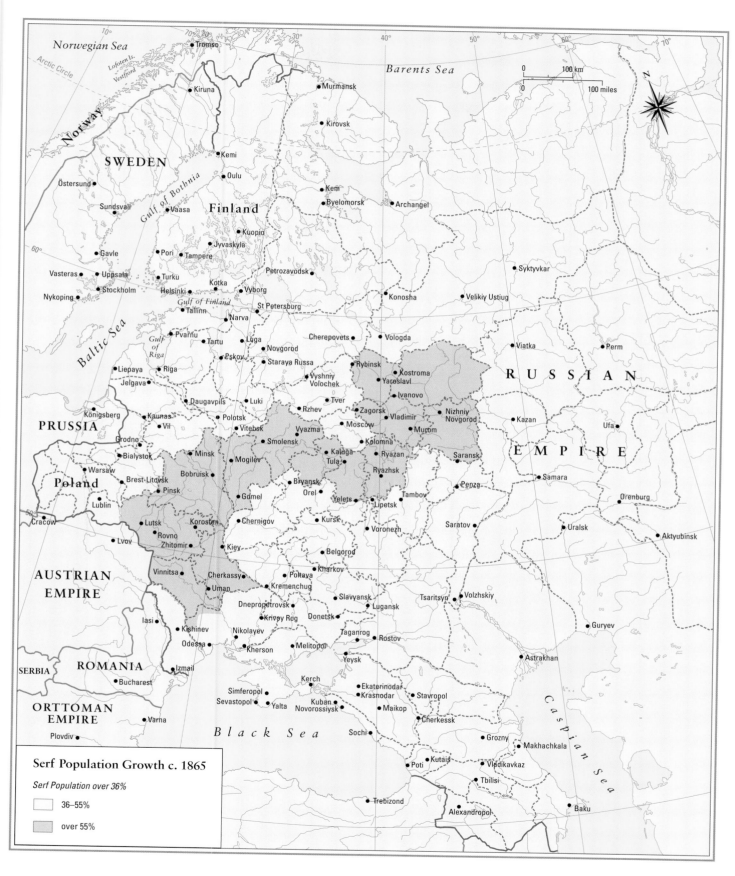

Norwegian Sea

Arctic Circle

Lofoten Is.
Vestfjord

Tromso

Kiruna

Barents Sea

Murmansk

N

0   100 km
0   100 miles

Kirovsk

NORWAY

SWEDEN

Östersund

Sundsvall

Vaasa

Kemi

Oulu

Finland

Kem

Byelomorsk

Archangel

Gulf of Bothnia

Kuopio

Jyvaskyla

Syktyvkar

Gavle

Pori

Tampere

Uppsala

Vasteras

Turku

Kotka

Petrozavodsk

Konosha

Velikiy Ustiug

Nykoping

Stockholm

Helsinki

Vyborg

Viatka

Perm

Baltic Sea

Gulf of Finland

Tallinn

Narva

St Petersburg

RUSSIAN

Pvarnu

Tartu

Luga

Cherepovets

Vologda

Gulf
of
Riga

Pskov

Novgorod

Rybinsk

Kostroma

Liepaya

Riga

Staraya Russa

Vyshniy
Volochek

Yaroslavl

Ivanovo

EMPIRE

Jelgava

Daugavpils

Luki

Rzhev

Tver

Zagorsk

Vladimir

Nizhniy
Novgorod

Königsberg

Kaunas

Polotsk

Vitebsk

Moscow

Murom

Kazan

Ufa

PRUSSIA

Vil

Vyazma

Smolensk

Kolomna

Grodno

Minsk

Mogilev

Kaluga

Ryazan

Saransk

Warsaw

Bialystok

Bobruisk

Tula

Ryazhsk

Brest-Litovsk

Bryansk

Orel

Tambov

Samara

Poland

Pinsk

Gomel

Yelets

Lipetsk

Penza

Lublin

Lutsk

Korosten

Chernigov

Kursk

Saratov

Uralsk

Orenburg

Cracow

Rovno

Zhitomir

Kiev

Voronezh

Aktyubinsk

AUSTRIAN
EMPIRE

Vinnitsa

Cherkassy

Belgorod

Lvov

Uman

Kharkov

Iasi

Kremenchug

Poltava

Slavyansk

Lugansk

Tsaritsyn

Volzhskiy

Kishinev

Dnepropetrovsk

Krivoy Rog

Donetsk

Nikolayev

Taganrog

Rostov

Guryev

Odessa

Kherson

Melitopol

Yeysk

Izmail

SERBIA

ROMANIA

Bucharest

Kerch

Ekaterinodar

Astrakhan

Simferopol

Krasnodar

Stavropol

ORTTOMAN
EMPIRE

Sevastopol

Yalta

Kuban
Novorossiysk

Maikop

Cherkessk

Caspian
Sea

Varna

Black Sea

Sochi

Grozny

Makhachkala

Plovdiv

Kutais

Vladikavkaz

Poti

Tbilisi

Trebizond

Baku

Alexandropol

Serf Population Growth c. 1865

Serf Population over 36%

☐ 36–55%

▨ over 55%

Russian Foreign Policy—China and Japan

In the mid-nineteenth century, Nicholas Muraviev-Amursky, Governor-General of Eastern Siberia, saw Siberia as a preserve for Russian colonization and agricultural development. He wanted to augment the naval station at Petropavlovsk on Kamchatka and assert a Russian presence in China. He feared that Britain, as a result of the Opium Wars, would forestall Russia in China, so in 1858 Muraviev forced the 1858 Treaty of Aigun on China, which gave Russia a foothold on the north bank of the Amur River, after which Khabarovsk was built. When British and French troops occupied Peking in 1860 to coerce China into enforcing the 1858 Treaties of Tientsin, a Russian envoy, General Ignatiev, secured the Maritime Provinces, east of the Ussuri River, for Russia. Russia, which now had a border with Korea, was allowed to construct a new naval base at Vladivostok. A dispute with Japan secured the island of Sakhalin in 1875.

Following the defeat of China in its war with Japan in 1894–95, Russia gained concessions to build the Chinese Eastern Railroad across Manchuria and, in 1898, to build a railroad from Harbin to Port Arthur in the Liaotung Peninsula. Japan had acquired this port at the end of the recent war, but had been forced to release it by the Great Powers. Russia snapped it up, leaving the Japanese furious. Russia then turned its attention to Korea, an area of great interest and concern for the Japanese since it afforded the most direct access to the Chinese mainland. The Russian government was unwisely contemptuous of Japan, despite its willingness to negotiate spheres of influence.

In February 1904 Japan launched a surprise torpedo attack on the Russian Far Eastern Fleet in Port Arthur, leaving two battleships and a cruiser damaged. The Russian government was militarily unprepared; the Trans-Siberian Railroad was incomplete and supplies to the Far East had to be transported across Lake Baikal by steamer. Japanese troops outnumbered Russian forces in the East Asia and were easily reinforceed by sea. The Japanese held naval superiority and possessed a number of good ports, in comparison with Russia's two widely distant naval bases of Port Arthur and Vladivostok.

After victories along the Yalu River and in Manchuria the Japanese besieged Port Arthur, which surrendered in December 1904 after a siege of 148 days. Russia was left with only one serviceable naval base, Vladivostok. The land war ended with the Battle of Mukden, in which the tsar's forces were resoundingly defeated. Meanwhile, the Russian Baltic fleet ran into the powerful fleet of

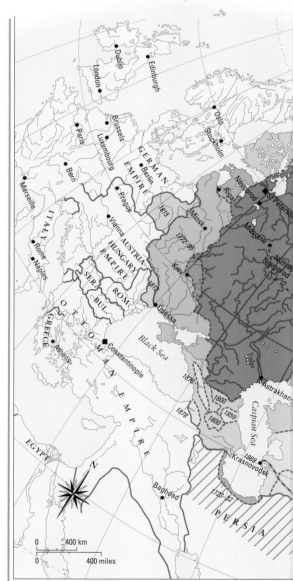

Russian Expansion into Asia to 1900

- Russian Empire, 1598
- Acquisitions, 1598–1689
- Acquisitions, 1689–1725 (Peter the Great)
- Acquisitions, 1725–1796
- Acquisitions, 1796–1855
- Acquisitions, 1855–1900
- Russian sphere of influence in Mongolia and China (1900–14) and in Persia (1907–21)
- Strategic railroads into Asia constructed by 1900

Fort Ross 1811–41

USA

CANADA

Alaska

Fort Wrangel 1834

Anadyr 1762

1800

Nizhni Kolymsk 1644

Nizhni Kamchatsk 1800

Okhotsk 1648

Petropavlovsk

Sea of Okhotsk

S i b e r i a

Yakutsk 1632

Lena

Murmansk

Ural Mountains

1598

Tobolsk

Omsk

Tomsk 1604

1689

Irtysh

1762

Yeniseisk 1619

1618

Yenisei

Chita

Irkutsk 1652

1853

1875–1905

Amur Region 1650–1689 to China 1689 Russian from 1858

Khabarovsk 1860

temporary occupation from 1900

Vladivostok 1860

Kazalinsk 1859

1800

1855

Manchuria

Urga

M o n g o l i a

Mukden

Sea of Japan

Tokyo

Tashkent

Kokand

Amu Darya

1895

Bukhara

ANISTAN

BRITISH INDIA

C H I N A

Beijing

Port Arthur 1898–1905

Kaesong

Yellow Sea

Kaifeng

Luoyang

Huang Ho

JAPAN

Admiral Togo in the Straits of Tsushima on 27 May 1905 where it was destroyed as a fighting force, with only four vessels reaching Vladivostok.

In August 1905, a peace treaty between the two powers was ratified in Portsmouth, New Hampshire. Russia now recognized Japan's interest in Korea, which was annexed by Japan in 1910.

Russia ceded to Japan the southern half of Sakhalin, control of the Liaotung Peninsula, together with Port Arthur and Dairen and extensive rights in south Manchuria. The Russian sphere of interest was confined to northern Manchuria, Outer Mongolia, and Sinkiang, while Japan's interests lay in Inner and southern Mongolia.

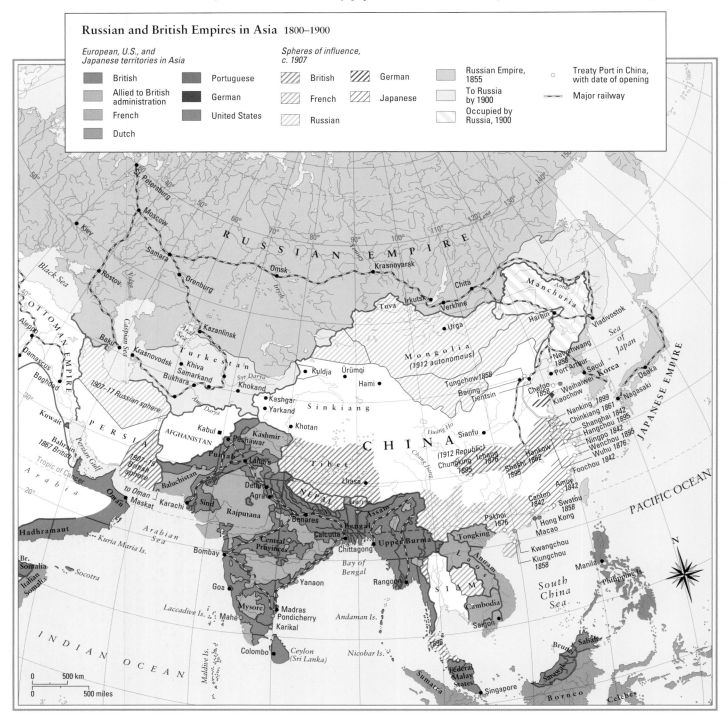

Russian and British Empires in Asia 1800–1900

European, U.S., and Japanese territories in Asia

- British
- Allied to British administration
- French
- Dutch
- Portuguese
- German
- United States

Spheres of influence, c. 1907

- British
- French
- Russian
- German
- Japanese

- Russian Empire, 1855
- To Russia by 1900
- Occupied by Russia, 1900

- Treaty Port in China, with date of opening
- Major railway

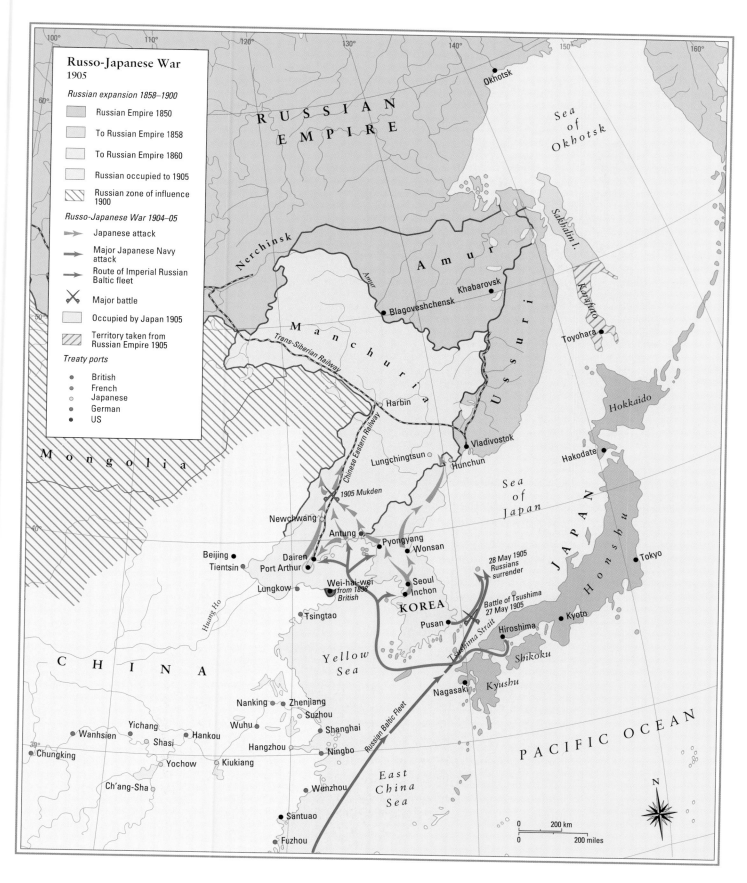

Russo-Japanese War
1905

Russian expansion 1858–1900

- Russian Empire 1850
- To Russian Empire 1858
- To Russian Empire 1860
- Russian occupied to 1905
- Russian zone of influence 1900

Russo-Japanese War 1904–05

- Japanese attack
- Major Japanese Navy attack
- Route of Imperial Russian Baltic fleet
- Major battle
- Occupied by Japan 1905
- Territory taken from Russian Empire 1905

Treaty ports

- British
- French
- Japanese
- German
- US

RUSSIAN EMPIRE

Sea of Okhotsk

Okhotsk

Nerchinsk

Amur

Khabarovsk

Amur

Blagoveshchensk

Sakhalin I.

Karafuto

Toyohara

Manchuria

Ussuri

Trans-Siberian Railway

Harbin

Chinese Eastern Railway

Vladivostok

Lungchingtsun

Hunchun

Mongolia

Sea of Japan

Hokkaido

Hakodate

1905 Mukden

Newchwang

Antung

Pyongyang

Wonsan

Beijing

Dairen

Port Arthur

Tientsin

Lungkow

Wei-hai-wei
from 1898 British

Seoul

Inchon

KOREA

Tsingtao

Pusan

28 May 1905
Russians surrender

Battle of Tsushima
27 May 1905

Tsushima Strait

JAPAN

Honshu

Tokyo

Kyoto

Hiroshima

Shikoku

CHINA

Yellow Sea

Nagasaki

Kyushu

Nanking

Zhenjiang

Suzhou

Wuhu

Shanghai

Yichang

Hankou

Wanhsien

Shasi

Hangzhou

Ningbo

Chungking

Yochow

Kiukiang

Russian Baltic Fleet

East China Sea

Ch'ang-Sha

Wenzhou

PACIFIC OCEAN

Santuao

Fuzhou

Huang Ho

0   200 km

0   200 miles

N

Imperial Expansion—Caucasus

This illustration by J. le Conte, dated 1873, shows various peoples from across the Caucasus region who were absorbed into the expanding Russian Empire.

The Caucasus Mountain range extends for some 600 miles between the Black and Caspian Seas. This region links Europe with western Asia and is a transit area for cultures, peoples, and religions. The inhabitants speak a wide range of languages and have been ruled by all the major historic empires. Early Russian concern with the Caucasus commenced with Peter the Great after Cossacks settled along the River Terek and the Kuban. During the reign of Catherine the Great, the Georgian King Hercules sought her protection from raiders from the mountain tribes of Dagestan. The 1783 Treaty of Georgievsk saw Hercules accepting Russian hegemony in return for a Russian guarantee of Georgian borders and independence. Alexander I reneged on the treaty and incorporated Georgia into Russia in 1801. Russian rule in Georgia was widely unpopular and insurrections followed, yet the ruler of neighboring Mingrelia allowed his lands to be incorporated into Russia in 1803.

Alexander I engaged in a desultory war with Persia; under the 1813 Treaty of Gulistan Russia acquired northern Azerbaijan, Dagestan, Shirvan, Shaki, Karabakh, and part of Talisk. The cities of Baku, Derbent, and Gandzha were ceded to Russia and Persia renounced all claims to Georgia, Mingrelia, Imeretia, and Abkhazia. Persia was pushed even further out of the Caucasus. In 1817, Russia advanced to the River Sunzha in the Chechnyan steppe and constructed a fort at Grozny in 1818. A Russian campaign led to the 1828 Treaty of Turkenchai when Persia ceded the khanates of Yerevan and Nakhichevan.

Wars with Turkey secured the remainder of the Caucasus. The 1828–29 war, precipitated by the Greek revolution, was ended by the Treaty of Adrianople, giving Akhaltsikh to Russia, which added it to Georgia. Other acquisitions were the northeastern shore of the Black Sea, containing the port of Anapa with the enclave ports at Poti and Sukhumi in Abkhazia. The Russo-Turkish war of 1877–78 gave Russia Ardahan, Kars, Batumi, and Bayazid, the latter being returned to Turkey at the 1878 Congress of Berlin, while Batumi was made a free port under Russian control.

Although Russia had incorporated the Caucasus into its empire, its writ and authority did not run throughout all this territory. In particular, two areas proved difficult to control: Circassia and Dagestan. Two campaigns secured eastern Circassia and another, in 1862, secured western Circassia and the various tribes were resettled on the plains or told to emigrate. Some 400,000 moved into the Ottoman Empire. In Dagestan Ghazi Mohammad (1828–34), Gamzat-bek (1832–34), and Imam Shamil (1834–59) were successive leaders of the Muslim Imamate. They preached a holy war against foreigners, secular rulers and landowners, such as Cossacks who were sometimes granted confiscated land. This insurrection encouraged Avars, Chechens, and Azeris to fight the Russians too. Russian campaigns against Imam Shamil, who had become a legendary leader of Caucasian resistance to Russian hegemony, cost them 12,000 casualties between 1840 and 1845. After the Crimean War ended, the Russians mounted a war of attrition in Dagestan, burning villages, clearing forests, and establishing fortified lines. Shamil was forced on to Mount Gunib, where he surrendered.

Russia could now develop the Caucasus. In the northern steppe lands colonization led to the growth of Russian settlements. The expansion of government meant career opportunities in the administration and for officers in the occupying forces. Russian courts were introduced and Islamic (Sharia) law was ousted. The economy developed considerably, and Russians and Armenians ran the rapidly expanding oil industry at Baku. Russian occupation was resented by the subject peoples, who rallied around their respective faiths and developed forms of nationalism, while socialism grew amongst industrial workers.

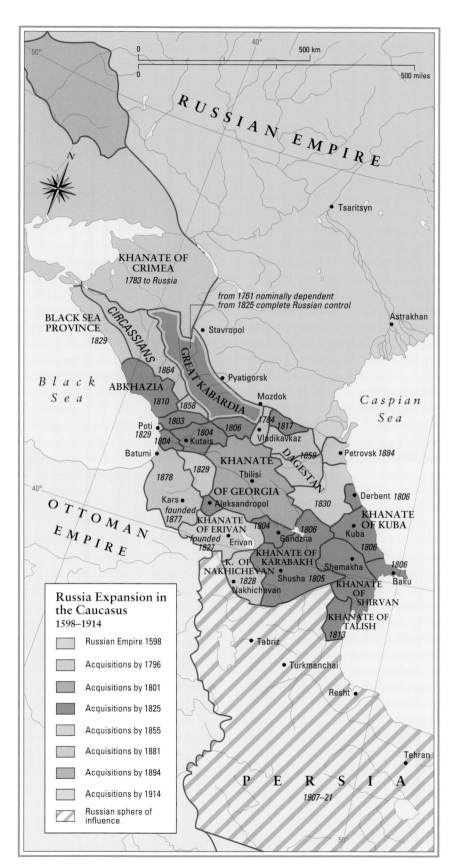

Russia Expansion in the Caucasus
1598–1914

- Russian Empire 1598
- Acquisitions by 1796
- Acquisitions by 1801
- Acquisitions by 1825
- Acquisitions by 1855
- Acquisitions by 1881
- Acquisitions by 1894
- Acquisitions by 1914
- Russian sphere of influence

Russia in Central Asia

This painting by Vasili Vereshchagin, dated 1870, shows the Sherdar Madrasah in Samarkand.

Russian expansion into Central Asia commenced with the subjugation of the Khazaks by 1847. The Crimean War impeded further enlargement of the Russian Empire in that region. The Russians dreamt of a thrust to the south that could push Russian borders up to Afghanistan and into the Pamirs adjacent to India. British control of India had been badly shaken by the 1857 Indian Mutiny, and it was possible that subversion or knowledge that the Russian army was nearby would entice the Indians to rebel again. This colonial adventure would depend upon Central Asian cooperation or annexation of key regions. In 1858, a former Russian diplomat in London, Count Nicholas Ignatiev, visited the khanates of Khiva and Bokhara; Khiva refused to allow Russian boats on its rivers, while Bokhara agreed to trade expansion.

In 1864 Russian forces moved to a fort at Alma-Ata in Kazak lands, built in 1854, and then two Russian army units advanced into Uzbek territory, taking the cities of Turkestan. The Uzbeks failed to fight tactically. As irregular cavalry, their mobility and hit-and-run tactics would have worn down slow-moving Russian infantry columns. Instead, they concentrated their forces in cities where they could be cut down by cannon-fire. After the Russian forces joined up, they took Chimkent but not Tashkent. The troops of Khokand failed in their counterattack to recapture Turkestan and in 1865 the Russians captured Tashkent after defeating Bokharan and Khokand forces at Niaz-bek. General Michael Cherniaev had only 2,000 men and twelve guns at Tashkent and faced 30,000 enemies but discipline and surprise tactics won victory. Khokand then accepted terms, losing some territory, paid an indemnity, and allowed in Russian traders.

In 1866, approximately 40,000 Bokharans faced General Romanovski at Yedshar where his 3,000 troops and twenty cannon dispersed the enemy. Khodjent was captured next. The Governor-General of Russian Turkestan at Tashkent invaded Bokharan lands in 1868 and fought a pitched battle at Samarkand, which was taken. In June 1868, a final conflict took place near Katta-kurgan. Bokhara now submitted and became a protectorate with the same peace conditions being accepted by Khokand. In 1873, Khiva was reduced to protectorate status while Khokand was annexed.

Russia's writ failed in a Turkmen region east of the Caspian Sea bordering Persia. This desert tribal area was difficult to traverse and the dominant and fierce Tekke people raided wherever they wanted and attacked Russian caravans. The Akhal oasis was a Tekke base as was the city of Merv, which had a citadel with five miles of walls about 80 feet high. In 1879, an attack on the oasis failed and the Russians were defeated at Dengil-Tepe but, in 1881, they took the fortress of Geok-Tepe, whereupon the Russians slaughtered the entire male population to encourage fear and surrender in Central Asia. Russia consolidated its rule after Merv surrendered by building a Trans-Caspian railroad linking Bokhara, Samarkand and Tashkent with Krasnovodsk on the Caspian and Samara, west of the Urals. The Pamirs were the last area to be annexed, but Russia and Britain gave the Wakkan mountain lands to Afghanistan to act as a buffer between the two imperial nations.

Russian rule in Central Asia brought peace and some economic progress. In particular, the cotton industry was developed and Russian and Ukrainian settlements mushroomed throughout the Kazak lands, pushing some tribal peoples off their pasturelands, which led to some resistance. The Khazaks continued a semi-nomadic existence until 1916 when the Russian government tried to impose conscription in Central Asia. At this point, the Khazaks erupted and thousands of people died.

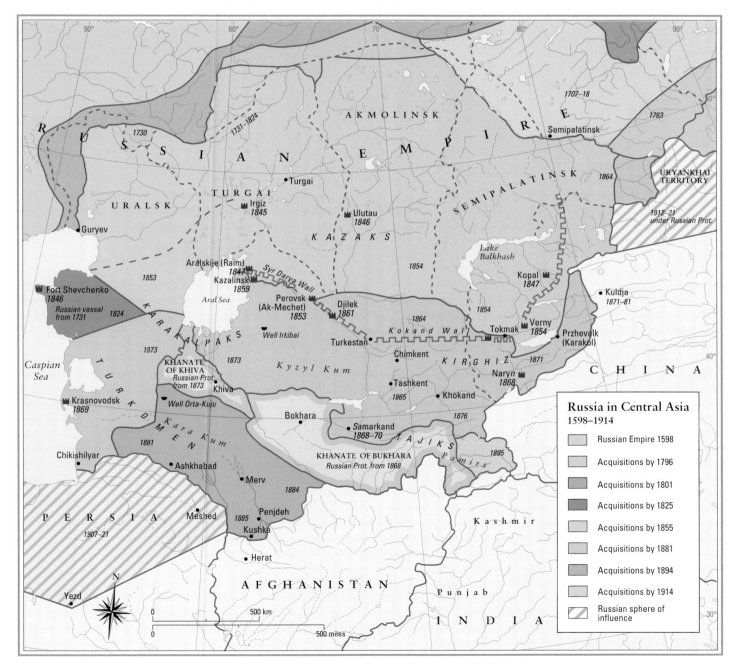

Russia in Central Asia
1598–1914

- Russian Empire 1598
- Acquisitions by 1796
- Acquisitions by 1801
- Acquisitions by 1825
- Acquisitions by 1855
- Acquisitions by 1881
- Acquisitions by 1894
- Acquisitions by 1914
- Russian sphere of influence

Poles, Finns, and Anti-Semitism

During the last half of the nineteenth century, nationalism, both Russian and non-Russian, played an increasing role in the empire's political life. Russian nationalists stressed that this was a Russian Empire and must prioritize the defense of Russian interests, culture, and language. The last two tsars, Alexander III and Nicholas II, sympathized with this view. Even moderate senior officials believed that the Empire's survival depended on the use of a single state language, Russian, in adminstration, army, courts, and schools. This policy was in conflict with rising nationalist sentiment among a number of non-Russian peoples. Initially confined to educated elites, by 1900 nationalism was spreading more widely among some of the non-Russian peoples in Russia's western borderlands.

When, following the Congress of Vienna, Russia acquired most of the Grand Duchy of Warsaw in 1815, Tsar Alexander I organized it as an autonomous kingdom of Poland, but in permanent union with the Russian Empire. Poland's constitution allowed a Diet, a separate administration, an army of 40,000 men, and official use of the Polish tongue. Nationalist activity generated a Polish insurrection in 1830 with Polish forces being defeated at Ostrolenka in 1831, after which Poland lost its Diet and national army. Polish universities were closed and Roman Catholic church lands were secularized. However, nationalism survived, fuelled by Romantic literature and poetry, authored by figures such as Adam Mickiewicz (1798–1855) and Joachim Lelewel (1786–1861). A new revolt broke out in 1863, which was crushed by 1864. As a result, Poland lost its autonomy, had a Russian administration re-established, and Warsaw University was Russified. Polish was banned in courtrooms and the Russian language was made compulsory in Polish schools. Writers and journalists were heavily censored and a

large Orthodox cathedral was built in Warsaw, symbolizing Russian domination. Nevertheless, dreams of independence were kept alive by the nationalist writings of Henryk Sienkiewicz (1846–1914), and by 1914 Polish nationalism, still a largely elite phenomenon even in 1863, had spread widely across the whole Polish population. Poland had to wait until the end of the First World War to become independent again.

Events in Finland demonstrated how Russia could manage to control a minority people in a peaceful manner. Finland had been annexed from Sweden in 1809, but retained its status as a Grand Duchy, with the title of Grand Duke being assumed by the tsar. The Finns kept a constitution and a Diet, which was not summoned until 1863, their Lutheran church, and their own schools. Initially, Russo-Finnish relations were good; the Finns were loyal to the tsar because Russians were regarded as political allies against the former governing Swedish minority, comprising only a tenth of the population, which had constituted the elites in commerce, administration, and the educational system. Taxes raised in Finland were spent in Finland and Russia and supported economic development in transport, silviculture, and agricultural credit banks.

Following the 1863 Polish uprising, the Finnish Diet was re-opened and the Diet voted money for elementary education, railroad construction, and currency reform, with Finland going on the gold standard, unlike Russia. The National Bank was placed under the control of the Diet and the political system grew in a modern and sophisticated manner. A benefit to Finland was that its soldiers could only serve in Finland. However, the 1890s witnessed creeping Russification, with the Diet stripped of nearly all its legislative functions. Yet after the 1905 Revolution, Finland was granted a unicameral parliament, using a universal male

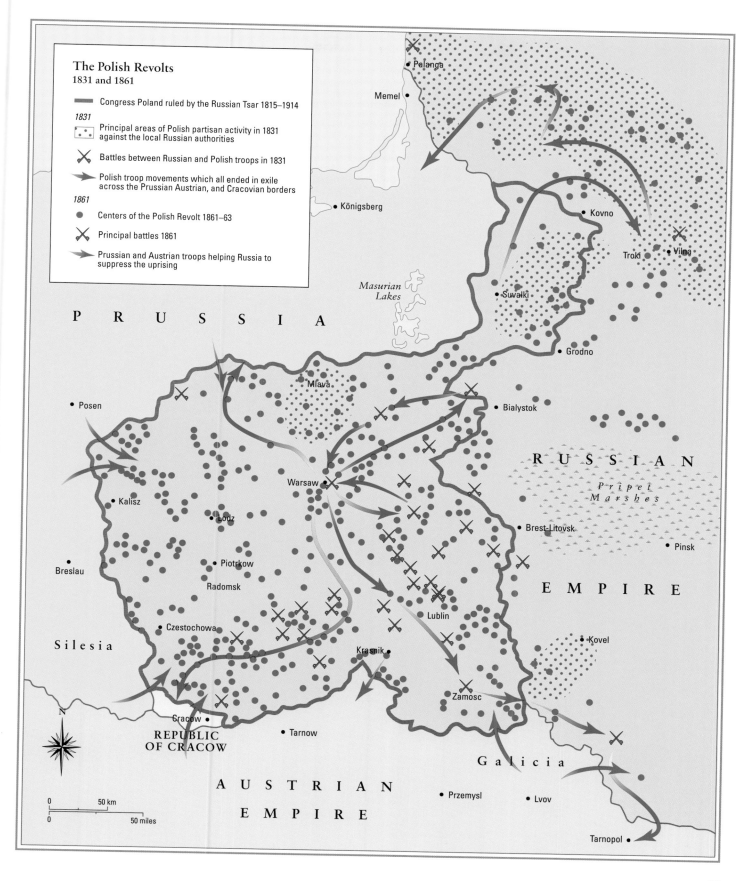

The Polish Revolts
1831 and 1861

Congress Poland ruled by the Russian Tsar 1815–1914

1831

Principal areas of Polish partisan activity in 1831 against the local Russian authorities

Battles between Russian and Polish troops in 1831

Polish troop movements which all ended in exile across the Prussian Austrian, and Cracovian borders

1861

Centers of the Polish Revolt 1861–63

Principal battles 1861

Prussian and Austrian troops helping Russia to suppress the uprising

PRUSSIA

Palanga

Memel

Königsberg

Kovno

Troki

Vilna

Suwalki

Masurian
Lakes

Grodno

Posen

Mlava

Bialystok

RUSSIAN

Kalisz

Warsaw

Pripet
Marshes

Lodz

Brest-Litovsk

Pinsk

Breslau

Piotrkow

EMPIRE

Radomsk

Lublin

Silesia

Czestochowa

Kovel

Krasnik

N

Zamosc

Cracow

REPUBLIC
OF CRACOW

Tarnow

Galicia

AUSTRIAN

Przemysl

Lvov

0   50 km

EMPIRE

0   50 miles

Tarnopol

and female franchise based upon proportional representation.

Jewish immigration into Europe dated back many centuries, with communities first established in the cities of the north Mediterranean. From there further communities were founded over western and central Europe. The persecution of European Jews began in the Middle Ages, driven by the crusading impulse that involved almost all of Christian Europe. Jews living along the Rhine and across France were attacked. Christian states deported Jews *en masse*, with few or no exceptions. Many of

these refugees found sanctuary in a more tolerant Poland—a state, in the 1400s, that covered a huge area of eastern Europe, looking remarkably like the Jewish Pale of settlement established in 1791 by Catherine the Great.

By 1815 the Russian Empire had expanded westward in Europe, inheriting from Poland a vast area of Jewish settlement numbering around 3 million. In 1835 further edicts forbade Jews to live in a 35-mile strip along the western border of the Pale of settlement and also banished Jews from the cities of Nikolyev and Sevastopol. By the 1860s, the Jewish pop-

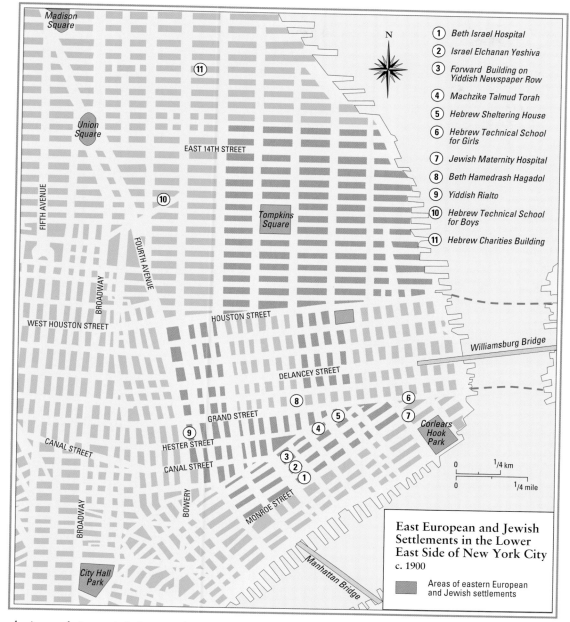

1. Beth Israel Hospital
2. Israel Elchanan Yeshiva
3. Forward Building on Yiddish Newspaper Row
4. Machzike Talmud Torah
5. Hebrew Sheltering House
6. Hebrew Technical School for Girls
7. Jewish Maternity Hospital
8. Beth Hamedrash Hagadol
9. Yiddish Rialto
10. Hebrew Technical School for Boys
11. Hebrew Charities Building

East European and Jewish Settlements in the Lower East Side of New York City c. 1900

Areas of eastern European and Jewish settlements

ulation of Imperial Russia had grown to around 4.5 million. The 1897 census gives a total of 5,189,401, or 4.13 percent of the total population. Many of the new Jewish arrivals had drifted southeastward from their core areas into the Ukraine, joining earlier Jewish communities and founding new ones. Jews were now an increasingly competitive element with locals. This caused anti-semitic incidents, which were mainly kept in check under Tsar Alexander II. In 1881 he was assassinated; and his successor, Alexander III, unleashed a tor-

rent of violence against the Jews—the "pogroms." A series of repressive laws discriminated against the Jews, and there were outbreaks of violence continuing in 1903–06, which were particularly severe in the Ukraine.

After 1880, many Jews chose emigration as their salvation. Over 2 million Jews left the Russian Empire heading for western Europe, South America, and South Africa. However, most of the emigrating Jews headed for the United States. By 1920 four times as many Jews lived in New York as lived in Warsaw.

Intellectuals and Revolutionaries in Nineteenth-Century Russia

The Russian tsars felt obliged to crush any critical ideas concerning politics and society lest they undermine the edifice of autocracy, which in the tsar's eyes was the only system of government capable of holding together and developing the Russian Empire, and of saving it from socialist and nationalist revolution. Nicholas I had observed the revolutionary ideas infecting Europe during the 1848 revolutions and was determined to protect Russia from any such contagion. He introduced systematic censorship, tighter controls over universities, and altered the curriculum to emphasize scientific subjects rather than the liberal arts. In 1849, the police arrested a group of intellectuals known as the Petrashevtsy Circle; 51 were exiled and fifteen, including Fedor Dostoevsky, were given the death sentence, which was later commuted to imprisonment.

When Alexander II began his reforms, Russian intellectuals were hopeful that they would continue but became even more critical of tsarism once reform fizzled out. One opposition group, the Populists, followed Alexander Herzen's (1812–70) advice in 1861 to "Go to the people" (*narod*) and find strength, stoicism, and purpose amongst the peasant masses. One of their teachers was Nicholas Chernyshevsky (1828–89), who believed that the evils of capitalism then destroying the West could be avoided if a society was created based upon a free, democratic body of peasant producers. He explored his ideas in a novel called *What Is To Be Done?* (1862). In the early 1870s the Narodniki moved into the countryside to help the oppressed, illiterate peasantry. The peasants were to be educated, improved, and civilized until they could run society for themselves. The Populists found the peasantry to be hostile and distrustful and were regarded with suspicion as they preached in the villages. They realized they were getting nowhere and eventually transformed themselves at the beginning of the twentieth century into the Social Revolutionary Party, which stood for the expropriation of the big estates in favor of the peasantry, cooperatives, and the strengthening of the existing village communities (*mir*) which owned collectively most of the land worked by peasants.

Another opposition strand was a cluster of terrorist organizations. Two examples of these were *Zemlya i Volya* (Land and Freedom) founded in 1876, and *Narodnaya Volya* (People's Will), established in 1879. Two major thinkers in the former were Peter Tkachev and Sergei Nechaev. They observed the failure of the Populists and decided that if the peasants would not overthrow autocracy then young revolutionaries must do it for them, fighting the government by utilizing conspiracy, terrorism, and assassination. One female member, Vera Zasulich (1849–1919), a member of the minor nobility, shot and wounded Theodore Trepov, the military governor of St. Petersburg. She was freed after being found not guilty by a jury and fled to Switzerland before being re-arrested. There, she converted to Marxism and worked with Leon Trotsky (1879–1940) and Vladimir Lenin (1870–1924).

People's Will had split from Land and Freedom and was more ruthless. This small group realized that a revolution was unlikely to occur and chose instead to undermine autocracy with a constant terror campaign. They funded themselves through robberies and were known to murder informers. They dedicated themselves to the assassination of Alexander II. Royal trains were attacked and one member, Stepan Khalturin, managed to smuggle explosives into the Winter Palace and exploded a mine under the dining room. The tsar happened to be late but 67 people were killed or wounded. Alexander managed to escape all the terrorist attacks against him. Repression grew and Alexander II was carefully guarded but, on 13 March 1881, two bombs were exploded, destroying the tsar's carriage. He died later from his injuries. In 1887, Vladimir Ulyanov, Lenin's older brother, attempted to kill Alexander III, failed, and was executed. The struggle between government and revolutionaries further polarized Russian political life and reduced the chances for more moderate and liberal groups to play a constructive role.

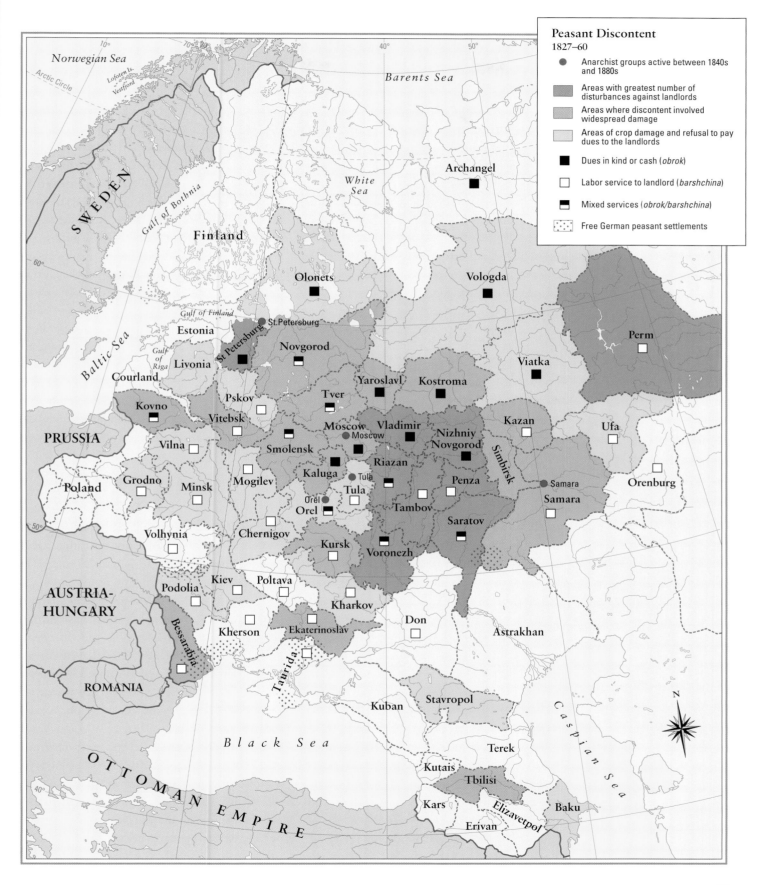

Peasant Discontent
1827–60

- ● Anarchist groups active between 1840s and 1880s
- Areas with greatest number of disturbances against landlords
- Areas where discontent involved widespread damage
- Areas of crop damage and refusal to pay dues to the landlords
- ■ Dues in kind or cash (*obrok*)
- □ Labor service to landlord (*barshchina*)
- ▬ Mixed services (*obrok/barshchina*)
- ⬚ Free German peasant settlements

Norwegian Sea

Arctic Circle

Lofoten Is.
Vestfjord

Barents Sea

SWEDEN

Gulf of Bothnia

Finland

White Sea

Archangel

Vologda

Perm

Olonets

Gulf of Finland

St. Petersburg

Estonia

Baltic Sea

Gulf of Riga

Livonia

Courland

Novgorod

Viatka

Pskov

Yaroslavl

Kostroma

Kovno

Vitebsk

Tver

Kazan

Ufa

PRUSSIA

Vilna

Smolensk

Moscow

Vladimir

Nizhniy Novgorod

Orenburg

Poland

Grodno

Minsk

Mogilev

Kaluga

Riazan

Simbirsk

Penza

Samara

Tula

Orel

Tambov

Saratov

Volhynia

Chernigov

Kursk

Voronezh

AUSTRIA-HUNGARY

Podolia

Kiev

Poltava

Kharkov

Don

Astrakhan

Kherson

Ekaterinoslav

Bessarabia

Taurida

Kuban

Stavropol

ROMANIA

Black Sea

Caspian Sea

OTTOMAN EMPIRE

Terek

Kutais

Tbilisi

Kars

Elizavetpol

Baku

Erivan

N

Economic Development and Its Effects

Defeat in the Crimea was based in large part on financial weakness and economic backwardness. The government after 1856 was therefore committed to a policy of rapid economic growth. In vast Russia the essential first step had to be the creation of a railroad network to link raw materials, producers, and markets. The first railroad linked St Petersburg to Pavlovsk, eventually tying Russia together, with lines radiating outwards from St Petersburg and Moscow to all the major cities and then into the Caucasus and Central Asia. This began from the 1850s and was the basis for rapid industrial growth, which commenced in the 1880s.

Economic growth was heavily dependent on foreign investment, first from Germany, and then France, with much funding originating in the Crédit Mobilier. The rise in home consumption as former peasants began to purchase more helped matters, as did the commencement of coal mining in Ukraine, drilling for oil at Baku in the Caucasus, and the upsurge in the textile industry and sugar beet refining in Poland. Presiding over this sudden development were two finance ministers—Ivan Vyshnegradsky (1886–92) and Sergei Witte (1892–1903). Ukraine became a center of economic growth, owing to the exploitation of coal and iron in the Donets Basin, and metal and refining factories mushroomed in Ukraine's Ekaterinoslav province. Alongside heavy industry, there was growth in light industries such as textiles, food, tobacco, and clothing, much of this being around Moscow and in the Baltic provinces. By 1906–14 Russian growth rates were the highest in Europe.

Various factors can explain the rapid increase in industrial growth. The emancipated peasantry provided a mobile labor force and generated a market for the purchase of consumer goods. The various ministers of finance, beginning with Nicholas K. Bunge (1881–87) helped generate an environment that fostered growth. A Peasant Land Bank was established (1883) and import duties were raised to check the consumption of foreign goods. Witte's eleven years as finance minister were the high point of a coherent policy of industrial growth, based on protectionism, government subsidies, and railroad construction. He placed the ruble on the gold standard in 1897, which attracted foreign investment. Grain exports, paid for in gold, were increased even when harvests were poor. The gold extracted could then be used to build up the gold reserves and pay off foreign debts and loans. Crucial to the Russian economy were the foreign firms setting up businesses in Russia, including Bell Telephone, Singer Sewing Machines, and the companies founded by Alfred Nobel in the Baku oil fields.

The agricultural sector of the economy fuelled the industrial areas through the massive increases in grain production and its export. This occurred despite widespread famine in 1891. The finance ministers only saw agriculture as an area to be exploited and the only institutions offering any help to the villages were local councils, "zemstva." This organization financed road construction, built bridges, provided a fire service, and generally sought to improve village infrastructure. Only in the period 1906–1914 did the central government inject large sums into peasant agriculture, education, and health.

Russian agricultural production grew greatly between 1861 and 1913. By 1913 Russia was challenging the USA for the position of the world's largest exporter of grain. Nevertheless in most of the Russian countryside farming methods and technology remained well behind Germany or Britain. The emancipation settlement had left some peasants with too little land, but by 1905 the key difficulty was that the huge increase in population was putting heavy pressure on the land available for farming.

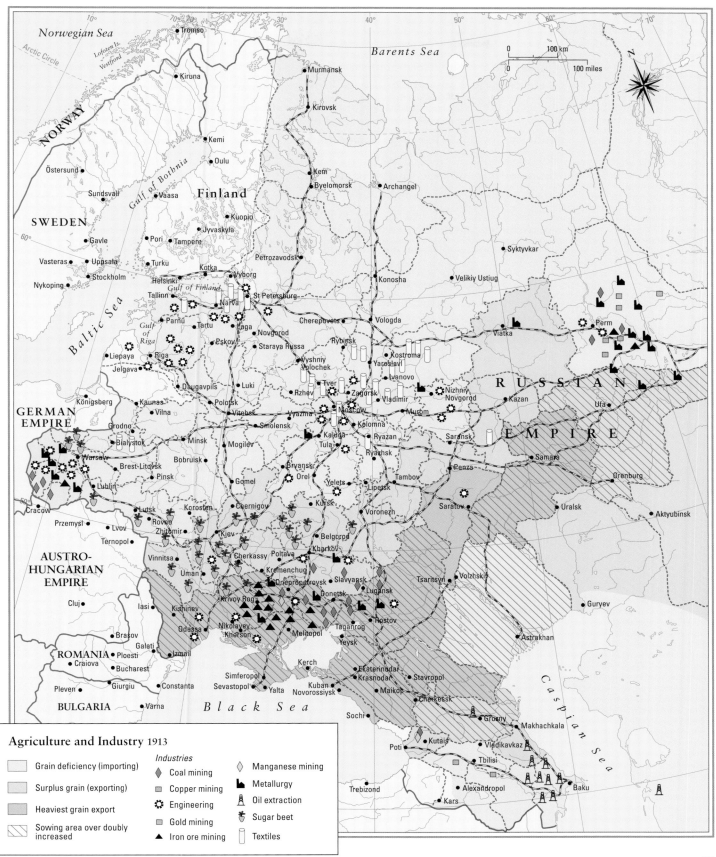

Agriculture and Industry 1913

- Grain deficiency (importing)
- Surplus grain (exporting)
- Heaviest grain export
- Sowing area over doubly increased

Industries
- ◆ Coal mining
- ▢ Copper mining
- ✿ Engineering
- ▢ Gold mining
- ▲ Iron ore mining
- ◇ Manganese mining
- ◣ Metallurgy
- ♨ Oil extraction
- 🥕 Sugar beet
- ▯ Textiles

Political Upheaval, 1905–1906

In 1905 there was a surge of political and social violence through vast swathes of the Russian Empire. The government had to cope with workers' strikes, peasant anarchy and violence, military and naval mutinies, and unrest amongst some national minorities. Ultimately, the government realized that opposition needed to be appeased and created a constitutional monarchy, a state parliament (duma), a multi-party system, and the 1906 constitution.

The major factors behind the revolution were peasant discontent, the working conditions and wages of the working class, the antagonism of ethnic groups who felt they were treated as exploited second class citizens, and the educated intelligentsia, many from the *zemstva* (local councils), who were critical of autocracy and demanded the political and civil rights enjoyed by other Europeans. This discontent created the general conditions for protest, but a spark was required to ignite revolution. The peasantry still resented the Emancipation Edict. Their expanding numbers meant increasing land hunger. They were also bearing the burden of industrialization, where grain was exported to pay for economic development. The peasants' rage exploded in 1905 and central and southern Russia bore the brunt of the violence, which included occasional murder of landlords, the torching of manor houses, and the killing of their livestock. This agricultural revolution was initially uncoordinated, although it did become politicized in some areas with the formation of a national Peasants' Union generated through the activities of the Social Revolutionary Party.

The national minorities had been subject to Russification, and resentment and hostility ran deep in Poland and the Baltic states and amongst the Jewish community. The urban areas were also ripe for revolution. Industrialization had concentrated the working class in a few centers where their living and working conditions were considered unsatisfactory. Strike activity could close down towns and hinder traffic on the railroads, but the law precluded unions. In such a situation, socialist ideas inevitably took hold, although workers' leaders failed to link their revolution with the agrarian unrest.

The trigger for the revolution came on 9 January 1905 when strikers in St. Petersburg marched to the Winter Palace to petition the tsar for a number of reforms, including freedom of speech, an end to redemption payments, and an eight-hour working day. Troops confronted the peaceful marchers, numbering between 50,000 and 100,000, and opened fire, killing and wounding several hundred people. This massacre, known as "Bloody Sunday," unleashed a wave of strikes through the empire. The General Strike that took place between 20–30 October precipitated the establishment of a St Petersburg Soviet by revolutionary politicians, led by Leon Trotsky (1879-1940). Army and navy mutinies erupted, symbolized by the famous seizure of the battleship *Potemkin* in the Black Sea on 14 June 1905, and were the greatest of all the threats to the regime's survival, which hung by a thread in the winter of 1905–06. In November 1905 an armed uprising occurred in Moscow, when large areas were seized by strikers who erected barricades to fight strike-breaking troops. However, the revolutionaries failed to seize the major railroad station so loyal troops could be brought in by train to combat the strikers. The Presnaya district saw terrible fighting in late 1905 and Russian troops caused a bloodbath before the fighting ended.

The concessions made by the tsar in the October Manifesto of 1905 (a parliament and civil rights) appeased much of the Russian upper and middle classes, many of whom were also terrified by the risk of anarchy and social revolution. Above all, most of the army remained loyal and suppressed the worker and peasant revolutions.

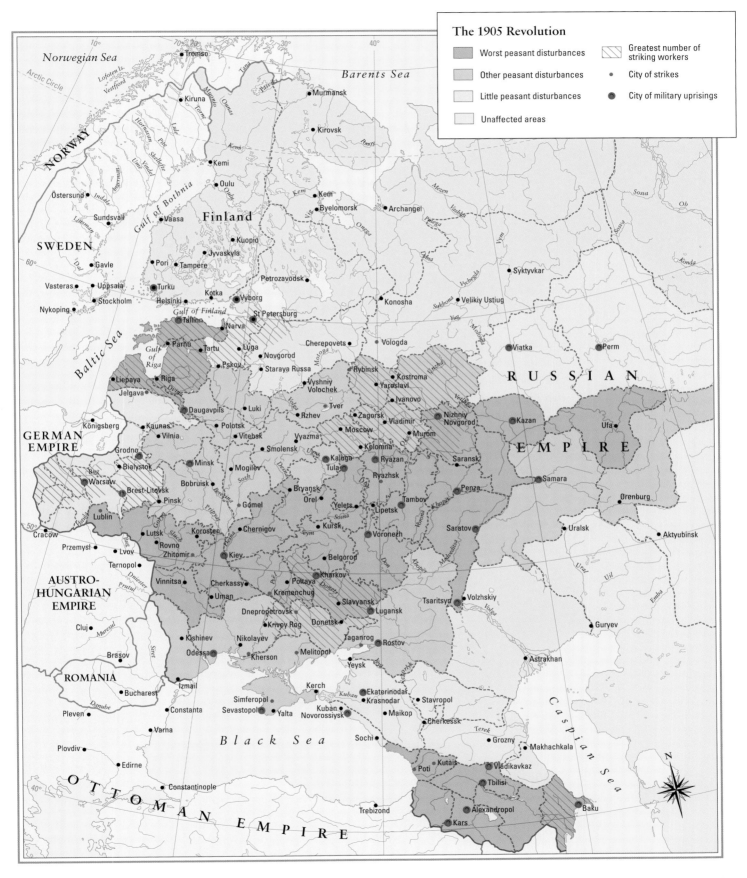

The 1905 Revolution

- Worst peasant disturbances
- Other peasant disturbances
- Little peasant disturbances
- Unaffected areas
- Greatest number of striking workers
- • City of strikes
- ● City of military uprisings

Norwegian Sea

Barents Sea

Arctic Circle

Tromso

Lofoten Is.

Vestfjord

Kiruna

Murmansk

Kemi

Kirovsk

NORWAY

Kemi

Östersund

Oulu

Byelomorsk

Archangel

Sundsvall

Vaasa

Finland

Kem

SWEDEN

Kuopio

Gavle

Jyvaskyla

Syktyvkar

Vasteras

Pori

Tampere

Uppsala

Petrozavodsk

Velikiy Ustiug

Stockholm

Turku

Kotka

Konosha

Viatka

Perm

Nykoping

Helsinki

Vyborg

St Petersburg

Gulf of Finland

Tallinn

Narva

Cherepovets

Vologda

Baltic Sea

Parnu

Tartu

Luga

Novgorod

Rybinsk

Kostroma

RUSSIAN

Gulf of Riga

Pskov

Staraya Russa

Yaroslavl

Riga

Vyshniy Volochek

Ivanovo

Liepaya

Luki

Tver

Zagorsk

Nizhniy Novgorod

Kazan

Ufa

EMPIRE

Jelgava

Daugavpils

Polotsk

Vladimir

Königsberg

Vitebsk

Vyazma

Moscow

Murom

Kaunas

Vilnia

Smolensk

Kolomna

GERMAN EMPIRE

Grodno

Minsk

Mogilev

Kaluga

Ryazan

Saransk

Samara

Bialystok

Bobruisk

Tula

Ryazhsk

Warsaw

Brest-Litovsk

Gomel

Bryansk

Orel

Penza

Orenburg

Pinsk

Yelets

Tambov

Lublin

Chernigov

Kursk

Lipetsk

Saratov

Cracow

Lutsk

Korosten

Voronezh

Uralsk

Przemysl

Rovno

Kiev

Belgorod

Aktyubinsk

Lvov

Zhitomir

AUSTRO-HUNGARIAN EMPIRE

Ternopol

Vinnitsa

Cherkassy

Kharkov

Cluj

Uman

Poltava

Tsaritsyn

Volzhskiy

Kremenchug

Brasov

Dnepropetrovsk

Slavyansk

Lugansk

Guryev

Krivoy Rog

Donetsk

Kishinev

Nikolayev

Taganrog

Rostov

ROMANIA

Odessa

Kherson

Melitopol

Astrakhan

Bucharest

Izmail

Yeysk

Pleven

Kerch

Ekaterinodar

Stavropol

Simferopol

Kuban

Krasnodar

Plovdiv

Sevastopol

Yalta

Novorossiysk

Maikop

Cherkessk

Varna

Black Sea

Sochi

Grozny

Makhachkala

Edirne

Kutais

Vladikavkaz

OTTOMAN EMPIRE

Constantinople

Poti

Tbilisi

Baku

Trebizond

Alexandropol

Kars

Caspian Sea

Kursk—a Province

Kursk was one of the 51 provinces of European Russia. In terms of size it was 33rd, in terms of population sixteenth. Kursk was an overwhelmingly flat, rural, and agricultural province. Its population of 3.13 million (1912) was 77 percent Russian and 22 percent Ukrainian. Along with thirty other provinces in European Russia Kursk was recorded as having no cities. The town of Kursk had a population of only 85,000 on the eve of the First World War but was nevertheless three times larger than the next biggest town. Just less than 23,000 people worked in factories, of which two employed over 1,000 workers each. In northern and central Russia, where the soil was poor, many peasants had traditionally supported themselves through cottage industries. In Kursk, and in the other five provinces of the so-called Central Agricultural Region, the rich Black Earth soils sustained a well-developed arable agriculture. Rye and oats were the two great crops though Kursk was famous for its fruit orchards and the very profitable sugar beet industry was growing rapidly in the pre-war years.

The administration of Kursk province was headed by the governor, in principle appointed by the tsar but in reality more often the nominee of the Minister of Internal Affairs, who was his direct boss. The governor was senior to the provincial representatives of the other central ministries but often had difficulties controlling them. The provinces were divided into fifteen districts. Even in 1914 the most important official at district level was the Marshal of the Nobility, elected by his fellow landowning nobles reflecting the close alliance between the monarchy and the landowning nobility on which the Russian Old Regime was based. In the decade before 1914 the government had attempted to reform this out-of-date system but ran into heavy opposition in a legislature dominated by landowners. Key areas of local government (e.g. primary education, health, roads) were the responsibility of the so-called zemstva, local councils elected by the population but with the franchise heavily tilted towards the propertied. The zemstvos usually worked effectively with the government to modernize the countryside in the pre-war decade: by 1911 Kursk had 2,446 schools with almost 175,000 pupils, and 121 hospitals but only 243 doctors. Nevertheless there was a built-in tension between elected local councils and an unelected core administration responsible only to the tsar.

Kursk's biggest problem in the early twentieth century was the growth of the population and therefore both deforestation and a shortage of land for farming. Between 1862 and 1904 Kursk's population grew by almost 50 percent and although by 1900 more than 400,000 people born in the province lived elsewhere (often in Siberia and the Caucasus) neither emigration nor the development of industry since 1880 had been able to absorb the growing rural population. In terms of the density of the rural population Kursk stood fifth among European Russia's provinces. Between 1877 and 1905 the average size of peasant farms shrank by 23 percent. Though Russian farming was backward by European standards, great improvements did occur in the last 30 years before the war, especially on the bigger noble estates: harvest yields per acre for spring sowings even on peasant land in Kursk much more than doubled in this period.

In Russia as a whole in 1905 nobles owned almost 132 million acres of land and peasants 435 million: this was roughly speaking the distribution in Kursk province too. Russian peasant-farmers therefore owned a far larger share of the land than in Prussia, let alone England. But in districts and parishes where big estates were concentrated there were outbreaks of arson, theft, and even the occasional murder during the revolution of 1905. In Kursk over 70 manor houses were torched and scores of peasants were killed and wounded in clashes with the army and police. As usual, disturbances were far worse in former serf villages than in areas inhabited by former state peasants, who had made up almost 60 percent of the Kursk peasantry when emancipation came in 1861. In the serf villages emancipation meant that the land had to

Russian Regions and Provinces c. 1860

be shared between nobles and peasants with both sides often feeling cheated. By 1915 nobles had sold more than half the land they had owned even after emancipation because making big agricultural estates profitable in Russia was often very difficult. On the other hand, in Kursk and elsewhere, it was generally the rich nobles who turned their estates into profitable capitalist enterprises who were most hated since they stopped letting land to peasants, introduced modern machinery, and banned the peasants from cutting wood and allowing their animals to roam in the forests which the landlords now began to develop as commercial enterprises.

After the suppression of the 1905 revolution reforms were introduced to modernize agriculture and develop rural education, health, and communications. But these would have required at least a generation to reduce rural tensions. When the monarchy fell in 1917 the peasants in Kursk as elsewhere took the opportunity to seize the gentry estates, greatly contributing to the collapse of the war effort, economy, and government in that year, and facilitating the Bolsheviks' seizure of power.

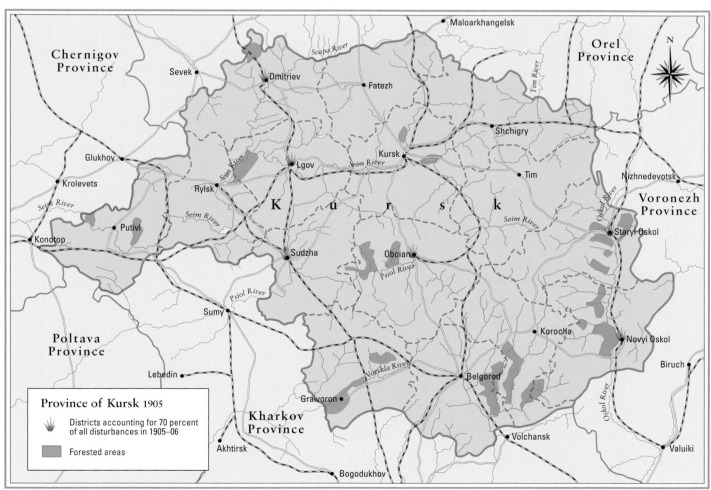

Province of Kursk 1905

Districts accounting for 70 percent of all disturbances in 1905–06

Forested areas

The First World War

The Imperial Russian Army on parade. The peacetime strength of Russia's army was over 1 million. On mobilization this would rise to over 3 million, drawn from all nationalities of the empire.

The background to the First World War was specifically the decline of the Ottoman (Turkish) and Habsburg (Austrian) empires and more generally the clash of empires and nationalisms across most of central, eastern, and southeastern Europe. In this sense the war fitted into a broader pattern of twentieth-century global history, one of whose key elements was precisely the struggle between empire and nationalism. By 1914 the Ottoman retreat from the Balkans was already causing acute tensions, but fear that the Ottoman empire might disintegrate completely and Constantinople come up for grabs made matters worse. Russia had enormous economic and strategic interests at stake: Russian exports and the security of its Black Sea region depended on the waterway which passed through the Ottoman capital and linked the Black Sea to the Mediterranean.

Growing German influence and interests in the Ottoman Empire scared the Russians. But the immediate cause of the war was the perception of Austrian leaders that unless they re-asserted their power in dramatic fashion their empire might soon go the same way as the Ottomans. Faced by relative geopolitical decline and growing nationalist challenges, Austria's rulers reacted in 1914 with a combination of desperation, arrogance, and miscalculation. Later in the twentieth century other rulers of empire faced similar challenges and sometimes (eg Suez 1956) reacted in similar fashion.

The only way to manage peacefully the enormous difficulties posed by the decline and possible collapse of empires whose territories covered much of Europe was for Russia and Germany to collaborate. Above all else the First World War occurred because they failed to do

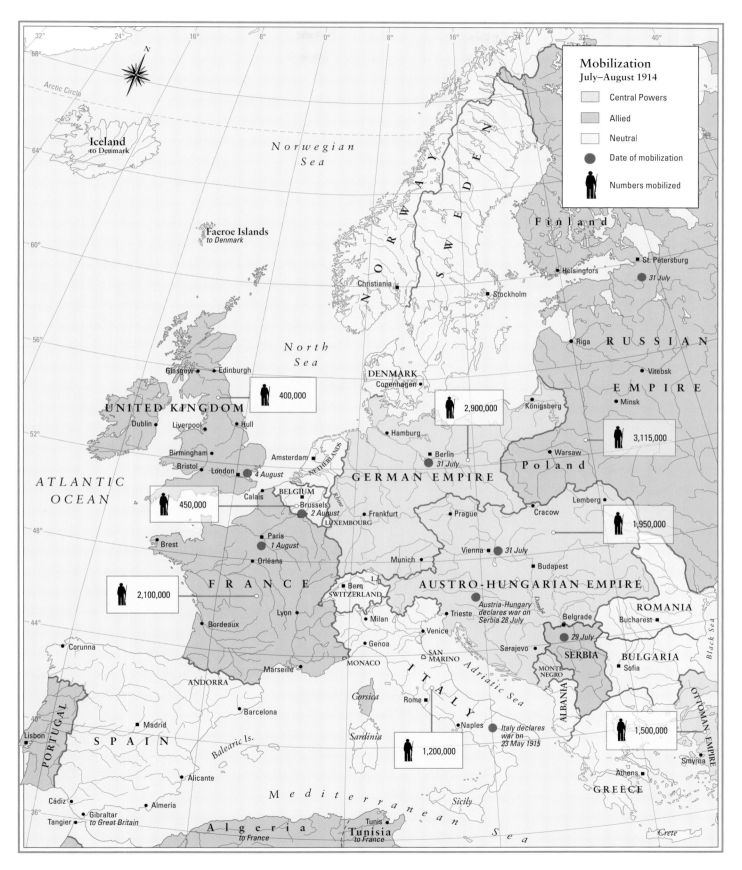

Mobilization
July–August 1914

Central Powers
Allied
Neutral
Date of mobilization
Numbers mobilized

Iceland
to Denmark

Arctic Circle

Norwegian
Sea

Faeroe Islands
to Denmark

N O R W A Y

S W E D E N

Finland

St. Petersburg
31 July

Helsingfors

R U S S I A N

Riga

E M P I R E

Vitebsk

Minsk

North
Sea

Glasgow   Edinburgh

DENMARK
Copenhagen

2,900,000

Königsberg

Warsaw

3,115,000

UNITED KINGDOM

Dublin   Liverpool   Hull
Birmingham
Bristol   Amsterdam
London   NETHERLANDS   GERMAN EMPIRE
4 August
BELGIUM
Calais
Brussels
2 August
LUXEMBOURG
Frankfurt

Hamburg

Berlin
31 July

Poland

Lemberg
Cracow

1,950,000

Prague

Vienna   31 July

400,000

450,000

ATLANTIC
OCEAN

Brest

Paris
1 August
Orléans

Munich

Budapest

2,100,000

F R A N C E

Lyon

Bern
SWITZERLAND

AUSTRO-HUNGARIAN EMPIRE

Austria-Hungary
declares war on
Serbia 28 July

ROMANIA

Bucharest

Trieste

Bordeaux

Milan

Venice

Belgrade
29 July

Black Sea

Corunna

Genoa

Sarajevo

SERBIA

BULGARIA

SAN
MARINO

MONTE-
NEGRO

Sofia

Marseille   MONACO

Adriatic Sea

ANDORRA

Corsica

I T A L Y

ALBANIA

OTTOMAN EMPIRE

Barcelona

Rome

1,500,000

Madrid

Sardinia

Naples

Italy declares
war on
23 May 1915

Smyrna

Lisbon
PORTUGAL

SPAIN

Balearic Is.

1,200,000

Athens

Alicante

GREECE

Cádiz   Almería

Tangier   Gibraltar
to Great Britain

M e d i t e r r a n e a n   S e a

Sicily

Crete

A l g e r i a
to France

Tunis
Tunisia
to France

97

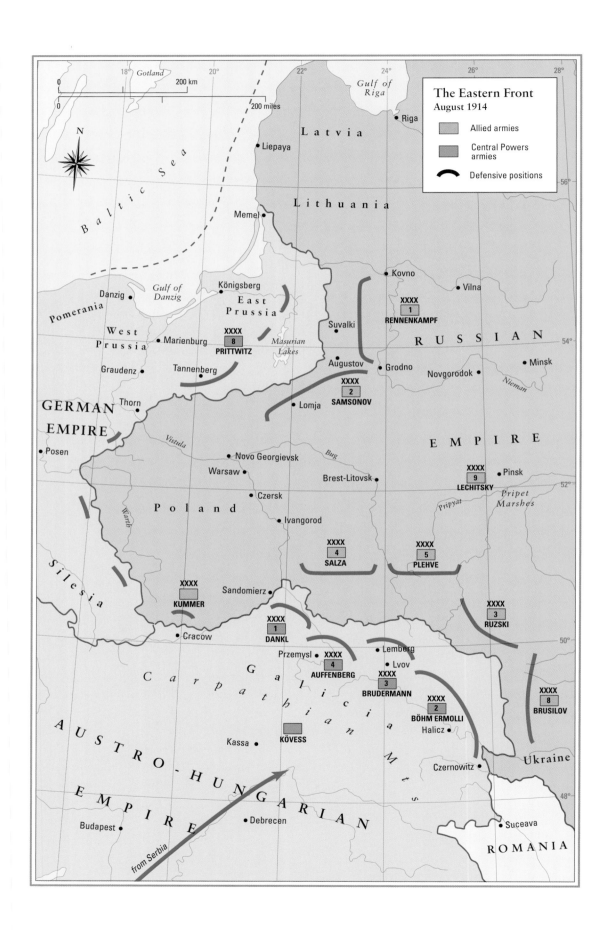

The Eastern Front
August 1914

Allied armies

Central Powers armies

Defensive positions

so. From 1813 until 1890 the alliance between Petersburg and Berlin had been one of the most stable elements in European politics. From the 1870s, however, relations began to sour. That was partly because of the growing importance of public opinion in both Germany and Russia. German liberals, socialists, and Jews disliked tsarism. In Russia liberals saw the Germany created by Bismarck as the pillar of European conservatism. They preferred France and even Britain as allies. More significant for the government was the fact that Russian nationalists resented not just growing German power after German unification in 1871 but also the prominent role of ethnic Germans (usually from the Baltic provinces) at court, in government and the armed forces, and in the economy.

In the 1880s Russia's Foreign Minister, Nikolai Giers, fought hard to beat off the pressure of public opinion and to hold to the conservative alliance of the Romanovs, Hohenzollerns, and Habsburgs. In the end, however, he was forced to concede. Above all this was because of shifts in the European balance of power and in the relations between the great powers. German unification and the rapid growth of the German economy in the second half of the nineteenth century made Germany the most powerful country in Europe. In 1879 Germany and Austria became allies, reversing almost 150 years of rivalry. Russia now faced a very powerful bloc of potential enemies on its western border. This border was flat, enormously long and without natural defenses. Still worse, the western borderlands were the gateway to core regions of Russian political and economic power (the Moscow and Petersburg regions) and to Ukraine, where in the decades before 1914 most of the empire's export agriculture, heavy industry, and coal mines were located. Not surprisingly, Russian military leaders were scared by the threat and pressed hard for an alliance with France that would ensure that Germany must fight on two fronts in the event of war. Many Russian diplomats also believed that an alliance with France was necessary to se-

cure a balance of power in Europe and to ensure that Germany and Austria respected Russian interests, above all in southeastern Europe (ie Constantinople and the Balkans).

The Franco-Russian alliance was finally signed in 1894 and remained the basis for Russian foreign and security policy down to 1917. In 1904 Britain moved towards France in the so-called Entente Cordiale. In 1907 a similar agreement linked Britain and Russia. Europe began to divide into two camps, the Triple Entente on one side and the Triple Alliance (Germany, Austria, and Italy) on the other. In themselves these two blocs by no means made war inevitable. However, they did contribute to further complicating the already very difficult problem of managing the many fears and conflicts of interest that were bound to arise as Europeans contemplated the growing problems and possible demise of the Ottoman and Habsburg empires.

The two Balkan wars of 1912 and 1913 drove Turkey from nearly all its European territories and its lands were divided up to enlarge the existing Balkan states and create Albania. The greatest beneficiaries of the Balkan wars were Serbia and Romania. Serbia was Russia's main ally in the Balkans and in 1913–14 Romania also began to move towards Russia. This was all the worse in Austrian eyes because large and dissatisfied Serb and Romanian minorities lived in the Habsburg Empire. In June 1914 a Bosnian Serb revolutionary murdered Archduke Franz Ferdinand, the heir to the Austrian throne, in Sarajevo. Austria used this as a pretext to destroy Serbian independence, thereby reasserting its power both in the Balkans and in the eyes of Slav and Romanian nationalists within its empire. Austria declared war on Serbia on 28 July 1914 and Russia intervened on behalf of its ally. Germany supported Austria, and France and Britain came into the war to stop Germany overturning the European balance of power and thereby endangering their own security. Turkey joined the war by attacking Russia in October 1914.

Russia invaded East Prussia to draw pressure off the French, who faced the great majority of the German army on the western front. The Russians were defeated at the battles of Tannenberg and the Masurian Lakes (August and September 1914). Further battles in Russian Poland between October 1914 and February 1915 ended in a stalemate. Although Russian hopes of invading Germany were thereby dashed and great losses incurred, the Russian advances did at least achieve a prime aim, which was to divert German armies eastwards and stop the Germans from knocking out France. In 1914 Russia inflicted major defeats on the Austrians in a series of offensives, occupied much of Galicia, and forced the Germans to come to Austria's assistance. In 1915 the Germans turned their attention and much of their army eastwards. Between May and September 1915 they and the Austrians inflicted heavy defeats and casualties on the Russians, in the process occupying Lithuania and Belorussia. Nevertheless the Russian army was far from destroyed and recovered much of its strength during the winter of 1915–16. Although the Russian offensive against the Germans at Lake Naroch in March 1916 failed, a second attack launched by General Aleksei Brusilov against the Austrians in June 1916 succeeded in spectacular fashion and for a time even threatened to knock Austria out of the war. Once again the Germans were forced to send large reinforcements to Austria's aid, thereby relieving pressure on French forces locked in combat with German armies at Verdun.

Although the Brusilov offensive inflicted over 750,000 casualties on the enemy the Russians themselves lost as many men or even more. The Germans and Austrians used their railroads to bring up their reinforcements whereas the advancing Russians could only move forward on foot or horseback. The Russians eventually over-stretched their supply lines. These were generic problems for attacking armies in the First World War, which explains why in tactical and operational terms the war often became a stalemate. The initial success of the Brusilov offensive brought Romania into the war but this proved disadvantageous to Russia since a German counter-offensive smashed the Romanian army and large Russian forces and supplies had to be sent to their aid. On the other hand the Russians scored many victories over the Turks and by the end of 1916 were driving deep into Anatolia.

At the beginning of 1917 the Russian army was far from defeated and in the absence of revolution within Russia could have made a big contribution to the allied war effort in that year. Nevertheless it is reckoned that even before the Brusilov offensive Russia had suffered approximately 5 million casualties during the war. In some units morale was beginning to dip, with soldiers beginning to lose faith in their commanders and in final victory. The Russian economy also faced great difficulties in sustaining the war effort, though by 1916 production of ammunition and weapons had grown impressively. By the end of 1916 inflation, food shortages, and the flood of refugees eastwards were badly affecting morale in the cities. Having taken over as commander-in-chief in September 1915, and after refusing demands for further liberalization of the political system, Nicholas II was blamed by the public for all Russia's wartime problems.

The capital had been renamed Petrograd in August 1914 to rid itself of the German-sounding Saint Petersburg. Unsurprisingly it was Petrograd, where the government had its home and where Russian political life was concentrated, that witnessed the sharpest and most dangerous opposition to the regime. Exaggerated criticism of the government's handling of the war (which actually was often much less incompetent than liberal opinion believed) and absurd rumors about the influence of Rasputin and other supposedly pro-German elements in Nicholas II's entourage spread down from the elites into the mass of the population. But the capital's workers were in any case the most radical in Russia. In the growing wave of

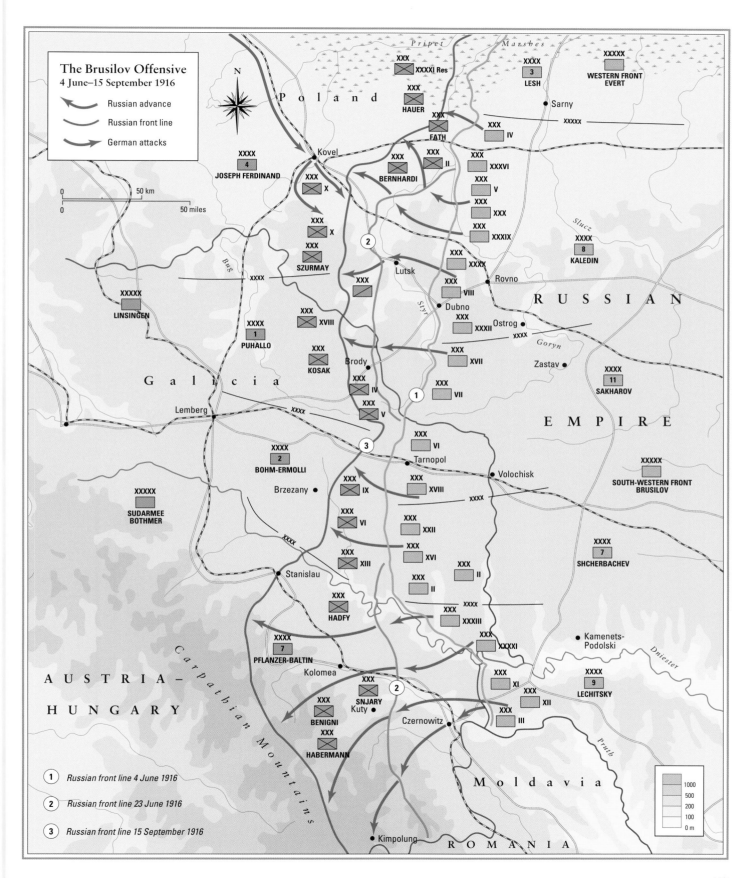

The Brusilov Offensive
4 June–15 September 1916

- Russian advance
- Russian front line
- German attacks

0 50 km
0 50 miles

P o l a n d

Pripet *Marshes*

XXX XXXXI Res

XXXX 3 LESH

XXXXX WESTERN FRONT EVERT

Sarny

XXX HAUER

XXX FATH

XXXXX

XXX IV

XXXX 4 JOSEPH FERDINAND

Kovel

XXX BERNHARDI

XXX II

XXX XXXVI

XXX X

XXX V

XXX X

XXX XXXIX

XXX SZURMAY

XXX

Lutsk

XXX

Rovno

XXXX 8 KALEDIN

XXXXX LINSINGEN

XXXX XXXXX

Bug

XXXX 1 PUHALLO

XXX XVIII

XXX VIII

Dubno

Styr

R U S S I A N

Slucz

XXX XXXII

Ostrog

XXXX

Goryn

G a l i c i a

XXX KOSAK

Brody

XXX IV

XXX XVII

Zastav

XXXX 11 SAKHAROV

E M P I R E

Lemberg

XXX V

XXX VII

1

3

XXXX 2 BOHM-ERMOLLI

XXX VI

Tarnopol

XXXXX SOUTH-WESTERN FRONT BRUSILOV

XXXXX SUDARMEE BOTHMER

XXX IX

Brzezany

Volochisk

XXX XVIII

XXXX

XXX VI

XXX XXII

XXX XIII

XXX XVI

XXXX 7 SHCHERBACHEV

Stanislau

XXX II

XXX II

XXX HADFY

XXX XXXIII

XXXX 7 PFLANZER-BALTIN

XXX XXXXI

Kamenets-Podolski

Dniester

Kolomea

XXX SNJARY

Kuty

2

XXX XI

XXX XII

XXXX 9 LECHITSKY

XXX BENIGNI

Czernowitz

XXX III

A U S T R I A –

H U N G A R Y

XXX HABERMANN

C a r p a t h i a n   M o u n t a i n s

Pruth

1 Russian front line 4 June 1916

2 Russian front line 23 June 1916

3 Russian front line 15 September 1916

M o l d a v i a

1000
500
200
100
0 m

Kimpolung   R O M A N I A

politically motivated strikes which swept Russia in the six months before the war, two-thirds were in the capital. Between 1907 and 1914 relations between management and labor in Saint Petersburg had been especially bitter, as managers sought to claw back concessions on hours of work, wages, and labor discipline forced on them during the 1905 revolution, and skilled metallurgical workers in particular tried to exploit employers' need for labor as defense contracts boomed. The capital had become a major industrial center in the pre-war decades and its shipyards and armaments firms were often enormous. Biggest of all was the Putilov works, which by 1917 employed almost 30,000 workers.

In February 1917 demonstrations broke out in Petrograd partly because of strikes and lockouts at the Putilov works but also because of food shortages. They turned quickly into a political protest against the regime. When Nicholas II ordered the garrison troops to suppress the demonstrations whole units mutinied. Within days the government had lost control of the capital and also faced mutinies in the Baltic fleet, during which many officers were killed. The liberal-conservative and liberal leaders in the parliament (duma) accepted the revolution and hoped to control it. The military high command had lost faith in Nicholas II and feared to undermine the war effort by sending troops from the front to crush the revolution in Petrograd and thereby incite civil war. Nor were they certain that their troops would be reliable

The Eastern Front
December 1916–March 1917

——— German, Austro-Hungarian, Bulgarian and Turkish front line

——▶ German, Austro-Hungarian, Bulgarian and Turkish attacks

- - ▶ German, Austro-Hungarian, Bulgarian and Turkish retreats

——— Russian and Romanian front line

——▶ Russian and Romanian attacks

- - ▶ Russian and Romanian retreats

[box] Marshes

if used to crush revolution. Believing that parliamentary leaders committed to victory over Germany could control and stabilize the home front, the high command abandoned Nicholas II, who was therefore forced to abdicate in early March. A so-called Provisional Government headed by a liberal, Prince Lvov, was set up to rule Russia and steer the war effort to victory.

The Provisional Government was hampered from the start by the power of the Petrograd Soviet, which immediately issued the Order Number One, greatly reducing officers' authority and quickly leading to a breakdown of discipline. Most peasants and workers had never been deeply committed to the war, or to the goals for which Russia's elites believed they were fighting. Lenin returned from Swiss exile in April 1917, having traveled across German territory in a "sealed train." From the German perspective this was a sensible policy, designed to sow confusion within Russia and undermine the war effort. The policy succeeded brilliantly. After Lenin's return the Bolsheviks adopted the call for immediate peace and mobilized great support partly for this reason. Meanwhile to broaden the Provisional Government's support and increase its effectiveness the moderate socialist, Alexander Kerensky (1881–1970), replaced Prince Lvov as premier in July 1917. Other moderate socialists (Mensheviks and Socialist Revolutionaries) became ministers too. With all the other main parties implicated in government and committed to continuing the war, the Bolsheviks were able to tap into the discontent of workers, peasants, and soldiers—not just against the war but also over increasingly difficult economic conditions.

Kerensky hoped that a new offensive, launched in July, would restore military morale and discipline, and bring the end of the war nearer. Instead, after advancing in some places, the offensive collapsed in the face of German reinforcements and supply problems. Even worse was the refusal of some units to go into action. The failure of the Kerensky offensive contributed to bitter recriminations between him and the military leadership. In late August and September relations broke down completely, with the new commander-in-chief, General Lavr Kornilov, demanding the restoration of authority both at the front and in the rear. There followed a confused episode—the so-called Kornilov revolt—though it remains unclear to this day whether Kornilov was actually seeking to replace Kerensky or whether he believed he was acting with the premier's consent. Whichever was true, the Kornilov revolt greatly strengthened the Bolsheviks. By the second half of 1917 both the army and the Russian home front were disintegrating. Military discipline collapsed under the impact of the failure of the offensive, the Kornilov revolt, and Bolshevik propaganda. In the interior peasants stopped exchanging food for worthless, ever-inflating paper money and turned their attention to seizing gentry land. Soldiers began to go hungry as supplies dried up and deserted in droves in order to participate in the land-grab. In the cities too class hatreds flared and workers began to take over factories, though this often had less to do with socialist fervor than with a desperate desire to stop owners closing down the factories in the face of labor militancy and the lack of the raw materials and energy supplies needed to keep the factories operational.

The Bolsheviks encouraged and exploited these conflicts and gained further support through their promise to end the war immediately. After coming to power in November 1917 they quickly began negotiations with Berlin and Vienna. Hostilities on the eastern front largely ceased in December as a result of an armistice though a final peace was not signed until March 1918 at Brest-Litovsk. The terms of the treaty, which were seen as treason to Russian interests by most educated Russians, played a big part in bringing on civil war in Russia. The Treaty of Brest-Litovsk also allowed Germany to move forces to the Western Front in the hope of destroying Britain and France in a massive offensive before large-scale American intervention made Germany's defeat inevitable.

The February Revolution and Provisional Government

The War Cabinet of the Provisional Government led by Alexander Kerensky, who can be seen sitting in the front row, fourth from the right.

The aftermath of the 1917 February Revolution saw Russia ruled by two different authorities: the Provisional Government initially comprising former duma members; and the Council of Workers' Deputies, that is the Petrograd Soviet, representing the working class. The new political landscape was populated by a number of political parties. The only significant non-localized party was now the liberal Constitutional Democrats (Kadets) and the Marxist Social Democrat Mensheviks and Bolsheviks, the latter being led by Vladimir Lenin. Added to these were the peasant-orientated Social Revolutionaries and anarchists, with many of the parties splitting into factions. Co-existing with the political parties were the peasantry who wanted land and the industrial workers, most of whom wanted peace and an eight-hour day and others who took over factories in direct action. Strikes increased, class consciousness consolidated, and hatred of the middle classes and former bosses hardened as politics polarized and the economy disintegrated.

Each part of the dual-authority system had differing views about the war. The Bolshevik-dominated Petrograd Soviet wished to end the war but the Provisional Government was determined to continue fighting to regain occupied territory and support Russia's allies. The Provisional Government believed that any Russian peace with Germany would not just result in the loss of

Russian territory but would also enable the Germans to concentrate all their forces on the Western Front, defeat the French and British, and become the dominant power in Europe.

Meanwhile, on the domestic front, the Provisional Government made no land settlement for the peasants, leaving such a reform for a future constituent assembly. Problems accrued amidst the national minorities. The Finns, Estonians, Latvians, and Ukrainians demanded independence, and Finland was beset with growing tensions between its own Social Democrats and an increasing right-wing block of parties, all arguing about where authority rested in Finland after the abdication of the tsar. There was now no Grand Duke and power rested with the Finnish Diet, yet the Russian Provisional Government persisted in denying the Finns their independence.

Russian society became increasingly polarized between socialists and middle-class groups and parties who saw in the recently appointed Commander-in-Chief General Lavr Kornilov (1870–1918) a symbol of order and discipline, issues that came to the fore in the summer of 1917. He wanted the death penalty to be reintroduced at the war front and for Bolshevik groups to be eradicated from the army so it could be restored as a fighting force. Evidence suggests that Kerensky ordered Kornilov to send an army corps to Petrograd to restore law and order and protect the Provisional Government from Soviet power. Accordingly, Kornilov moved on the capital, but a rail workers' strike, which stopped the railways working, effectively defended the capital. Bolshevik prisoners were freed from prison and the Bolshevik Red Guards armed. The coup petered out, Kornilov was imprisoned (seemingly betrayed by the Provisional Government), and the Bolsheviks did not return their weapons to the government, making them the most powerful group in Petrograd.

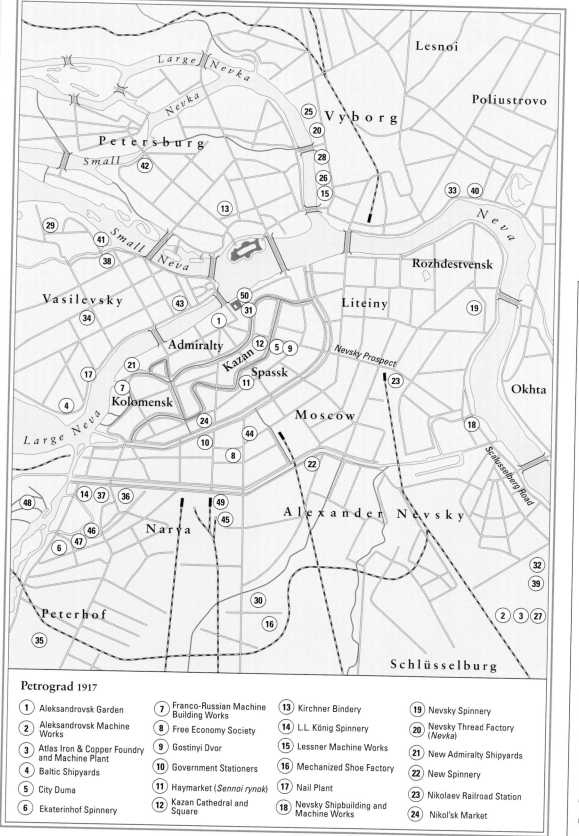

Petrograd 1917

1 Aleksandrovsk Garden
2 Aleksandrovsk Machine Works
3 Atlas Iron & Copper Foundry and Machine Plant
4 Baltic Shipyards
5 City Duma
6 Ekaterinhof Spinnery
7 Franco-Russian Machine Building Works
8 Free Economy Society
9 Gostinyi Dvor
10 Government Stationers
11 Haymarket (*Sennoi rynok*)
12 Kazan Cathedral and Square
13 Kirchner Bindery
14 L.L. König Spinnery
15 Lessner Machine Works
16 Mechanized Shoe Factory
17 Nail Plant
18 Nevsky Shipbuilding and Machine Works
19 Nevsky Spinnery
20 Nevsky Thread Factory (*Nevka*)
21 New Admiralty Shipyards
22 New Spinnery
23 Nikolaev Railroad Station
24 Nikol'sk Market

25 Nikol'sk Weaving Factory
26 Nobel' Plant
27 Obukhov Steel Mill
28 Old Sampson Spinning and Weaving Factory
29 Osipov Leather Works
30 Ozoling Machine Plant
31 Palace Square
32 Paul Factory
33 Phoenix Machine Construction Works
34 Possel' Horseshoe Works
35 Putilov Plant or Works
36 Russian-American Rubber Factory
37 Russian Spinnery
38 Siemens & Halske Electric Works
39 Spassk & Petrovsk Cotton Mills
40 St Petersburg Metal Works
41 St Petersburg Pipe Works
42 St Petersburg Rolling & Wire Mill
43 St Petersburg University
44 Technology Institution
45 Train Car Construction Plant
46 Triumphal Arch (Narva Gates)
47 Triumphal Spinnery
48 Voronin, Liutsh & Cheshire Weaving Factory
49 Warsaw Railroad Station
50 Winter Palace

From Red October to Brest-Litovsk: The Consolidation of Bolshevik Power

The Bolsheviks gained kudos in their defense of the February Revolution against the Kornilov coup, with voters swinging behind them and electing Bolshevik majorities to the Petrograd, Moscow and many other soviets. The Social Revolutionaries split, with the Left Social Revolutionaries joining the Bolsheviks in attacks on the Provisional Government. Trotsky, an independent Menshevik, also switched his allegiance to the Bolsheviks. The main issue exercising the Bolsheviks was the timing of a second revolution, with Lenin holding out for backing from a Congress of Soviets that would generate some socialist legitimacy in the eyes of other revolutionary parties; the Congress was due in October.

Despite the fact that the Bolsheviks led the revolution to success, they operated in a milieu that was ripe for change. The old elites were frag-

mented and the tsar had proved inept in wartime, which robbed the dynasty of all prestige and made any support for preserving the monarchy unlikely. Increasing hunger, hostility towards the war, and class hatred provided the environment for revolutionary outbreaks to occur throughout the country, irrespective of what happened in the capital. Strikes spread with some 2.4 million workers striking from March to October. Striking workers began to add revolutionary political demands to the normal requests for better pay and shorter hours.

In mid-October, a Military Revolutionary Committee of the Petrograd soviet was established under the leadership of Trotsky. Confusing propaganda was issued that Kerensky was planning to surrender Petrograd to the Germans. Meanwhile, Trotsky ordered arms from weapons factories to be issued to

A young officer of the Moscow garrison talks to his revolutionary soldiers, October 1917.

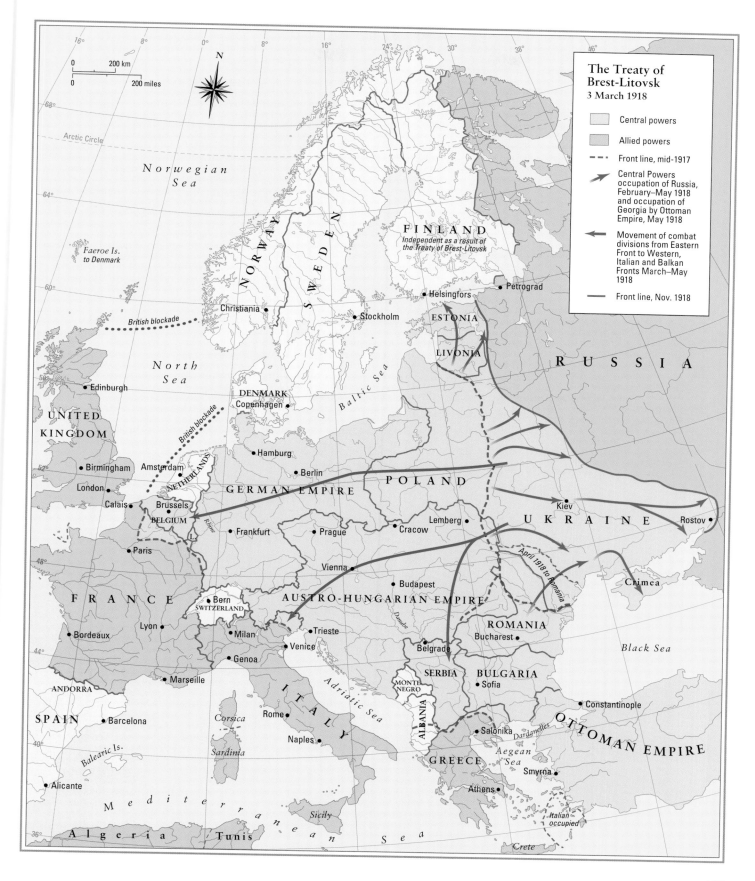

The Treaty of
Brest-Litovsk
3 March 1918

Central powers

Allied powers

Front line, mid-1917

Central Powers
occupation of Russia,
February–May 1918
and occupation of
Georgia by Ottoman
Empire, May 1918

Movement of combat
divisions from Eastern
Front to Western,
Italian and Balkan
Fronts March–May
1918

Front line, Nov. 1918

Lenin, born Vladimir Ilyich Ulyanov into a wealthy family on 22 April 1870. He became chairman of the Council of People's Commissar of the Russian SFSR on 8 November 1917. He remained in office until his death on 21 January 1924.

Red Guards while he planned how to seize key points within the city. On 23 October, Bolsheviks overran the garrison of the Peter and Paul Fortress and on the night of 25 October Trotsky spoke to the Soviet Congress about the need to defend Petrograd from Kerensky. In their propaganda, the Bolsheviks accused all parties in the Provisional Government of being counter-revolutionaries. Simultaneously, Red Guard units marched on specific targets all over the city. They seized the bridges over the Neva, which linked the heart of Petrograd to the islands, as well as the telegraph station. The next day the Red Guards occupied the railroad stations, the electrical station, the state bank, and the main post office. On the final day the Winter Palace, which housed the Provisional Government, was captured. Sergei Eisenstein's film *October* (1927) portrays the event as a massive storming of the palace, a heroic action of great violence. In reality, it was rather a placid affair and practically bloodless. The Military Revolutionary Committee proclaimed the overthrow of the government and declared an immediate end to the war, stating that all land belonged to the peasants. The Bolshevik coup caused few casualties but hundreds of thousands died during the civil war that followed.

The revolution of Red October was a localized urban coup d'état, which was essentially a Petrograd revolution, but nonetheless the radicalization of the workers, soldiers, and peasants spread the revolution to many other areas, leaving the Bolsheviks in control of pockets of territory. The Bolsheviks had to consolidate their control. They had criticized the Provisional Government for not holding elections to a Constituent Assembly and so elections to this institution were held in November. The Social Revolutionaries achieved the greatest number of seats while the Bolsheviks won about 25 percent of the vote, mainly from urban areas. The Constituent Assembly convened on 18 January 1918, with debates lasting just a day before Vladimir Ulyanov Lenin (1870–1924) dissolved it. Lenin launched a dictatorship, a far cry from

any form of Socialist democracy. Meanwhile, Kerensky had fled, wondering how his father's school pupil and family friend, Lenin, had won.

On 10 July 1918, the Bolsheviks, now the Communist Party, published the first constitution of the new state, named the Russian Soviet Federated Socialist Republic. Six days later, Tsar Nicholas II and his family were murdered at Ekaterinburg. It soon became clear that the Bolshevik leadership were determined that the Party's role should be monopolistic and that terror would be used to deter non-believers. Democracy was dead, the regime claimed to be socialist and vowed to destroy capitalism. Noone knew how a new economy should be developed or even what its shape would be.

As for the war, an armistice was arranged but the Bolsheviks were so slow in negotiating a peace treaty that the Germans started advancing again deep into the Ukraine and also threatened Petrograd. Peace negotiations recommenced in March 1918 with the peacemakers meeting at Brest-Litovsk. The Russians acknowledged the independence of Finland and gave up the lands that would become Estonia, Latvia, and Lithuania, as well as Belarus and the Ukraine. In reality, these would become political and economic clients of Germany and Austria. Territory from Turkey in the Russo-Turkish War of 1877–78 was to be returned. Thus, Russia lost vast numbers of people, the Ukrainian grain basket, and its industrial heartland.

The treaty, however harsh, gave the Bolsheviks a breathing space to face their internal enemies and Allied interventionist forces. The treaty lasted only eight and a half months; because of Germany's defeat on the Western Front, the Western allies destroyed the German military machine and forced Germany to renounce the Treaty of Brest-Litovsk, thereby doing Lenin a great service. The Baltic States won their independence in 1918 as did Poland while Finland engaged in a civil war, during which the Bolsheviks were defeated with the help of Germany.

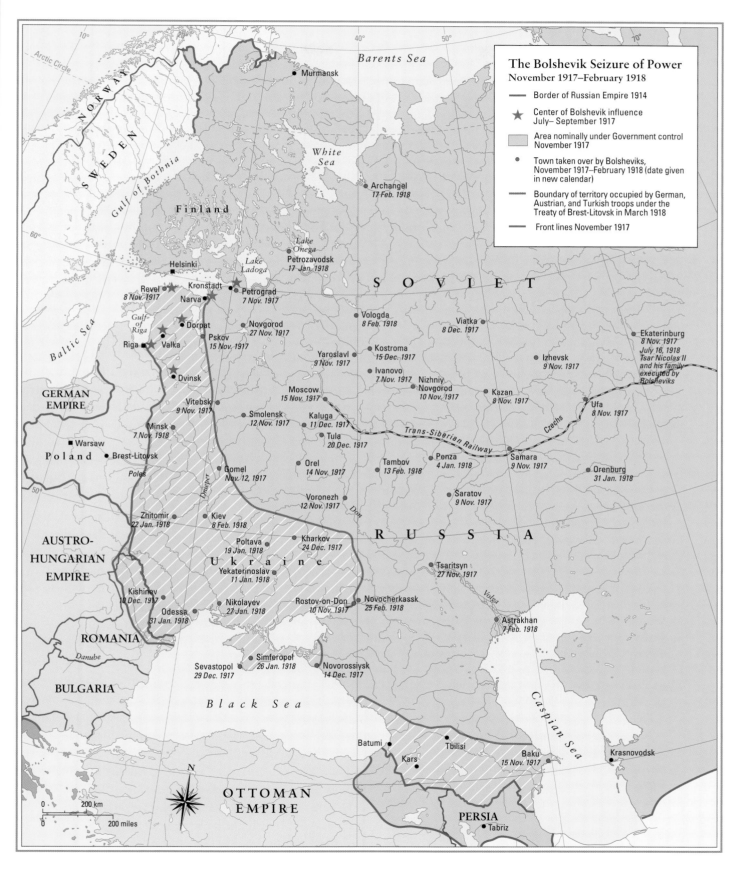

The Bolshevik Seizure of Power
November 1917–February 1918

— Border of Russian Empire 1914

★ Center of Bolshevik influence July– September 1917

Area nominally under Government control November 1917

• Town taken over by Bolsheviks, November 1917–February 1918 (date given in new calendar)

— Boundary of territory occupied by German, Austrian, and Turkish troops under the Treaty of Brest-Litovsk in March 1918

— Front lines November 1917

Arctic Circle

NORWAY

SWEDEN

Barents Sea

Murmansk

Gulf of Bothnia

Finland

White Sea

Archangel
17 Feb. 1918

Lake Onega

Petrozavodsk
17 Jan. 1918

Helsinki

Lake Ladoga

S O V I E T

Revel
8 Nov. 1917

Kronstadt

Petrograd
7 Nov. 1917

Narva

Gulf of Riga

Dorpat

Novgorod
27 Nov. 1917

Vologda
8 Feb. 1918

Viatka
8 Dec. 1917

Ekaterinburg
8 Nov. 1917
July 16, 1918
Tsar Nicolas II
and his family
executed by
Bolsheviks

Baltic Sea

Riga

Valka

Pskov
15 Nov. 1917

Yaroslavl
9 Nov. 1917

Kostroma
15 Dec. 1917

Izhevsk
9 Nov. 1917

Dvinsk

Ivanovo
7 Nov. 1917

Kazan
8 Nov. 1917

Ufa
8 Nov. 1917

Czechs

GERMAN
EMPIRE

Vitebsk
9 Nov. 1917

Moscow
15 Nov. 1917

Nizhniy
Novgorod
10 Nov. 1917

Smolensk
12 Nov. 1917

Trans-Siberian Railway

Minsk
7 Nov. 1918

Kaluga
11 Dec. 1917

Warsaw

Tula
20 Dec. 1917

Penza
4 Jan. 1918

Samara
9 Nov. 1917

Orenburg
31 Jan. 1918

Poland

Brest-Litovsk

Orel
14 Nov. 1917

Poles

Gomel
Nov. 12, 1917

Dnieper

Tambov
13 Feb. 1918

Saratov
9 Nov. 1917

Voronezh
12 Nov. 1917

R U S S I A

Don

Zhitomir
22 Jan. 1918

Kiev
8 Feb. 1918

AUSTRO-
HUNGARIAN
EMPIRE

Poltava
19 Jan. 1918

Kharkov
24 Dec. 1917

Tsaritsyn
27 Nov. 1917

U k r a i n e

Yekaterinoslav
11 Jan. 1918

Volga

Kishinev
10 Dec. 1917

Nikolayev
27 Jan. 1918

Rostov-on-Don
10 Nov. 1917

Novocherkassk
25 Feb. 1918

Odessa
31 Jan. 1918

Astrakhan
7 Feb. 1918

ROMANIA

Simferopol
26 Jan. 1918

Sevastopol
29 Dec. 1917

Novorossiysk
14 Dec. 1917

BULGARIA

Danube

Caspian Sea

B l a c k   S e a

Batumi

Tbilisi

Baku
15 Nov. 1917

Krasnovodsk

N

Kars

OTTOMAN
EMPIRE

PERSIA

Tabriz

0   200 km

0   200 miles

The Russian Civil War

The Bolshevik coup inaugurated a period of violence known as the Russian civil war, during which the Bolsheviks fought for survival and sought to impose their rule over all of Russia. Opposition to the Bolsheviks, which had started before the scattering of the Constituent Assembly, grew rapidly. The press had been gagged in late 1917, key political figures had been arrested, and revolutionary tribunals established. The secret police, or Cheka, created in December that year and placed under the supervision of Felix Dzerzhinsky (1877–1926), operated outside the law in punishing opponents of the regime. The Cheka established terror and the first concentration camps, later to become Stalin's Gulag. Mensheviks, left-wing Social Revolutionaries, and anarchists rose up against the Bolsheviks in many localities, such as the Volga town of Yaroslavl. In the summer of 1918 Fanya Kaplan (1890–1918), a socialist revolutionary, shot Lenin in the shoulder and jaw.

Violence spread throughout Russia between communist and anti-communist forces. The anti-communist forces, known as the Whites, comprised a large variety of groups, whose attempts to defeat the "Reds", or Bolsheviks, were entirely uncoordinated. General Kornilov escaped prison and travelled south to form the Volunteer Army, which captured Ekaterinodar in March. Kornilov was killed and succeeded by Anton Denikin (1872–1947), a former tsarist general. The latter operated in southern Russia but his army was finally pushed back to the Crimea, where he held out for a time. The peasants were suspicious of the Whites' intent, fearing that the Whites would bring back the landlords, and even built an anarchist, or Black, Army in Ukraine, led by Nestor Makhno (1888–1935). He fought any faction that attempted to control Ukraine and would ally with anyone to achieve this purpose. His army won a number of victories and for a time controlled much of Ukraine but after defeating the Whites the Bolsheviks were able to concentrate on other enemies. Makhno was crushed and eventually fled to Romania and subsequently France. Warfare in southern Russia was accompanied by anti-Jewish pogroms and tens of thousands were killed.

The Whites fielded armies around the periphery of Russia in the Baltic, Caucasus, Central Asia, Crimea, Siberia, and Ukraine. Those fighting in the far north welcomed the intervention of the Allied countries, which sent troops through the ports of Murmansk and Arkhangel to guard wartime supplies that they had sent to the Provisional Government. Elsewhere, the Czech Legion, consisting of Czech expatriates who had settled in Ukraine as well as Czechs who were drafted into the Austrian army and became Russian prisoners-of-war, roamed the Trans-Siberian Railroad, hoping to quit Russia and be sent to fight in France with the intention of demanding a Czechoslovak state at any peace table. In the Far East, the British, Americans, and Japanese fielded troops. The Japanese dreamt of controlling Siberia as far as Lake Baikal. Allied interventionist forces were widespread: there were French in the Crimea and British in Batum, Baku and Krasnovodsk in Turkmenistan.

The Reds found it difficult to win over the peasants who sought to avoid conscription into the Red Army. Many non-Russians served with the Bolsheviks and, lacking their own officers, the Red Army coerced former tsarist officers to join them, often holding their wives and children hostage. Trotsky was the Commissar of War and exerted harsh disciplinarian measures, with deserters being shot and "White" villages burned.

Some of the most vicious fighting in the Civil War took place in Ukraine, with villages being burnt, class warfare on the increase, and battles between armored trains. Some of these events are depicted in the four-volume *And*

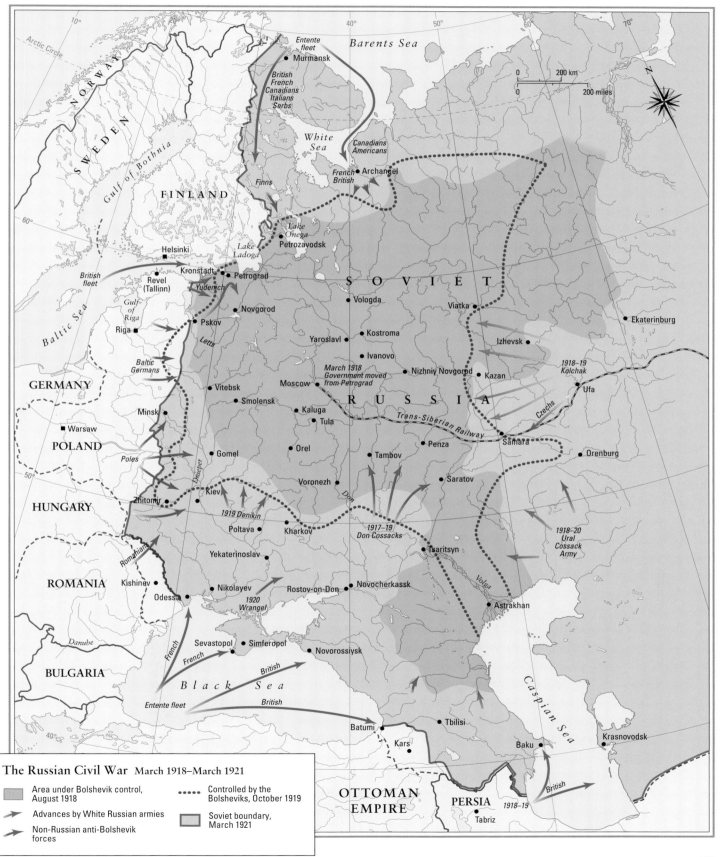

The Russian Civil War March 1918–March 1921

- Area under Bolshevik control, August 1918
- Advances by White Russian armies
- Non-Russian anti-Bolshevik forces
- Controlled by the Bolsheviks, October 1919
- Soviet boundary, March 1921

The Russo–Polish War
February 1919–March 1920

— Poland created at the Treaty of Brest-Litovsk in 1917 to be under the economic domination of Germany

--- Curzon Line 1919

◄— Main Russian attacks

◄-- Russian retreats

▶— Polish counterattacks

Poland after 1921

Quiet Flows the Don series written by Michael Sholokhov (1905–84). Elsewhere, the tsarist General Yudenich (1862–1933) mounted an attack on Petrograd from Estonia in 1919 but Trotsky organized the defense of the city and Yudenich was driven back. The overall White leader was supposedly Admiral Kolchak, who led the counter-revolutionary movement in Siberia. But Kolchak never had the means to create an effective government in enormous Siberia, let alone coordinate the whole White movement strung out around the immense periphery of the former Russian Empire.

The Reds also faced the Poles in the Russo-Polish War of 1920–21 and each side's fortunes ebbed and flowed until the 1921 Treaty of Riga by which Poland was paid an indemnity and a large bloc of territory around Pinsk was gained. Poland also took some Lithuanian territory around Grodno and Vilnius. All of these lands would be fought over again during the Second World War.

Meanwhile, Siberia fell under the sway of various warlords, some of whom collaborated with Japanese invaders. Three were extremely cruel and violent men: Gregory Semyonov (1890–1946), Ivan Kalmykov (1890–1920), and Roman von Ungern-Sternberg (1885–1921). The Civil War petered out as the Allied interventionists left Russia.

A legacy of the Civil War was the Bolshevik loss of Russian territories forfeited during the confusion of war. In Finland, Marshal Mannerheim led White Finnish troops against Bolsheviks who were either shot or placed in internment camps. Finnish independence was gained and a border Treaty of Tartu with Russia determined the country's extent. Estonia, Latvia, and Lithuania became independent after brief wars of independence, aided by British officers, notably Lieutenant-Colonel Harold Alexander who subsequently became Lord Alexander of Tunis.

The Red Army's ultimate victory in the civil war can be attributed to its control of the heart of Russia, with its vast reserves of population and industrial resources, its unified command, and its hold on the core of the railroad system. It was far harder to coordinate the White counter-revolutionary armies around Russia's periphery. Lenin was also a far more astute politician than the White generals. Russian nationalism, the core White ideology, alienated non-Russians, who often preferred the semi-autonomy that Lenin promised to non-Russians who supported the Bolshevik cause.

The New States of Eastern Europe
c. 1921

- Territory lost by Germany
- Territory lost by Russia (Soviet Union after 1917)
- Territory lost by Bulgaria
- States and territories created from the former Austro-Hungarian Empire
- → Battles and campaigns fought by emerging states
- — Borders recognized 1920–22
- *6 December 1917* Date of Independence or state formation

The Aftermath: From War Communism to NEP and the Creation of a Police State

Russia had suffered intensely during the First World War, revolutions, and civil war and experienced devastating violence. The Red Terror inaugurated an even more destructive force as enemies of the state were executed in the tens of thousands. In August 1918 the first concentration camp, inspired by Lenin, was constructed in the province of Penza. The camps were execution centers as well as prisons and labor camps. In the camp at Kholmogory, which was under the command of Mikhail Kedrov (1878–1941), political prisoners were drowned en masse in June 1920 and the psychotic commander was known to have massacred school children. In 1921 the Red Army ruthlessly crushed the sailors' revolt against Communist rule at Kronstadt.

The Tenth Party Congress, meeting in March 1921, reinforced the Leninist concept of democratic centralism by which an issue could be freely debated within the Party but all members had to unconditionally stick to the majority decision. The Congress also agreed with Lenin's dictum that factionalism was banned and all other parties were proscribed. In reality, the Party was increasingly run by a self-appointed oligarchy backed up by an ever-increasing secret police, the Cheka. This organization, which became the GPU (State Political Administration, and then OGPU (Unified State Political Administration) continued its campaign against dissenters even after the Red Terror ended. The terror remained latent until Stalin began his purges and elimination of enemies.

Lenin introduced the New Economic Policy at the Tenth Party Congress. During the civil war, Russia had been subjected to "War Communism." Special requisitioning squads were sent into the countryside to seize peasant produce in order to feed the towns and the army. The civil war had devastated the countryside causing a great loss of livestock and agricultural equipment, a reduction in manpower and a shortage of chemical and animal fertilizers. Less land was cultivated and the growing of industrial crops, such as flax, diminished in favor of grain. The destruction of the big estates and of many of the largest peasant farms also inevitably reduced the marketing of foodstuffs. War communism caused great hardship and, with the drought of 1920, famine spread and maybe as many as ten million people died. Foreign relief aid helped limit the distress but matters were so dire that one retailer resorted to selling human flesh. The new policy introduced a mixed socialist and capitalist economy with a low tax on agricultural products as an incentive for the peasants to produce more and sell it on the open market. Politically, the intention was to reduce peasant grievances against the Party. Lenin realized that a free market could provide the goods that the population craved, in the process reducing public opposition to the regime and giving the Party time to regain its strength after the strains of the civil war.

The state would now control foreign trade, banking, the railroad network, and all major industries. Recovery in the industrial sector was sluggish because of inexperience in planning and direction. The rural sector produced grain surpluses but the peasants were prone to producing a surplus only when urban goods were available and cheap. The peasants thus remained a class enemy of the Party and this turned into violence in the late 1920s. A major phenomenon of NEP was the private businessmen who were allowed to become shopkeepers and market traders. Altogether NEP enabled the industrial and agricultural sectors to recover to the levels of 1913 by 1926.

A consequence of Bolshevik survival was the growth of a vast bureaucratic machine. Many of the Bolsheviks who operated this machine believed that socialism would not survive amidst the reforms of the NEP. The industrialization process kept the urban working classes under control, but the peasant was still a danger to be removed and arguments over how this could be achieved fueled the political infighting after Lenin's death.

ORGANIZING STATE SECURITY

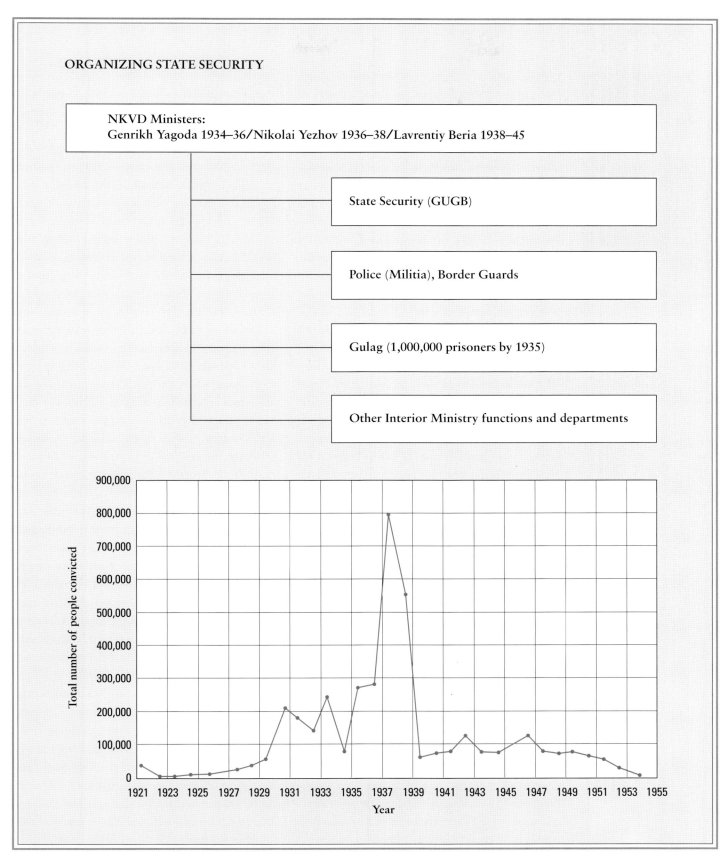

NKVD Ministers:
Genrikh Yagoda 1934–36/Nikolai Yezhov 1936–38/Lavrentiy Beria 1938–45

State Security (GUGB)

Police (Militia), Border Guards

Gulag (1,000,000 prisoners by 1935)

Other Interior Ministry functions and departments

Stalin's Rise to Power

Joseph Stalin, born on 18 December 1878 as Ioseb Besarionis Dze Jugashvili of Georgian parentage. He ruled the Soviet Union from the mid-1920s until his death in 1953.

Between the Twelfth and Seventeenth Party Congresses (1923–34), certain basic features of the Soviet regime were established: politically, a small oligarchy of party leaders took control; economically, there was total dedication to building an advanced industrial economy; and, socially, the Communist Party sought to subordinate all aspects of social life to its control. In December 1934 the assassination of Sergei Kirov (1886–1934), the Leningrad Party leader, marked the beginning of the Stalinist period, when the remains of any collective decision-making were removed and a one-man dictatorship destroyed the oligarchy.

Before 1922, Joseph Stalin (1878–1953) had been appointed People's Commissar for the Nationalities (1917), a member of the Politburo (the executive branch of the Bolshevik Party), liaison officer between the Politburo and Bureau of Organization (Orgburo) in 1919, Head of the Workers' and Peasants' Inspectorate, and General Secretary of the Party in 1922. As Commissar for Nationalities, he managed many millions of non-Russians and established a power base in the border regions where he was involved in local intrigues, winning much personal support.

By virtue of his administrative positions, Stalin controlled every branch of the Party, including those that had the task of eliminating inefficiency and corruption. He was a political auditor who had to train an elite of reliable socialist bureaucrats for the new regime. Immense powers of patronage enabled him to place his people throughout the governmental machinery, constructing a massive bureaucracy policed by himself and his personnel. As General Secretary, he set the agenda for Politburo meetings, managing to manipulate, discipline, and pack local committees with his supporters, and he could use the Central Committee as a counterweight to the Politburo. Above all, through his control of Party committees at every level, Stalin could control who was "elected" to Party Congress and therefore to the Party Central Committee. Control of these institutions was to play a crucial part in his victory in the struggles between Bolshevik leaders in the 1920s.

Lenin had doubts about Stalin's motives and methods but illness prevented him from doing anything. He suffered his first stroke in May 1922, and died in January 1924. Lenin's demise shattered the Party leadership. Excepting the strong-willed Stalin and Trotsky, the members deferred to Lenin's awesome and overwhelming personality. During his illness, a triumvirate was formed comprising Stalin, Gregory Zinoviev (1883–1936), Chairman of the Communist International, and Lev Kamenev (1883–1936), Moscow Party leader. These three men confronted Trotsky, whom they feared because of his control of the Red Army.

The mutual hostility between Trotsky and Stalin was inflamed by the Stalin-inspired cult of Lenin, with Stalin claiming to be Lenin's heir. Stalin stirred up a fear of a reactionary movement or coup, with Trotsky becoming a Russian Bonaparte. Trotsky was also criticized for his views on permanent revolution, which made the Bolshevik revolution dependent on successful left-wing revolutions in other countries. Stalin retaliated by introducing the concept of "socialism in one country," which emphasized the creative role of the Party in building a new society within the USSR. This line, combining pragmatism with hints even of Russian nationalism, appealed to many of the ex-workers and peasants who rose to senior positions in the 1920s and 1930s.

The triumvirate broke down, with Zinoviev and Kamenev joining Trotsky, who resigned as Commissar for War in 1925. Stalin linked himself to other Bolshevik politicians and enlarged the Politburo to include personal supporters. He then expelled his enemies from the Politburo, and Trotsky and Zinoviev were expelled from the Party. Trotsky was exiled to Alma Ata and then from the Soviet Union, and was eventually murdered in Mexico in 1940 by a Stalinist agent.

The Failure of International Revolution and the Rise of Fascism 1919–35

Revolutionary attempts by non-Russian Communists to seize power 1918–23—all suppressed by armed forces

Communist propaganda centers receiving money from Petrograd encouraging Communist activity

Countries of the Moscow Comintern Congress of 1920 whose delegates first demanded freedom for their own Communist parties

Democratic countries

Repressive or conservative countries

Fascist countries

Communist dictatorship

Right-wing activity

0   200 km
0   200 miles

Norwegian Sea

North Sea

ATLANTIC OCEAN

NORWAY

SWEDEN

FINLAND

Oslo

Stockholm

Helsinki

Leningrad
(*Petrograd renamed 1924*)

Tallinn

ESTONIA

Riga

LATVIA

LITHUANIA

Kaunas

U.S.S.R.

DENMARK
Copenhagen

Königsberg

East Prussia

Danzig
free city under League of Nations

Warsaw

Brest-Litovsk

UNITED KINGDOM

Dublin

IRELAND

London

Amsterdam

NETHERLANDS

Hamburg

Bremen

Berlin

GERMANY

Essen

Brussels

BELGIUM

Rhine

Frankfurt

POLAND

Cracow

Lvov

Prague

CZECHOSLOVAKIA

Paris

FRANCE

SAAR
autonomous under League of Nations

Bavaria

Vienna

AUSTRIA

Budapest

HUNGARY

ROMANIA

Bern
SWITZ.

Geneva

Trieste

Venice

Belgrade

Bucharest

Danube

YUGOSLAVIA

ANDORRA

PORTUGAL

SPAIN

Madrid

Lisbon

Balearic Is.

ITALY

Rome

Adriatic Sea

BULGARIA

Sofia

Istanbul

ALBANIA

GREECE

Athens

Aegean Sea

TURKEY

Black Sea

Italian occupied

Gibraltar
to Great Britain

Tangier
International zone

Morocco

to France

Algeria

Tunisia

Mediterranean Sea

Libya
to Italy

The Purges

The purges commenced in 1932 when critics of Stalin, the Ryutin Group, were expelled from the Party and dissident workers were arrested and dubbed "wreckers" and "spies" in an attempt to discipline the workforce and divert attention from failures of policy during the industrialization process. In 1934, Stalin was wary of the Leningrad Party boss, Sergei Kirov, who had a strong following. In the Party, Kirov had a reputation for relative moderation, and for wishing to alleviate terror and the great suffering inflicted by collectivization and rapid industrialization. When Kirov was murdered in 1934, Stalin blamed terrorists or foreign agents and instigated a reign of terror, mass arrests, and deportations, with repression intensifying after 1936. Stalin decided to kill all Party members whose past might make them opponents or aspirants to power and pressure and surveillance increased. The increasing fear of war with Nazi Germany may have been a factor in Stalin's determination to destroy all "enemies within."

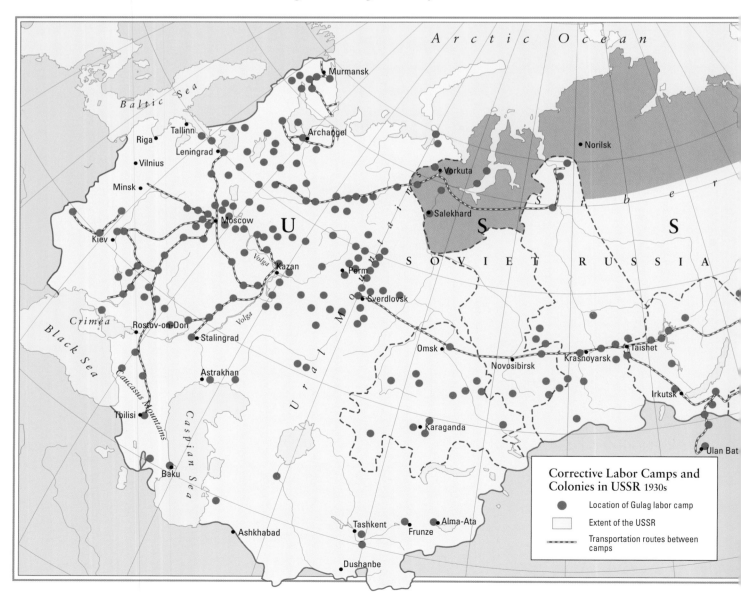

Corrective Labor Camps and Colonies in USSR 1930s

- Location of Gulag labor camp
- Extent of the USSR
- Transportation routes between camps

During this period, leaders of the revolution were publicly tried and confessed to unimaginable crimes—collaboration with Trotsky and associations with German and Japanese intelligence operatives in a series of planned wrecking and sabotage activities. Prison camps were built and mobilized to liquidate all opposition and dissident groups, whether actual, imagined, or potential.

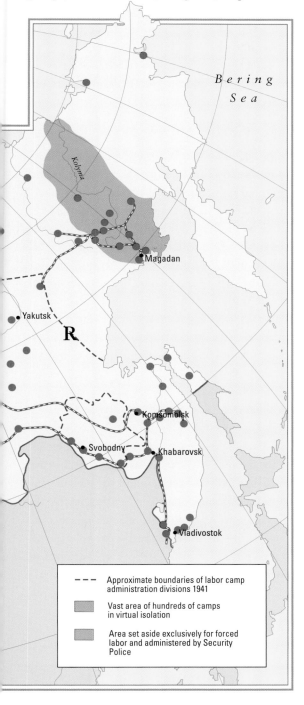

--- Approximate boundaries of labor camp administration divisions 1941

Vast area of hundreds of camps in virtual isolation

Area set aside exclusively for forced labor and administered by Security Police

Lenin's entire Politburo, with the exception of Trotsky and Stalin, was executed and the majority of the Central Committee was eliminated. The old Bolshevik revolutionaries, together with many Party members from its upper and middle echelons, were wiped out. In addition, Stalin had 1,100 out of 2,000 Party Congress members executed, destroying the old Party in a malicious frenzy.

The military were also targeted. Most of the armed forces' top leaders were destroyed, including Tukhachevsky, Chief of the Red Army, and Admiral Orlov, Commander of the Red Fleet. Half the generals and 35,000 officers were imprisoned or killed. The navy and air force suffered a similar fate. The Red Army was left crippled, disorganized, poorly commanded, and totally demoralized. All this was demonstrated conclusively when the Finnish armed forces repelled sustained attacks by the Red Army in the Winter War of 1939–40.

A large proportion of managers, scientists, and engineers went to prison, thereby damaging the economy. All Party and state leaders in the constituent republics were accused of treason or bourgeois nationalism and purged, together with regional Party secretaries and general apparatchiks. People with contacts abroad were shot and even teachers of foreign languages were purged. All those who were linked or married to the accused were purged, and ultimately the purgers were also purged. Genrikh Yagoda, head of the NKVD, was shot. His successor, Nichols Ezhov Yezhov was purged and replaced by Lavrenti Beria (1899–1953).

A system of gulag "corrective" labor camps spread across the entire country with some ten million people inhabiting them at one time or another, and a million or more executions before the German invasion in 1941. Prisoners provided slave labor for construction projects in geographically hostile areas. Entire ethnic groups were moved into Siberia and Central Asia and after the Second World War returning prisoners of war were sent to the camps, as were Polish and Baltic elites. Young, ambitious men like Nikita Khrushchev (1894–1971) and Leonid Brezhnev (1906–1982) were able to use the death of the Bolshevik old guard to pursue political career opportunities.

Stalin's Collectivization

The collectivization of agriculture, the First Five-Year Plan, and industrialization all followed the Party's abandonment of NEP. Collectivization was an integral part of industrialization and took place for a number of reasons, both economic and political. In economic terms, Stalin believed that squeezing agriculture was the only way to shift resources to industry. In political terms, the peasantry were destroyed as an autonomous entity. Stalin sought to consolidate the Soviet regime and to provide socialism with an economic base by instigating a second economic revolution to transform Russia and legitimate it socio-economically through the creation of a large proletariat.

The peasantry was essentially conservative, non-socialist, and interested in higher food prices, some industrial products, and consumer goods. So, wealthier peasants were seen as a threat to socialism and were equated with the bourgeois aspects of the New Economic Policy. These "kulaks" would be subjected to the totalitarian logic of violence, dynamism, and speed. Collectivization was used by Stalin to consolidate his political authority over the Party and government, and to coerce a reluctant peasantry in a rural country where an urban Party had seized power. Collectivization was essentially a coup d'état against the peasantry, imprisoning them in large-scale farms where they could be dominated effectively.

A Party debate over the pace of collectivization ensued. Since the peasants were harvesting less grain in 1928 than during the height of NEP, two options existed: either to coerce peasants into providing food or to entice them back in to the market by raising food prices. Stalin opted for speed and coercion. Accordingly, collectivization was launched on 7 November 1929 with little thought about how it was to be achieved and urban Party officials, who patently misunderstood rural life, implemented the policy. Stalin offered poor peasants collective farms that would be endowed with confiscated kulak property. The kulaks became the victims of an economic war with some one and a half million moved from their homes elsewhere and 900,000 sent to prison camps to work on dam and canal construction in the gulag system.

The peasants resisted collectivization in numerous ways and young Party members and workers were sent into the country to discipline the peasantry in a class war. The peasants retaliated by slaughtering livestock, with half the population of cattle, pigs, sheep, and goats eliminated. Horse numbers were also halved, thereby reducing horse-drawn traction and tractors had to be manufactured and distributed to the new collective farms to plug the shortfall before collectivization could really develop. Resistance in the north Caucasus, Ukraine, and Kazakhstan was especially intense with resultant mass starvation. The Khazaks lost 90 percent of their livestock and a quarter of this nomadic population died, as did five million Ukrainians. Some people resorted to cannibalism.

Collectivization effectively re-enserfed the peasants in a hierarchical revolution from above; a system of almost complete control ensured that people were moved into towns and labor camps. The state destroyed churches and mosques and both clergy and the richer peasants largely vanished from Soviet society. The peasants were eventually given private plots (two-thirds of an acre) and were able to produce enough food to provide an agricultural surplus, which was invested in industry. However, taxation of private peasants would probably have allowed more investment than collectivization. Collectivization effectively destroyed the old Russian peasant world and Soviet agriculture never recovered from the damage done by Stalin.

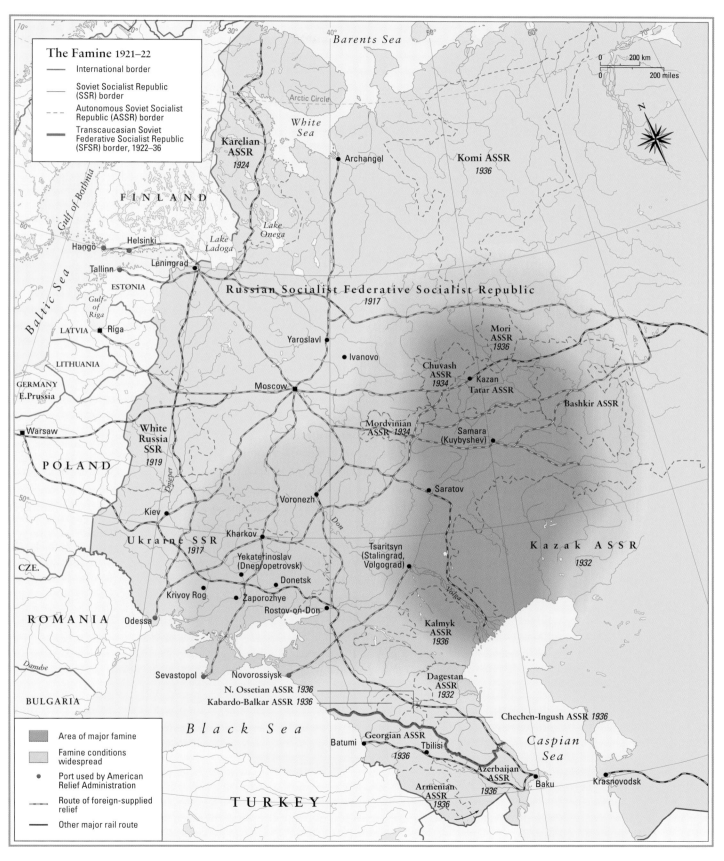

The Famine 1921–22

——	International border
——	Soviet Socialist Republic (SSR) border
- - -	Autonomous Soviet Socialist Republic (ASSR) border
▬▬	Transcaucasian Soviet Federative Socialist Republic (SFSR) border, 1922–36

Barents Sea

Arctic Circle

White Sea

Karelian ASSR *1924*

Archangel

Komi ASSR *1936*

0   200 km
0   200 miles

N

FINLAND

Gulf of Bothnia

Lake Onega

Helsinki

Hangö

Lake Ladoga

Tallinn

Leningrad

ESTONIA

Baltic Sea

Gulf of Riga

Russian Socialist Federative Socialist Republic *1917*

LATVIA   Riga

Yaroslavl

Mori ASSR *1936*

LITHUANIA

Ivanovo

Chuvash ASSR *1934*

Kazan
Tatar ASSR

GERMANY E.Prussia

Moscow

Bashkir ASSR

Warsaw

White Russia SSR *1919*

Dnieper

Mordvinian ASSR *1934*

Samara (Kuybyshev)

POLAND

Kiev

Voronezh

Don

Saratov

Ukraine SSR *1917*

Kharkov

Kazak ASSR *1932*

CZE.

Yekaterinoslav (Dnepropetrovsk)

Donetsk

Tsaritsyn (Stalingrad, Volgograd)

Krivoy Rog

Zaporozhye

Rostov-on-Don

Volga

ROMANIA

Odessa

Kalmyk ASSR *1936*

Sevastopol

Novorossiysk

Dagestan ASSR *1932*

N. Ossetian ASSR *1936*

Kabardo-Balkar ASSR *1936*

Chechen-Ingush ASSR *1936*

BULGARIA

Black Sea

Batumi

Georgian ASSR *1936*

Tbilisi

Caspian Sea

Azerbaijan ASSR *1936*

Baku

Krasnovodsk

Armenian ASSR *1936*

TURKEY

▨	Area of major famine
▧	Famine conditions widespread
●	Port used by American Relief Administration
┅┅	Route of foreign-supplied relief
——	Other major rail route

Industrialization

Industrialization was the second concurrent strand, along with collectivization, in Stalin's great economic strategy, which was so innovative in its scale and method. Stalin was alarmed by the West's war potential and fearful for the USSR. He planned to construct a vast iron, steel, and oil industry as the basis for heavy industrial growth. Indeed, he sought to emulate and surpass the industrial revolutions of Western Europe and the USA. Heavy industry and a virtual war economy would project the Soviet Union into a secure and defensible future. The Great Depression in the West gave Russia a lead-time in which to catch up while the capitalist world stagnated. Stalin's new planned, command economy was the first of its kind in peacetime. Resources would be concentrated on heavy industry at the expense of consumer goods, housing, and agriculture. Emphasis would be placed on capital goods, such as coal mines and steel mills, with keynote projects such as the hydro-electric plant on Dnieper Dam. It was claimed that collectivization would free the peasants of 500 million gold rubles in annual rent payments and this would help finance industrialization.

The First Five-Year Plan commenced in October 1928 and it visualized a great leap forward. The transformation would be financed by peasant rural surpluses, by saving the interest on annulled tsarist debts, and by the state taking management of all the mills, factories, banks, and modes of transportation seized from their previous capitalist owners. The people would, it was claimed, have to suffer in the short run, but their sacrifices would lead to the creation of a prosperous socialist version of urban industrial modernity. The plans established output targets, which were set by the state planning authority, Gosplan, and while the target figures lay in the realm of fantasy, the achievements were still incredible. For example, if 1928 production is expressed as 100, then by 1940 crude steel production had risen to 500, coal to 600, oil to 200, electricity to 900, and metal cutting machine tools to 2,900.

The first plan developed traditional industrial areas such as Moscow, Leningrad, and the Don Basin but engineering projects also occurred elsewhere. New industrial centers were developed at the iron and steel mill at Magnitogorsk in the Urals, the metallurgical combine at Kuznetsk in the Kuzbas, and at the Stalingrad Tractor Works on the Volga. The Second Five-Year Plan (1933–37) continued prioritizing heavy industry and the defense complex, which increased its productivity threefold with the help of a large influx of newly trained scientists and engineers. Production of consumer goods was increased but remained minimal and the peasants were still coerced and exploited. Inequalities crept in when pay increases and apartments were allocated to shock brigade leaders and Stakhanovites (a workers' movement that focused on "socialist competition" and rewarded workers who went beyond their quotas). Occasionally, retaliatory lynchings ensued. The Third Five-Year Plan, adopted in 1939, was cut short by war. However, the industrial base of the Soviet Union had been established, enabling the country to resist and finally push out the Germans during the Great Patriotic War.

Russia survived the war by moving much of its heavy industry to the east, out of range of the Germans. As for agriculture, the destruction of life and property during the war was immense. By 1953, output per head in foodstuffs was less than in the last days of tsarism. In 1946, Stalin launched a plan of national reconstruction to develop the industrial areas of central and eastern Russia, the areas that had been so important for the war effort. The plan was helped by the seizure of equipment from Germany and occupied eastern and central Europe. By 1948, Soviet factories had regained pre-war production levels, and by 1952 had well surpassed them.

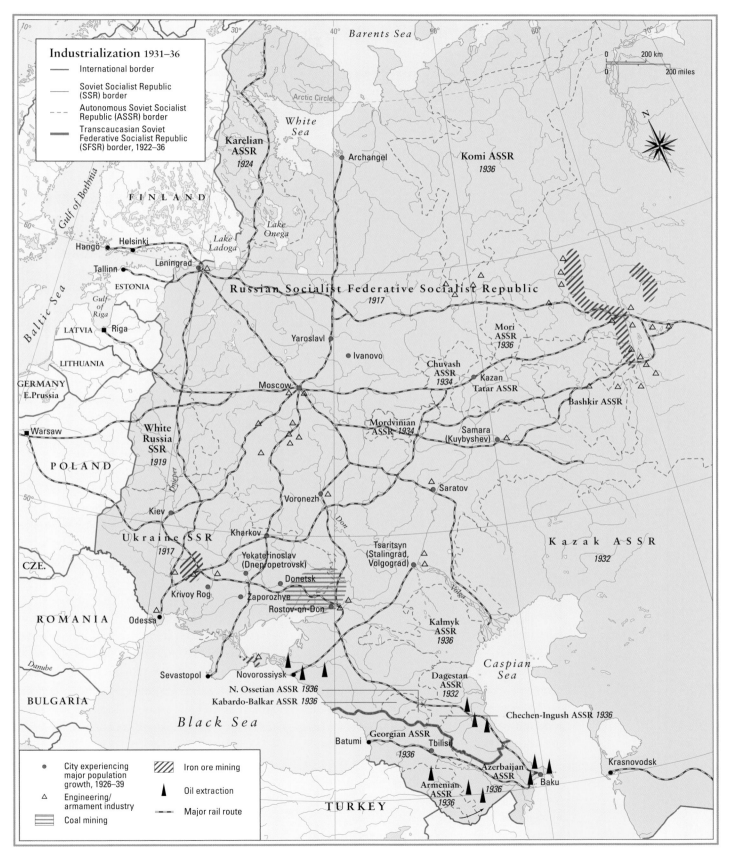

Industrialization 1931–36

———	International border
———	Soviet Socialist Republic (SSR) border
- - -	Autonomous Soviet Socialist Republic (ASSR) border
━━━	Transcaucasian Soviet Federative Socialist Republic (SFSR) border, 1922–36

Barents Sea

White Sea

Arctic Circle

Karelian ASSR *1924*

Komi ASSR *1936*

Archangel

Gulf of Bothnia

FINLAND

Lake Onega

Lake Ladoga

Hangö   Helsinki

Leningrad

Tallinn

ESTONIA

Baltic Sea

Gulf of Riga

LATVIA   Riga

LITHUANIA

GERMANY
E.Prussia

Russian Socialist Federative Socialist Republic *1917*

Yaroslavl

Ivanovo

Mori ASSR *1936*

Chuvash ASSR *1934*   Kazan
Tatar ASSR

Bashkir ASSR

Moscow

Warsaw

White Russia SSR *1919*

Dnieper

POLAND

Mordvinian ASSR *1934*

Samara (Kuybyshev)

Saratov

CZE.

Kiev

Ukraine SSR *1917*

Kharkov

Voronezh

Don

Tsaritsyn (Stalingrad, Volgograd)

Kazak ASSR *1932*

Yekaterinoslav (Dnepropetrovsk)

Donetsk

Krivoy Rog

Zaporozhye
Rostov-on-Don

ROMANIA

Odessa

Volga

Kalmyk ASSR *1936*

Danube

Sevastopol   Novorossiysk

N. Ossetian ASSR *1936*

Kabardo-Balkar ASSR *1936*

BULGARIA

Black Sea

Dagestan ASSR *1932*

Chechen-Ingush ASSR *1936*

Caspian Sea

Batumi   Georgian ASSR *1936*   Tbilisi

Azerbaijan ASSR *1936*   Baku

Krasnovodsk

Armenian ASSR *1936*

TURKEY

●	City experiencing major population growth, 1926–39
△	Engineering/armament industry
▤	Coal mining
▨	Iron ore mining
▲	Oil extraction
┅┅┅	Major rail route

0   200 km
0   200 miles

N

Roads to War

In 1914 Germany and Russia were the two most powerful countries on the European continent. To some extent the First World War began as a conflict between them over which of them was to control Eastern and Central Europe. By supreme and unpredictable irony the war resulted in the defeat of both Germany and Russia. The post-war order created at Versailles in 1919 was based on the defeat of both powers and at their expense. But although Russia and Germany were temporarily weakened, the underlying geopolitical reality of their potential power remained. When they regained their previous power in the 1930s the Versailles order in east and central Europe was bound to collapse.

Faced by Hitler, Stalin had the same options as Nicholas II before 1914: either to ally with Britain and France against Germany or to seek security by persuading the Germans to expand westwards. Strong mutual distrust between liberal and capitalist Britain and France on the one hand and Communist Russia on the other was a major reason why a renewed Franco-British-Russian alliance was not created against Germany.

In 1918–21 a new map of eastern Europe was drawn. A large Poland established itself at the expense of both Russia and Germany; Finland had gained its independence, as had the Baltic Republics of Estonia, Latvia, and Lithuania. Bessarabia had been lost to the new Republic of Romania, and the Kars area of the Caucasus had been taken by the new Republic of Turkey. At the end of the Russian Civil War the Ukraine was regained by the Soviets and the USSR's frontiers were effectively established in the Caucasus and Asia.

The new Soviet Russia and its federated states, however, were now diplomatically isolated from the western powers. Germany also suffered under the Treaty of Versailles, undergoing a reduction of territory, and a partial occupation, with its armed forces compulsorily reduced, and its industry forbidden to develop new weapons of war. The two states found themselves with common interests.

Germany sought to evade the military consequences of the Versailles Treaty, while Soviet Russia was eager to modernize and develop the Red Army and was interested in importing technical expertise. At an international trade conference held in Genoa, Italy, the Soviet and German contingents slipped quietly away and agreed to what became the Treaty Rapallo, signed on 16 April 1922. This recognized that both states' claims against each other—both territorial and financial— were rescinded, and decreed that diplomatic and trade relations be restored.

Against this background Johannes Friederich "Hans" von Seeckt became Chief of Staff of the Reichswehr (German Army) and from 1920–26 served as Commander in Chief. He appointed General Kurt van Schleicher, who later became the penultimate chancellor of the Weimar Republic, to negotiate with Leonid Borisovich Krasin, Bolshevik politician and diplomat, at the time the peoples' commissar for trade and industry. They created a secret agreement for Germany to supply the Soviets with the technology to develop their arms industry while evading the terms of the Versailles Treaty, which effectively had disarmed Germany. A German company, GEFU, was created and through this enterprise millions of Reichmarks were made available for German companies to design and build new weapons deep inside Russia. The Junkers Aircraft Company developed and produced the K30 Bomber at Fili, south of Moscow, Krupps tested new artillery near Rostov-on-Don, poison gas developments were undertaken near Samara, and the Kazan Military Academy was busy developing armored warfare techniques involving new tank designs, and welcomed German officers to all its courses.

Despite Soviet-German cooperation, both states were aware of each other's developments and they created their own theories of mobile warfare. In Germany the army that transformed from the Reichswehr to the Wehrmacht was operationally and tactically the product of von Seekt in the 1920s, its vision of combined arms operations continuing to develop in the 1930s. It was this army with which Germany went to war in September 1939.

Meanwhile in the Soviet Union the arms industry developed in an amazingly short time. The first Soviet-designed tank—the MS-1—left the factory in 1929. Just four years later Soviet industry was turning out 3,000 tanks and armored vehicles per year. This plentiful supply of equipment provided the basis for creating a mechanized force. The first armored brigade was announced in 1930 and by 1932 the Red Army had formed two mechanized corps—a full three years before Germany had created its first Panzer Division. By the mid-1930s, the Soviet Union led the world in tank production and the deployment of mechanized forces. The Red Army had a peacetime army of 1.5 million men by 1938.

Among the military leaders modernizing the

Red Army were battle-hardened soldiers like Mikhail Tukhachevsky, an ex-Imperial Army Officer, now risen to High Command in the Red Army. He, along with others, developed the theory of "deep battle," which viewed the offensive as a series of successive operations that deployed large mechanized force to punch through the enemy front deep into enemy territory, supported by air power and mobile infantry. But by stressing offensive warfare the Soviet army had not fully elaborated a defensive operations doctrine.

With the rise of Hitler and the Nazis, the secret military cooperation came to an end. The two states, with their rival political philosophies, would fight a war by proxy in the Spanish Civil War and the Soviets grew increasingly anxious about the territorial growth and influence of Nazi Germany. From the mid-1930s attempt were made to create an alliance with Britain and France. During the Munich crisis the Soviet Union was not

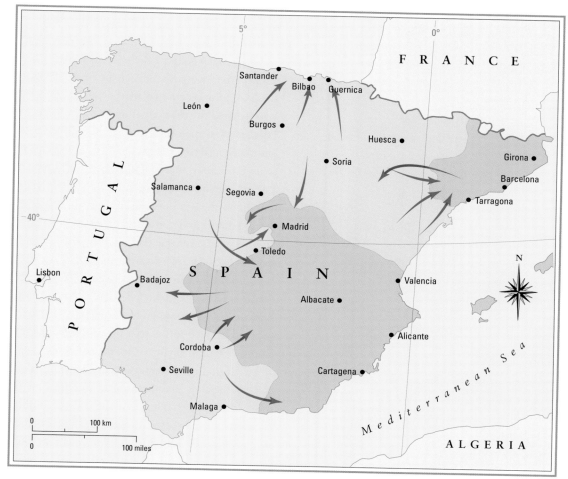

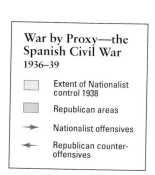

**War by Proxy—the
Spanish Civil War
1936–39**

Extent of Nationalist control 1938

Republican areas

Nationalist offensives

Republican counter-offensives

even invited to the negotiating table. Nevertheless, Soviet diplomats continued discussions with Britain and France, which eventually came to nought, failing on the Soviet request for the right of passage through Poland in the event of a German attack on Poland, but also, most fundamentally, on the correct Soviet belief that if the USSR went to war with Germany in alliance with France and Britain it would have to do the lion's share of the fighting.

Meanwhile, Stalin had decided that a compromise with Germany could offer an alternative security solution and instructed simultaneous negotiations to begin in May. These were led by a new commissar for foreign affairs, Viacheslav Molotov, one of the few senior survivors of Stalin's great purges. Firstly a trade and credit agreement was arranged, this was followed, and eventually ratified, in a political agreement. The details were agreed, on the German side, by foreign minister Joachim von Ribbentrop on 24 August and the Molotov-Ribbentrop agreement was announced to a stunned world. This agreement contained a series of secret protocols; eastern Europe was carved up into spheres of

influence. As a result of this, the Soviet Union occupied Estonia, Latvia, Lithuania, and Bessarabia, and a demarcation line was also agreed running through Poland.

The Red Army's new operating techniques were tested in the Far East by Japanese forces at Lake Khasan in a series of skirmishes and in a major battle at Khalkin Gol, on the river border between Mongolia and the Japanese satellite-state of Manchukuo (Manchuria). Japanese forces occupied an area around the village of Nomonhan, challenging Soviet strength in the area. After initial clashes, command of the Soviet forces was taken over by Corps Commander George Zhukov, one of Tukhachevsky's most brilliant students. The ensuing battle was a triumph for Zhukov and mobile warfare. By 27 August 1939 the battle was over and the Japanese signed an agreement to end hostilities on 15 September. Meanwhile, twelve days earlier, Germany and Soviet forces had attacked Poland. For Europe, the Second World War had begun.

For the Soviet Union the non-aggression pact with Germany enabled the state to move its borders further west, thereby acquiring a broader shield for the defense of the Soviet heartland. It also reduced the chances of a two-front German-Japanese war against the Soviet Union. Above all, Stalin believed that the pact had bought the USSR time. He never doubted that Hitler would remain a deadly enemy and threat to the USSR. But he believed that the war between Britain and France on the one hand and Germany on the other would last for years, taking the same course towards stalemate on the Western Front as had the First World War. During this time, while all Soviet communism's rivals weakened themselves through war, the USSR would be free to develop its economy and armed forces to a position of unassailable power and security. Stalin was nonplussed when Germany won the war in the West in six weeks, thereby establishing its domination of most of the European continent and placing the USSR in a position of acute danger. To do him justice, not just the British and French but also most German generals were equally surprised.

Political Agreements
1938–39

British and French guarantees for Poland, Greece, Romania and Turkey, 1939

Copenhagen declaration of neutrality, July 1938

Axis, May 1939

German-Soviet Non-Aggression Pact, 23 August 1939

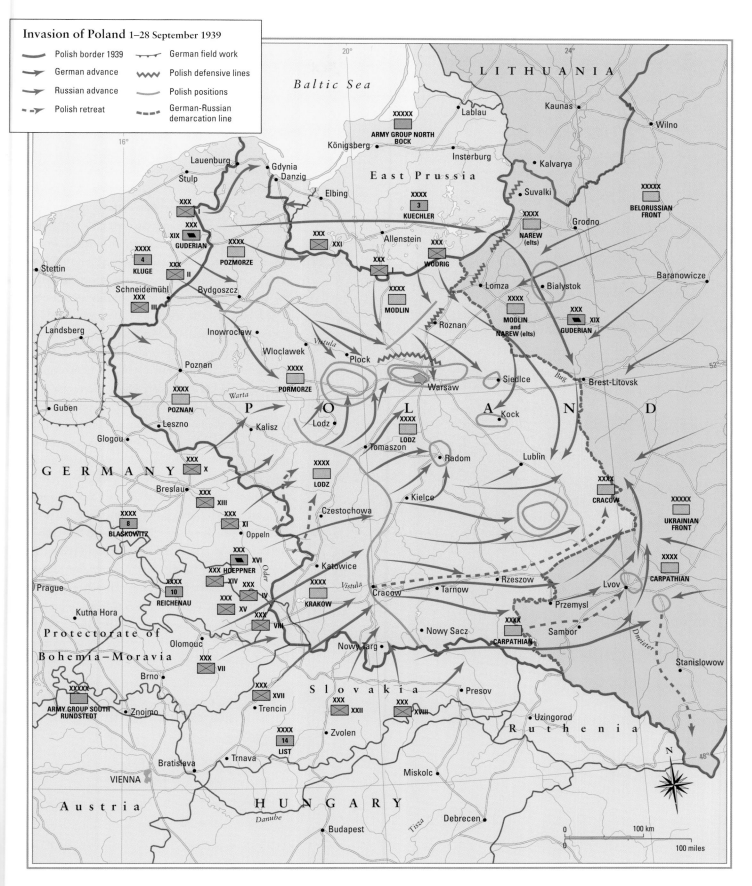

Invasion of Poland 1–28 September 1939

⌒	Polish border 1939	⌒	German field work
→	German advance	⩓⩓⩓	Polish defensive lines
→	Russian advance	⌒	Polish positions
⇢	Polish retreat	⇢	German-Russian demarcation line

The Winter War

The post-purge Red Army hastened to muster its forces to advance its claims to eastern Poland. On 5 September Moscow called up its Reservists, and on 17 September the Red Army crossed the Polish border, intending to follow its military philosophy by quickly penetrating the Polish defenses. The deployed Soviet forces experienced many difficulties—especially in logistics; delays in obtaining fuel for the mobile columns held back many intended advances. The bulk of the Polish Army was engaging German forces in the west. The few Polish forces defending the east managed to inflict casualties on the Red Army; almost 1,000 killed and 2,000 wounded. As the Polish state died, German occupation forces and the NKVD began their work—slaughtering untold thousands in the west and around 14,500 Polish officers and NCOs in the Katyn Forest in the east.

In October 1939, the Soviet government approached Finland for a number of concessions, including border adjustments and a 30-year lease on the strategic Hanko Peninsula. For a while Finnish representatives bargained with Moscow. On 3 November Molotov broke off negotiations and, after a carefully created border incident, Moscow ended its non-aggression treaty on 28 November. Soviet forces attacked the following day. The Finnish armed forces were vastly outnumbered, but at least they were prepared for a winter war. Once again, at short notice, the Red Army was ordered to prepare for a campaign intended to last twelve days. It would take 105 days for the Red Army to overwhelm Finnish resistance.

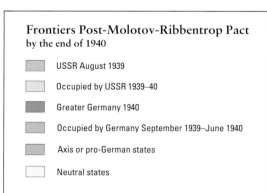

Frontiers Post-Molotov-Ribbentrop Pact
by the end of 1940

- USSR August 1939
- Occupied by USSR 1939–40
- Greater Germany 1940
- Occupied by Germany September 1939–June 1940
- Axis or pro-German states
- Neutral states

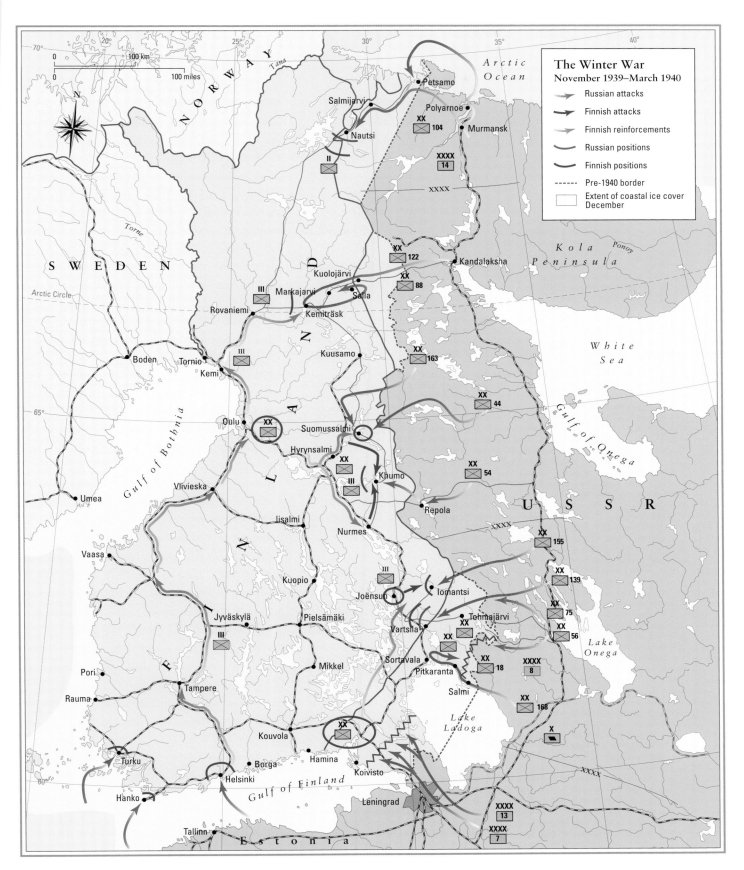

The Winter War
November 1939–March 1940

→ Russian attacks
→ Finnish attacks
→ Finnish reinforcements
⌒ Russian positions
⌒ Finnish positions
---- Pre-1940 border
▭ Extent of coastal ice cover December

The Great Patriotic War

The impact of the purges on the Red Army's performance in Poland and Finland was obvious. Out of the senior officer corps of around 80,000, 30,000 had been shot or imprisoned—these included three out of five marshals, all deputy defense commissars, all commanders of military districts, the commanders and chiefs of staff of the navy and air force, fourteen out of sixteen army commanders, 60 out of 67 corps commanders, and 136 out of 199 divisional commanders. Officers continued to disappear with alarming regularity up to the moment Germany invaded in June 1941.

After the lackluster performance of the Red Army, reforms were instigated. The political commissars, who had grown in power during the purges, were again reduced to a subordinate position, restoring the unity in the command structure frequently missing in the Finnish campaign, and improving the situation for professional officers. A new severe code of military justice was introduced, which gave the Red Army commanders a great deal of the authority that the tsarist army had once enjoyed.

By June 1940, in line with the Molotov-Ribbentrop Pact, the Soviet Union forced the Baltic States—Lithunania, Latvia, and Estonia—into mutual assistance agreements, allowing Soviet forces into their territories. Germany, now focused on redeploying the bulk of its forces to face France and Britain in the west, was unable or unwilling to support the Baltic States—they did, after all, fall into the Soviet sphere of influence.

Further south, again in line with the Molotov-Ribbentrop accords, Stalin pressurized the Romanian government to give up the region of Bessarabia. Romania refused and Stalin ordered immediate military action. The 9th Army, commanded by Major-General I.V. Boldim, attacked on 28 June, and Bessarabia was quickly overrun. The long border between the USSR and the Axis powers to the west was now established.

In July 1940, General A.M. Vasilevsky, Deputy Chief of the General Staff Operations Department, posited a possible German attack along the Minsk-Smolensk axis north of the great Pripet Marshes. The Soviet mobilization plan was adjusted to meet this threat. However, after Marshal K. A. Meretskov became Chief of the General Staff in August 1940, a re-evaluation took place, envisioning a German thrust south of the great marshes into the rich land of the Ukraine, and the mobilization plan was adjusted. Three months later a war game was organized to test the revised plan. To everyone's consternation, Stalin's in particular, the outcome demonstrated that the General Staff had underestimated German offensive potential and the Red Army's defensive preparation and skills were distinctly lacking.

By April 1941 Soviet intelligence had detected German offensive preparations, but during this period of deteriorating relations Soviet diplomats acted as if peace and cooperation continued. Stalin, who remained desperate for peace, implemented partial mobilization, but forbade the border military districts from undertaking any defensive measures that could be misinterpreted by Germany. On 13 May the General Staff ordered 28 rifle divisions to move toward the border areas. Between late May and early June 800,000 reservists were called to fill out reserve divisions and man fortified areas. Despite three years of preparation and these prudent moves, the Red Army was unprepared, poorly equipped, and badly deployed.

By the evening of 21 June 1941, almost 3.5 million men, 3,000 tanks, and 2,800 aircraft, divided into three army groups—the largest invasion force in history—had assembled on the western border. Facing them were 2.9 million men with up to 19,000 tanks—mostly obsolete—and the Red Air force with 8,000 aircraft, which were being re-equipped.

Operation Barbarossa began shortly after Hitler's Jurisdiction Decree, which exempted German soldiers from prosecution if they committed crimes against Soviet citizens. This, together with unrelenting propaganda, set the scene for a murderous campaign.

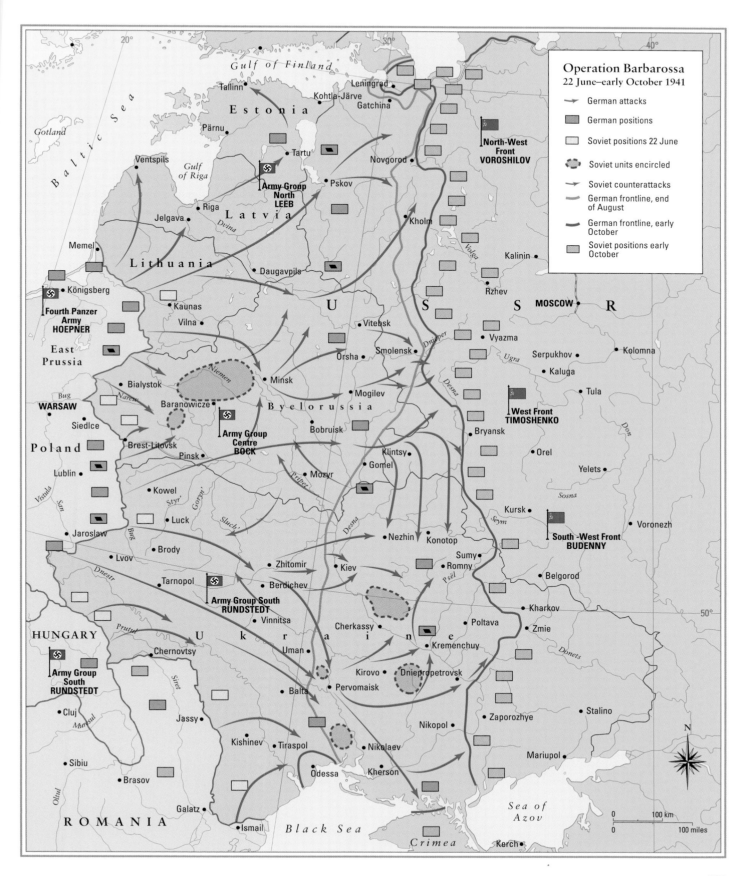

Operation Barbarossa
22 June–early October 1941

→ German attacks

▬ German positions

▯ Soviet positions 22 June

⬮ Soviet units encircled

→ Soviet counterattacks

▬ German frontline, end of August

▬ German frontline, early October

▬ Soviet positions early October

Gulf of Finland

Baltic Sea

Gotland

Leningrad
Tallinn
Kohtla-Järve
Gatchina
Estonia
Pärnu
Tartu
Novgorod
North-West Front VOROSHILOV

Ventspils
Gulf of Riga
Pskov

Riga
Latvia
Army Group North LEEB
Kholm

Jelgava
Dvina
Daugavpils

Memel
Lithuania
Kalinin
Rzhev

Königsberg
Kaunas
Vitebsk
Smolensk
Dnieper
MOSCOW

Fourth Panzer Army HOEPNER
Vilna
Vyazma
Serpukhov
Kolomna

East Prussia
Niemen
Orsha
Ugra
Kaluga
Tula

Bialystok
Narew
Minsk
Byelorussia
Mogilev
Desna

WARSAW
Baranowicze
West Front TIMOSHENKO

Siedlce
Army Group Centre BOCK
Bobruisk
Bryansk

Poland
Brest-Litovsk
Pinsk
Pripet
Klintsy
Gomel
Orel

Lublin
Kowel
Styr'
Gorym'
Mozyr
Desna
Yelets

Jaroslaw
Sluch'
Luck
Nezhin
Konotop
Kursk
Sosna
Voronezh

Lvov
Brody
Seym
South-West Front BUDENNY

Dnestr
Tarnopol
Zhitomir
Kiev
Sumy
Romny
Belgorod

Army Group South RUNDSTEDT
Berdichev
Psël
Poltava

HUNGARY
Prutul
Vinnitsa
Cherkassy
Kremenchuy
Kharkov
Zmie

Chernovtsy
Ukraine
Uman
Kirovo
Dniepropetrovsk
Donets

Army Group South RUNDSTEDT
Siret
Balta
Pervomaisk
Nikopol
Zaporozhye
Stalino

Cluj
Muresul
Kishinev
Tiraspol
Nikolaev
Mariupol

Sibiu
Jassy
Odessa
Kherson
N

Brasov
Galatz
Sea of Azov

Oltul
ROMANIA
Ismail
Black Sea
Crimea
Kerch
0 100 km
0 100 miles

20°   30°   40°   50°

U   S   S   R

After Stalin recovered from the shock of invasion, he called on Soviet citizens to commit to a "relentless struggle." On 3 July he announced a "patriotic war," which included a scorched-earth policy—everything not obliterated by the fighting was to be destroyed by Soviet forces. Stalin issued an order that the Red Army should not cede any territory to the enemy. The effect of this order, in the face of the most experienced army of the age, was to reduce what little tactical effort the Red Army could have made to almost nothing, and dooming its soldiers to captivity and death. The German advance continued, encircling hundreds of thousands of Soviet troops. The Panzer divisions led the way, followed by the infantry, while logistic units coped with ever lengthening lines of supply.

Despite terrible losses, there was no Soviet collapse. As the Red Army retreated, a massive effort was organized to move productive industry eastward. Around 50,000 factories and workshops were painstakingly dismantled, packed onto railroad wagons, and, wherever possible with their key workers, sent eastward.

Vast numbers of Soviet prisoners fell into German hands during Operation Barbarossa. By the end of the Russo-German war, the Red Army's missing and prisoners-of-war reached 4,559,000.

The German occupation of the Soviet Union was brutal in the extreme, with extermination squads roaming the countryside. Many villagers fled to the forests, often becoming partisans. Over 80 percent of those taken prisoner by the Germans did not survive their captivity.

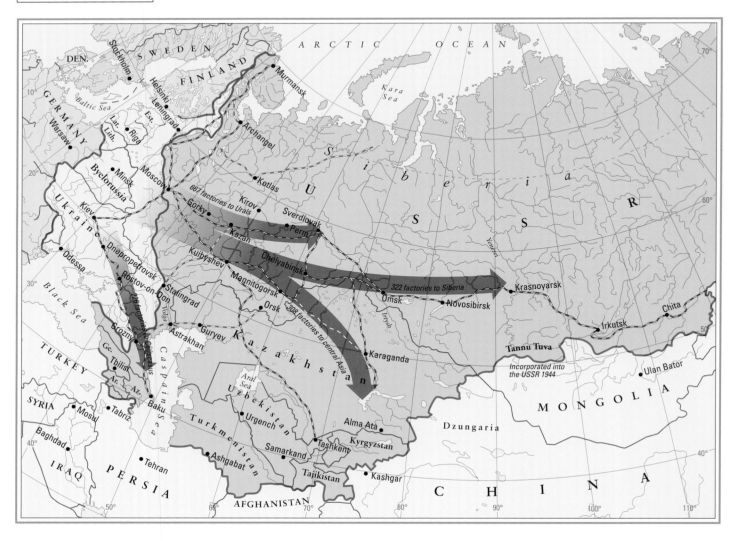

Dispersion of Soviet Industry 1941–42

— Boundary of USSR 1941
— German front line 1941–42
—•—•— Strategic railroads
—•—•— Added railroads 1941–45
▨ Unoccupied USSR
☐ Neutral

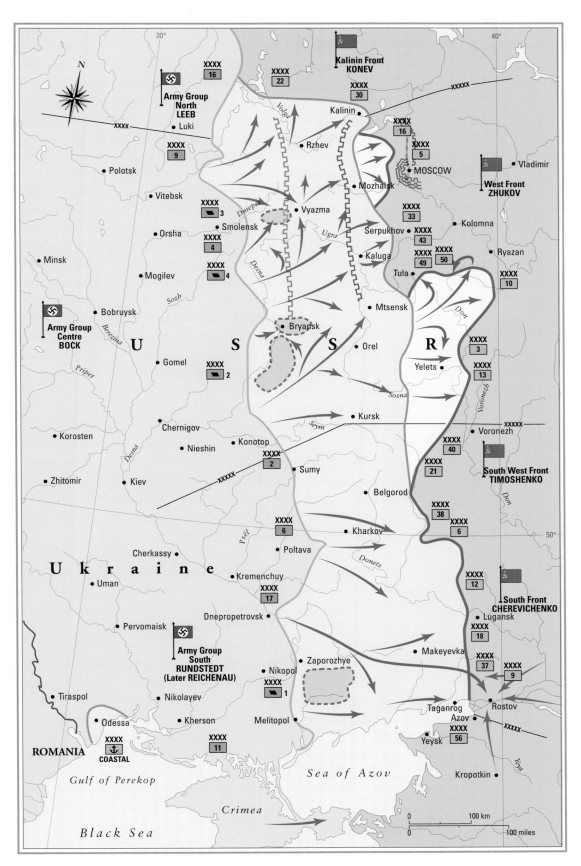

The Barbarossa plan deployed three Army Groups—North, commanded by von Leeb; Center, under von Bock; and South, led by von Rundstedt. Army Groups North and Center accounted for the bulk of the German field armies and were concentrated north of the Pripet Marshes. Army Group North was to advance through the Baltic States and on to Leningrad. Army Group Center's mission was to advance into Byelorussia, destroying the Soviet defending forces, then to assist Army Group North to capture or besiege Leningrad.

Meanwhile, Army Group South would attack from Romania. Its northern flank, where most of its Panzer formations were located, attacked south of the Pripet Marshes toward Kiev, then on to the Donets Basin.

As the German army advanced eastward, gaps appeared and widened between the leading Panzer formations and the supporting infantry, mostly advancing on foot. The front line also widened north-south, and forces had to be committed to hold tactically important supply lines, slowing the advance.

German High Command had planned to destroy, or capture, the bulk of the Soviet defending armies before they could withdraw into the Russian interior. Despite the fact that millions of Soviet soldiers had been killed or taken prisoner, the Red Army had not lost its cohesion. As division after division was destroyed on the battlefield, the Soviet population and its heavy industry supplied new recruits and weapons to equip and formto form and equip replacements. By the end of July the number of Soviet divisions had risen from 170 to 212. Though few of the new formations were at full strength or fully equipped, the Soviet will to resist and fight back was undiminished. Importantly, despite the purges, new talent was appearing in the officer corps; German assessment of the "purge effect" was not quite what they had hoped for.

Army Group North largely ran to plan, as did Army Group Center, capturing some 280,000 men at Minsk. However, this took days, delaying the advance on Smolensk, not taken until 17/18 July.

Now Hitler intervened; Army High Command wanted to press on to Moscow, Hitler insisted that a Panzer Group be sent to Leningrad, while another Panzer Group be sent south into the Ukraine where the offensive was falling behind schedule. Reinforced, German forces broke the Red Army's resistance in the region, while further south the Romanian 4th Army besieged Odessa on 5 August. Odessa held out until early October. Panzer Groups I and II maneuvered, trapping 650,000 Red Army troops in the Kiev Pocket. General Kirponos, Commander of the Red Army's Southwest Front, was killed at this time, completing the breakdown of command and control in the region. At the opposite end of the 621-mile (1000 km) front Army Group North captured Novgorod and by 8 September reached Lake Ladoga, effectively cutting off Leningrad, beginning its 872-day siege.

Hitler now looked again at Moscow, and determined that Soviet resistance was nearing its end. He authorized an operation to envelop Vyazma to be followed by an advance toward Moscow. Most of September was spent re-organizing, bringing up supplies and preparing for Operation Typhoon (the advance to Moscow). This operation began on 30 September and followed the usual German pattern, with the Panzer forces pushing forward and creating new encirclements, to be dealt with by the following infantry.

German High Command placed great faith in the expected collapse of Soviet resistance, which failed to happen. October brought the rains of the fall, the season of mud when most unmetalized Russian roads became impassable. On the Soviet side, new divisions were forming, grouped into armies and deployed into the Stavka Reserve. Stalin now became convinced that Japan would strike south into the Pacific and southeast Asia, thus allowing trained and experienced divisions to be moved from the Far East to the Moscow front. The Soviets were gaining strength—each German advance seemed more difficult and expensive. By 19 October Moscow was declared under siege. However, Soviet counterattacks were launched at Kalinin and Misensk.

In early November German High Command

finally admitted that the Soviet Union could not be defeated in 1941. However, the Germans fought on in an attempt to retain the initiative—advance units almost reached the outer limits of Moscow. The Russian winter had now arrived and the planned Soviet counteroffensive, and the freezing temperatures, sapped the German soldiers' will to fight and immobilized much of their equipment. Soviet equipment worked, designed to cope with extreme cold. German units retreated, leaving behind a large proportion of their equipment.

Hitler demanded no withdrawals, while his commanders insisted on freedom of movement. Hitler's reaction was to dismiss his army group commanders as well as several army commanders during the first month of the Soviet counteroffensives. In the end he assumed direct command of the German Army himself.

The Caucasus
June–November 1942

- → German attacks
- ⇢ German retreat
- ⌒ German front line
- ⇢ Russian retreat
- ⛏ Oilfield

The Soviets launched three armies in their counteroffensive on 6 December, which included a new formation—the "Shock Army"—specifically formed for counteroffensive attacks. German positions north and south of Moscow collapsed and the Red Army launched a wider offensive. By the spring both sides had fought themselves into a stalemate. The Soviets now faced the invaders reinvigorated and behind defense in depth.

In the winter of 1941, Hitler ordered his mauled armies to stand fast along an eastern front that stretched from the Baltic to the Black Sea. In the south, German forces had occupied most of the Crimean peninsula and reached Taganrog on the Sea of Azov.

Stalin met the Stavka on 5 January 1942, and outlined his plans. The German defeat before Moscow encouraged Stalin to initiate premature offensives. During November and December there had been local offensives at Tikhvin, near Leningrad, and north of Rostov-on-Don, that had brought some success. Now Stalin wanted offensives to relieve Leningrad, and liberate the Donbass and the Crimea; however, events overtook these ambitions. The Southwest Front had launched an attack in the Kursk area on 1 January aimed at Army Group South—this developed into a struggle to recapture Kharkhov. The Red Army created a 20-mile deep salient in the German line. In a textbook response the German counterattack

Stalingrad
January 1942– February 1943

- ➤ Russian attacks
- ➤ German counter-attacks
- ⇢ German retreats
- ⌣ German front lines
- ⊥ Russian artillery concentrations
- ⇛ Russian fighter interception
- ➤ Luftwaffe air lift

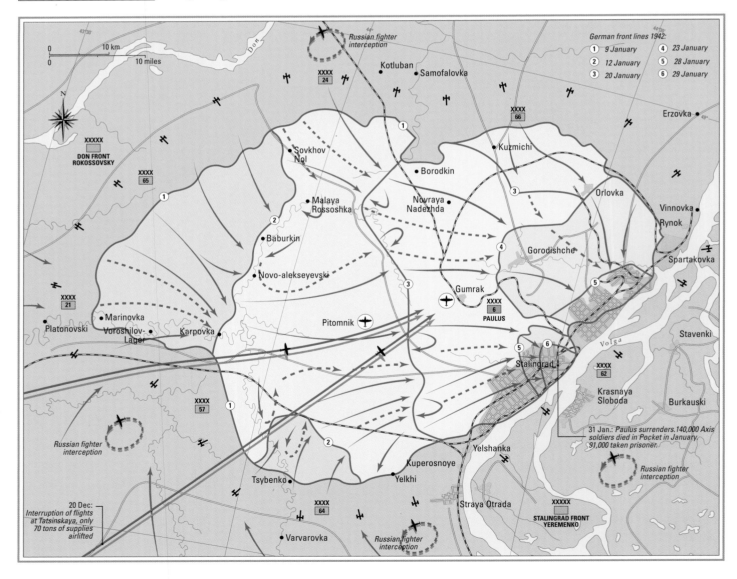

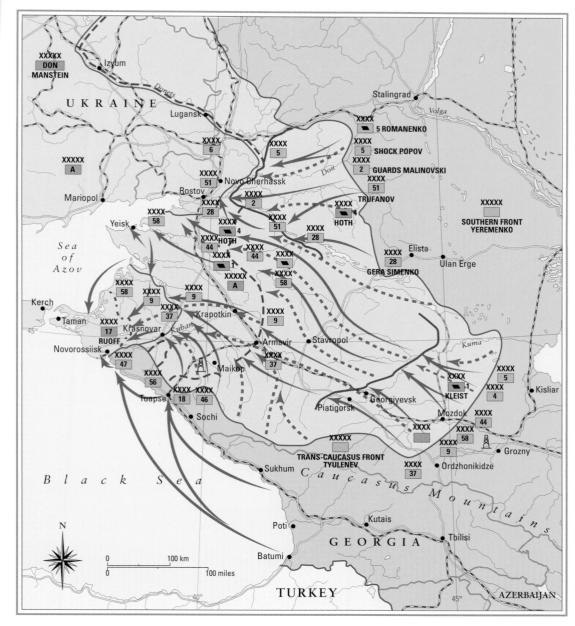

North Caucasus
January–April 1943

→ Soviet attacks

╌╌► German retreat

⌒ German position at the beginning of January

▬ Soviet front line 16 January

╌ ╌ Soviet front line 24 January

· · · German position 4 February

· – · Soviet front line 4 April

⛟ Oilfield

pinched off the salient. The usual Hitler/Stalin mantra of "no retreat," cost the Red Army 200,000 prisoners, only some 22,000 escaped.

Further south, the Red Army launched an amphibious landing at Kerch, in the eastern Crimea, which ultimately failed. The Great Fortress at Sevastopol held out until July, now all of Crimea and most of Ukraine was in the hands of the invaders.

The amphibious Soviet plan had misfired and the Red Army fell back to behind the Northern Donets. Hitler, however, had new plans—a south-

easterly advance toward the oil-rich regions of the Caucasus, the capture of which would help fuel his war machine. Operation Blue, launched in the spring of 1942, drove toward Stalingrad and the lower Volga, led by the 6th Army under General Friedrich Paulus, and the 4th Panzer under General Hoth. Stalingrad, formerly Tsaritsyn, had an association with Stalin that went back to the Civil War when he was active in its defense, it now bore his name. A city sprawling for miles along the west bank of the River Volga, it was a crucial industrial and communications center for

Russian Front 4 July 1943 — Soviet Frontline, 4 July

the Soviet war effort. This would be the scene of one of the most titanic battles of the Second World War. The capture would be a great propaganda prize for Hitler and deny the Volga route to northern Russia from the Caucasus oilfields.

The battle for the city began with the usual German air strikes, followed by an advance by Panzer units, with infantry following behind. Stalin ordered that no citizens were to leave; they were badly needed at the numerous munitions plants. It was believed that the sight of these workers' loyalty as they manned their machines would give the defending troops a boost in morale. As German units entered the city, the fighting became increasingly bitter.

By 23 August, the Germans had advanced to the banks of the Volga in the north and southern parts of the city. In the center, the Soviets held out, Stalin issued his order—"not a step back." Reinforcements were sent across the Volga and little by little after vicious hand-to-hand street fighting, the Soviets enlarged their enclave. Street-by-street, building-by-building, the fighting ebbed and flowed. The hill that dominates Stalingrad, Mamayev Kurgan, changed hands many times, incurring horrific casualties by both sides.

Hitler's obsession with capturing Stalingrad was about to cost him the 6th Army, the largest and best equipped German army deployed in Russia. On 19 November, three Soviet armies, under General Nikolai Vatutin, attacked the Romanian 3rd Army guarding the northern flank. By the end of the day, the Soviets had broken through. On the following day, another assault launched against the southern flank—Operation Uranus—was underway. Two days later the pincers closed, cutting off 250,000 Germans along with thousands of Romanians.

As the Soviet encirclement increasingly constricted the German/Axis enclave, attempts were made to supply the surrounded force by air—it failed—and to try to break the siege. The 4th Panzer Army launched an attack with back-up from the other Panzer divisions, this also failed. Ultimately, on 2 February 1943, the German and Axis troops in Stalingrad surrendered. The battle

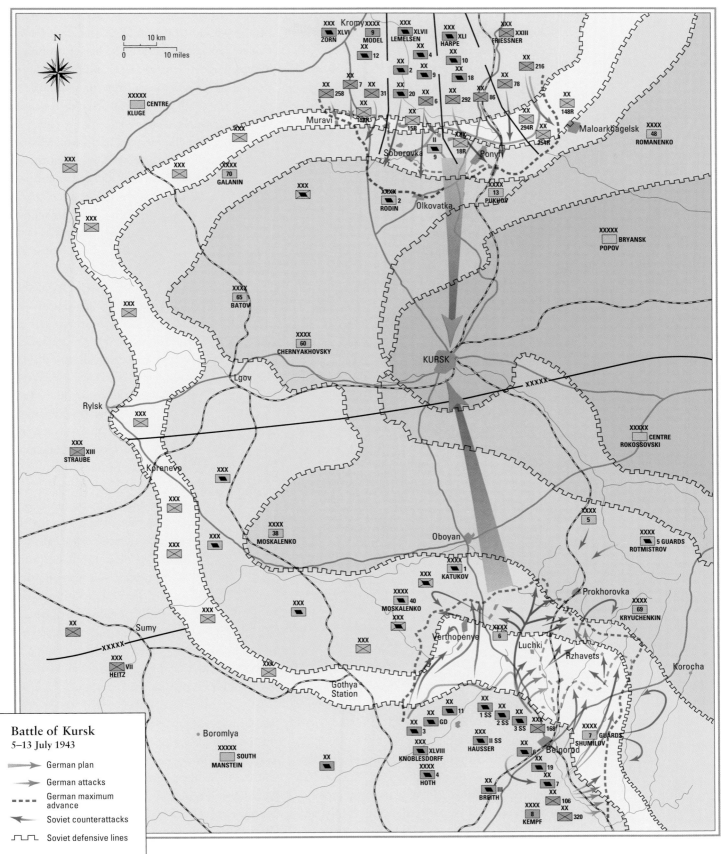

Battle of Kursk
5–13 July 1943

→ German plan
→ German attacks
-- German maximum advance
← Soviet counterattacks
⊓⊔ Soviet defensive lines

had cost the Axis 850,000 casualties, and the Soviets around 1,200,000 but no one quite knows the exact number.

By the time of the victory at Stalingrad, Leningrad's long torment was at least alleviated. On 12–18 January 1943, Operation Iskra created a 12-mile-wide strip along the southern shore of Lake Ladoga along which, still under enemy fire, a limited supply route was opened to the city.

The Red Army, after defeating the Germans before Moscow, winning at Stalingrad, and clearing the Caucasus, was growing in strength, and receiving new equipment, and it was a different and more confident force than that of 1941. The German/Axis armies were now declining in strength.

In January 1943, the Red Army pushed German forces westward to the Lower Don and to a line east of Belgorod to Kursk. The Red Army's advance continued into the western Donets area; here the battle for Kharkov was fought out with the aim of destroying German Army Group B, concentrated to the south of the city. Kharkov was librated on 16 February only to be counterattacked by the German 4th Panzer Army joined by the 1st Panzer Army. The Soviet forces were severely treated and pushed back, losing 23,000 dead, but only 9000 captured. Most Red Army soldiers retreated across the frozen Donets River. On 7 March, the German counterattacks continued, hoping to break into the heart of Voronezh. The Soviet Voronezh front fell back, forming the southern front of the Kursk salient. This salient would be an ideal point from which the Red Army could attack into the flanks of German Army Groups South and Center. The rationale behind the German Operation Zitadelle was to attack this salient as soon as possible.

On 18 June, Hitler decided to proceed with Operation Zitadelle. Meanwhile, the Red Army had been busy creating a series of defensive lines up to 200 miles deep—the tactical zone (at divisional level) was 10 to 12 miles deep. The German plan included Walter Model's 9th Army, made up of XX and XXIII Corps, and XLI, XLVI, and XLVII Panzer Corps, attacking from the north, while Hermann Hoth's 4th Panzer Army, with its LII Corps, XLVIII Panzer Corps, and II SS Panzer Corps, and supported by Armee-Abteilung Kempf, with III Panzer Corps, XLII Corps, and Corp Raus, would attack from the south. Facing them in the north was Central Front commanded by Konstantin Rokossovski, in the south by Voronezh Front commanded by Nikolai Vatutin.

The Lucy spy ring, an anti-Nazi espionage operation run from Switzerland, had had given Soviet High Command the approximate time of the German attack. The Red Army was dug in, prepared, and waiting. Just before the Germans launched their attack, Soviet artillery fired the largest "counterpreparation" bombardment recorded to date, hitting German forces as they prepared to attack. Though shaken, Hoth's 4th Panzer Army attacked in the south at 5:00am. Thirty minutes later Model's 9th Army moved forward in the north, both forces leading with their tanks, with infantry following. They moved into withering anti-tank fire. In the north the attack stalled after just 8 miles; in the south the attack was also held in the Soviet defenses. Now was the moment the Soviets deployed the armored counterattacks; the largest tank battle of the Second World War occurred at the village of Prokhorovka.

The Soviet counterattack launched on 12 July and quickly recovered the ground lost to the German attacks. A full counteroffensive began on 3 August. This gigantic battle and its following Soviet offensive was the end of German initiatives on the eastern front. The Red Army was now poised to move into the Ukraine and Crimea.

During the months from July to December 1943, the Red Army undertook, and won one of the great battles of the Soviet-German war. The Soviet plan involved five "fronts," or army groups, comprising 2,600,000 men, 50,000 guns, and heavy mortars over 2400 tanks, and mobile assault guns, all supported by almost 2800 aircraft. Confronting this huge force were elements of Army Group Center, commanded by Field Marshal von Kluge, and units from Army Group South, commanded by Erich von Manstein. The total German forces assembled were 1,240,000

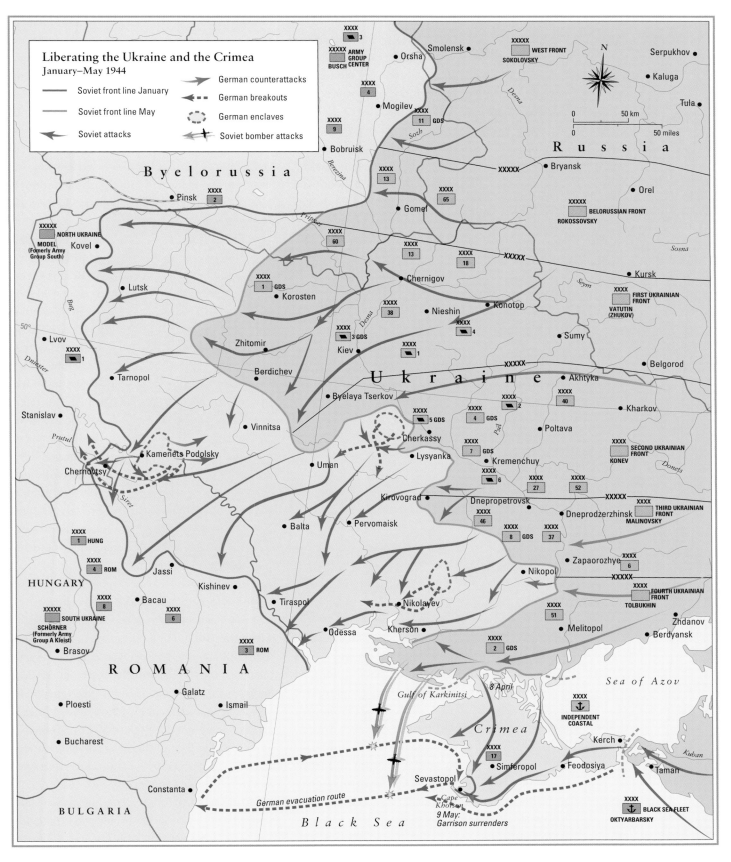

Liberating the Ukraine and the Crimea
January–May 1944

—— Soviet front line January

—— Soviet front line May

⬅ Soviet attacks

➡ German counterattacks

⇢ German breakouts

◌ German enclaves

✦ Soviet bomber attacks

Russia

Smolensk

Orsha

Serpukhov

Kaluga

Tula

Mogilev

Bobruisk

Bryansk

Orel

Byelorussia

Pinsk

Gomel

Kursk

Belgorod

Kovel

Lutsk

Korosten

Chernigov

Nieshin

Konotop

Sumy

NORTH UKRAINE MODEL (Formerly Army Group South)

Lvov

Zhitomir

Kiev

Akhtyka

Kharkov

FIRST UKRAINIAN FRONT VATUTIN (ZHUKOV)

Tarnopol

Berdichev

Ukraine

Byelaya Tserkov

Poltava

Stanislav

Vinnitsa

Cherkassy

Lysyanka

Kremenchuy

SECOND UKRAINIAN FRONT KONEV

Kamenets Podolsky

Uman

Kirovograd

Dnepropetrovsk

Dneprodzerzhinsk

THIRD UKRAINIAN FRONT MALINOVSKY

Chernovtsy

Balta

Pervomaisk

Zaparozhye

Nikopol

FOURTH UKRAINIAN FRONT TOLBUKHIN

HUNG

ROM

Jassi

Kishinev

Bacau

Tiraspol

Nikolayev

Kherson

Melitopol

Zhdanov

Berdyansk

HUNGARY

SOUTH UKRAINE SCHÖRNER (Formerly Army Group A Kleist)

Brasov

ROMANIA

Galatz

Odessa

ROM

Ploesti

Ismail

Gulf of Karkinitsi

Sea of Azov

8 April

INDEPENDENT COASTAL

Kerch

Taman

Bucharest

Crimea

Simferopol

Feodosiya

Constanta

Sevastopol

German evacuation route

Cape Khoison

9 May: Garrison surrenders

BLACK SEA FLEET OKTYARBARSKY

BULGARIA

Black Sea

ARMY GROUP CENTER BUSCH

WEST FRONT SOKOLOVSKY

BELORUSSIAN FRONT ROKOSSOVSKY

N

0   50 km

0   50 miles

men, 12,600 guns, 2100 tanks, and around 2100 aircraft. The Soviet offensive covered a huge area, from the Pripet Marshes, in the north, to the Sea of Azov, in the south. Operations began in the south on 13 August, with the right wing of the Steppe Front launching an attack in the direction of Krasnograd; three days later attacks were launched from a bridgehead on the northern Donets River, part of the Donbass Offensive, which lasted until 22 September. The Southwest Front reached the River Dnieper, south of the city of Dneprepetrovsk by December.

As usual, Hitler opposed any plan to give ground and shorten the defensive line but he did agree to Army Group South's withdrawal to Melitopol and the River Dnieper. Also four division were moved from Army Group Center to Army Group South.

Meanwhile, on 26 August, the Soviet Central Front attacked Army Group Center. By 31 August, the Red Army achieved a significant breakthrough south of Sevsk. By the beginning of September, Center and Voronezh fronts were advancing on Kiev. The Voronezh front deployed a mobile battle group, forging ahead of the main group of armies. This force reached the Dnieper River on the night of 21 September. On the following day, small bridgeheads were established on the west bank of the river, around which fierce struggles developed—the Soviets held. By October there were 23 bridgeheads, which the German forces fought hard to contain, though eventually the defense failed. On 12 October the Voronezh front—renamed 1st Ukraine Front—attacked toward Kiev, finally recapturing the city on 6 November after fierce fighting. To the south, a massive group of Soviet forces attacked from the Zaporozhe bridgehead and along the northern coastline of the Sea of Azov, isolating the German 17th Army and many other units in the Crimea.

By the end of 1943 the Soviets had consolidated their conquests and were ready to launch new offensive operations. The Germans hoped that the onset of winter would slow down their enemies, giving time for re-equipment and reinforcements to arrive—their hopes were dashed.

On Christmas Eve 1943, attacks were launched by the 1st Ukrainian Front toward Zhitomir, Korosten, and Berdichev. These attacks, collectively known as "West Bank Ukraine" (west of the Dnieper River), lasted from 24 December 1943 to 17 April 1944, and were fought over a 900-mile front. The positions of the German 8th and 1st Panzer armies were threatened. Hitler, with his usual bluster, forbade his army to retreat and they were surrounded. The Germans counterattacked, almost reaching the encircled forces. On the night of 16/17 February, the German force attempted to break out; after vicious fighting around 20,000 exhausted men escaped Soviet captivity.

The 1st Ukrainian Front, now under the command of George Zhukov, attacked on 4 March. The next day it was joined by the 3rd Ukrainian Front. Facing this massive onslaught there was little German commanders could do. It seemed likely that the Red Army advance would cut off Kamenets–Podolsky. Despite local counterattacks and stubborn resistance, German and Axis forces were being pushed westward.

Between 11 and 13 March, Stavka approved Zhukov's plan to advance over the Dniester River and on to Chernevtsy on the Romanian border. The effect of this move was to cut off, almost, German forces in Poland and Byelorussia from those in southern Russia and Romania. The latter forces fell back into Romania and toward the southern Carpathians.

During March and early April, massive Soviet forces were gathered to the north and east of Crimea. Their object was the German garrison, which was still holding out, made up of the 17th Army and a number of Romanian divisions. Launched on 8 April, the offensive from Perekop, in the north, and from the Kerch peninsula, in the east, had, in an amazingly short time, cornered the Axis armies in the fortress base of Sevastopol by 5 May. On 9 May the Axis garrison surrendered; a few escaped by sea, but 25,000 survivors went into captivity.

To the north, at long last, the Soviets were now ready to launch attacks that would end Leningrad's long siege. The offensive launched on 14 January

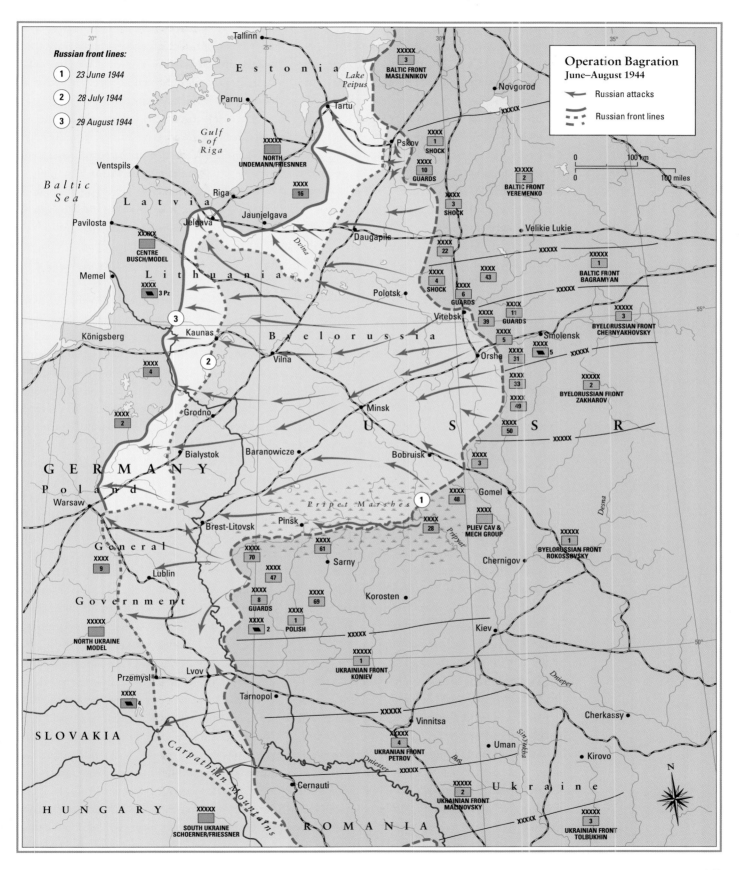

Russian front lines:
1. 23 June 1944
2. 28 July 1944
3. 29 August 1944

Operation Bagration
June–August 1944

Russian attacks
Russian front lines

0   100 km
0   100 miles

1944 and was supported by some 35,000 partisans intent on disrupting German communications and lines of supply. By 1 March the Red Army had reached the borders of Latvia and was into Estonia. Leningrad's long torment was over.

By the spring of 1944 Soviet planning for the Byelorussia operation began. A huge salient left by Soviet advances in the north and south was left occupied by German Army Group Center, still close to the heartlands of Russia. The principal objectives of the operation now called "Bagration" after Prince Bagration, a hero of the war against Napoleon in 1812, was to destroy Army Group Center. To achieve this, the Red Army assembled its forces of 1,400,000 men, 31,000 guns and large mortars, 5200 tanks, supported by over 5000 aircraft. Soviet High Command were well aware that their western allies planned a major landing in France in the late spring. They timed the operation to begin on 22 June, thus maximizing the effect on Germany of having to fight a "two fronts" war.

The operation began on the night of 19/20 June, with partisans' attacks once again aimed at German communications and supply lines. On the night of 21/22 June air attacks began and the Red Army reconnaissance units infiltrated along sparsely-held forward German positions. On 23 June the main attack was launched. These dates were not lost on anyone, being almost three years to the day since the German invasion of the Soviet Union. Each front and Army had been given achievable objectives of around 93 miles (150 kilometers) from their start line, but so successful was the attack and the following advance, that they quickly developed new objectives of 155 miles (250 km) from the start line.

Major German forces were surrounded and destroyed at Minsk. Between 5 and 11 July, what was left of the once mighty Army Group Center fell back, heading westward. General Walter Model, now in command, requested permission to withdraw from the city of Vilna (Vilnius); Hitler, as usual, refused. The city fell on 13 July followed by Pinsk on 14 July, and Grodno on 16 July. By 20 July the Red Army had achieved its objective and destroyed Army Group Center; of its 67 divisions, 17

had been annihilated, the remaining 50 were down to less than half strength. Operation Bagration had underwritten the main objective of warfare in classic style in that the destruction of the enemy's main forces must be the objective.

After this massive achievement the Soviet advance began to lose momentum, eventually reaching the pre-war borders of eastern Prussia, and coming to a temporary halt within clear sight of Warsaw. The Warsaw uprising began on 1 August 1944 and General Rokossovski failed to help the Poles. For a time Stalin forbade Allied aircraft the right to land and refuel in an attempt to supply the Polish Home Army by air; the outcome was a disaster for the Poles.

Vengeful Soviet armies were moving across the Balkans destroying German allies. By September 1944, Romania was overrun. By the end of October, now accompanied by new Romanian allies, the Soviets were approaching Budapest. The attack on the city was launched on 29 October; the city fell on 13 February 1945. Hitler ordered a counterattack—"Spring Awakening"—after ten days of bitter fighting, and, bogged down in mud, it failed. Soviet forces and their new allies resumed their advance, by 4 April they were within a few miles of Vienna. The city was surrounded and by 5 April fierce street fighting raged in the suburbs. By 13 April the Red Army took control of the city; 130,000 German troops were taken prisoner. Attention now turned north; the Red Army had advanced across western Poland and into pre-war Germany, taking the Baltic coastal areas and part of Silesia. A determined German counterattack was beaten off along the River Oder.

The Soviets were now poised for the final attack on Berlin. Stalin gave the order for the city to be taken by 1 May—May Day. Before the final push, the Red Army redeployed its forces. Zhnkov's 1st Byelorussian Front was placed southeast of Berlin, flanked in the north by Rokossovski's 2nd Belorussian Front, and to the south, Ivan Konev's 1st Ukrainian Front. In all, the forces comprised 2,500,000 men, 6250 tanks, 41,600 guns and heavy mortars, and over 7000 aircraft. Facing these enormous forces were 33 under-strength division groups of Hitler Youth and the old men of the Volksturm. The three Soviet fronts fought through the German defense lines and by 20 April, Hitler's birthday, were able to bring the city center under artillery fire. On 25 April the city was surrounded. Inside Berlin, its depleted garrison fought on and the ring finally closed. On 30 April, Hitler committed suicide. The city surrendered on 2 May. Some German formations fought on in the west of Prague, finally surrendering on 11 May, three days after the western allies' and two days after the Soviets' victory celebrations in Europe. Now Soviet forces were required, by treaty, to join the ongoing Allied war in the Pacific.

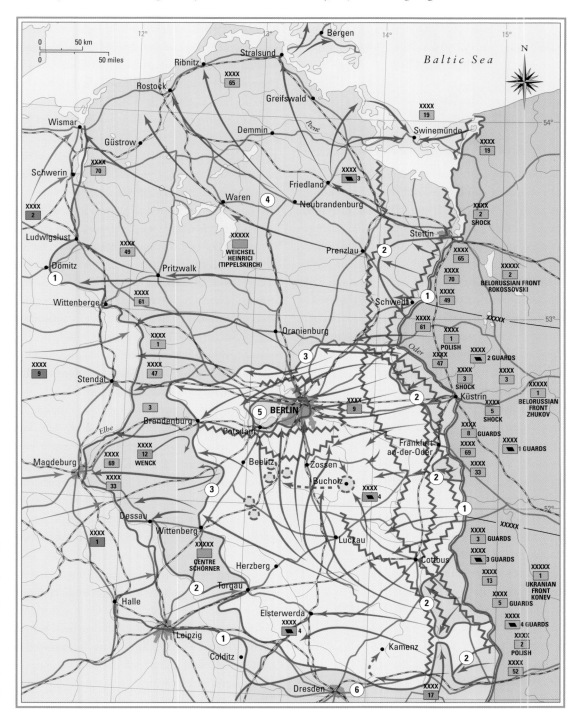

The Fall of Berlin
15 April—6 May 1945

→ Russian advance

→ Allied advance

→ German counterattack

⌣ Allied front line

⋁⋁ German defensive line

⊂⊃ German pockets

Allied front lines:

① 15 April

② 18 April

③ 25 April

④ 28 April – 1 May

Axis front line:

⑤ 2 May

⑥ 8 May

Manchuria

Soviet tanks move through the streets of Harbin in September 1945.

At the Yalta Conference in February 1945, the Soviet leadership had agreed that, three months after the defeat of Germany, despite a non-aggression treaty dating from April 1941 and not due to expire until 1946, they would attack Japan.

For their part, the Japanese had concluded that the Soviet attack would happen at the earliest opportunity, after the defeat of Germany. The breach of the treaty was rationalized by the Soviets as necessary under the terms of their responsibility to the United Nations and on the pressing request of the western Allies at the Potsdam Conference.

The Soviet plan called for four attacks; the main thrusts were in Manchuria with amphibious attacks on northern Korea, the Sakhalin Islands, and along the Kurile Islands. The enormous force, under the command of Marshal A. M. Vasilevsky, was made up of three fronts—Transbaikal, 1st and 2nd Far East—and comprised 1,500,000 men, 5000 tanks, and tens of thousands of guns. They were from a battle-hardened army, their commanders were well-rehearsed in operations on a vast scale.

They were opposed by around 1,000,000 men, over 1000 tanks, and 1800 aircraft of the Kwangtung Army. This was an army of occupation, lightly-equipped with relatively few tanks, heavy guns, or aircraft. It was designed to fight insurgency battles and control the local popula-

tion, but it was still a capable fighting force, well positoned behind prepared defenses, and still constituted one of the largest field armies available to Japan. It was outnumbered by the massive group of armies being gathered against it.

On 8 August, earlier than the Japanese had expected, the Soviet declaration of war and attack was launched. The main thrust was from the Gobi Desert of Mongolia by the Transbaikal Front, thus avoiding the main areas of Japanese defenses. A supporting attack was launched by the 1st Far Eastern Front, while the 2nd Far Eastern Front secured the Amur River region. The theater of war was the size of western Europe. The Japanese were caught completely off balance, believing that the Soviets could not bring such a large force across the practically roadless terrain of eastern Mongolia. In fact the Stavka had planned for an operation in early to mid-August and had made every effort to conceal the build-up of forces around Manchuria. Many units crossed Siberia in their own transport to avoid overuse of the strategically important Trans-Siberian railroad. The fighting in Manchuria came to an end quickly, around 17 August, though some Japanese units fought on until 1 September.

The impact of the Soviet campaign in Manchuria was politically profound. The fact that the Soviets had broken their non-aggression pact, removed any chance that Japan could negotiate a peace treaty via the auspices of the Soviet Union. This, together with the nuclear attacks by the United States on the home islands of Japan, emphasized to the Japanese High Command the utter hopelessness of their position.

The Soviet Union, however, was not a party to the 1951 Peace Treaty with Japan and remained without a final settlement. The Soviet occupation of Manchuria, Port Arthur, and northern Korea, north of the 38th Parallel, was unopposed—almost. Sakhalin Island and the Kurile Islands, which had been lost in 1905, were re-occupied. The Manchurian campaign constituted the largest single defeat suffered by Japan in the Second World War. Korea was divided along the 38th Parallel, occupied by a Soviet military government in the north and a United States military government in the south.

The prosecution of the war in Europe and eastern Asia had extended Soviet power westward into central Europe, and within a few days march

of Peking (Beijing). The cost had been enormous; military losses were around 9 million, civilian losses were put at about 18 million, probably more (accurate figures are difficult to establish as experts disagree). Thousands of villages and country towns were virtually obliterated in eastern Europe, some never to be reborn. Total war casualties lie somewhere between 27 and 30 million.

Soviet Invasion of Manchuria
September 1945

— Soviet frontline on 1 September
— Japanese frontline 1 September
← Soviet advances

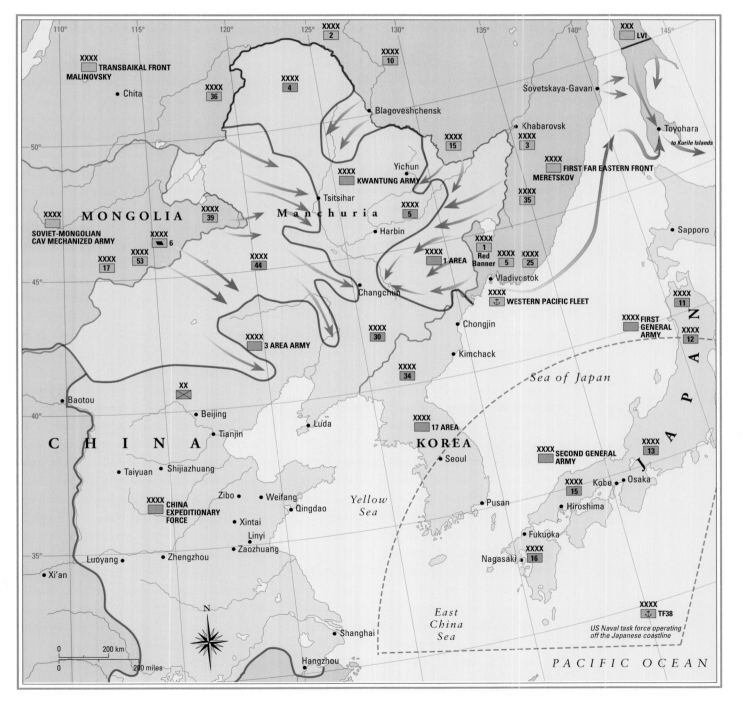

Postwar Europe

In the aftermath of the Second World War, Europe was confronted with new dangers posed by the growth of two superpowers, the USA and USSR, and struggled to prevent a resurgent Germany emerging to destabilize the continent for a third time. In 1947 Great Britain and France signed the Dunkirk Treaty against Germany, which was translated into the 1948 Brussels Treaty that created the Western European Union (WEU), with the inclusion of Belgium, the Netherlands, and Luxembourg.

European politicians realized that a more potent threat than Germany was emerging. The Soviet Union had shifted its border westward by seizing parts of Finland, Estonia, Latvia, Lithuania, eastern Poland, Ruthenia, and Bessarabia (in Romania). Additionally, the new postwar states of Poland, Czechoslovakia, Hungary, Romania, and Bulgaria were turned into communist puppet states while Germany, alongside neighboring Austria, was divided among four occupying powers.

The democratic governments of Europe were apprehensive about Soviet plans, which they visualized as monolithic world communism on the march, which had to be resisted. Communist trade unions in France and Italy, prominent in wartime resistance movements, were so feared by the USA that it began to finance the establishment of competing Christian trade unions. In 1947 Britain, aided by the Americans, fought communists in Greece. In Asia the Soviet Union had only just withdrawn its support from Iranian separatists, while the Iranian communist Tudeh Party was backing moves to give the Soviets oil concessions in Iran. Further east, Mao Zedong's 1949 victory in the Chinese civil war was followed by the Chinese occupation of Tibet.

The lessons for Europe were that each individual state was unable to defend itself and—bearing in mind the financial resources that Europeans had expended in wartime and the cities, towns, and villages that had been devastated and pillaged by war and occupation—cooperation was essential for security. Britain had prioritized wartime survival over costs incurred by military activity and owed an enormous debt to the USA.

At this time the USA entered the scene with two major policies, the Truman Doctrine and the Marshall Plan. The 1947 Truman Doctrine aimed to support free peoples resisting violence or outside pressure, with special emphasis on Turkey and Greece. As Stalin contemplated the devastating aftermath of the Second World War in Russia—between 15 to 25 million war dead, 1,700 cities and 70,000 villages destroyed—his paranoid suspicion of the capitalist West created the basis for the Cold War. Matters were inflamed by Winston Churchill's Iron Curtain Speech at Fulton, Missouri, and by an American diplomat in Moscow, George Kennan, whose "Long Telegram" stated that the Soviet Union would only respond to force and containment, not to the prewar concept of appeasement. Secondly, America devised the Marshall Plan, which provided finance for a European economic recovery package to aid development. The plan was intended to stabilize economic chaos, which local communist parties might exploit for their electoral or revolutionary benefit. The Soviets refused the offer of Marshall aid, deeming it to be dollar imperialism. Aid certainly helped extend American markets in Western Europe, but its goals were political.

In 1945 the United Nations was established in response to the Second World War, adopting the Universal Declaration of Human Rights in 1948, which remains largely on paper in most countries. The WEU emerged as the military arm of the Council of Europe, which contained most western European countries. Finally, the USA joined member nations of the WEU to create the North Atlantic Treaty Organization (1949), which soon added Italy, Denmark, Norway, Iceland, Portugal, Canada, Greece, and Turkey to its membership. NATO became the keystone of the alliance between the USA and Western Europe in the Cold War and afterwards.

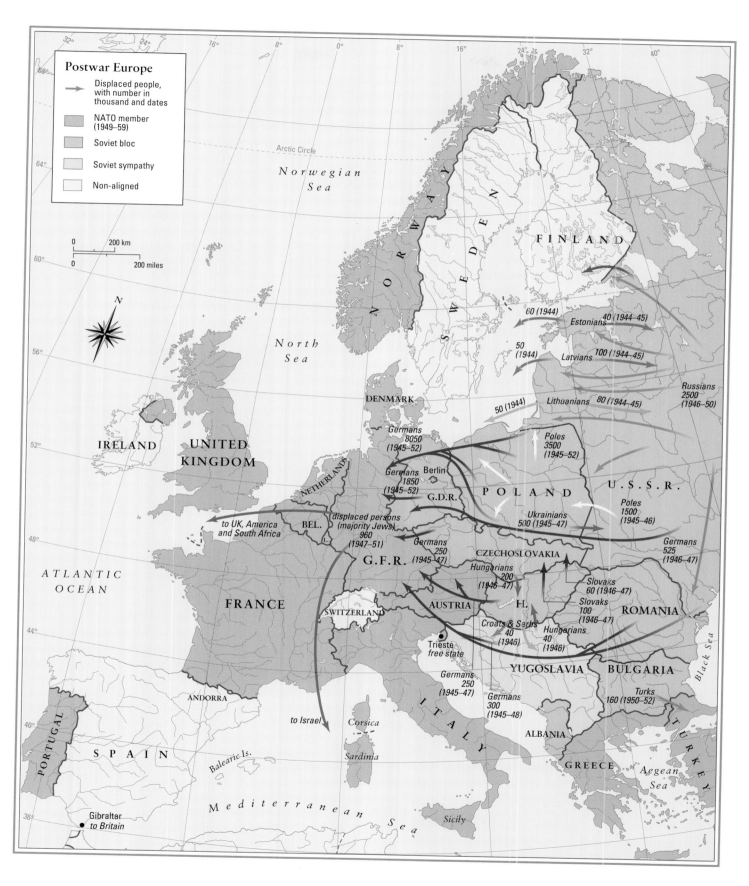

Postwar Europe

→ Displaced people, with number in thousand and dates

NATO member (1949–59)

Soviet bloc

Soviet sympathy

Non-aligned

0   200 km
0   200 miles

Norwegian Sea

Arctic Circle

N O R W A Y

S W E D E N

FINLAND

North Sea

DENMARK

IRELAND

UNITED KINGDOM

60 (1944)

50 (1944)

Estonians   40 (1944–45)

Latvians   100 (1944–45)

Russians 2500 (1946–50)

50 (1944)   Lithuanians   80 (1944–45)

Germans 8050 (1945–52)

Poles 3500 (1945–52)

U.S.S.R.

Germans 1850 (1945–52)   Berlin

G.D.R.   P O L A N D

Poles 1500 (1945–46)

NETHERLANDS

ATLANTIC OCEAN

to UK, America and South Africa   BEL.   L.   displaced persons (majority Jews) 960 (1947–51)

Ukrainians 500 (1945–47)

Germans 525 (1946–47)

Germans 250 (1945–47)   CZECHOSLOVAKIA

G.F.R.

Hungarians 200 (1946–47)

Slovaks 60 (1946–47)

Slovaks 100 (1946–47)

FRANCE

SWITZERLAND

AUSTRIA   H.   ROMANIA

Croats & Serbs 40 (1946)   Hungarians 40 (1946)

Trieste free state

Germans 250 (1945–47)

to Israel   Corsica

Germans 300 (1945–48)   YUGOSLAVIA   BULGARIA

Turks 160 (1950–52)

ANDORRA

PORTUGAL   S P A I N   *Balearic Is.*   Sardinia

ALBANIA   *Black Sea*

GREECE   TURKEY   *Aegean Sea*

Gibraltar *to Britain*

I T A L Y

Mediterranean Sea   Sicily

Khrushchev—De-Stalinization, Thaw, and Reform

After Stalin died in 1953, the various members of the Politburo decided to repudiate the past dictatorship and establish a new political system where no one person could have absolute power. This de-Stalinization process sought to restore so-called Leninist norms in the life of the Party, and Lenin became the object of a new cult and a source of legitimacy. Stalin's pictures and statues were destroyed and his books removed from libraries. Then, in February 1956, at the Twentieth Party Congress, Nikita Khrushchev (1894–1971), First Secretary of the Party, delivered an anti-Stalin speech. This action can be regarded as a step in the power struggle that began with Stalin's death.

The new collective leadership included George Malenkov (1902–88), Premier of the Soviet Union, Viacheslav Molotov (1890–1986), Commissar of Foreign Affairs, Lazarus Kaganovich (1893–1991), Secretary of the Moscow Party Committee and former First Secretary of the Ukrainian Party Committee, Anastasius Mikoyan (1895–1978), Commissar for Foreign and Internal Trade, Lavrenti Beria (1899–1953), head of the secret police, and Nikita Khrushchev. Of this group, Beria and Khrushchev were the most ambitious to acquire supreme personal power. Beria's ambitions and power most terrified the other leaders and in 1953 they colluded in executing him. The removal of Beria facilitated Khrushchev's rise to supreme power.

Khrushchev had risen in the Party under the patronage of Kaganovich in Ukraine and became a secretary of the Central Committee of the Party and First Secretary of the Moscow Party. Like the other contenders, Khrushchev confronted an array of problems. The Korean War was ongoing and the USA was becoming the major enemy. The terror system, which existed at a pathological level, needed to be alleviated. The damages caused by war to the economy, housing, and services needed repairing. Industrial planning was over-centralized and agriculture suffered from poor mechanization and low harvests.

The leaders had sought to provide answers to these problems and discussions of future policies be-

came the forum for conflict, with Khrushchev stressing the role of the Party against state institutions and personality cults. He used de-Stalinization to discredit the Politburo and when he was outvoted in the Politburo over economic policy, he appealed to a plenary session of the Central Committee whose provincial members were flown in by Marshal Zhukov. His enemies were ousted from their positions and given minor tasks to perform elsewhere, leaving the Politburo packed with Khrushchev's protégés.

Khrushchev attained the pinnacle of power in 1958 when agricultural production had been raised through the Virgin Lands campaign, which brought vast areas of arid land in Asiatic Russia under cul-

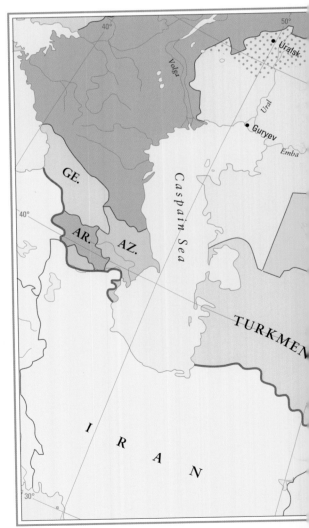

tivation by flooding Kazak territory with Russian and Ukrainian colonists. He presided over the launching of the Sputnik satellite. He visited President Dwight D. Eisenhower (1890–1969) in September 1959, but when he interrupted a meeting of the United Nations general assembly in 1960 with angry outbursts, his image suffered, both in Russia and abroad. In 1961 he introduced a new Party program that antagonized Party members and Chinese communists because he denied the inevitability of war with the capitalist world and made naïve promises about the rapid onset of full communism. The enormous risks taken by Khrushchev in the Cuban Missile Crisis confirmed his reputation among his colleagues for one-way and reckless decision-making.

Agricultural policy, including the Virgin Lands scheme, ran into trouble which further damaged Khrushchev's reputation. Stalin's Machine Tractor Stations were abolished, and skilled tractor engineers were divided amongst collective farms, further reducing agricultural output and leading to a rise in food prices, which affected the general population. Khrushchev changed Party organization, constantly decentralizing and then re-centralizing regional industrial management, causing administrative chaos and upsetting people's careers. Khrushchev reduced defense expenditure, antagonizing the Red Army. Ultimately, Khrushchev forfeited the support he had held in 1957 within the Party elite and was ousted in 1964 in a manner which suggested that true collective leadership based on the power of the Central Committee had replaced one-man rule for good.

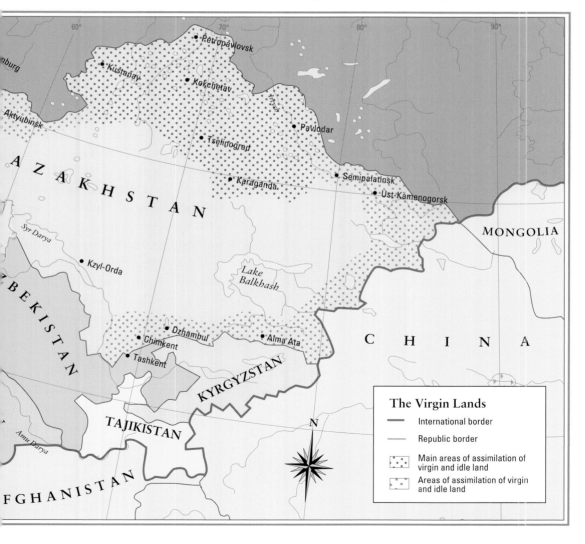

The Virgin Lands

— International border

— Republic border

Main areas of assimilation of virgin and idle land

Areas of assimilation of virgin and idle land

Operation Anadyr

Operation Anadyr was the Soviet code name for the placement, between June and October 1962, of missiles, airplanes, and troops in Cuba to protect that state and threaten the USA. The Soviet leader Nikita Khrushchev was convinced that the United States' growing lead in developing and deploying strategic missiles could be countered by placing Soviet missiles in Cuba. Khrushchev faced a strategic situation where the US was perceived to have a powerful first strike capability that placed the Soviet Union at a huge disadvantage. The USSR possessed only twenty ICBMs, which could hit the USA from inside Soviet territory, and a newer variant would only come on stream in 1965. So, Soviet nuclear capability rested on medium and intermediate ballistic missiles that could reach American allies and most of Alaska but not the other mainland 48 states. Moving existing nuclear weapons to locations from which they could reach American targets was a possible solution.

Khrushchev had made the American/British/French democratic zone of West Berlin the main arena of the Cold War and wanted to bring it into the Soviet orbit, since the East Germans and Soviets considered that western control over a part of Berlin posed a great threat to East Germany. Khrushchev calculated that if the Americans did not react to missile deployments in Cuba, then he could force the West out of Berlin using these Cuban missiles as a deterrent to western counter-measures in Berlin. The Americans would be forced to bargain with the Soviets after learning of the missiles' presence; Khrushchev could trade missiles for Berlin. Since Berlin was strategically more important than Cuba, the trade would be a win for Khrushchev. Finally, Khrushchev was reacting in part to the nuclear threat of obsolescent US Jupiter intermediate-range ballistic missiles, which the USA had deployed in Turkey in 1962.

Cuban President Fidel Castro was convinced that the USA would invade Cuba to wipe out the defeat at the Bay of Pigs (the ill-fated invasion of Cuban territory in April 1961 by a group of Cuban exiles trained and financed by the CIA). Khrushchev thought likewise and the two leaders agreed to place nuclear missiles secretly in Cuba. The Cuban-Soviet operation was uncovered by a US Air Force U-2 spy plane, which, in October 1962, took clear photographs of medium-range and intermediate-range ballistic missiles. The USA chose not to invade Cuba but established a blockade by air and sea to prevent further military supplies entering Cuba. President John F. Kennedy (1917–63) declared that the USA would not allow offensive weapons into Cuba and that the weapons already on Cuba must be removed. The USA was not alone in its actions; other nations offered naval vessels, airplanes and land facilities. These states included Argentina, Venezuela, Trinidad and Tobago, Dominica, and Colombia; all operated on the defense provisions of the Rio Treaty (1947). US resolve was further demonstrated when 23 nuclear-armed B-52s were stationed to orbit points within striking distance of the Soviet Union so the latter could see the threat.

Protracted negotiations followed and Kennedy and Khrushchev reached agreement. The USSR would dismantle its weapons and return them to the Soviet Union, subject to United Nations verification, in exchange for a US declaration and agreement never to invade Cuba without direct provocation. The USA also secretly agreed to remove its Jupiter missiles deployed in Turkey and Italy; these were not known to exist by the American public. The blockade was formally ended on 20 November 1962 and because the crisis had brought the USA and USSR to the brink of war, a Moscow-Washington hotline was established so dangerous situations could be defused as quickly as possible. Khrushchev's adventurism and aggressive brinkmanship partially explains his fall from power two years later.

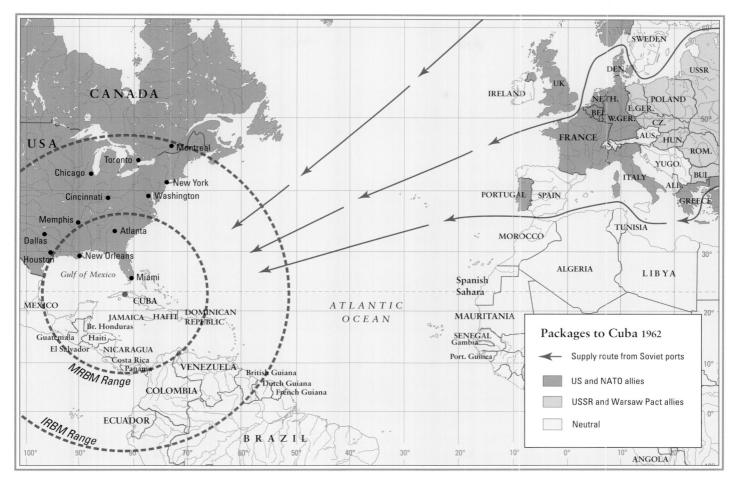

Packages to Cuba 1962

← Supply route from Soviet ports

US and NATO allies

USSR and Warsaw Pact allies

Neutral

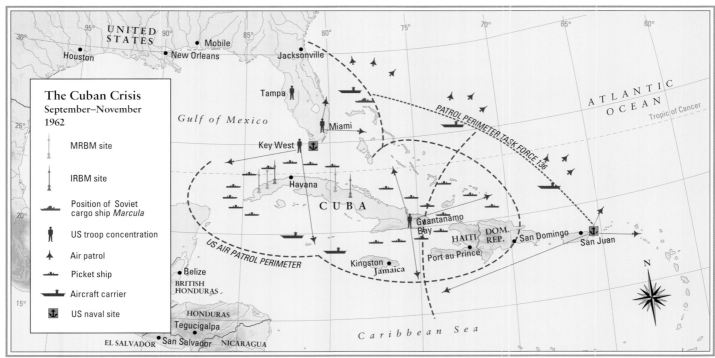

The Cuban Crisis

September–November 1962

⚊ MRBM site

⚊ IRBM site

⚊ Position of Soviet cargo ship *Marcula*

☺ US troop concentration

✈ Air patrol

⚓ Picket ship

⚓ Aircraft carrier

⚓ US naval site

Brezhnev and Stagnation

In October 1964, a new collective leadership emerged, centered upon Leonid Brezhnev (1906–82) as First Party Secretary and Alexis Kosygin (1904–80) as Prime Minister. Throughout his leadership, Brezhnev functioned as the presiding officer of an oligarchy which, with the passing of time, became transmogrified into a gerontocracy. The new leaders possessed a different style of rule to that of Khrushchev, maintaining a very cautious and aloof manner that always sought a consensus in policy-making. There was never any Brezhnev programme as such but he appeared as a spokesman of a united leadership. Even when the invasion of Czechoslovakia took place in 1968, the decision to implement this policy appeared as a Politburo decision when in fact there was united substantial opposition. The regime came to be the antithesis of Khrushchev's; a break with the past was promised with no "subjective" policies, no empty-headed ideas. The leaders would be men of the golden mean, ultimately culminating in immobilism. Khrushchev's "voluntarism" would be corrected.

As the Party's General Secretary, Brezhnev rapidly became the primus inter pares by the 1970s. Khrushchev's economic failures were to be put right by reforms ushered in by his colleague Alexis Kosygin, premier of the Soviet Union. However, these reforms failed, partially due to the obstructionist nature of the Soviet bureaucracy and the desire of managers to be told what to do. The USSR was lagging behind the West in terms of technological development and western firms were encouraged to open plants in the Soviet Union, as Italian Fiat did to produce Lada cars. Yet the regime failed to improve the ossified command economy and the government survived by using the profits from oil, gas, and gold sales to purchase essentials, such as food, abroad. This policy increasingly depended on the existence of high energy prices in world markets after the creation of OPEC and the 1973 Arab-Israel war.

Agriculture was also suffering and, as a result of a series of poor harvests, grain was imported from the USA or Canada, a measure that ensured that peasants would not be forced to slaughter domestic livestock. Fortunately for the USSR, the peasants lavished care on their private plots, producing 25 percent of all meat and dairy produce and in some years 40 percent of the potato crop. A major problem with agriculture was the continued state insistence on monoculture. In Central Asia, where cotton was cultivated, vast irrigation schemes drained much of the Aral Sea while pesticides caused severe health and ecological problems in Uzbekistan, Kazakhstan, and Turkmenistan.

Brezhnev conducted hard-line policies in eastern Europe that led to the invasion of Czechoslovakia in 1968, and these conservative attitudes permeated the USSR. Political arrests increased, with accusations of bourgeois ideology, deviationism, and bourgeois nationalism. The secret police were not invasive but violence could still be used against Soviet citizens. When food prices and supplies rose or collapsed, there were popular protests, such as the demonstration at Novocherkassk in 1962, when troops killed 26 and wounded over 80. Despite Brezhnev promulgating a new constitution in 1977, which guaranteed free speech, the right of assembly, and freedom of press and conscience, dissenting writers were still arrested. Baptists and Jehovah's Witnesses were persecuted while nationalist dissent was growing, especially in the Baltic Republics.

Family living conditions were cramped and women's pay was two-thirds that of men yet, despite economic stagnation, the Siberian oil, gas, and coalfields were developed by Western finance and space technology was highly advanced. Despite the personality cult that was encouraged around him, Brezhnev was essentially a mediocre personality, who presided over a country reliant on a black economy and a Party that was unravelling at the seams. Nevertheless, for most Soviet citizens the 1960s and 1970s were a time of stability, peace, and rising living standards.

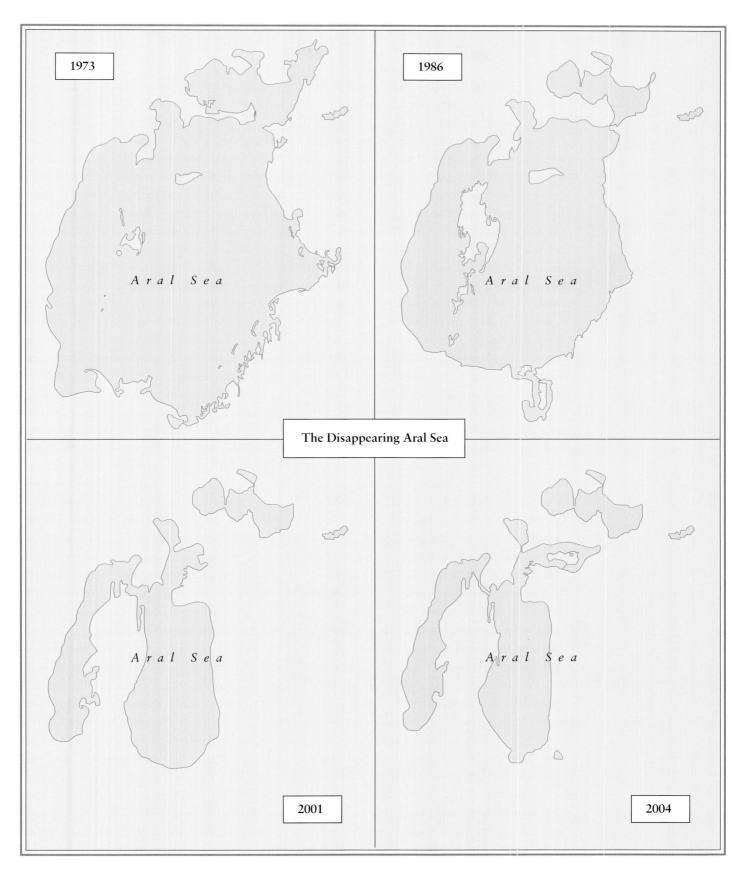

1973

1986

A r a l   S e a

A r a l   S e a

The Disappearing Aral Sea

A r a l   S e a

A r a l   S e a

2001

2004

Russia in Eastern Europe—Disintegrating Empire

At the end of the Great Patriotic War Stalin determined that the Soviet-occupied areas—Poland, Hungary, Romania, Bulgaria, Albania, and East Germany—should come under strong communist domination. These so-called people's democracies were subjected to nationalization policies, the collectivization of agriculture, attacks on the Church, and the imprisonment of many non-communists. The Soviet Empire had acquired a Soviet bloc, but the sheer speed of its construction meant that it contained many weaknesses. The creation of the Cominform (Communist Information Bureau) in October 1947, Comecon (Council for Mutual Economic Assistance) in January 1949, and the Warsaw Pact in May 1955 merely papered over the cracks in this ramshackle edifice. Protests in East Berlin in 1953, in Poland and Hungary in 1956, in Czechoslovakia in 1968, and the development of Solidarity in Poland from 1980, all presaged the collapse of the Soviet bloc in 1989.

Popular disturbances in East Berlin after Stalin died in 1953 resulted in 42 executions and 28,000 arrests. More serious revolts occurred in 1956 in Hungary and Poland. Poland was fervently Roman Catholic, but the authorities forced the Polish primate, Cardinal Stefan Wyszynski (1901–81), to retire into a monastery. In June 1956 industrial riots took place at Poznan. With Khrushchev's de-Stalinization, the Soviet presence in Poland was questioned and reform was on the agenda, as debated in the Party newspaper, *Nowe Drogi*. In this situation, Wladyslaw Gomulka (1905–82), a formerly purged secretary-general of the Party was reinstated as first Party secretary and he cleverly placed himself at the forefront of the reform movement. He then sought to reconstruct the Central Committee of the Party, presenting this as the Polish Party's own commitment to reform, rather than reacting to outside pressure. Gomulka persuaded a high-powered Soviet delegation, which had flown to Warsaw, that he was in control and that Poland would neither threaten the strategic interests of the USSR nor leave the Warsaw Pact. He reassured the Soviets that socialism would continue to flourish.

In Hungary, conflicts developed between hard-liners, moderates, and reformers, with political confusion growing. The key opposition figure was Imre Nagy (1896–1958), appointed Chairman of the Council of Ministers by popular reformist acclaim. However, unlike Gomulka, Nagy never managed to contain the reform movement, which spread throughout the country and turned into rebellion. Nagy was forced to demand a multi-party system, an end to Warsaw Pact membership, complete independence, and neutrality. Soviet security interests were now affected and Soviet troops marched on Budapest and crushed the rebellion. Estimates suggest that some 16,000 Hungarians were killed or wounded. Nagy was executed and replaced by János Kádár (1912–89).

By 1968, Czechoslovakia was an economically stagnant state and its leader Antonin Novotny (1904–75) was too Stalinist to countenance reform. In October 1967, the Slovak leader, Alexander Dubcek (1921–92) took over opposition leadership in the Central Committee, but his situation was similar to that of Nagy and he could not control the demands of the liberal opposition. The "Prague Spring" ended when the Soviet army led Warsaw Pact forces into Czechoslovakia, where they met no resistance. Dubcek was arrested, but not executed; his successor, Gustáv Husák (1913–91), showed little of the flexibility or continued openness to limited reform of his Hungarian counterpart, János Kádár.

In 1989 communism collapsed throughout eastern Europe. Poland's industrial unrest had led to the formation of a new trade union, Solidarity, backed by the Roman Catholic Church. The union's leader, Lech Walesa (born 1943) won political and civic freedom in Poland, where democratic elections were held in June 1989. In Czechoslovakia Václav Havel (1936–2011) led the "Velvet Revolution," while Secretary-General Nicolae Ceausescu of Romania was executed in a rebellion on Christmas Day 1989. Frontiers were opened all over the former Soviet bloc and masses of refugees crossed into western Europe.

NORWAY

SWEDEN

North Sea

DENMARK

Baltic Sea

• Riga

• Klaypeda (Memel)

• Kaliningrad

Gdánsk •

• Rostock

• Szczecin

East Berlin •

POLAND

• Warsaw

EAST GERMANY

• Posnan

• Lodz

Halle •

Dresden •

• Wroclaw

Lublin •

Kiev •

NETHERLANDS

BELGIUM

L.

WEST GERMANY

• Prague

CZECHOSLOVAKIA

• Cracow

Przemysl •

• Lvov

U. S. S. R.

FRANCE

• Brno

• Kosice

Bratislava •

Debrecen •

Gyor •

• Budapest

Jassy •

AUSTRIA

HUNGARY

• Cluj

SWITZERLAND

• Pecs

• Arad

ROMANIA

• Zagreb

• Bucharest

Rijeka •

Belgrade •

Constanza •

YUGOSLAVIA

Danube

Black Sea

Varna •

Split •

BULGARIA

Burgas •

• Kotor

• Sofia

ITALY

Adriatic Sea

ALBANIA

TURKEY

Durres • Tirana

Vione •

Aegean Sea

GREECE

Sicily

The Soviet Union in Eastern Europe
1949–68

- Soviet Union from 1945
- Principal areas of anti-Soviet protest and revolt 1953–68—crushed by Soviet intervention
- Only European Communist state entirely free from Soviet intervention since 1949
- Only European Communist state within Soviet bloc pursuing independent policy since 1968
- Only European Communist state aligned with China refusing contact with Soviet Union
- Only European Communist state to accept Soviet guidance with equanimity
- ● Warsaw Pact member
- Members of NATO
- Neutral countries

The Cold War—Defending the Soviet Union

The first crisis of the Cold War occurred in Germany. Postwar hostility between wartime allies meant that the Allied Control Council in Germany did not function properly from the outset. Matters came to a head in the summer of 1948 in Berlin when the US, France, and Britain decided to unite their different zones of jurisdiction within a single economic unit. The Soviet authorities withdrew from the Allied Control Council and blockaded the overland supply of the city, which lay 110 miles within Soviet territory. The Soviets announced that the four-power administration

The First Defense Rhine-Alps-Piave Line

→ Direction of Soviet attack

NATO Army areas

NATO member (1949–59)

Soviet bloc

Soviet sympathy

Non-aligned

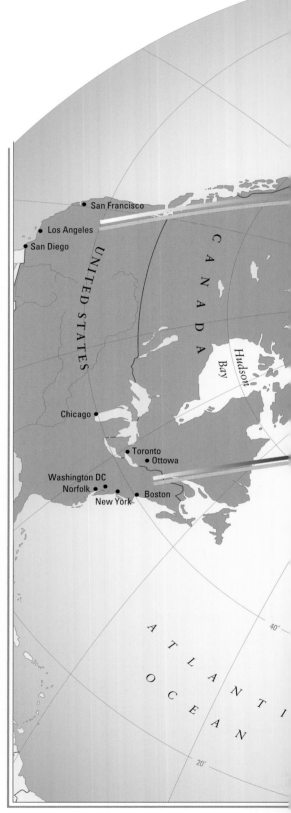

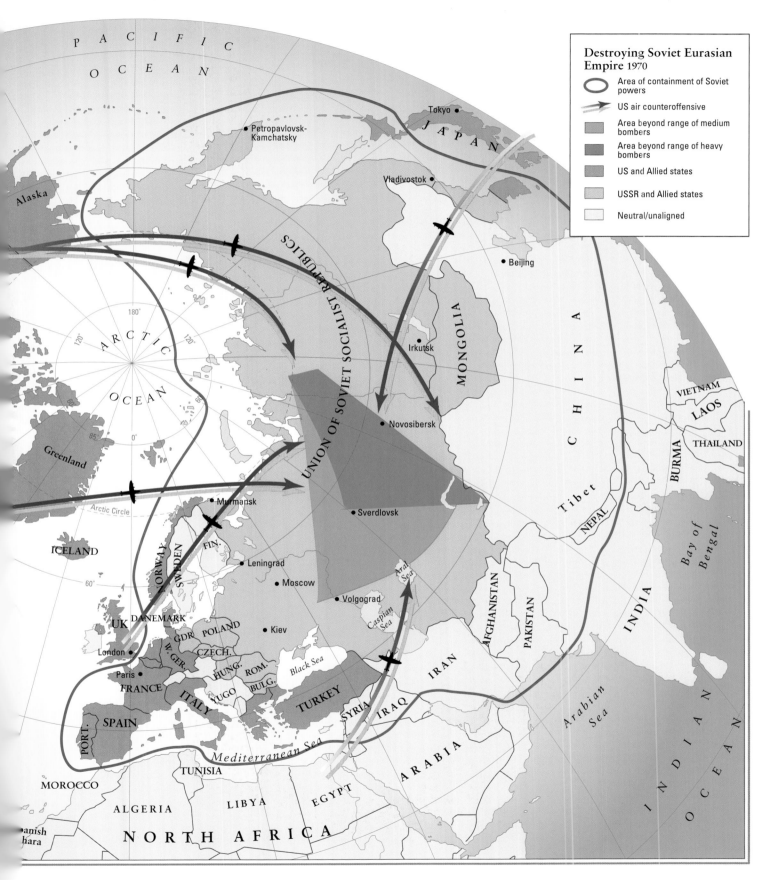

Destroying Soviet Eurasian Empire 1970

⬭ Area of containment of Soviet powers

➤ US air counteroffensive

Area beyond range of medium bombers

Area beyond range of heavy bombers

US and Allied states

USSR and Allied states

Neutral/unaligned

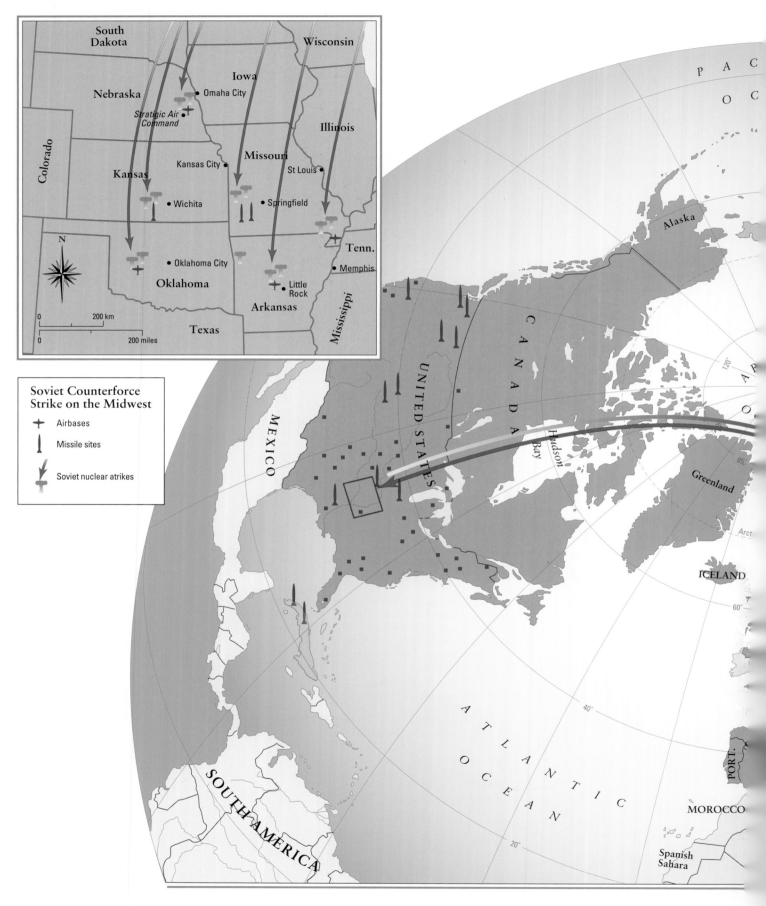

South
Dakota

Wisconsin

Iowa

Nebraska

● Omaha City

Stratigic Air
Command ●

Illinois

Colorado

Kansas

Missouri

Kansas City ●

St Louis ●

● Wichita

● Springfield

● Oklahoma City

Oklahoma

Tenn.

● Memphis

Little
Rock

Arkansas

Texas

Mississippi

N

0   200 km

0   200 miles

**Soviet Counterforce
Strike on the Midwest**

✈ Airbases

| Missile sites

↓ Soviet nuclear atrikes

PACIFIC OCEAN

Alaska

CANADA

UNITED STATES

Hudson Bay

Greenland

Arct

MEXICO

ICELAND

ATLANTIC OCEAN

SOUTH AMERICA

PORT.

MOROCCO

Spanish
Sahara

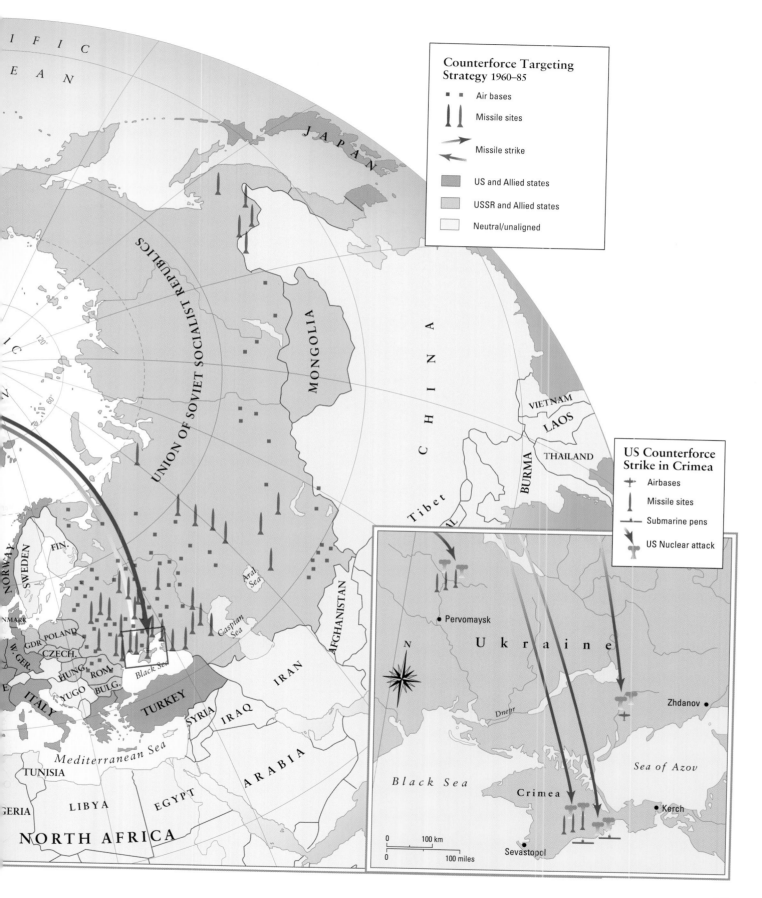

Counterforce Targeting Strategy 1960–85

- ▪▪ Air bases
- Missile sites
- → Missile strike
- ← Missile strike
- US and Allied states
- USSR and Allied states
- Neutral/unaligned

US Counterforce Strike in Crimea

- Airbases
- Missile sites
- Submarine pens
- US Nuclear attack

PACIFIC OCEAN

JAPAN

UNION OF SOVIET SOCIALIST REPUBLICS

MONGOLIA

CHINA

VIETNAM

LAOS

BURMA

THAILAND

Tibet

NEPAL

NORWAY

SWEDEN

FIN.

DENMARK

W. GER.

GDR

POLAND

CZECH.

HUNG.

ROM.

YUGO.

BULG.

ITALY

Black Sea

TURKEY

SYRIA

IRAQ

IRAN

AFGHANISTAN

Aral Sea

Caspian Sea

ARABIA

Mediterranean Sea

TUNISIA

ALGERIA

LIBYA

EGYPT

NORTH AFRICA

Pervomaysk

U k r a i n e

Dnepr

Zhdanov

Sea of Azov

Black Sea

Crimea

Kerch

Sevastopol

N

0   100 km
0   100 miles

of the city—a provocative window on capitalism in the communist zone—had ceased. On 26 June the US and Britain began to supply the city with food and other vital supplies by air—the Berlin "airlift."

In response, the Soviet army of occupation in East Germany was increased to 40 divisions (far outstripping the eight divisions in the Allied sectors). Three groups of US strategic bombers were sent to Britain, and tensions were high. The airlift lasted for eleven months, costing $224 million. Eventually, in May 1949, the Soviets lifted the blockade, a response to countermeasures imposed by the Allies on East German communications and a trade embargo on all Eastern bloc exports. The airlift had

demonstrated the Allies' willingness to take on the Soviet Union and oppose further Soviet expansion. In May 1949 the Federal Republic of Germany, with its capital in Bonn, was established in the western zones, while the German Democratic Republic was established in the Soviet zone later that year.

Cold War hostilities intensified in 1949 when the USA and its ideological allies established the North Atlantic Treaty Organization. In 1949, the USSR exploded its first atomic bomb while Mao Zedong achieved a communist victory in China. In 1950, a Russo-Chinese friendship treaty was signed and China invaded Tibet. The American policy of containment of world communism was manifested during the Korean War (1950–53) when the USA used the United Nations to prevent North Korea capturing the South. In 1953 Stalin died and tensions eased; the USSR signed the Austrian State Treaty in 1955 withdrawing its occupation forces and also left its base at Porkkala in Finland. These peaceful events were countered by the creation of the Warsaw Pact (1955) and the admission of West Germany into NATO (1955).

The USSR became involved in various crises. In 1961, the USA backed the failed invasion of communist Cuba in the Bay of Pigs fiasco. This eventually was linked to the pivotal Cuban Missile Crisis (1962), when a US spy plane detected Soviet nuclear-tipped missiles in Cuba, and the USA and USSR, each with the powers of mutual mass destruction, confronted each other over a tense 13 days. The Middle East became an arena for the USA and USSR to become engaged in a proxy war between Israel and the Arab states, which sucked vast quantities of arms from Russia at enormous expense. Dangers were so evident that the superpowers commenced the first SALT (Strategic Arms Limitation Talks) in 1972.

The Soviet Union gained a number of propaganda coups during the 1970s. In the wake of American defeat in Vietnam and the blow dealt by the 1973 "oil shock" to the international

The Soviet Conquest of Europe
(D + 90 Days)

— Direction of Soviet attack
— Initial Allied defenses
NATO member (1949–59)
Soviet bloc
Soviet sympathy
Neutral

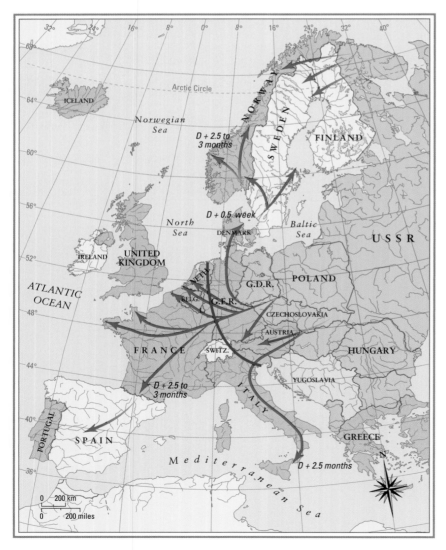

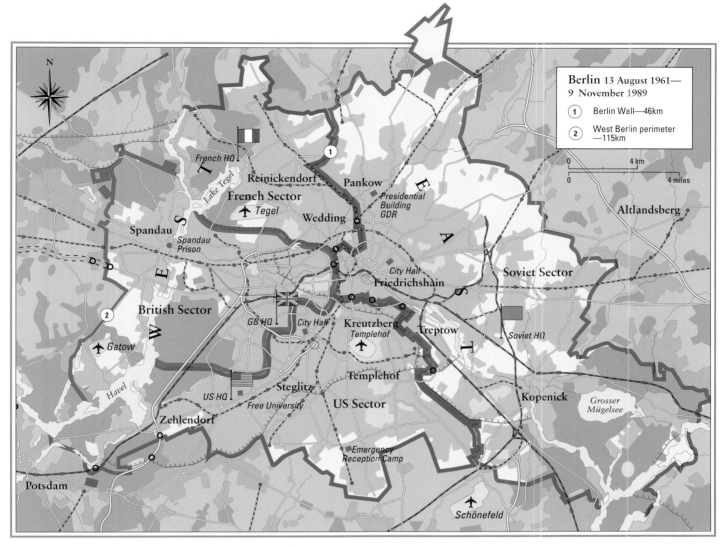

Berlin 13 August 1961—
9 November 1989

① Berlin Wall—46km

② West Berlin perimeter
—115km

capitalist economy it was possible briefly to believe that history was moving in Soviet Communism's favor. In 1975, communist North Vietnam defeated the South and Soviet-backed regimes were established in Mozambique and Angola. In 1978, a coup d'état brought a Marxist government to Afghanistan, which the USSR invaded on behalf of the new government in December 1979, causing a breakdown in relations with the USA and the commencement of the Second Cold War. During this period pro-Soviet regimes came to power in parts of Africa. In 1985, General-Secretary Mikhail Gorbachev (born 1931) achieved power and introduced a new way of thinking into Soviet foreign and security policy. He withdrew troops from Afghanistan between 1986 and 1989 and cooperated with the UN over the 1990 Gulf War.

Air Relief for Berlin
12 June 1948—12 May 1949

◻ Under Soviet Administration

--- Boundary for sectors and
responsibility area

⬚ Air corridors

Soviet Intellectuals, Dissent, and Samizdat Culture

The nature of dissent in Soviet politics changed after Khrushchev fell from power. Within the Party conservatism ruled, any space for open debate was closed, and Khrushchev's "off-and-on" policy of denouncing aspects of Stalinism ceased. Any new critique of the regime would come from intellectual dissidents, whose situation was parlous, as was demonstrated by the trial in 1965 of two writers, Julius Daniel and Andrei Siniavsky, who were sent to the labor camps.

Emergent dissent could be categorized in several ways: campaigns for individual rights; nationalist and ethnic movements; support for religion. Those determined to uphold individual rights wished to follow their personal activities independent of state surveillance or control. Dissidents could be pro-capitalist, liberal-democrat, or seeking greater rights within the framework of the Soviet political system. Dissident protests and petitions during the 1960s took various forms. Civil rights activists sought Soviet legality, the possibility of public meetings and demonstrations, free literary activity and criticism, the dissemination of literature, the right to make legal appeals. Dissidents disseminated illegal *samizdat* (self-published manuscripts), or *magnitizdat* (material on the old-fashioned magnetic tape), and *tamizdat* (material published abroad and then sometimes smuggled into the USSR).

One major dissident was nuclear physicist Andrei Sakharov (1921–89), who developed a convergence philosophy, maintaining that Lenin's socialism was a humane dream that had been perverted by Stalin and his successors. He maintained that the USSR demonstrated the vitality of socialism and had achieved a great deal for the people—materially, culturally, and socially—and enhanced the moral significance of labor. He thought that socialism and capitalism could learn from each other and develop together in détente but the USSR needed democratization.

Alexander Solzhenitsyn (1918–2008) was an important novelist who condemned Stalinism in his *One Day in the Life of Ivan Denisovich* (1962). Other work offended the authorities and he was expelled from the USSR in 1974 for writing *The Gulag Archipelago* about the concentration camp system. He thought that Orthodox Christianity was the only force to spiritually heal Russia and wanted a Russian state based partly on the Slavophile ideals of nineteenth-century liberal-conservative thnkers.

Major groups of people who had been deported during the Great Patriotic War from the

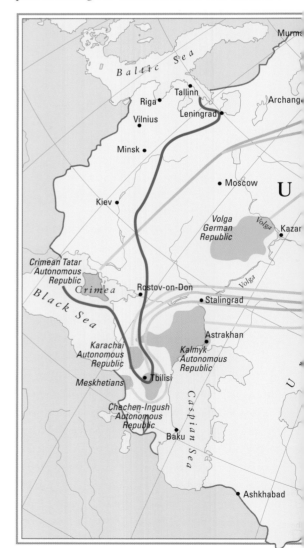

Volga, Crimea, and Caucasus began to return to their homelands in 1956: the Kalmyks, Chechen, Ingush, and Balkars. The Crimean Tatars were only allowed back after 1967. Ukrainian dissident writers supported Ukrainian cultural autonomy. Some protesters claimed that the Ukrainian language was penalized in educational institutions and that Ukrainians living outside their republic were unable to find Ukrainian libraries and newspapers. Two leading Ukrainian activists were Ivan Dziuba (born 1931) and Viacheslav Chornovil (1937–99). Elsewhere, Jews complain about anti-Semitism, employment and educational discrimination, the destruction of religious and cultural movements, and from the 1970s, agitated for emigration to the USA or Israel.

Khrushchevian repression of churches spawned demands by religious movements to end persecution. The legality of church closures was questioned, as was the harassment of worshippers. Religious leaders in the Russian Orthodox Church who were "enemies of the state" were denounced, while Evangelical Christian Baptists, the Catholics in Lithuania, and the Ukrainian Uniate Church were persecuted. Jehovah's Witnesses were especially feared for their ideology and True Christians were proscribed.

Andrei Amalrik, who detailed dissent in Russia in *Will the Soviet Union Survive until 1984?* (1970), was sentenced to three years in a labor camp in Kolyma and was exiled in 1976 rather than face further incarceration.

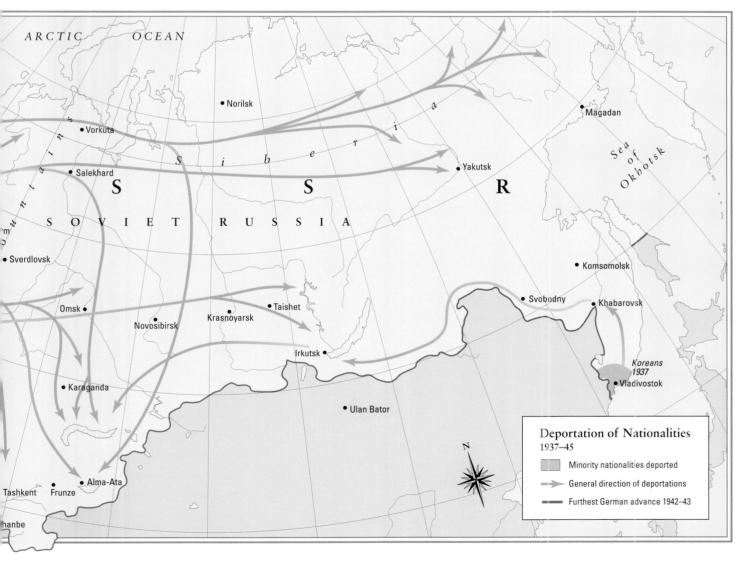

Deportation of Nationalities
1937–45

- Minority nationalities deported
- General direction of deportations
- Furthest German advance 1942–43

Interregnum—Andropov, Early Perestroika, and Chernenko

When Brezhnev died in 1982, the former KGB Chairman, Yuri Andropov (1914–84), became the new Secretary-General. He was an intelligent, hard-line communist who had encouraged the invasion of Hungary in 1956 and, in the KGB, advocated the trials of numerous dissidents and the deportation of Solzhenitsyn. He realized that the USSR was economically stagnant and thought that firmer Party discipline, the application of more technology, and a crackdown on absenteeism and alcoholism would solve Russia's economic problems. Andropov was only in power for fifteen months, dying before he could implement his program of "conservative reform" or confront the institutional resistance and inertia it would face.

Andropov also faced foreign policy issues. The Soviet Union backed General Wojciech Jaruzelski (1923–2014) in his introduction of martial law and crackdown on Solidarity. This avoided the Politburo's nightmare of having to send the Soviet army into Poland. The USSR poured arms into the anti-Israel countries of Syria, Iraq, and Libya and to the Palestinian Liberation Organization. Elsewhere the Soviet occupation of Afghanistan came at an enormous cost and the rural pacification campaigns proved to be a Soviet Vietnam. During the Second Cold War in 1979, the USSR deployed SS-20 intermediate missiles aimed at Western Europe. In retaliation, in 1983, the USA and NATO were determined to station ground-launched cruise missiles and Pershing ballistic missiles in Europe. Andropov subsequently broke off strategic arms reduction talks and US-USSR tensions grew.

Relations with China deteriorated because Andropov refused to sign a treaty with China to rationalize the border on the Ussuri River where conflict had commenced on Damyansky Island in 1969. The cost to the Soviet Union of deploying troops along the border with China was immense. Possibly the most damaging incident for

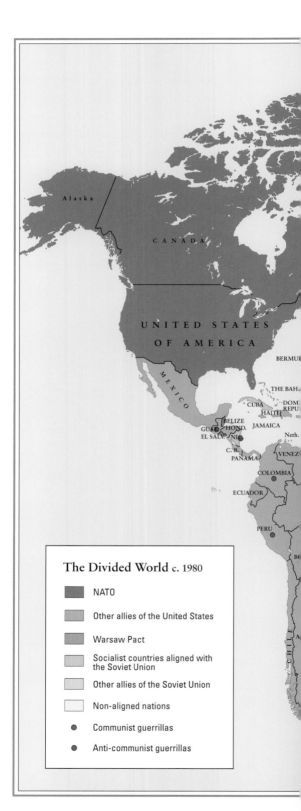

The Divided World c. 1980

- NATO
- Other allies of the United States
- Warsaw Pact
- Socialist countries aligned with the Soviet Union
- Other allies of the Soviet Union
- Non-aligned nations
- ● Communist guerrillas
- ● Anti-communist guerrillas

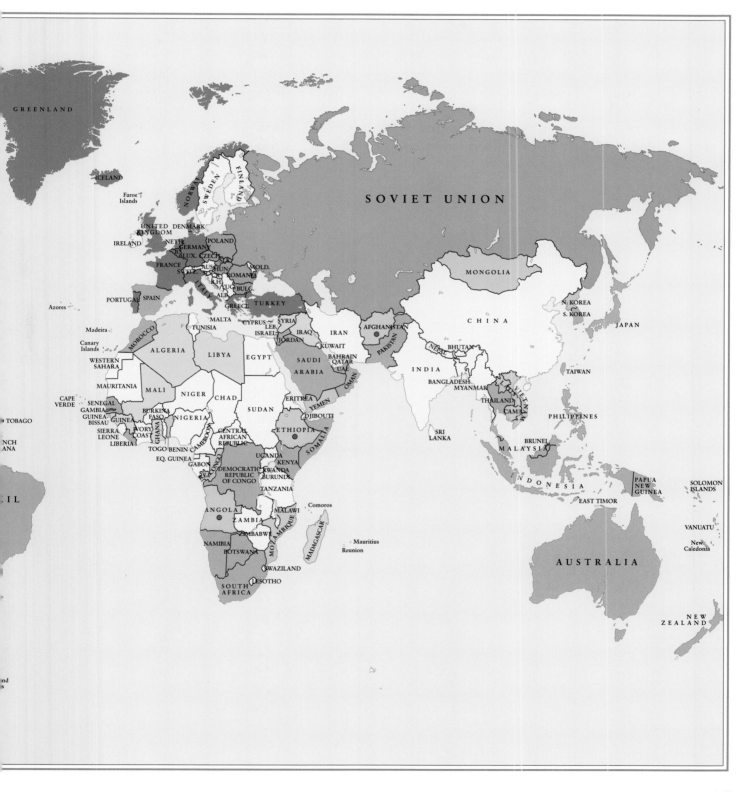

Andropov, heightening Cold War tensions, was in 1983, when a Soviet fighter shot down a South Korean jumbo jet, KAL 007, after stalking it for two hours. All 269 passengers and crew were killed, including 61 US citizens. All aspects of foreign policy relationships deteriorated while US President Ronald Reagan (1911–2004) dubbed the Soviet Union as the "evil empire."

Andropov died in February 1984, suffering from heart and kidney problems. Brezhnevite forces resurfaced and Marshal Dmitry Ustinov (1908–84) acted as kingmaker, as he had done

with Andropov, and backed Konstantin Chernenko (1911–85) as General-Secretary. Chernenko was poorly educated and lacked intellect and self-confidence but he had the common sense to recognize the qualities of Mikhail Gorbachev (born 1931), despite the fact that Andropov had been grooming Gorbachev as his heir. Chernenko gave him responsibility for the Central Committee Secretariat and agriculture, thereby making him his official deputy. In 1984 Gorbachev became Chairman of the Foreign Committee of the USSR.

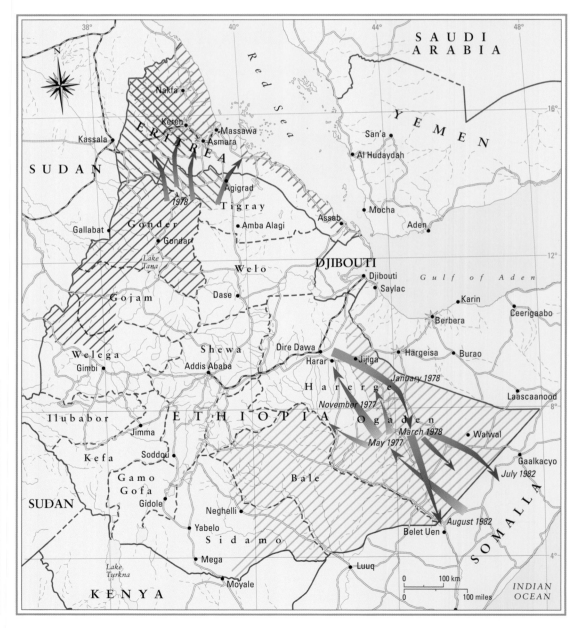

Chernenko faced immense difficulties in domestic and foreign policy. Solidarity still caused trouble in Poland while dissenters in Hungary, Bulgaria, and Czechoslovakia were confronting their respective communist regimes. The Afghan war was a constant drain on manpower and finances. In Africa the Soviets backed the People's Movement for the Liberation of Angola (MPLA), flying in Cuban troops to help them become victorious in the civil war there. This new left-wing regime confronted South African incursions in hot pursuit of Namibian insurgents. Cuban troops were also ferried into Ethiopia to support Lieutenant Colonel Mengistu Haile Marian in his fight against Ogaden Somali secessionists. Elsewhere, the costs of bolstering socialist-style regimes across the world burdened the USSR, as did the need to subsidize the Soviet indirect empire in Eastern Europe, above all by cheap Soviet energy. When Chernenko died on 10 March 1985 and Gorbachev became General Secretary of the Party, the USSR was suffering from imperial overstretch.

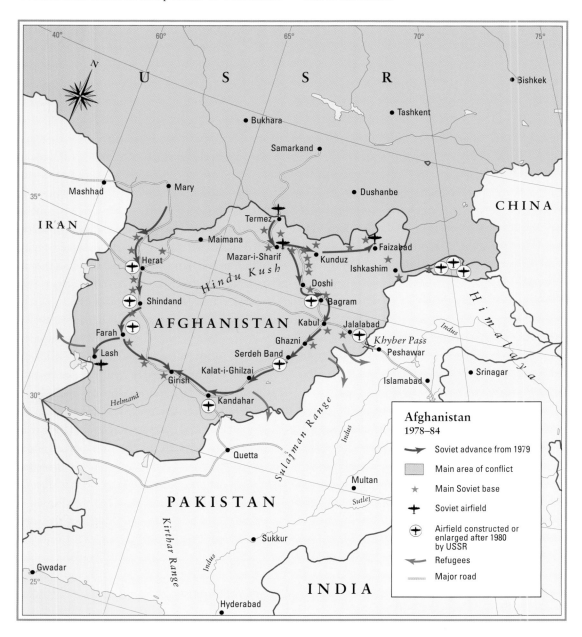

Gorbachev: From Reform to Failure

Mikhail Gorbachev became General-Secretary of the Communist Party on 11 March 1985. He was the first Russian leader not to have been tainted by the experiences of Stalinism and the Second World War. He was well educated, with a law degree, and he gained power as a new generation of educated men in power started to question the existing gerontocracy and its methods of political control. At the same time, Soviet society was undergoing modernization, and new interest groups were emerging: for example, mothers complained about the treatment of their sons in the army in Afghanistan, where the dead were placed in body bags without dog-tags to identify the bodies; an environmental group condemned the growth of industry on the shores of Lake Baikal. This new political environment was potentially supportive of the policies that Gorbachev sought to introduce to combat a declining economy and severe imperial overstretch, and to meet the challenge of competing with a cripplingly expensive new generation of American military technology. The USA was spending vast sums on its weapons research and development programs with the aim of being a generation ahead of any other country in its weapons technology. This spending helped fuel a spiral of insecurity, with the USSR attempting to compete in this research but without the cash and technology necessary to implement it. The USA was deliberately draining the USSR of resources.

Gorbachev faced a mammoth task in turning around a dislocated economy. Soviet citizens survived by using a black economy to subsidize their legal salaries. It was impossible to ask ordinary citizens to end these illegal transactions without having something to put in its place that would guarantee an adequate lifestyle. Soviet citizens were innately conservative and suspicious. Used to a totalitarian state, with secret police lurking and eavesdropping, they retained their security by maintaining a dual persona, with a public face and a private one. Gorbachev attempted to intro-duce reforms to this conservative and untrusting population that would allow the Communist Party to mend its ways and make the USSR more efficient and less corrupt all the way up to its highest echelons of power. These reforms were known as "perestroika," "glasnost," democratization, and 'new thinking' in foreign policy.

Perestroika, or restructuring, was an attempt to root out corruption and make the command economy work by overcoming stagnation and inefficiency. Officials who were wedded to the old order and its thinking would be sacked. Symptomatic of this policy was the replacement of Foreign Minister Andrei Gromyko (1909–89), who had held the same office for 28 years, with Eduard Shevardnadze (1928–2014), the First Secretary of the Georgian Communist Party. Gorbachev increased the pace of de-Stalinization by rehabilitating more victims of Stalin's dictatorship. Andrei Sakharov (1921–89), the nuclear physicist and human rights activist, was invited back to the capital from his internal exile in Gorky.

Glasnost, or openness, was intended to make politics and society more transparent, so that information was freely available and problems were no longer covered up. An example of administrative failure followed the 1986 Chernobyl nuclear disaster, when news of the event was not announced until two days after the explosion, meaning that many people were affected by radiation. Greater freedom of speech was allowed and the press became freer. People were allowed to congregate and glasnost accelerated liberal debate, which gained momentum much more quickly than Gorbachev had intended. Democratization must not be understood as the launch of a multi-party system but the beginning of a multi-candidate electoral system where more than one communist candidate would stand for each constituency, with the intention of stimulating debate, removing corrupt and incompetent officials, and returning the best possible candidate.

In June 1988, at the Communist Party's

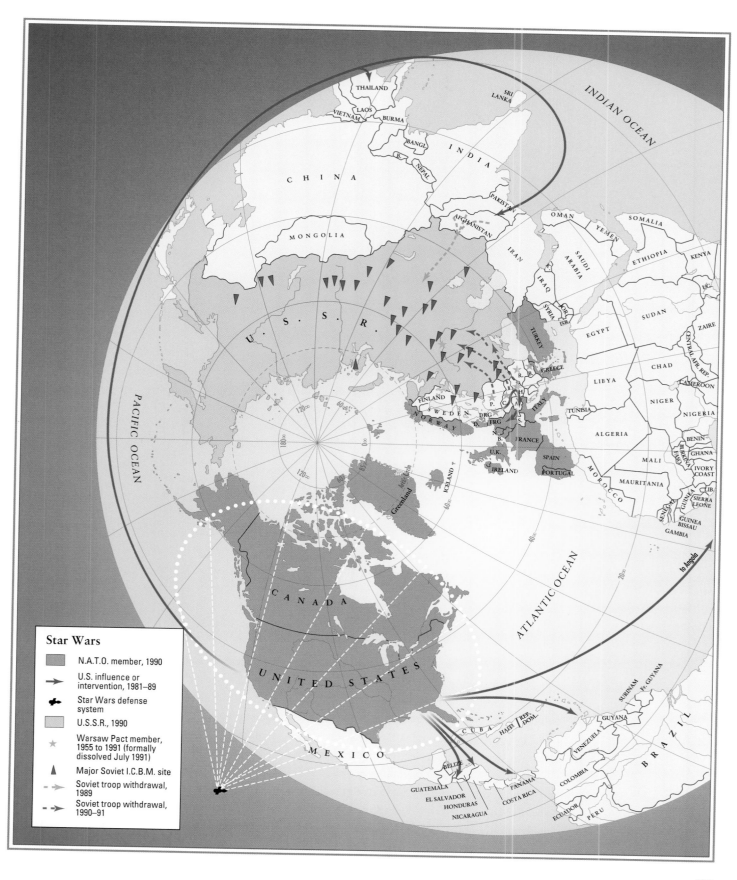

Star Wars

- N.A.T.O. member, 1990
- U.S. influence or intervention, 1981–89
- Star Wars defense system
- U.S.S.R., 1990
- Warsaw Pact member, 1955 to 1991 (formally dissolved July 1991)
- Major Soviet I.C.B.M. site
- Soviet troop withdrawal, 1989
- Soviet troop withdrawal, 1990–91

Mikhail Sergeyevich Gorbachev was the eighth and final leader of the Soviet Union. He was Head of State from 1988 until 1991.

Conference, Gorbachev initiated a series of radical reforms in an attempt to minimize Party control of the government apparatus. There would be a new executive presidential system and a new legislature called the Congress of People's Deputies. The pace of reform was staggering; elections to the Congress would take place in March and April 1989. Gorbachev became the Chairman of the Supreme Soviet in May 1989 and in March 1990 was elected President of the Soviet Union by the Congress. The work of the Congress was hampered at the outset because the candidates who were elected did not meet Gorbachev's expectations. The deputies returned from the big cities, especially Moscow and Leningrad, were extremely radical and wanted a faster pace of reform than Gorbachev was prepared to endorse. The provinces returned conservatives and members of the communist nomenklatura that Gorbachev wanted to disband. These deputies became tenacious obstacles to change.

In foreign affairs, Gorbachev abandoned the Leninist doctrines that had defined relations with the capitalist West as zero-sum game. He sought arms reduction, collaboration with the Western powers, and the end of the Cold War. He was determined to pull out Russian troops from Afghanistan and this was achieved by February 1989. To reduce tension in Europe, Gorbachev and Shevardnadze met President Reagan of the USA and signed the Intermediate-range Nuclear Forces Treaty (1987), which attempted to reduce nuclear forces in Europe by eradicating all intermediate nuclear missiles such as the Soviet SS-20s and American Pershing and cruise missiles. Soviet resources, used to support regimes in Africa and Central America, were withdrawn. These policies found favor in the West, leading Gorbachev, in 1990, to receive the Nobel Peace Prize. In Eastern Europe, he refused to coerce populations that were seeking freedom and the Berlin Wall was opened in 1989. The Eastern European states were allowed to go their separate ways, which was achieved peacefully except in Romania, where the Communist leader Nicolae Ceausescu and his wife were executed on Christmas Day 1989.

Inevitably, Gorbachev's reforms had implications for political stability in many non-Russian republics of the USSR where Soviet rule had often rested largely on fear and inertia. This was above all true in the Baltic republics. The often free and fair elections for republican governments in early 1990 were a major step in deepening the Soviet domestic crisis and ultimately in destroying the USSR. In 1990, the Lithuanian Sajudis Movement won a majority in the Lithuanian parliament and declared independence. Soviet forces acted violently in the Baltic States, tarnishing Gorbachev's reputation.

Tempers were also reaching boiling point in the Caucasus and Central Asia where nationalist fervor rose. Gorbachev hoped to bring all the republics into a new Union, which would allow much more autonomy to the individual republics, through a treaty to replace previous constitutions in the Soviet Union. Boris Yeltsin was elected president of the Russian Republic and his subsequent efforts to assert Russian control over Russian resources was an enormous threat to the survival of the Soviet central ministries. It was to end this threat and avert the collapse of the USSR that the heads of the army, KGB, and other key institutions sought to overthrow Gorbachev in a putsch in August 1991 while he was holidaying in the Crimea. Conspirators from the regular police, KGB, and armed forces, along with the Chairman of the Supreme Soviet of the USSR Anatoly Lukyanov, Vice-President Yanaev, Prime Minister Pavlov, and Gorbachev's military advisor Sergei Akhromeev, placed Gorbachev under house arrest. Gorbachev was rescued and flown back to Moscow but he was broken politically. The various Soviet republics declared themselves independent and the Russian Federation took over the Soviet tools of power. On 25 December, Gorbachev resigned and Yeltsin moved into his office on 27 December 1991.

The collapse of both Soviet communism and of the Soviet Union in the six short years after Gorbachev assumed power in a stable and conservative country astonished both the Soviet population and the world. Gorbachev's reform program was the cause of the USSR's collapse. Introducing significant market elements into the Soviet command economy was an inherently very difficult process with great potential for destabilization, but Gorbachev's cause was helped neither by contradictions between aspects of his economic policy or the plunge in world oil prices. Political liberalization at precisely the moment when failed economic reforms were grievously lowering mass living standards contributed greatly to the collapse of the USSR but so too did the fact that Gorbachev and his advisers greatly over estimated the legitimacy and popular support for the Soviet Union in many of the non-Russian republics. Economic, governmental, political, and nationalist crises fed each other in a spiral that could only have been stopped—if at all—by the use of massive repression by 1991. Gorbachev was partly responsible for the collapse of the USSR in 1991, but by his commitment to legality and refusal to sanction the massive use of force he was also responsible for the fact that the collapse occurred with minimum bloodshed.

The Yeltsin Saga

Boris Yeltsin's Russian presidency, which began in June 1991, was characterized by a conflict with conservative anti-reform politicians. These remnants of a past political age constantly strove to impeach or depose him, generating an increasing arbitrariness in Yeltsin's attempts, which were not always successful, to increase his power.

Yeltsin (1931–2007) had risen to power rapidly and stormily. He had joined the Communist Party in 1961 and by 1976 was the first secretary of the Sverdlovsk District Party Central Committee. Gorbachev summoned him to Moscow in 1985 to join the Politburo and to eliminate corruption in the Moscow Party. Becoming Party leader of Moscow, Yeltsin was a talented reformer and a populist figure, who chose to travel by public bus rather than Party car. However, he soon fell foul of conservatives, led by Yegor Ligachev (born 1920). In 1986, Yeltsin spoke out against the nomenklatura, Party privileges in relation to cars, food, clothes, imported goods, and even clinics, and criticized the bureaucratic caste in charge of the Soviet Union. This challenge resulted in Yeltsin's removal from both the Moscow leadership and the Politburo.

Despite his fate, Yeltsin had become widely known as a political maverick, an outspoken critic of corruption and inefficiency, and a political mover with much popular support, especially amongst the miners. Once Gorbachev's reforms resulted in free elections, Yeltsin could use this popularity. In March 1989, Yeltsin was elected by one of the Moscow districts to the new Congress of People's Deputies, winning nearly 90 percent of the vote against a Party-backed candidate. In May 1990, he was voted in as Chairman of the RSFSR Supreme Soviet and in July resigned from the Communist Party. Yeltsin participated in anti-government demonstrations and stimulated opposition to the government. In June 1991, he was elected President of the RFSFR and, when hard-liners attempted a coup in August, he led the resistance in a dramatic series of events outside the Russian White House and emerged as the dominant political figure in the USSR, marginalizing Gorbachev in the process. In November, Yeltsin abolished the Communist Party of the Soviet Union and on 8 December founded the Commonwealth of Independent States, and the USSR ceased to exist.

Yeltsin's tasks were to eradicate the budget deficit and make the ruble internationally convertible to attract foreign investment. Additionally, prices were to be stabilized to reduce inflation so that economic growth could be financed out of savings, investment, and taxes, providing the taxes could be extracted from state enterprises. Although Yeltsin was unable to rely on consistent parliamentary support, he managed to survive votes of no confidence and impeachment. The economy continued to disintegrate and neo-communists criticized the regime, as did a multiplicity of badly organized interest groups, which formed the beginnings of a party system, with names such as Democratic Choice and National Salvation Front. The Constitutional Court also lifted Yeltsin's ban on the Communist Party of the Soviet Union.

In order to pay off national debts and consolidate pensions, Yeltsin chose to privatize part of the economy. Each citizen was rewarded with a voucher rated at 10,000 rubles to be used to buy shares in specifically chosen state enterprises. The major part of the Russian economy was valued at only $9 billion. Businessmen who had money began to buy up these vouchers using middlemen, and acquired vast profits in such transactions, especially men like Boris Berezovsky (1946–2013), Roman Abramovitch (born 1966), Mikhail Khodorkovsky (born 1963), and Vladimir Potanin (born 1961). Thus were the oligarchs created and they started to bankroll political parties and finance Yeltsin's election campaigns. In this way, Berezovsky became part of Yeltsin's "political family." Another privatization scheme was implemented before elections in 1996 because Yeltsin needed funds to pay government salary arrears and improve the living standards of voters. The oligarchs would lend money and be given deeds to remaining state industries as surety. This "loans for shares" scheme stated that if the government defaulted on repayments, then the oligarchs would own the state industries outright.

Yeltsin, appalled by the opposition that confronted him, decided that the country needed a new constitution, giving him more power. A referendum agreed with the concept of a new constitution and Yeltsin convened a Constituent Assembly. Chaos broke out politically and Vice-President Alexander Rutskoi (born 1947) led some 100 deputies to the White House in 1993 with hundreds of armed supporters. The electricity, water, and telephone services were cut off while Yeltsin declared a state of emergency, ordering the army to attack the White House, which was subsequently shelled. Nearly 150 people were killed and hundreds wounded before the hard-liners of Rutskoi were crushed. Despite having stifled the opposition, Yeltsin faced fierce competition in all subsequent elections. In July 1995, he suffered a heart attack, followed by surgery and illness. Yeltsin realized that he could not continue as President and began to groom Vladimir Putin for a high political role. In 1998, Yeltsin appointed Putin head of the Federal Security Service (FSB), one of the successor agencies to the KGB, and later Putin was appointed Prime Minister of the Russian Federation. In December 1999, Yeltsin resigned and in elections that followed Putin became President.

Yeltsin had faced many serious issues beyond the domestic sphere. Russia had to redefine its role in relation to the former Warsaw Pact countries and the erstwhile Soviet Republics. Ideology was apparently eradicated from foreign policy, with a commitment instead to maintaining Russia's geopolitical position

and stability on its borders. The Commonwealth of Independent States would become a major element in mediating local conflicts in the Caucasus and Central Asia. The loss of much of the Black Sea and Caspian coastlines, and several ports, as well as the Baltic States, compromised Russian security. Russian borders were less defensible than those of the Soviet Union and Yeltsin was forced to walk the tightrope of distinguishing between security and empire.

As far as weapons reductions were concerned, in March 1992, former Warsaw Pact and NATO countries agreed to allow reconnaissance flights over their countries to verify arms control and weapons reduction. More talks took place and both sides agreed to reduce their nuclear arsenal by two-thirds over ten years; this agreement was formalized by the START II Treaty.

The fear of NATO expansion into Eastern Europe, and threat of containment, was a major issue confronting Yeltsin. In November 1991, to assuage Russian apprehension, the North Atlantic Co-operation Council was established. This was a forum for consultation between NATO, Eastern Europe, and the former Soviet republics, which could mediate disputes between signatories. In June 1994, Russia signed the Partnership for Peace initiative, which offered NATO shared exercises with former Soviet republics and joint peacekeeping missions. As well as strengthening ties with NATO, Russia formed an economic union with Belarus and Kazakhstan in April 1996, known as the Community of Sovereign Republics, a measure to control Belarus' $500 million indebtedness to Russia. By the end of the Yeltsin era, inflation was pegged back, the money supply controlled, and foreign investment had been procured, especially in the gas and oil industries. But the years between 1987 and 2000 had seen a dramatic collapse in living standards and welfare services, the elimination of Soviet-era savings and pensions, and a dramatic decrease in male life-expectancy. For most Russians these had been deeply traumatic and distressing years.

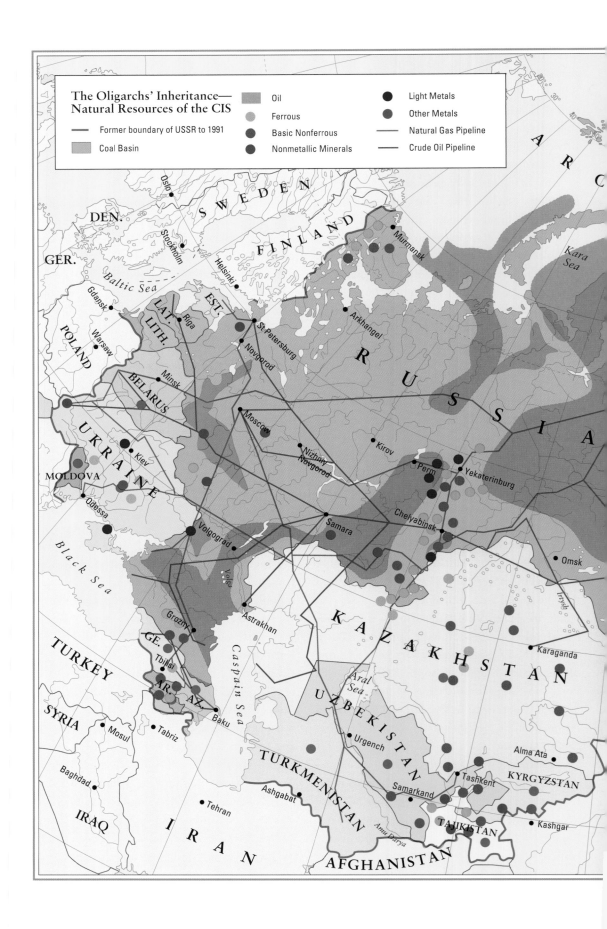

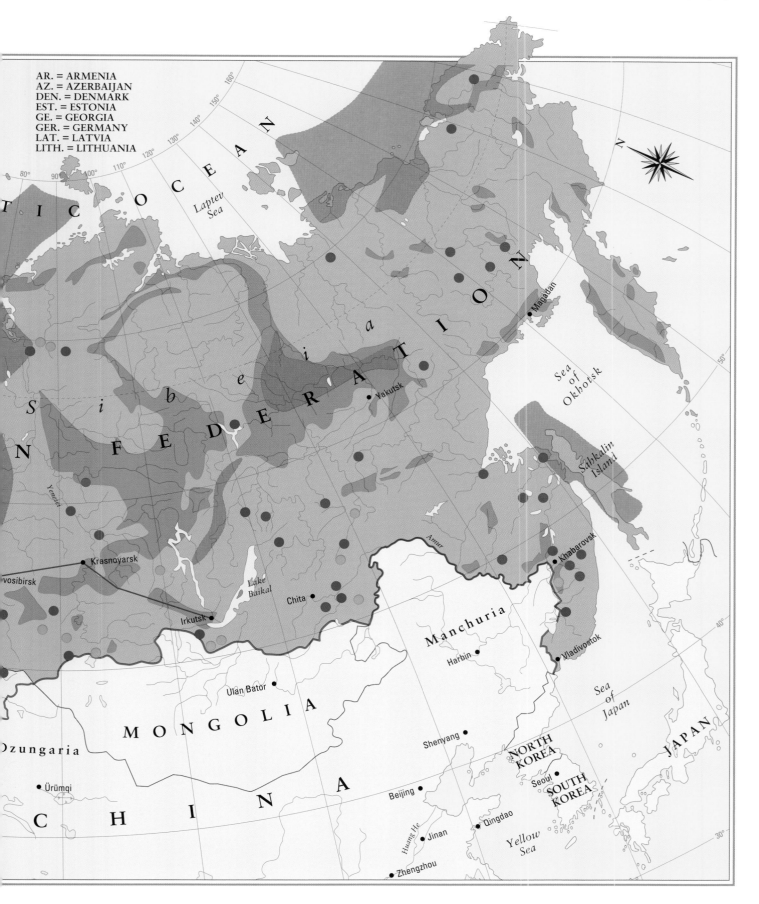

AR. = ARMENIA
AZ. = AZERBAIJAN
DEN. = DENMARK
EST. = ESTONIA
GE. = GEORGIA
GER. = GERMANY
LAT. = LATVIA
LITH. = LITHUANIA

ARCTIC OCEAN

Laptev
Sea

Siberia

RUSSIAN FEDERATION

Yenisei

Yakutsk

Magadan

Sea
of
Okhotsk

Sakhalin
Island

Amur

Krasnoyarsk

Novosibirsk

Lake
Baikal

Chita

Khabarovsk

Irkutsk

Manchuria

Vladivostok

Ulan Bator

MONGOLIA

Harbin

Sea
of
Japan

JAPAN

Dzungaria

Shenyang

NORTH
KOREA

Ürümqi

CHINA

Beijing

Seoul

SOUTH
KOREA

Huang He

Jinan

Qingdao

Yellow
Sea

Zhengzhou

Nationalities and the Near Abroad

The USSR was a complex federation of over a hundred nationalities and ethnic groups, each with its own language and culture. More than 150 languages and dialects were spoken in the Soviet Union. These peoples were spread throughout fifteen Union Republics, and 38 Autonomous Republics, Regions, and Areas within these Union Republics. Within the Soviet Union, by far the largest of the Union Republics was the Russian Soviet Federated Socialist Republic (Russia), with a population of 147 million souls. Next came the Ukrainian SSR with nearly 52 million. Had the Soviet Union survived into the mid- and late-1990s, its population would have been approximately 291 million. Each administrative area was meant to contain a named concentration of one or two ethnic groups but they normally contained an ethnic mix. For example, the Yakut ASSR in Siberia had a total population of 1.1 million, comprising 35.6 percent native Yakuts, 50.3 percent Russians, with the remainder being Ukrainian, Evenki, Eveni, and Yukagir. In the Dagestan ASSR the ethnic mix comprised Avars, Aguls, Dargins, Kumyks, Laks, Lezgins, Rutuls, Tabasarans, and Russians, with the Avars forming the largest group (27.5 percent).

Theoretically, all non-Russian Union republics were the equal of the Russian Republic, but, in practice, Moscow and the RSFSR were dominant. The leader of a Union Republic would tend to be a local national, but his deputy was almost always a Russian as would be the head of the local KGB. The network of nomenklatura posts was used to monitor local developments closely and this process was facilitated by the Stalinist policy of encouraging ethnic Russians to migrate to other republics to dilute the local population in demographic terms. This project has now rebounded, with Russians living in the successor republics and sometimes being treated as second-class citizens by the titular nationality.

Having launched his reforms without much sensitivity to their impact in the non-Russian republics, Gorbachev soon faced mounting nationalist unrest as repression ended and non-Russians were free to air their grievances and, in 1990, to elect their own republican governments. The Khazaks, Ukrainians, Crimean Tatars, and Baltic peoples mounted ethnic demonstrations, and in the Caucasus there was a flare-up over the status of Nagorno-Karabakh. The last years of Soviet rule saw many non-Russian republics showing their anger and resentment against the economic, ethnic, political, and cultural policies of the Soviet Union. Perestroika gave no material benefits to the expectations aroused by glasnost. Some republics had suffered from the Soviet policy of forcing them to adopt monoculture. In the Uzbek Republic, for example, intensive cotton-cultivation—demanded by Moscow so that cotton surpluses could be exported for hard currency—depleted the soil, denying local peoples the option of growing more cereals, fruit, and vegetables.

Some nationalities complained about previous Russification policies. These included the Baltic peoples, where Latvians existed in equal numbers to Russians, and Estonians comprised some two-thirds of the population. The Baltic peoples confronted Soviet power, arguing that they were illegally incorporated into Stalin's Russia after the Nazi-Soviet Pact. The Baltic populations pursued their independence peacefully, as was demonstrated by a 2-million-strong human chain, which joined hands in August 1989 and linked the capitals of Vilnius, Riga, and Tallinn. Indeed, events in Estonia were often described as the "singing revolution." Despite some violence in Vilnius, where Soviet troops seized the TV station and soldiers attacked the Latvian Ministry of the Interior, Gorbachev opted for a policy of coercion, for example the oil blockade to Lithuania in April

1990. Despite these measures, the Baltic States gained their independence in 1991 with little bloodshed. But denial of automatic citizenship to Russians resident in Latvia and Estonia was a source of dispute both within these republics and between them and Russia.

Not all republics have experienced independence so peacefully. The Persian-speaking Tajiks comprise nearly two-thirds of Tajikistan's population, with Russians being the most influential minority (7.6 percent). On independence in 1991, the old political order remained in charge but was confronted by opposition centered on the Islamic Movement Party, which sought the creation of an Islamic state. Fighting broke out between the Islamic democrats and the communists led by President Rahmon Nabiyev (1930–93), who had been leader of the Tajik Communist Party. With arms supplied by Afghanistan, the opposition won control of Dushanbe, the capital. However, Russian and Uzbek forces supported the pro-communists and rapidly dominated the country, allowing the old order to re-establish its authority. Islamic political movements were suppressed and banned and Russian military units remained in the country, alongside forces from Uzbekistan, Kyrgystan and Kazakhstan, as a CIS peacekeeping force. These troops combated opposition raids from Afghanistan in order to prevent any Islamic fundamentalist bridgeheads being established in Central Asia. One problem stemming from this civil war was the fear of Russians resident in Tajikistan, who began leaving in droves. By 1994, estimates suggested that two-thirds of the Russians had left with thousands more preparing to do so. The situation in Tajikistan was mirrored by a countervailing situation in Uzbekistan where Tajiks have demonstrated against the Turkic-speaking majority Uzbeks. Disputes over who should step in to fill the power vacuum left by the Russian retreat from empire have beset Central Asia and the Caucasus.

The geostrategic position of Russia in Europe is dominated by open access to the Baltic and Black Seas and, to defend its borders, Russia announced the formation of a Russian Federation army in 1992. The former Union Republics feared that Russia would seek to dominate any integrated new military organization, turning the CIS into a replacement for the Warsaw Pact.

There has been a developing debate within Russia about the nature of Russia's borders and defense, the condition of Russians living in the "near abroad," and whether Russia should reinvent its empire. Some Russian politicians, noticeably Alexander Rutskoi, erstwhile vice-president of Russia, refuse to accept the collapse of the Soviet Union. The maverick leader of the Liberal Democratic Party, Vladimir Zhirinovsky (born 1947), dismissed as a neo-fascist by some, rejected Baltic independence and wanted to reclaim the "near abroad," but would sell the western Ukraine to Poland. The nationalist writer Alexander Solzhenitsyn thought that the Russian-inhabited regions of northern Kazakhstan should be stripped from that republic and become part of the Russian Federation. In 1994, Foreign Minister Andrei Kosyrev (born 1951) argued that withdrawal from the former republics would leave a power vacuum to be filled by potentially hostile powers, but this has not yet happened in most cases. Other commentators have felt that Russia should withdraw into itself and adopt an isolationist stance to avoid being sucked into a new Afghan War in, for example, Moldova or Georgia. The opposing view is that a "historic" Russia should link with Ukraine and Belarus to form a Slav bloc with common linguistic and cultural ties. The present Russian stance is not to allow outside countries to interfere in the Near Abroad, to continue to interfere in the internal affairs of the NATO states in the Baltic, confront the Ukraine, and probably strengthen relations with China which signed an energy deal with Russia worth $4 billion in 2014.

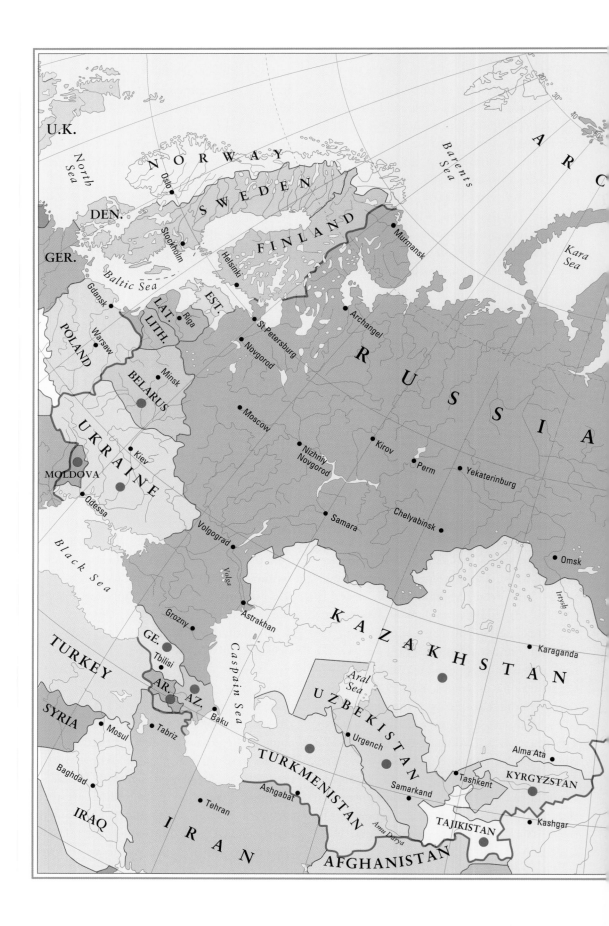

AR. = ARMENIA
AZ. = AZERBAIJAN
DEN. = DENMARK
EST. = ESTONIA
GE. = GEORGIA
GER. = GERMANY
LAT. = LATVIA
LITH. = LITHUANIA
U.K. = UNITED KINGDOM

USSR to Russian Federation

— Former boundary of USSR to 1991

● Member of Commonwealth
of Independent States from 1991

A R C T I C   O C E A N

Laptev
Sea

S i b e r i a

F E D E R A T I O N

Yenesei

Magadan

Sea
of
Okhotsk

Yakutsk

Sakhalin
Island

Krasnoyarsk

Amur

Khabarovsk

Novosibirsk

Lake
Baikal

Chita

Irkutsk

Manchuria

Vladivostok

Harbin

Ulan Bator

M O N G O L I A

Sea
of
Japan

J A P A N

Dzungaria

Shenyang

NORTH
KOREA

Ürümqi

Seoul

SOUTH
KOREA

C H I N A

Beijing

Huang He

Jinan

Qingdao

Yellow
Sea

Zhengzhou

181

Conflict in the Caucasus

Centrifugal forces have plagued the USSR and its successor states in the Caucasus. The region's ethnic structure is complex, the inhabitants belonging to different linguistic groups and sometimes different language families. Furthermore, both Armenia and Georgia have viewed themselves as Christian islands in a Muslim sea. Additionally, many native Caucasians live outside their territorial units in other Caucasian lands or even adjacent areas of Russia. Ethnic violence has broken out in the Chechen Wars, in conflict between Armenia and Azerbaijan over Nagorno-Karabakh, and in the disintegration of Georgia when Abkhazia, Adzharia and South Ossetia have attempted to secede.

At the 1956 Twentieth Party Congress, Khrushchev attacked Stalin, scolding him for the forced mass resettlement of entire Caucasian peoples to Central Asia during the Great Patriotic War. These included the Chechens, who were accused of collaborating with German occupation forces during that war. All those peoples were rehabilitated and allowed to return to their homelands in 1957. The Chechens were naturally hostile to the Soviet authorities and held together by bonds of loyalty: to religion, with a strong Sufi content in their Sunni faith; to clan, villages, and extended kinship groups; and to codes of honor, culture, and vendetta. While the Ingush and Chechen people share religious and cultural ties, the resistance of the Ingushetian people to Moscow has not been as violent as that of their Chechen counterparts.

On 27 November 1990, the Chechen-Ingush Supreme Soviet declared its sovereignty within the Russian Federation. The Chechen National Congress, an informal body, elected Major-General Jokhar Dudayev (1944–96) as chairman of its executive committee, and in September 1991 deposed the Supreme Soviet. Dudayev was elected president but he lacked a substantial majority, largely being supported by the highland clans and not in the lowland and urban areas. Separation from Ingushetia was declared but not recognized by Russia. Yeltsin did nothing until Dudayev apparently turned into a dictator, ruling by armed force. In December 1994, Yeltsin ordered an invasion to regain control and protect the Chechen section of the Caspian-Black Sea oil pipelines and the refinery in the Chechen capital, Grozny, which was a linkage point to the Tengiz oilfield in Kazakhstan. The Chechens fought back, using guerrilla tactics against ill-trained Russian conscripts and even raided into Russia to attack villages in retaliation for the wanton killing of Chechen civilians. The capital was flattened and Dudayev killed. A peace was then concluded with the new Chechen leader Zelimkhan Yandarbiyev (1952–2004), a poet and author, in May 1996.

Russia's defeat allowed Chechnyan independence but the state was soon dominated by warlords, with hostage-taking becoming a major source of revenue. In 1999, the Islamic International Brigade, containing Chechen rebels, supported separatist rebels in the neighboring republic of Dagestan. A series of terrorist attacks on Moscow apartment blocks was blamed on the Chechens and the Russian army invaded Chechnya in October 1999 to commence the Second Chechen War. The Chechen regime collapsed as Grozny and most regions were captured. However, the insurgents continued terror activities: in October 2002 they held a Moscow theater under siege for three days and some 130 hostages died; in September 2004 they captured a school in Beslan, North Ossetia. Russian forces stormed the school and wiped out the terrorists but several hundred hostages died, including 186 children.

The insurgency lasted until 2009 when the Russian counter-terrorism operation ended after two important separatist leaders were killed. Chechnya was then reintegrated into Russia but was provided with limited internal autonomy. A Chechen referendum supported this move with a vast turnout and approval rating, a situation that was criticized by many journalists as a sham. Insurgency continues on an intermittent basis and one separatist group, the Caucasus Emirate, wishes

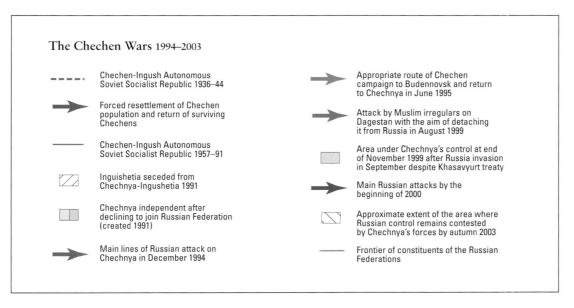

The Chechen Wars 1936–44

- - - - · Chechen-Ingush Autonomous Soviet Socialist Republic 1936–44

➡ Forced resettlement of Chechen population and return of surviving Chechens

—— Chechen-Ingush Autonomous Soviet Socialist Republic 1957–91

▨ Inguishetia seceded from Chechnya-Ingushetia 1991

▨ Chechnya independent after declining to join Russian Federation (created 1991)

➡ Main lines of Russian attack on Chechnya in December 1994

➡ Appropriate route of Chechen campaign to Budennovsk and return to Chechnya in June 1995

➡ Attack by Muslim irregulars on Dagestan with the aim of detaching it from Russia in August 1999

▨ Area under Chechnya's control at end of November 1999 after Russia invasion in September despite Khasavyurt treaty

➡ Main Russian attacks by the beginning of 2000

▨ Approximate extent of the area where Russian control remains contested by Chechnya's forces by autumn 2003

—— Frontier of constituents of the Russian Federations

1 The entire Chechen population deported to Central Asia, Chechen-Ingush ASSR abolished in 1944.

2 Surviving Chechens allowed to return, Chechen-Ingush ASSR Re-established in 1957.

3 Taken by Russian forces in January 1995, retaken by Chechens in August 1996. Taken by Russia after having obliterated Grozny (Jokhan) by prolonged bombardment in February 2000.

4 Treaty between Chechnya and Russia in August 1996, ends First Chechen War by recognizing Chechnya's de facto independence. Final status to be decided within five years. Chechnya, invaded again by Russia in 1999, anxious about the militant Islam, insurgence continues.

to expel Russians and create a militant Islamicist state. Some members have travelled to Syria to fight against President Bashar al-Assad alongside the Islamic State of Iraq and the Levant (ISIS), but have since split from it.

The different ways in which Moscow approaches separatism and calls for autonomy suggest that different factions operate diverse policies towards the ethnic republics. A bilateral treaty was signed between Tatarstan and Russia in February 1994, allowing substantial autonomy to Tartarstan. Likewise, a treaty between Russia and Bashkorostan gave this small republic control over its rich economy and resources. The liberal method of dealing with some autonomous republics is a contrast to the policy of hardline repression pursued in Chechnya and some other areas of the republics, and is usually in response to armed separatist insurrection.

Nagorno-Karabakh and Nakichevan have been a source of conflict between Armenia and Azerbaijan. Armenian incorporation into the Soviet state occurred during a troubled time. Mass genocide, in 1915, of Anatolian Armenians by the Ottoman Empire was followed by famine, disease, and death for 20 percent of the population of Russian Armenia. Since then, demographic growth has replaced those losses, but attitudes towards Islam, blamed for the genocide, are hostile and Armenians feel surrounded by enemies. The neighboring Azeris' Turkic language makes them close to Turkey, the old enemy. This past compounds the problems of borders. The autonomous region of Nagorno-Karabakh was created in 1923 within the territory of Azerbaijan and is mainly inhabited by Armenians. The region of Nakhichevan bordering Iran—once an integral part of medieval Armenia but later settled by Azeris—was given to Azerbaijan but is entirely cut off from it by Armenia.

During the disruption of the Gorbachev period, with the growth of ethnic nationalism, Armenians considered that the situation in Nagorno-Karabakh was an affront to their honor, culture, and identity. The advent of glasnost increased expectations of border rectifications and Moscow's reluctance to implement this led to anti-Moscow sentiment. On the other hand, the Azeris believe Nagorno-Karabakh is theirs. Karabakh was part of Persia until 1828, when it was ceded to Russia. When the Red Army entered Transcaucasia in 1920, Nagorno-Karabakh and Nakhichevan were allotted to Armenia but then given to Azerbaijan in 1921. Nakhichevan was progressively de-Armenianized and Armenians were afraid that similar policies would be pursued in Nagorno-Karabakh. Karabakh was part of historic Armenia, retaining its Armenian populace, but was a recent birthplace of Azeri culture and national identity in the nineteenth century.

The Nagorno-Karabakh issue flared up in 1998 with anti-Armenian riots in Sumgait in Azerbaijan. In retaliation, Armenia pushed out some 200,000 Azeris, generating a huge refugee problem in Baku.

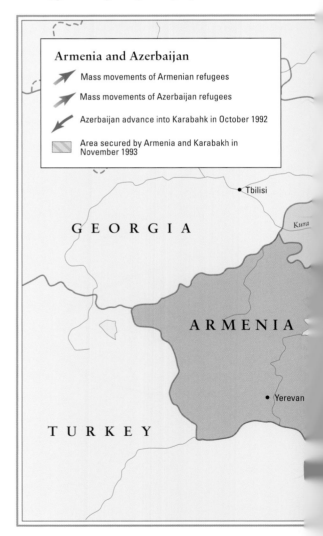

Armenia and Azerbaijan

➤ Mass movements of Armenian refugees

➤ Mass movements of Azerbaijan refugees

➤ Azerbaijan advance into Karabahk in October 1992

▨ Area secured by Armenia and Karabakh in November 1993

The Kremlin placed Nagorno-Karabakh under its direct rule in early 1989 but returned authority to Azerbaijan in late 1989. The following year, the Armenian Supreme Soviet included Nagorno-Karabakh in its budget and allowed its residents to vote in Armenian parliamentary elections. After Armenia became independent in 1991, events progressed rapidly. In May 1992, Armenian troops seized Azerbaijani Susha, attacked Nakhichevan, and captured Lachin, thereby creating a corridor between Armenia and Nagorno-Karabakh. By the end of 1993, Karabakh was well defended by forces armed with Soviet weapons. In exchange for constructing two Russian military bases in Armenia, Russian military assistance was accelerated while former Soviet officers were included in Karabakh forces. To defend the Lachin Corridor, Armenian

troops destroyed many Azeri villages and towns, generating another million refugees. Eventually, a ceasefire was negotiated and peace talks have been ongoing ever since, but to no avail. Meanwhile, the disputed territory has become the de facto independent Republic of Nagorno-Karabakh and is defended by an alert, well-disciplined armed force, needed to protect the small state from occasional Azeri breaches of the ceasefire.

A third Caucasian powder keg is the ethnic jigsaw of Georgia, with Georgians, Armenians, Russians, Azeris, Ossetians, Abkhazians, Adzhars, and Greeks living cheek by jowl. This mixture was stirred into a witch's brew by the growth of intense nationalism during perestroika and glasnost. Previously, in the 1970s, the Abkhazians agitated against Georgian discrimination and Moscow

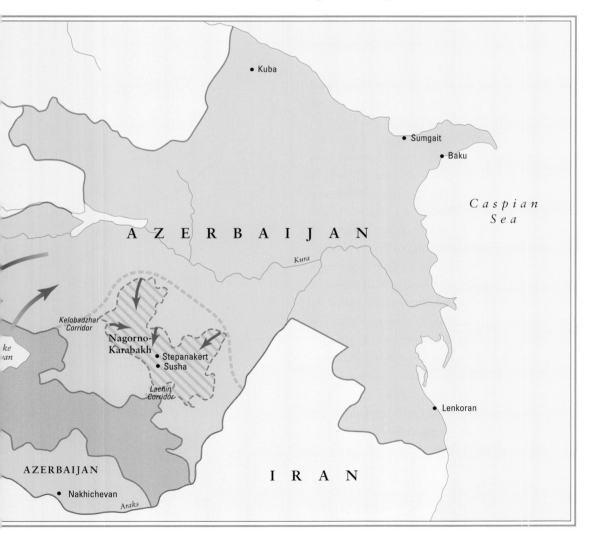

forced concessions from the Georgians. In 1979, the Sukhumi Pedagogical Institute was granted a new status as the Abkhazian State University. Further demands for the right to secede and to end the use of Georgian as a state language in the Abkhaz Autonomous Republic stimulated Georgian nationalism; the Georgians claimed that they were being discriminated against and there were debates over the nature of Georgian citizenship and ethnic policy generally. President Zviad Gamsakhurdia (1939–93) even suggested that the Ossetes of South Ossetia should move to North Ossetia in the Russian Federation. South Ossetia declared its independence and the Georgian government "abolished" the South Ossetian Autonomous Region. Brutal fighting followed, which was stopped by a peacekeeping force led by Russia. Since 1996, South Ossetia has held its own elections and remains outside Georgian authority and protected by Russia.

A major problem for Georgia was the paranoid character of the increasingly authoritarian Gamsakhurdia. His policies of Georgianization offended ethnic minorities and his Christianization campaign antagonized Georgian Muslims, such as the Adzharians, who inhabited their own autonomous republic. Elsewhere, the Abkhazian Unity organization opposed Georgia's 1989 decree that the Georgian language had a superior status and in August 1990 the Abkhazian Supreme Soviet declared independence. Georgian troops invaded Abkhazia under the pretext of protecting supply routes in the Georgian civil war between the forces of the now ousted Gamsakhurdia and a Military Council. In August 1992, Georgian units attacked the Abkhazian parliament building and a brushfire war developed. One interesting event was the call by the Confederation of Mountain Peoples of the Caucasus to send volunteers to help defend Abkhazia; certainly, Chechens fought there. By October 1992, Abkhaz fighters had secured half of Abkhazia and by July 1993 the situation was so dangerous that the United Nations agreed that Russia could send in peacekeeping forces. By September 1993, Abkhazian troops had retaken the whole country including the capital, Sukhumi.

Russian aid certainly secured Abkhazian independence, which created at least 200,000 Georgian refugees. In June 1994, Yeltsin enlarged Russian peacekeeping forces.

The Abkhazians felt free to organize themselves politically. Their parliament elected Vladislav Ardzinba (1945–2010) as the first president of the republic and a new constitution was adopted which maintained that Abkhazia was a sovereign state and a subject of international law. The mandate of Russian peacekeeping forces was extended until 1997 and Abkhazia remains de facto independent and is monitored by a UN Observer Mission in Georgia (UNOMIG). Apart from its enemies having Russian protection, personnel and hardware, the

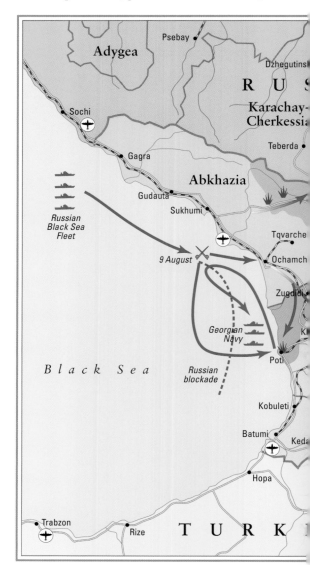

Georgian civil war weakened the state to such an extent that for a time the southern areas of Georgia were ruled by local Armenians or Azeris and much of the rest by local clan-based satraps, many of them resentful of central government authority.

Since then, Georgian bargains with Russia have secured Russia three military bases in Georgia in return for a training and supply package. Limited military cooperation with NATO in its Partnership for Peace program was a step towards respectability on the world stage, as was an International Monetary Fund loan worth approximately US$40 million at the end of 1994. A shift in attitude occurred in September 1997 when Abkhazia was prepared to sign a protocol for the establishment of a union state of equal partnership with Georgia; key policy areas, such as foreign affairs, defense, and foreign economic relations would be jointly administered. This policy foundered and fighting has occasionally broken out, noticeably in the South Ossetian War in 2008. Russian forces remain in Abkhazia.

In time, central government control was restored in ethnically Georgian areas and a democratic regime was consolidated, but this has reduced neither internal political conflict in Georgia nor the standoff between Georgia and the de facto independent regions of Abkhazia and South Ossetia. When the Georgian government attempted to reassert control over South Ossetia by force in 2008, it was stopped by Russian military intervention.

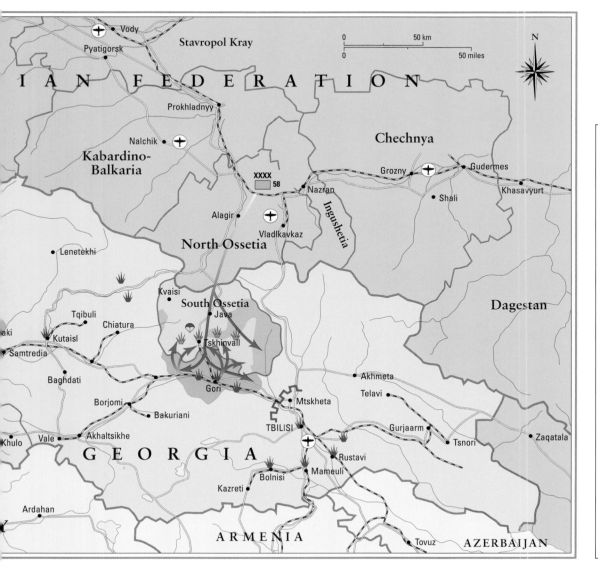

Russo-Georgian War
7–12 August 2008

Georgian offensive 7–10 August

Russian counteroffensive 8–16 August

Area shelled by Georgian artillery

Russian air attacks

Russian naval movements

Georgian naval movements

Territory controlled by the breakaway republics of Abkhazia and South Ossetia prior to the war

Abkhazia and South Ossetia territory loyal to the Georgian government that was lost to the separatists and Russian forces

Georgian territory (outside Abkhazia and South Ossetia) occupied by the Russian army

Georgian defensive position after 11 August

Russian airborne forces

Naval engagements

Airports

Russia, NATO, and the New European Order

When the Soviet Union dissolved into its constituent republics in December 1991, the geopolitical structure of Europe changed. The Russian Federation hoped to establish a Commonwealth of Independent States comprising all the former Soviet republics, but only a limited version emerged. While Soviet Cold War organizations such as the Warsaw Pact and Comecon vanished, the West retained its North Atlantic Treaty Organization and the European Union. In this fluid situation the former Cold War enemies needed to achieve or keep national security while NATO had to find a new role in the world.

In 1994 NATO offered former Warsaw Pact members the Partnership for Peace program, which allowed them to participate in joint exercises and peacekeeping operations. The Russians viewed this move with suspicion.

Europe faced its first post-Cold War challenge when Yugoslavia collapsed and a series of wars followed involving the successor states of Slovenia, Croatia, Bosnia-Herzegovina, Kosovo, and eventually Serbia, which was bombed by NATO in 1999. The Bosnian War commenced in 1992 and the scale of the violence led the United Nations, on 9 October 1992, to order a no-fly zone over Bosnia-Herzegovina, which NATO began enforcing in April 1993. When the 1995 Dayton Agreement ended the war, NATO stationed a UN-mandated force in the region known as IFOR (Implementation Force) which developed into SFOR (Stabilization Force). Serbia had been allied with Russia but the Russian Federation joined in IFOR, SFOR, and then in Kosovo. Russian co-operation showed that, despite damage done to Serbia, Russia was willing to engage in peacekeeping operations with its former Cold War enemies. But the West's decision to create an independent Kosovan state angered Moscow and fed a Russian belief that the Western powers flouted international law when it suited them.

Russia also resented the move of its former satellites towards NATO, which was enlarged by the membership of Poland, Hungary, and the Czech

New European Order 1993

——— Western border of the USSR to 1991

- - - Former satellite states of the USSR

■ Independent 1991

■ Independent 1992

□ Independent 1993

━━━ Yugoslavia to 1991

━━━ Czechoslovakia to 1993

■ NATO members by 1990

Republic in 1999 and by Bulgaria, Slovakia, Slovenia, and Romania in 2004. In 2004 Estonia, Latvia, and Lithuania also joined NATO, bringing that military organization right to the Russian border, which was seen as an alarming development and as the most flagrant breach of what Moscow believed had been a Western promise to Gorbachev not to extend NATO eastwards. Albania and Croatia joined NATO in 2009, and Moscow deeply feared that other states—above all Ukraine—would do so in the future.

However, in the aftermath of the 2001 attacks on the World Trade Center, Russia's supportive reaction led to a thaw in relations. In 2002 the NATO-Russia Council was established, giving Russia an equal role in shaping policy toward terrorist threats.

Since losing the buffer zone of Eastern Europe and the Baltic States to NATO, Russia has attempted to create a new redoubt against the West. A military treaty with Belarus has pushed a massive salient westward, outflanking the three Baltic countries to the north and Ukraine, with its pro-European tendencies, to the south. Russia has also prepared its own version of the Monroe Doctrine, which proclaimed, in 1823, that efforts by European powers to interfere in the Americas would be met by US intervention. Russia has provided peacekeeping troops to resolve ethnic conflict in the former USSR in Moldova and Georgia (South Ossetia and Abkhazia), lest others intervene. This type of policy commenced when Russian troops were deployed in Tajikistan to defend the country from guerrilla fighters from Afghanistan. Russia also increases its power and influence by recognizing separatist regions as sovereign republics. Russia can use its supplies of oil and gas to ensure that small states trade with Russia to create Russian hegemony.

Other security policies are a common defense agreement with Kazakhstan and a number of military bases abroad that Russia maintains. These comprise: troop compounds in South Ossetia and Abkhazia; air bases in Belarus and Armenia; a peacekeeping operation in Transnistria; and bases in Tajikistan, Kazakhstan, and Kyrgyzstan. Russia is also seeking naval facilities around the world to complement those in Syria and Vietnam.

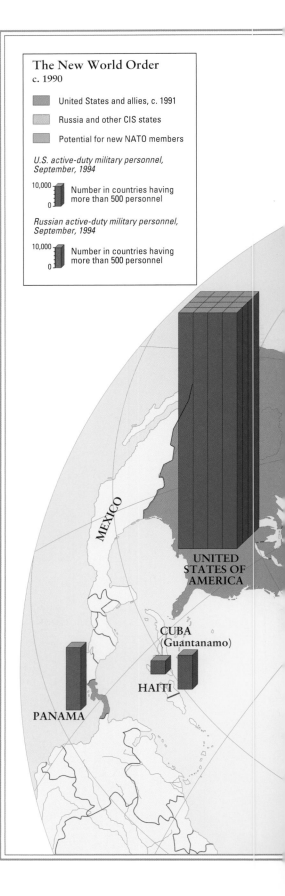

The New World Order
c. 1990

United States and allies, c. 1991

Russia and other CIS states

Potential for new NATO members

U.S. active-duty military personnel, September, 1994

10,000
0
Number in countries having more than 500 personnel

Russian active-duty military personnel, September, 1994

10,000
0
Number in countries having more than 500 personnel

MEXICO

UNITED STATES OF AMERICA

CUBA
(Guantanamo)

HAITI

PANAMA

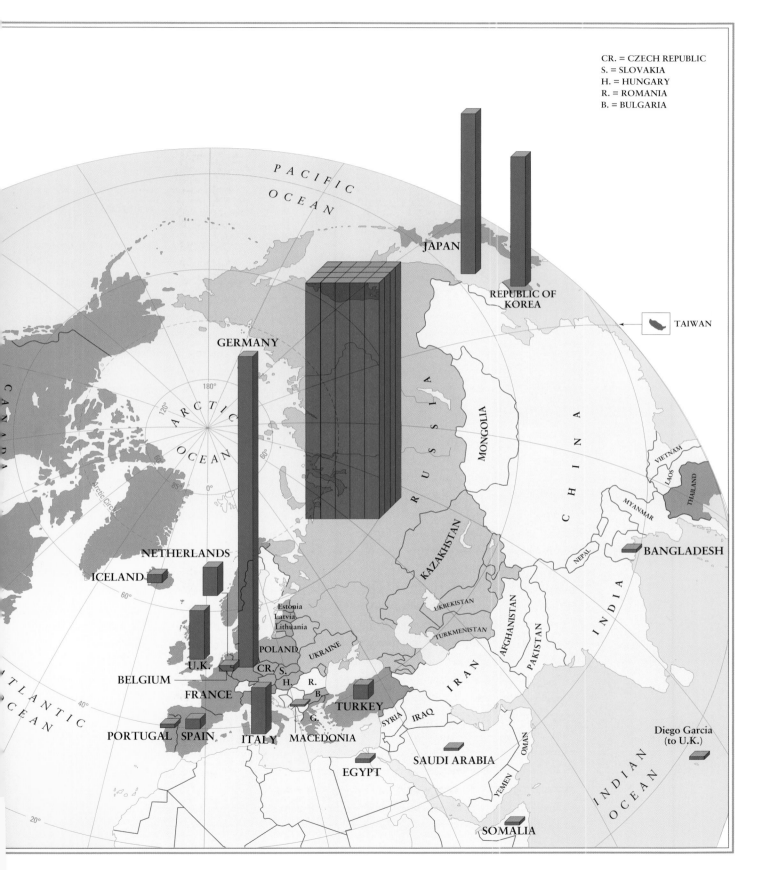

CR. = CZECH REPUBLIC
S. = SLOVAKIA
H. = HUNGARY
R. = ROMANIA
B. = BULGARIA

The Putin Era

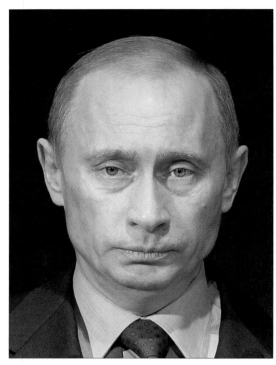

Vladimir Vladimirovich Putin spent 25 years in the KGB after graduating in Law from university, spending several of those years as a spy in the Cold War. He became Russian President in 2000.

Vladimir Putin graduated from the law faculty of Leningrad University and was then recruited into the KGB's espionage operations and posted to Dresden in East Germany for fifteen years. His task, allegedly, was to audit the political loyalties of Soviet officers and soldiers stationed there. In 1990 Putin retired from the KGB to work for Anatoly Sobchak (1937–2000), one of his old university tutors, a liberal and St. Petersburg's first mayor. After Sobchak's failure in the 1996 elections, Putin relocated to Moscow to become deputy to Pavel Borodin (born 1946), Yeltsin's political manager. By March 1997 Putin was head of the Kremlin's Control Department, which monitored relations with Russia's 89 regions. He prevented regional leaders seceding from Russia and this earned him the soubriquet "imperialist." In July 1998, he was moved to run the Federal Security Service (FSB), the KGB's successor. Sponsored by Anatoly Chubais (born 1955), he was also appointed to the Security Council, the advisory organization that helps to coordinate the armed forces and security apparatus.

The stage was now set for a battle royal between the oligarchs, who required Putin to defend their interests. Their backing would determine the outcome of the presidential race. The lines were drawn between the Yeltsin "family" and new enemies. Yeltsin first fought the duma, which evolved into a conflict between a reinvigorated Communist Party and Yeltsin supporters. An alliance between regional leaders and certain politicians was a key factor in apportioning political power in Russia. The periphery was pulling away from the political center and former links were being weakened. The election would decide any new power center.

However, Yeltsin had a plan of his own. He realized that the economy was in meltdown and he needed a successor who would be strong, ruthless, and not a communist. Putin, who had become prime minister in 1999, was achieving public acclaim for the way in which he conducted the Second Chechen War during his premiership. Then, on 31 December 1999, Yeltsin announced that he intended to resign and that Putin would take over the duties of president until the next presidential election in a few months time. Meanwhile a new party, Unity, had been cobbled together to back Putin in the elections. On 26 March 2000, Putin won 52.94 percent of the vote, while his most dangerous rival, the communist Gennady Zyuganov (born 1944) only gained 29.21 percent. Compared with the sick old man Yeltsin, Putin appeared as a teetotaling, tough character.

The Chechen War was the arena that consolidated Putin's reputation. Some insurgents from an earlier conflict in Dagestan had fled to Chechnya to use it as a base for Islamicist rebels. When several apartment blocks were blown up in Russian cities in September 1999 Putin accused the Chechens and utilized the events as a casus belli to attack Chechnya. Bombings and invasion followed. Political opponents, including former FSB officer Alexander Litvinenko (1962–2000), accused FSB officers of causing the explosions to provide Putin with reasons for attacking the republic. This story never went away: Litvinenko fled to England where he

Russian Oil Exports

Oil pipeline

Proposed oil pipeline

Gas pipeline

Proposed gas pipeline

Russian-dominated pipeline
(all or most of the oil or gas
moving through these pipelines
is from Russia)

Tanker terminal

worked with the exiled oligarch Boris Berenovsky, who repeated the allegations. When Litvinenko died after being poisioned by radioactive polonium-210, relations between Moscow and London soured. Journalist Anna Politkovskaya (1958–2006), who wrote about the incident, was shot dead in a lift in her apartment block on 7 October 2006, having worked for the highly critical *Novaya Gazeta*. She was one of some 300 journalists who have been killed or disappeared since 1993. The message seems to be that criticism of the Kremlin can result in terrible punishment.

Autocracy was on the march, demonstrated by the Kremlin's undemocratic move against the 89 federal regions of Russia. Their leaders would no longer be elected but appointed by the Kremlin. These federal regions were then grouped into eight federal districts, each administered by an envoy appointed by

the president, who would liaise between the Kremlin and regions to ensure regional compliance. A further occasion of government hostility towards criticism had occurred when the nuclear submarine *Kursk* sank in the Barents Sea in August 2000. Putin was on holiday at Sochi on the Black Sea and waited five days before he broke his holiday to make public statements, a poor exercise in public relations. Oligarch Vladimir Gusinsky's NTV Channel criticized the

Kremlin's handling of the situation. Putin was aware how Yeltsin had suffered from media handling, so Gusinsky was pressured into handing his media operations to the state and was held under arrest until he completed the hand-over documentation after which he fled to Israel. In the following years all independent mass-media outlets were closed down or acquired by the state, and freedom of speech was severely constrained.

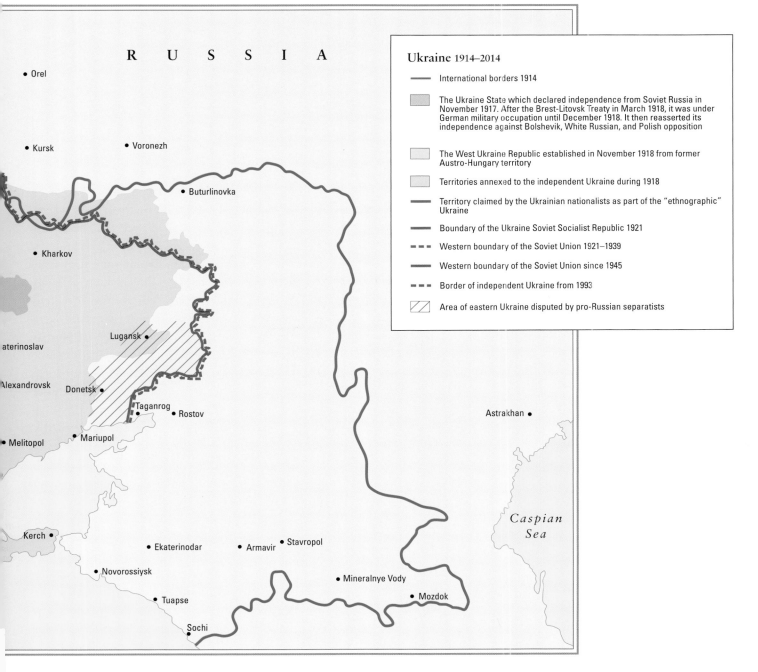

Ukraine 1914–2014

—— International borders 1914

     The Ukraine State which declared independence from Soviet Russia in November 1917. After the Brest-Litovsk Treaty in March 1918, it was under German military occupation until December 1918. It then reasserted its independence against Bolshevik, White Russian, and Polish opposition

     The West Ukraine Republic established in November 1918 from former Austro-Hungary territory

     Territories annexed to the independent Ukraine during 1918

—— Territory claimed by the Ukrainian nationalists as part of the "ethnographic" Ukraine

—— Boundary of the Ukraine Soviet Socialist Republic 1921

--- Western boundary of the Soviet Union 1921–1939

—— Western boundary of the Soviet Union since 1945

--- Border of independent Ukraine from 1993

     Area of eastern Ukraine disputed by pro-Russian separatists

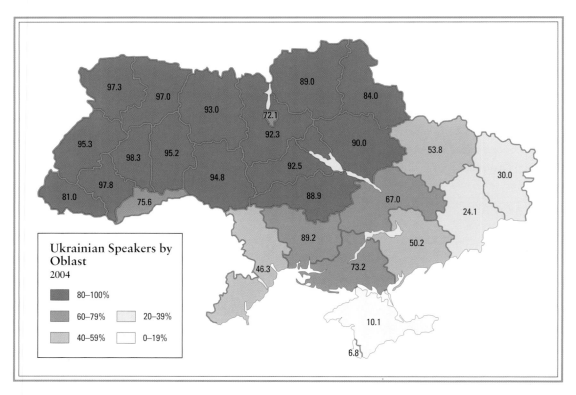

Ukrainian Speakers by Oblast
2004

- 80–100%
- 60–79%
- 40–59%
- 20–39%
- 0–19%

Putin was determined to rein in the power of other oligarchs and summoned them to the Kremlin in summer 2000. He intended to strike a deal whereby they agreed to keep out of politics in return for him not interfering with their business interests nor overturning the privatization process that had given them their wealth. They would not be able to fund political parties, seek political power, criticize or attack Putin. Berezovsky, who had bankrolled Putin's election, now considered Putin a dangerous *parvenu*, and decamped to London. Roman Abramovich agreed to abide by Putin's rules, and although he also traveled to London, where he bought Chelsea Football Club, he is free to return to Russia whenever he wishes.

One of the richest oligarchs, Mikhail Khodorkovsky, felt he was above the rules. During Yeltsin's privatization, Khodorkovsky had gained possession of the Yukos oil company, which owns 20 percent of Russia's oil. Khodorkovsky financed several political parties and hoped to play a major role in politics. In October 2003, Putin had the businessman arrested. His assets were frozen and he was presented with reassessed tax bills that he could not pay owing to the freeze. Yukos was thus bank-

rupted and Khodorkovsky was tried and sentenced to eight years in a labor camp. The state now owned Yukos assets and sold them off cheaply to oil companies owned by the government, ensuring that the state sector of the economy was now strengthened. In 2009, a new trial was held accusing the oligarch of embezzlement and money laundering. Found guilty, he was sentenced to fourteen years' imprisonment, thereby keeping him away from two more presidential elections. As this suggests, Russian courts obey the orders of the political leadership.

Putin gathered more power as he removed or "purged" the liberals who constituted the political elite at the time he became president. The old liberal order of ministers and administrators was gradually replaced by men drawn from Putin's colleagues when he worked in St Petersburg and by personnel drawn from the KGB and FSB. These "siloviki," or "strongmen," normally adopted a Russian nationalist and statist position. National unity and integrity plus a strong state were considered essential ingredients in ruling a country extending 6,000 miles from west to east. The most prominent of this group were presidential aides

Viktor Ivanov (born 1950) and Igor Sechin (born 1960) and defense minister Sergei Ivanov (born 1953). Various estimates have been made as to how many of these so-called siloviki hold positions in the higher reaches of government, which range from 30 to 70 percent.

Although the public were delighted to see the oligarchs receive their comeuppance, they have been replaced by virtually more of the same. The siloviki appear to be a replacement class serving its own corporate interests by running the state. Igor Sechin is still head of Rosneft, the huge oil company that took over many Yukos assets, while Sergei Ivanov runs Russia's largest arms manufacturers. Others run the state export bank and the railroads while Dmitri Medvedev (born 1965), who became president after Putin completed his second presidential term, was a former chairman of the state gas monopoly, Gazprom.

Putin's presidential successes have focused on ending the economic meltdown under Yeltsin. The reduction of income tax and other economic concessions together with the demand for Russian oil and gas resulted in economic growth every year until 2008. This enabled the government to pay salaries on time, restore some welfare services, and improve urban living standards. Together with an ending of the political instability of the 1990s and a reassertion of Russian interests in the international context, this contributed to Putin's popularity.

Gas pipelines from Russia to Germany have created energy dependence on Russia in Europe while another gas line stretches to the Pacific to feed China, Japan, and Korea. The steady growth rates meant that Russia gained self-confidence and could act in a fairly aggressive way on the world stage and towards former constituent republics of the USSR. As European countries needed Russian oil and gas they were hardly critical of alleged human rights abuses and the unusual use of the judiciary to eliminate those criticizing Kremlin policy.

When NATO expanded into East and Central Europe, the United States considered placing a missile shield in those countries, eliciting a damning response from Putin, who realized that the Russian Federation could be the only real target. Furthermore, Putin accused the US of fishing in troubled waters in Ukraine, which was in the Russian sphere of interest. The Russians have responded by renewing strategic bombers on long flights and once again projecting Russian naval power into the Mediterranean. In Ukraine, Putin threw his verbal support behind Viktor Yanukovych (born 1950) in the 2004 presidential elections, the results of which were later declared rigged by the Ukrainian Supreme Court. The subsequent Orange Revolution brought two anti-Russian candidates to power, Viktor Yushchenko (born 1954) and Yulia Tymoshenko (born 1960). Fortunately for Moscow, Yushchenko and Tymoshenko then fell out, bungling the chances for democratic stabilization and allowing the return to power of Viktor Yanukovych. To put pressure on Ukraine, Russian supplies of gas were briefly turned off in 2006 and 2009 in response to Ukraine's increasingly friendly relations towards the United States and NATO.

When Putin's second presidency ran out in 2008, a deal was done by which Dmitri Medvedev would stand with Putin's backing and that of his party, Yedinstvo, which had carried 66 percent of the vote in the 2007 duma elections. Medvedev won 70 percent of the vote, became president and appointed Putin as his prime minister. The next presidential election was in March 2012 and Putin stood while Medvedev agreed not to stand. However, the duma elections on 4 December 2011 saw Putin's party, United Russia, lose its constitutional two-thirds majority, although it retained an absolute majority. Against a background of accusations of electoral fraud, with dead people apparently voting in some constituencies, demonstrations were held in Moscow demanding new elections and the resignation of Putin. Putin won 63.6 percent of the vote in March 2012 and has continued to run a strong, increasingly authoritarian (though not totalitarian) government. The annexation of Crimea in 2014 greatly enhanced Putin's flagging popularity though at the expense of inciting Western sanctions and harming Russia's already stagnating economy.

Russia's Shadow Empire

When the Soviet Union fragmented in 1991, millions of people went to bed in one country and awoke in a different one. As a result, the Russian people became one of the biggest ethnic groups in the world to be divided by borders. Partly because of economic migration and planned resettlement programs during the Soviet era, Russian speakers extended into territories that were historically a part of the Russian Empire, such as Kazakhstan. President Putin has vowed to defend all ethnic Russians wherever they live. He is also prepared to project Russian power into former regions of the Russian Empire. This nationalist tone raises the cohesiveness of Russian-speaking populations in Russia's neighbors and inside Russia itself.

In Estonia and Latvia, the language issue is important. Twenty-six percent of Latvia's population are Russian-speakers who initially faced difficulties gaining citizenship. Government policies have relaxed but Russian-speakers are now protesting against plans to teach certain secondary school subjects in Latvian alone. Estonia initiated a language test for acquiring citizenship, which was seen as discrimination, and this has now relaxed with the Russian population, which accounts for a quarter of the whole, gradually acquiring Estonian citizenship. Interestingly, Putin has announced new pensions for Soviet-era veterans living in the Baltics and Russian diplomats have been distributing Russian passports to ethnic Russians. These are attempts to exert Russian influence in the Baltic region, where both Estonia and Latvia are members of NATO.

Putin has publicly stated that the area of Moldova known as Transnistria or Trans-Dniestr comprises parts of old Russian Bessarabia, as do parts of Ukraine, and he calls these areas "Novorossiya", or New Russia. The secessionist Republic of Transnistria is defended not by just its own troops but by Russian military units stationed there and this is set to continue for the next twenty years. When the Crimea acceded to the

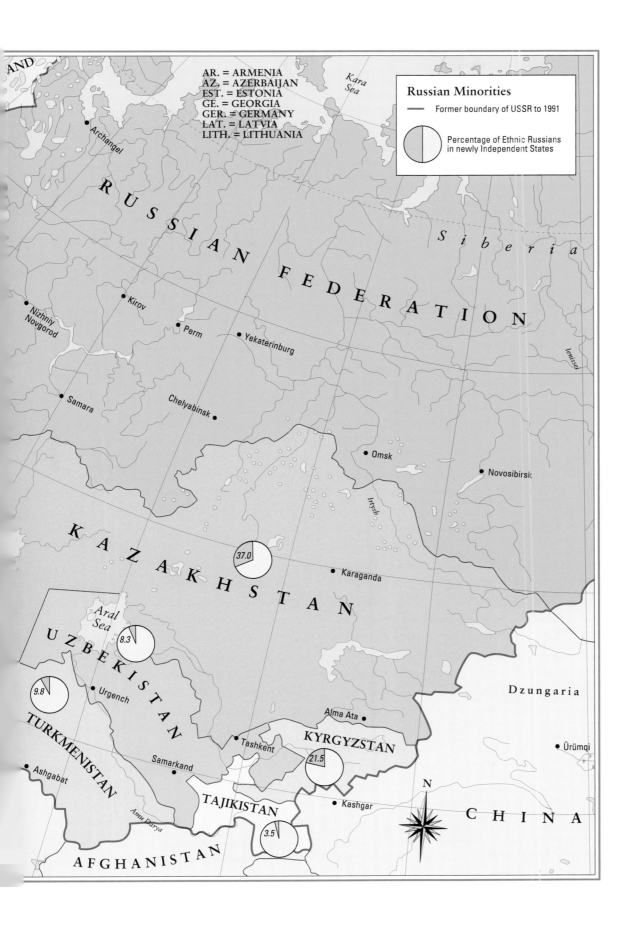

AR. = ARMENIA
AZ. = AZERBAIJAN
EST. = ESTONIA
GE. = GEORGIA
GER. = GERMANY
LAT. = LATVIA
LITH. = LITHUANIA

Russian Minorities

— Former boundary of USSR to 1991

Percentage of Ethnic Russians
in newly Independent States

Kara Sea

Siberia

RUSSIAN FEDERATION

• Archangel

• Kirov

• Nizhniy Novgorod

• Perm

• Yekaterinburg

• Samara

Chelyabinsk •

• Omsk

• Novosibirsk

Irtysh

Ienissei

KAZAKHSTAN

37.0

• Karaganda

Aral Sea

UZBEKISTAN

8.3

9.8

• Urgench

Dzungaria

TURKMENISTAN

• Alma Ata

KYRGYZSTAN

• Ashgabat

Samarkand •

• Tashkent

21.5

• Ürümqi

N

TAJIKISTAN

• Kashgar

CHINA

Amu Darya

3.5

AFGHANISTAN

A protester waves a pro-Russian flag in central Sevastopol, March 2014.

Russian Federation in March 2014, the head of the Transnistrian parliament asked to join the Russian Federation. In some ways, Putin might be seen as "gathering the lands of Rus," as had Ivan III and Basil III of Muscovy. The only countries recognizing Transnistrian independence are the Republics of South Ossetia, Abkhazia, and Nagorno-Karabakh.

The Caucasus has been a region of conflict with Russian forces engaged in Georgia. South Ossetians separatists fought with the Georgians in the 1991–92 South Ossetian War, which ended with part of South Ossetia under the control of a Russian-backed, but internationally unrecognized, government. A joint peacekeeping force of South Ossetians, Russians, and Georgians was stationed in the region and and a similar situation existed in Abkhazia after the 1992–93 war for Abkhazian independence from Georgia. Violence recommenced in April 2008 when South Ossetians attacked Georgian villages. The Georgians launched a full-scale military operation on 7/8 August, provoking regular and airborne Russian troops to enter South Ossetia to drive out the Georgians. Simultaneously, the Abkhazians and Russians attacked the only piece of Abkhazia still in Georgian hands, the Kodori Gorge. Russian planes bombed various Georgian targets and a Russian naval blockade of the Georgian coast was established with one Georgian missile boat being sunk. After the war, Russian troops were stationed in both Abkhazia and South Ossetia and Russian air defense missile systems were sited in both republics. The Russian ruble is the currency unit of Abkhazia while the South Ossetian economy is heavily reliant on Russian aid and on serving the Russians deployed in the republic.

Russia remains Armenia's patron, which has upset Azerbaijan in disputes with Armenia over the sovereignty of the Republic of Nagorno-Karabakh. Russia supplies arms, and engages in officer training with Armenia's army. Russia has military bases in Armenia and a defense agreement signed in August 2010 ensures a Russian military presence until 2044, with Russia committed to supplying modern weaponry and mili-

tary hardware at reduced prices.

In Kazakhstan, ethnic Russians constituted some 40 percent of the population in 1979. In 2009, this number had shrunk to 23.7 percent, with most Russians living in north Kazakhstan where they comprise over half the population. Policies promoting the Kazakh language meant that some jobs are inaccessible to ethnic Russians and their concerns reached Putin's ears. However, the Russian Federation has obtained leverage in Kazakhstan because Kazakhstan, Russia, and Belarus signed the Eurasian Economic Union treaty in May 2014. Putin's stated goal is to enlarge the Union to include all post-Soviet states.

The most important events in the Russian Federation's "expansion" occurred in 2014 in the Crimea and Ukraine. In Ukraine the desire to join the European Union sparked fierce debates, with some citizens preferring closer ties with the Russian Federation. Ethnic Russians in Ukraine, some 17 percent of the population, felt threatened because Russian was not an official language. Pro-European Ukrainians took to the streets and in February 2014 the violence led to the impeachment of President Viktor Yanukovych (born 1950), who fled the country. The replacement president was Petro Poroshenko (born 1965) who wanted to regularize relations with Russia and end unrest in the country.

An interim government was formed but not accepted by Putin. Pro-Russian forces in the Crimea, which had a majority of Russian inhabitants, gradually took control of the peninsula, and seized the Crimean parliament. The parliament voted to dismiss the Crimean government, replace its prime minister, and decided to hold a referendum on Crimea's autonomy from the Ukraine. The outcome of the vote, the validity of which has been questioned, was to declare independence from Ukraine and the parliament asked to join the Russian Federation. A treaty of accession was signed by Crimea, the federal city of Sevastopol and the Russian Federation on 18 March. Ukrainian forces were evicted from their Crimean bases and were withdrawn from the region.

The firmly Russian areas of Ukraine in the

eastern cities, located in the provinces of Donetsk and Lugansk, established pro-Russian militias, which have seized administrative buildings in the cities and declared the founding of the Donetsk People's Republic and the Lugansk People's Republic, both of which have joined in the self-proclaimed Federal State of Novorossiya. These separatists have occupied tracts of eastern Ukraine and are alleged to have received support from Russian Federation military units, weaponry, and finance. Putin has been accused of deliberately destabilizing Ukraine, which already has a large outstanding energy debt owed to Russia. Fierce fighting has seen rebel-held lands recaptured and then seized again. Ceasefires break down and it is feared that if rebel and Ukrainian forces withdraw from the front lines then a de facto statelet of Novorossiya will remain behind, propped up by the Russian Federation, with a Ukrainian army in-

capable of combating Russian forces.

It appears that Putin is not seeking to rebuild the Soviet Union but to create economic union in Asia. Armenia, Tajikistan, and Kyrgyzstan will probably join the Eurasia Union next and Uzbekistan is supportive. Others expressing a wish to join are the Republics of Transnistria, South Ossetia, Abkhazia, and also the Autonomous Territorial Unit of Gaugauzia in Moldova. Putin has succeeded in boosting Russian consciousness and self-confidence and in protecting Russians in other countries as a means of pressuring these states to create a shadow empire. However, war in the Donbass, where the Russian Federation claims to have no troops stationed, has led to the spectre of Russian casualties returning to Russian soil. Putin must also take notice of the anti-war protest marches that occurred in Moscow in fall 2014, which condemned intervention in Ukraine.

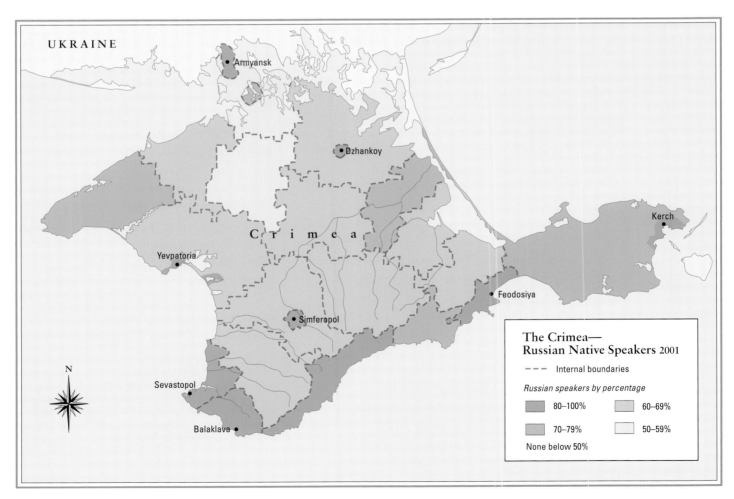

The Crimea—
Russian Native Speakers 2001

– – – Internal boundaries

Russian speakers by percentage

- 80–100%
- 70–79%
- 60–69%
- 50–59%
- None below 50%

RUSSIAN RULERS

TRADITIONAL FOUNDER OF THE RURIK
DYNASTY IN NOVGOROD

Ryurik

REIGNS OF THE PRINCES AND GRAND
PRINCES OF KIEV, 900s–1240

Igor ?–945

Sviatoslav, 945–72

Iaropolk I, 972–80

Vladimir I, Saint, 980–1019

Sviatopolk, 1015–19

Iaroslav I, the Wise and Mstislav I, the Brave
1019–36

Iaroslav I, the Wise (ruling alone), 1037–54

Iziaslav I, 1054–76, 1078

Sviatoslav II, 1076–78

Vsevolod I, 1078–94

Sviatopolk II, 1094–1113

Vladimir II Monomakh, 1113–25

Mstislav II, the Great, 1125–32

Iaropolk II, 1132–39

Vsevolod II of Chernigov, 1138–46

Iziaslav II of Volynia, 1146–54

Iuri Dolgoruky of Rostov–Suzdal, 1155–57

Rostislav of Smolensk, 1158–67

Iziaslav III of Volnyia, 1167–69

Gleb of Southern Pereyaslavl, 1169–71

Iaroslav of Volynia, 1172–74

Sviatoslav of Chernigov, 1174–94

Ryurik, of Smolensk, 1194–1203, 1205–11

Roman of Volynia, 1203–05

Vsevolod Chermny of Chernigov, 1211–12

Mstislav of Smolensk, 1212–23

Vladimir of Smolensk, 1223–1236, 1236–38

Yaroslav of Northern Pereyaslavl, 1236

Mikhail of Chernigov, 1236–39

Danilo of Halych–Volynia, 1239–40

REIGNS OF THE GRAND PRINCES OF
VLADIMIR, 1155–1327

Andrei, Bogolyubsky, 1155–74

Vsevolod, Big Nest, 1176

Iuri, 1212–16, 1218–38

Konstantin, 1216–18

Iaroslav, 1238–46

Sviatoslav, 1246–47

Andrei, 1247–52

Alexander Nevsky, 1252–63

Iaroslav, 1264–72

Basil Yaroslavich, 1272–76

Dmitrii, 1277–94

Andrei, 1294–1304

Mikhail of Tver, Saint, 1304–18

Iuri of Moscow, 1318–22

Dmitrii of Tver, 1322–26

Alexander of Tver, 1326–27

REIGNS OF THE GRAND PRINCES OF
VLADIMIR & MOSCOW, 1326–1547

Ivan I, Kalita, 1328–41

Simeon, the Proud, 1341–53

Ivan II, 1353–59

Dmitrii Donskoi, 1359–89

Basil I, 1389–1425

Basil II, 1425–33, 1434, 1434–35, 1447–62

Iuri, 1433, 1434

Dmitrii Shemyaka, 1445–47

Ivan III, the Great, 1462–1505

Basil III, 1505–33

Ivan IV, 1533–47, (–1584)

REIGNS OF THE RUSSIAN TSARS, EMPERORS, & EMPRESSES

Ivan IV, Grozny, (1533) 1547–84

Theodore I, 1584–98

Boris Gudonov, 1598–1605

False Dmitrii, 1605–06

Basil Shuisky, 1606–10

Interregnum, 1611–12

Michael Romanov, 1613–45

Alexis, 1645–76

Theodore II, 1676–82

Peter I and Ivan V, 1686–96

Peter I (sole ruler), the Great, 1696–1725

Catherine I, 1725–27

Peter II, 1727–30

Anna, 1730–40

Ivan VI, 1740–41

Elizabeth, 1741–61

Peter III, 1761–62

Catherine II, the Great, 1762–96

Paul I, 1796–1801

Alexander I, 1801–25

Nicholas I, 1825–55

Alexander II, 1855–81

Alexander III, 1881–94

Nicholas II, 1894–1917

LEADERS OF THE RUSSIAN PROVISIONAL GOVERNMENT, 1917

Prince George Lvov

Alexander Kerensky

SOVIET LEADERS

Vladimir Lenin, 1917–24

Joseph Stalin, 1928–53

Nikita Khrushchev, 1953–64

Leonid Brezhnev, 1964–82

Iuri Andropov, 1982–84

Konstantin Chernenko, 1984–85

Mikhail Gorbachev, 1985–91

LEADERS OF THE RUSSIAN REPUBLIC, 1991–

Boris Yeltsin, 1991–99

Vladimir Putin, 2000–2008

Dmitri Medvedev, 2008–12

Vladimir Putin, 2012–

GLOSSARY

ASSR

An Autonomous Soviet Socialist Republic, normally housing a minority within a union republic, with a higher status than an oblast (housing a small ethnic group) and an okrug (an autonomous administrative area in the north housing indigenous people). Examples of ASSRs are Abkhaz ASSR and Chechen-Ingush ASSR.

Black Hundreds

Ultra-nationalist, conservative supporters of the Romanovs. They were noted for their xenophobia, anti-Semitism and incitement of pogroms.

Bolshevik

From the Russian term meaning "one of the majority," the Bolsheviks emerged as a faction of the Social-Democratic Party in 1903, under the leadership of Lenin, and ultimately seized political power in 1917. The Bolsheviks were a highly centralized, disciplined party, who considered themselves the leaders of Russia's revolutionary working class.

Boyar

Wealthiest elite in Kievan Rus. Moscow boyars became the ruling class.

Brussels Treaty

A treaty signed in March 1948 between the UK, France, Belgium, and Luxemburg. It contained a mutual defense clause.

Causus belli

Cause of war

Cheka

(Extraordinary Commission to Combat Counterrevolution, Sabotage and Speculation). A Soviet state security organization, created in 1917, and headed by Felix Dzerzhinsky. As the military and security arm of the Bolsheviks, the Cheka played a significant role in the Red Terror, and became notorious for torture and summary execution.

CIS (Commonwealth of Independent States)

An association of sovereign states, formed by Russia and eleven republics that were formerly part of the Soviet Union. The city of Minsk in Belarus is the administrative center. The CIS coordinates members' policies on foreign relations, defense, economics, environmental protection, and law enforcement.

Comecon

Council for Mutual Economic Assistance, which lasted from 1949 to 1991. Initial members were the USSR and the Eastern bloc.

Cominform

Information Bureau of the Communist and Workers' Parties. Founded in 1947, this Soviet-dominated organization sought to coordinate Communist Parties around the world.

Comintern (Communist International)

An international communist organization founded in 1918 to "fight by all available means, including armed force, for the overthrow of the international bourgeoisie and for the creation of an international Soviet republic as a transition stage to the complete abolition of the State."

Composite bow

A bow made from wood, horn, and sinew, sometimes known as a re-curved bow. This weapon was used by horse archers of the steppes.

Druzhina

The band of warriors who followed Rus leaders in exacting tribute.

Duma

A council of boyars advising the grand dukes and tsars of Russia. It was discontinued by Peter I and reinvented as a limited parliamentary assembly after 1905.

Dunkirk Treaty

Treaty signed on 4 March 1947 between France and the UK as a Treaty of Alliance and Mutual Assistance against a possible German attack after World War Two but really aimed at the USSR.

Glasnost

This term, meaning openness and transparency in government, was used by Mikhail Gorbachev in an attack on corruption.

GPU

The successor to the Cheka, this political police

agency (State Political Administration) was formed in 1926 and was succeeded by the NKVD in 1934. The GPU became the OGPU (Unified State Political Administration), under the Council of People's Commissars of the USSR.

Gulag
(Chief Administration of Corrective Labor Camps). This term refers to the Soviet system of transit, detention, and forced labor camps that housed the political prisoners of the Soviet Union from the 1920s to the 1950s. The Gulag was under the control of the secret police (OGPU, NKVD and KGB) and, by 1936, housed some five million prisoners. The majority of the camps, which housed between 2,000 and 10,000 prisoners, were "corrective labor camps," and it is estimated that, because of the harsh conditions in which they lived and near starvation, 10 percent of the Gulag population died each year.

Kadet
Informal name for the Constitutional Democratic Party of the Russian Empire, which was a political home for intellectuals, professionals, university academics, and lawyers.

KGB
(Committee for State Security). The main government security agency for the USSR from 1954–91, responsible for internal intelligence, security and the secret police. The KGB was divided into approximately 20 directorates, and was an army service, governed by army regulations.

Kulak
The word means "tight-fist" and refers to the independent farmers who benefitted from the Stolypin land reforms (1906–17). The term was used by Stalin to designate class enemies.

League of Armed Neutrality
Catherine II created the first League of Armed Neutrality during the American War of Independence in March 1780. She contended that neutral countries could trade with belligerent countries except in weapons and military supplies. It was joined by Denmark, Sweden, Prussia, the Holy Roman Empire, the Netherlands, Portugal, the Kingdom of the Two Sicilies, and the Ottoman Empire.

Menshevik
From the Russian term meaning "one of the minority," the Menshevikes were a minority faction of the Social-Democratic Party, who split from the Lenin-dominated majority (Bolsheviks) in 1903. They were led by Julius Martov, and maintained that the proletariat could not dominate a bourgeois revolution and sought to establish a liberal, capitalist regime. After the 1917 revolution the Mensheviks were disunited and were unable to form a legal opposition.

Miklagarð
This Viking name for Constantinople means "big city".

Mir
A self-governing community of peasant households.

Nakaz
An Enlightenment-based set of legal principles written by Catherine II.

Narodniki
A group of nineteenth-century socialists who believed that educating the peasantry with their ideas would move the masses to demand reform and so liberalize Russia.

NATO
North Atlantic Treaty Organization. Signed on 4 April 1949 as a mutual defense organization against an external threat. NATO became the main Cold War defense against the USSR and its allies.

Nazi-Soviet Pact
A treaty of non-aggression between the USSR and Hitler's Germany. A secret clause existed allowing the partition of Poland and the division of the Baltic States, Finland, and Romania into spheres of interest.

New Economic Policy (NEP)
A Leninist economic policy, also referred to as "state capitalism," which was introduced after the Russian Civil War of 1917–22. The complete nationalization of industry, instituted under War Communism, was partially reversed, and some individuals were allowed to own private enterprises, while the state continued to control banks, large industries, and foreign trade. NEP was succeeded by Stalin's policy of collectivization.

NKVD

(The People's Commissariat of Internal Affairs). The NKVD was the successor to the GPU, and was established in 1934. The NKVD was effectively a secret police organization, which was not subject to Party control or the law, and became a direct instrument of Stalin for use against the party and the country during the Great Terror of the 1930s.

Nomenklatura

The nomenklatura were members of the Communist Party who held all the important posts in the administration, government, industry, agriculture, and education. They were chosen for their tasks by the upper echelons of the Party, and according to Trotsky they were a caste operating as if they owned the state. The Yugoslavian Communist Milovan Djilas called them a new class in his book of that name and was imprisoned for his thoughts.

Oblast

A type of administrative division in the Russian Federation, which has a governor and locally elected legislature.

Oprichniki

The terror organization used by Ivan the Terrible, numbering some 6,000 men, who killed Ivan's actual enemies and those who were suspected of being so.

Oprichnina

The area of Russia set apart by Ivan IV for his personal rule.

Orgburo

The Organizational Bureau, immediately beneath the Politburo in the Communist Party hierarchy, supervised the work of local party committees and was empowered to appoint Communist cadres. The Orgburo was elected by plenums of the Central Committee, and was in place from 1919–52, when its functions were transferred to the Secretariat.

Perestroika

This policy, introduced by Mikhail Gorbachev, aimed at restructuring the political and economic system of the USSR in order to make the command economy more efficient.

Pogrom

This is a violent riot or attack on an ethnic or religious group, being most noticeably anti-Semitic in Russia. Pogroms resulted in the deaths of many Jews and the emigration of others.

Politburo

The policy-making body of the Communist Party, first established by the Bolsheviks in 1917, with seven members. The chairman of the Politburo was also the general secretary of the Communist Party, but did not necessarily hold a state office, such as prime minister. The members of the Politburo were elected by delegates of the Communist Party Congress, usually held every four to five years. In 1991, following the break-up of the Soviet Union, the Politburo was dissolved.

Pomestie

A piece of land given by the grand duke or tsar in exchange for service.

Primary Chronicle

This chronicle is a history of Kiev from about 850 to 1110 and was written in Kiev in approximately 1113.

RSFSR

Russian Soviet Federative Socialist Republic, commonly referred to as Soviet Russia or the Russian Federation, which was a sovereign state from 1917–22.

Ryutin Affair

In 1932 a group of communists, led by Martemyan Ryutin, who were opposed to Stalin's regime, distributed inflammatory pamphlets to workers and opposition members, arguing for an end to forced collectivization, the slowing down of industrialization, and the expulsion of Stalin as Soviet leader. The group was arrested in September 1932 and expelled from the Party.

Satrap

The name given to a governor of a province in the ancient Median and Persian Empires.

Soviet

Before the 1917 revolution, the term "soviet" referred to any government council. After 1917 it refers to a local council, originally elected only by manual workers, with certain powers of local administration, or to a higher council elected by a local council, which formed part of a hierarchy of soviets culminating in the Supreme Soviet.

(SSR) Soviet Socialist Republic
These ethnically based administrative units were subordinate to the Soviet government. Towards the end of the Soviet era, there were fifteen Soviet republics (excluding the Russian Federation), each with their own Communist Party, branches of the Red Army and Commissariats for foreign affairs and defense. All of the former republics that existed during the final decades of the Soviet Union are now independent states.

Stakhanovite
Named after Alexis Stakhanov, a coal miner who was reported in 1935 to have overfulfilled his daily quota by 1400 percent. Other workers soon achieved "Stakhanovite" results, and these achievements were used by the government to raise production quotas further.

Stavka
A term referring to the high command of Russian forces in both the Russian Empire and the Soviet Union.

Streltsy
From the 16th–18th centuries these units of armed guardsmen ("musketeers") formed the tsar's personal bodyguard and, through performing police and security duties, wielded considerable political influence.

Syndicalism
A type of socialist economic organization in which the workers own and run a factory for their own profit.

Trudovik
A breakaway group of Social Revolutionaries that became a party in elections to the Duma. Alexander Kerensky was a Trudovik.

Truman Doctrine
This was a pledge made by US President Harry S. Truman to support any country militarily and economically if it was threatened by communism or

the Soviet Union.

Tumen
A Mongol military unit of 10,000 men.

Varangian Guard
An elite bodyguard of the Byzantine emperor, comprising men of Scandinavian origin and subsequently Anglo-Saxons after the 1066 Norman invasion of England. Harold Hardrada of Denmark served in the Guard.

Warsaw Pact
The pact was a mutual defense system in the eight communist countries of Europe and was the counterpart to NATO in the Cold War.

Western European Union
This union took place in October 1954 when Italy and West Germany joined the Brussels Treaty.

Zemsky Sobor
The first Russian parliament of "Estates General," which assembled in the 16th and 17th centuries. Convened by the tsar, these sporadic gatherings included three estates: the clergy, boyars, and gentry (including merchants and townspeople). They varied in size from 200 to over 500 in 1614. The first full zemsky sobor was convened in 1549, during the reign of Ivan the Terrible. When the Romanovs came to power in the 17th century, the sobor gradually lost power, and the last assembly was held in 1684.

Zemstva
Plural of zemstvo. A form of limited local self-government from the 1860s. Their boards looked after roads and bridges, prisons, hospitals, and schools, and promoted new agricultural techniques and commerce.

BIBLIOGRAPHY

GENERAL WORKS

Bartlett, Roger P., *A History of Russia*, Palgrave Macmillan, Basingstoke, 2004

Bartlett, Vincent, *A History of Russian Economic Thought*, Routledge, London, 2009

Berdiaev, Nikolai, et al., *Vekhi*, M. E. Sharpe, New York, 1994

Blinnikov, Mikhail S., *A Geography of Russia and its Neighbours*, Routledge, London, 2011

Breyfogle, Nicholas B., Schrader, Abby & Sunderland, Willard (eds), *Peopling the Russian Periphery. Borderland Colonisation in Eurasian History*, Routledge, London, 2007

Channon, John & Hudson, Robert, *The Penguin Historical Atlas of Russia*, Penguin, Harmondsworth, 1995

Dewdney, John, *A Geography of the Soviet Union*, Pergamon, Oxford, 1971

Figes, Orlando, *Natasha's Dance: A Cultural History of Russia*, Penguin, London, 2003

Franklin, Simon & Widdis, Emma, *National Identity in Russian Culture: An Introduction*, Cambridge University Press, Cambridge, 2004

Freeze, Gregory L., *Russia. A History*, Oxford University Press, Oxford, 2009

Gilbert, Martin, *The Routledge Atlas of Russian History*, Routledge, London, 2007

Gleason, Abbott (ed), *A Companion to Russian History*, Blackwell, Oxford, 2007

Hoetzsch, Otto, *The Evolution of Russia*, Thames & Hudson, London, 1966

Hosking, Geoffrey, *A History of the Soviet Union*, Fontana, London, 1985

Hosking, Geoffrey, *Russia and the Russians: From Earliest Times to the Present*, Penguin Books, London, 2002

Hosking, Geoffrey, *Russia—People and Empire*, Harvard University Press, Cambridge, MA., 1998

Josephson, Paul et al, *An Environmental History of Russia*, Cambridge University Press, New York, NY, 2013

Kappeler, Andreas, *The Russian Empire: a Multi-ethnic History*, Longman, Harlow, 2001

Lieven, Dominic, *Empire: the Russian Empire and its Rivals*, John Murray, London, 2001

Lieven, Dominic (ed), *Cambridge History of Russia, Vol. 2, Imperial Russia, 1689–1917*, Cambridge University Press, Cambridge, 2006

McAuley, Mary, *Soviet Politics, 1917–1991*, Oxford University Press, Oxford, 1992

Mastiugina, Tatiana, *An Ethnic History of Russia: Pre-revolutionary Times to the Present*, Greenwood Press, Westport, CT, 1996

Miliukov, Paul, *The History of Russia: From the Beginnings to the Empire of Peter the Great. (vol. 1)*, Funk and Wagnalls, New York, 1968

Milner-Gulland, Robin, *The Russians*, Wiley-Blackwell, Oxford, 1999

Perrie, Maureen (ed), *The Cambridge History of Russia, Volume I, From Early Rus' to 1689*, Cambridge University Press, Cambridge, 2008

Riasanovsky, Nicholas V., *A History of Russia*, Oxford University Press, New York, 1969

Service, Robert, *A History of Modern Russia, From Nicholas I to Putin*, Penguin, London, 2003

Sixsmith, Martin, *Russia: A 1,000 Year Chronicle of the Wild West*, BBC Books, London, 2012

Suny, Ronald Grigor, *Cambridge History of Russia, Vol 3, The Twentieth Century*, Cambridge University Press, Cambridge, 2006

Tolz, Vera, *Russia*, Arnold, London, 2001

THE SLAVS AND THE KIEVAN RUS

Barford, P. M., *The Early Slavs: Culture and Society in Early Medieval Eastern Europe*, British Museum Press, London, 2001

Bronsted, *The Vikings*, Penguin Books, Harmondsworth, 1973

Chaliand, Gérard, *Nomadic Empires: From Mongolia to the Danube*, Transaction Publishers, New Brunswick, NJ, 2004

Christian, David, *A History of Russia, Central Asia and Mongolia, vol. I, Inner Eurasia from Pre-history to the Mongol Empire*, Blackwell, Oxford, 1998

Clarkson, J.D., *A History of Russia from the Ninth Century,*

Longman, London, 1962

Dolukhanov, Pavel, *The Early Slavs: Eastern Europe from the Initial Settlement to the Kievan Rus*, Routledge, London, 1996

Fennell, John, *The Crisis of Medieval Russia, 1200–1304*, Longman, New York, NY, 1983

Franklin, Simon & Shepard, Jonathan, *The Emergence of Rus, 750–1200*, Longman, London, 1996

Halperin, Charles J., *Russia and the Golden Horde: The Mongol Impact on Medieval Russian History*, John Wiley and Sons, Hoboken, NJ, 1987

Obolensky, Dimitri, *Byzantium and the Slavs*, St. Vladimir's Seminary Press, Crestwood, NY, 1994

Obolensky, Dimitri, *The Byzantine Commonwealth: Eastern Europe, 500–1453*, Cardinal, London, 1974

Rice, Tamara T., *The Scythians*, Thames & Hudson, New York, NY, 1961

Sedlar, Jean W., *East Central Europe in the Middle Ages, 1000–1500*, University of Washington Press, Seattle, WA, 1994

Vernadsky, George, *Kievan Russia*, Yale University Press, London, 1972

MUSCOVY

Blum, Jerome, *Lord and Peasant in Russia: From the Ninth to the Nineteenth Century*, Princeton University Press, Princeton, New Jersey, 1961

Crumney, Robert O., *The Formation of Muscovy*, Longman, London, 1987

De Hartog, Leo, *Russia and the Mongol Yoke: The History of the Russian Principalities and the Golden Horde, 1221–1502*, British Academy Press, London, 1996

De Madariaga, Isobel, *Ivan the Terrible*, Yale University Press, London, 2006

Dunning, Chester, S. L., *Russia's First Civil War. The Time of Troubles and the Founding of the Romanov Dynasty*, Pennsylvania State University Press, University Park, PA, 2001

Khodarkovsky, Michael, *Russia's Steppe Frontier. The Making of a Colonial Empire, 1500–1800*, Indiana University Press, Bloomington, IN, 2003

Kollman, Nancy S., *Kinship and Politics: The Making of the Muscovite Political System, 1345–1547*, Stanford University Press, Stanford, CA, 1987

Longworth, Philip, *Alexis, Tsar of All the Russias*, F. Watts, New York, NY, 1984

Martin, Janet, *Medieval Russia, 980–1584*, Cambridge University Press, Cambridge, 2007

Ostrowski, Donald, *Muscovy and the Mongols. Cross-cultural Influences on the Steppe Frontier, 1304–1589*, Cambridge University Press, Cambridge, 2002

Pavlov, Andrei P., *Ivan the Terrible*, Pearson/Longman, London, 2003

Perrie, Maureen, *Pretenders and Popular Monarchism in Early Modern Russia. The False Tsars of the Time of Troubles*, Cambridge University Press, Cambridge, 1995

Skrynikov, Ruslan G., *Ivan the Terrible*, Academic International Press, Gulf Breeze, FL, 1981

THE ROMANOVS, 1613–1825

Anderson, M. S., *Peter the Great*, Longman, New York, NY, 2000

Boeck, Brian J., *Imperial Boundaries. Cossack Communities and Empire Building in the Age of Peter the Great*, Cambridge University Press, Cambridge, 2009

Bushkovitch, Paul, *Peter the Great*, Rowman & Littlefield, Oxford, 2003

Cracraft, James, *The Revolution of Peter the Great*, Harvard University Press, Cambridge, MA, 2003

De Madariaga, Isobel, *Catherine the Great: A Short History*, Yale University Press, London, 2002

Dixon, Simon, *Catherine the Great*, Longman, Harlow, 2001

Dixon, Simon, *The Modernisation of Russia, 1676–1825*, Cambridge University Press, Cambridge, 1999

Hartley, Janet, *Alexander I*, Longman, London, 1994

Hartley, Janet, *A Social History of the Russian Empire, 1650–1825*, Longman, London, 1993

Hughes, Lindsey, *Russia in the Age of Peter the Great*, Yale University Press, Harmondsworth, 2000

Hughes, Lindsey, *Sophia, Regent of Russia, 1657–1704*, Yale University Press, New Haven, CT, 2000

Kahan, Arcadius, *The Plow, the Hammer and the Knout: An Economic History of Eighteenth Century Russia*, University of Chicago Press, Chicago, Il, 1985

Kamenskii, Aleksandr, and Griffiths, David, *The Russian Empire in the Eighteenth Century: Tradition and Modernisation*, M.E. Sharpe, New York, NY, 1997

Konstam, Angus, *Poltava 1709*, Osprey Publishing, Oxford, 1994

LeDonne, John P., *The Russian Empire and the World, 1700–1917: the Geopolitics of Expansion and Containment*, Oxford University Press, New York, 1997

Lieven, Dominic, *Russia Against Napoleon. The Battle for Europe, 1807–1814*, Penguin Books, London, 2010

Longworth, Philip, *Alexis, Tsar of All the Russias*, F. Watts, New York, NY, 1984

Pipes, Richard, *Russia under the Old Regime*, Penguin, Harmondsworth, 1995

Riasanovsky, Nicholas, *Nicholas I and Official Nationality in Russia, 1835–1855*, University of California Press, Berkeley, CA, 1992

Stiles, Andrina, *Russia, Poland and the Ottoman Empire, 1725–1860*, Hodder and Stoughton, London, 1991

REACTION AND REFORM, 1825–1906

Crisp, Olga & Edmondson, Linda, (eds), *Civil Rights in Imperial Russia*, Oxford University Press, Oxford, 1989

Eklof, B., Bushnell, J. and Zakharova, L. (eds), *Russia's Great Reforms 1855–1881*, Indiana University Press, Bloomington, 1994

Emmons, Terence, *The Russian Landed Gentry and the Peasant Emancipation of 1861*, Cambridge University Press, Cambridge, 2008

Emmons, Terence and Vucinich, Wayne S., *The Zemstvo in Russia. An Experiment in Local Self-government*, Cambridge University Press, Cambridge, 2011

Lieven, Dominic, *Nicholas II, Emperor of all the Russias*, John Murray, London, 1993

Lincoln, W. Bruce, *Nicholas I*, Indiana University Press, Bloomington, IN, 1978

Nish, Ian, *The Origins of the Russo-Japanese War*, Longman, Harlow, 1985

Polunov, Alexander, Zakharova, Larissa and Shetz, Marshall, S., *Russia in the Nineteenth Century: Autocracy, Reform and Social Change, 1814–1914*, M. E. Sharpe, Armonk, NY, 2005

Saunders, D., *Russia in the Age of Reaction and Reform, 1801–1881*, Longman, London, 1992

Small, Hugh, *The Crimean War: Queen Victoria's War with the Russian Tsars*, Tempus Publishing Ltd., Stroud, 2007

Waldron, Peter, *Russia of the Tsars*, Thames & Hudson, London, 2011

Wallace, Sir Donald, *Russia on the Eve of War and Revolution*, Random House, New York, 1961

RUSSIAN REVOLUTION AND AFTERMATH

Acton, Edward, *Rethinking the Russian Revolution*, Edward Arnold, London, 1990

Acton, Edward, Cherniaev, Vladimir and Rosenberg, William (eds), *Critical Companion to the Russian Revolution 1914–1921*, Edward Arnold, London, 1997

Balzer, Harley, D., *Russia's Missing Middle Class. The Professions in Russian History*, M. E. Sharpe, Arnonk, New York and London, 1996

Brooks, Jeffrey and Chernyavsky, George, *Lenin and the Making of the Soviet State: A Brief History with Documents*, Palgrave Macmillan, Basingstoke, 2007

Carr, Edward H. and Davies, R., *The Russian Revolution from Lenin to Stalin, 1917–1929*, Palgrave Macmillan, Basingstoke, 2003

Figes, Orlando, *A People's Tragedy: The Russian Revolution, 1891–1924*, Pimlico, London, 1997

Gatrell, Peter, *The Tsarist Economy 1850–1917*, Batsford, London, 1986

Gatrell, Peter, *Russia's First World War: A Social and Economic History*, Longman, London, 2005

Keegan, John, *The First World War*, Random House, London, 1998

Lenin, Vladimir, I., *The State and Revolution*, Penguin Books, Harmondsworth, 1992

Lieven, Dominic, *Towards the Flame: Empire, War and the End of Tsarist Russia*, Penguin, London, 2015

Lincoln, W. Bruce, *In War's Dark Shadow: The Russians before the Great War*, Oxford University Press, Oxford, 1994

Lockhart, Bruce, *Memoirs of a British Agent*, Macmillan, London, 1985

Mawdsley, Evan, *The Russian Civil War*, Birlinn Ltd., Edinburgh, 2008

Miller, Martin A., *The Russian Revolution: The Essential Readings*, Wiley-Blackwell, Oxford, 2000

Pipes, Richard, *The Russian Revolution, 1899–1919*, Fontana, London, 1992

Pipes, Richard, *Russia under the Bolshevik Regime, 1919–1924*, Fontana, London, 1995

Read, Christopher, *Lenin: A Revolutionary Life*, Routledge, London, 2005

Read, Christopher, *Revolution in Russia, 1914–22: The Collapse of Tsarism and the Establishment of Soviet Power*, Palgrave Macmillan, Basingstoke, 2013

Reed, John, *Ten Days That Shook the World*, Penguin Books, Harmondsworth, 1966

Sanborn, Joshua A., *Imperial Apocalypse: The Great War and the Destruction of the Russian Empire*, Oxford University Press, Oxford, 2014

Service, Robert, *The Russian Revolution, 1900–1927*, Macmillan, London, 1991

Service, Robert, *Trotsky*, Pan Books, London, 2010

Smele, Jonathan, D., *The 'Russian' Civil Wars 1916–1926: Ten Tears that Shook the World*, C. Hurst & Co. Publishers, London, 2015

Stone, Norman, *The Eastern Front, 1914–1917*, Penguin Books, London, 2008

Swain, Geoffrey, *Trotsky and the Russian Revolution*, Routledge, London, 2014

Thatcher, Ian D., *Trotsky*, Routledge, London, 2003

Wade, Rex A. (ed), *Revolutionary Russia: New Approaches to the Russian Revolution of 1917*, Routledge, London, 2004

STALIN, HIS REGIME, AND WORLD WAR II

Alliluyeva, Svetlana, *Twenty Letters to a Friend*, Hutchinson, London, 1967

Applebaum, Anne, *Gulag: A History of the Soviet Camps*, Penguin, London, 2004

Applebaum, Anne, *Iron Curtain: The Crushing of Eastern Europe, 1944–56*, Penguin, London, 2013

Barber, John, *The Soviet Home Front, 1941–1945: A Social and Economic History of the USSR in World War II*, Longman, London, 1991

Bethel, Nicholas, *The Last Secret*, Futura, London, 1976

Beevor, Antony, *Stalingrad*, Penguin, London, 2007

Bullock, Alan, *Hitler and Stalin: Parallel Lives*, HarperCollins, London, 1991

Carruthers, Bob and Erickson, John, *Russian Front, 1941–45*, Orion, London, 2000

Clark, Lloyd, *Kursk. The Greatest Battle*, Headline Review, London, 2012

Erickson, John, *The Road to Berlin*, Cassell Military, London, 2003

Erickson, *The Road to Stalingrad*, Cassell Military, London, 2003

Fitzpatrick, Sheila, *Everyday Stalinism: Ordinary Life in Extraordinary Times, Soviet Russia in the 1930s*, Oxford University Press, Oxford, 1999

Forczyk, Robert, *Where the Iron Crosses Grow. The Crimea 1941–44*, Osprey Publishing, Oxford, 2014

Geliately, Robert, *Stalin's Curse: Battling for Communism in War and Cold War*, Oxford University Press, Oxford, 2013

Getty, J. Arch, Naumov, Oleg V., and Sher, Benjamin, *The Road to Terror: Stalin and the Self-destruction of the Bolsheviks, 1932–1939*, Yale University Press, London, 2010

Harrison, Mark, *Soviet Planning in Peace and War 1938–1945*, Cambridge University Press, Cambridge, 1985

Hughes, Gwyneth and Welfare, Simon, *Red Empire: The Forbidden History of the USSR*, Weidenfeld & Nicolson, London, 1990

Kotkin, Stephen, *Magnetic Mountain: Stalinism as a Civilization*, University of California Press, Berkeley, 1995

Kotkin, Stephen, *Stalin: Paradoxes of Power 1878–1928*, Allen Lane, London, 2014

Moorhouse, Roger, *The Devils' Alliance: Hitler's Pact with Stalin, 1939–1941*, Bodley Head, London, 2014

Nettl, J.P., *The Soviet Achievement*, Thames and Hudson, London, 1967

Newton, Steven H., *German Battle Tactics on the Russian Front, 1941–45*, Schiffer Publishing Ltd., Atglen, PA, 2004

Overy, Richard, *Russia's War*, Penguin, London, 2010

Priestland, David, *Stalinism and the Politics of Mobilisation. Ideas, Power and Terror in Inter-war Russia*, Oxford University Press, Oxford, 2007

Solzhenitsyn, Alexandr, *One Day in the Life of Ivan Denisovich*, Penguin Books, Harmondsworth, 1972

Solzhenitsyn, Alexandr, *Rebuilding Russia*, The Harvill Press, London, 1991

Zaloga, Steven J., *The Red Army of the Great Patriotic War, 1941–45*, Osprey Publishing, Oxford, 1989

Zubkova, Elena, *Russia After the War: Hopes, Illusions, and Disappointments, 1945–1957*, M.E. Sharpe, Armonk, 1998

KHRUSHCHEV TO CHERNENKO

Bacon, Edwin et al., *Brezhnev Reconsidered*, Palgrave Macmillan, Basingstoke, 2003

Braithwaite, Rodric, *Afgantsy. The Russians in Afghanistan, 1979–1989*, Profile Books, London, 2012

Filzer, Donald, *The Khrushchev Era – Destalinisation and the Limits of Reform in the USSR, 1953–1964*, Macmillan, London, 1993

Fursenko, Alexander, and Nattali, Timothy, *'One Hell of a Gamble': Khrushchev, Castro and Kennedy, 1958–1964*, W.W. Norton, New York, 1997

Khrushchev, Nikita (Trans. Strobe Talbot), *Khrushchev Remembers*, Sphere, London, 1971

Litván, György (ed), *The Hungarian Revolution of 1956: Reform, Revolt, and Repression, 1953–1963*, Longman, London, 1996

Smith, Jeremy & Ilič, Melanie, *Soviet State and Society under Nikita Khrushchev*, Routledge, London, 2008

The Programme of the Communist Party of the Soviet Union, Novosti, Moscow, 1986

Taubman, William et al., *Nikita Khrushchev*, Yale University Press, London, 2000

Tompson, William, *Khrushchev – A Political Life*, Macmillan, London, 1995

Volkogonov, Dmitri A., *The Rise and Fall of the Soviet Empire: Political Leaders from Lenin to Gorbachev*, HarperCollins, London, 1990

Zemtsov, Ilya, *Chernenko, the Last Bolshevik: Soviet Union on the Eve of Perestroika*, Transaction Publishers, Piscataway, NJ, 1989

GORBACHEV, YELTSIN, AND THE END OF THE USSR

Andrews, Josephine, *When Majorities Fail: the Russian Parliament 1990–1993*, Cambridge University Press, Cambridge, 2002

Breslauer, George, *Gorbachev and Yeltsin as Leaders*, Cambridge University Press, Cambridge, 2002

Brown, Archie, The Gorbachev Factor, Oxford University Press, Oxford, 1996

Chubais, Igor & Ogden, J. Alexander, *From the Russian Idea to the Idea of Russia: How We Must Overcome the Crisis of Ideas*, Harvard University Press, Cambridge, MA, 1998

Clark, Bruce, *An Empire's New Clothes: The End of Russia's Liberal Dream*, Vintage, London, 1995

Davies, Robert W., *Soviet History in the Yeltsin Era*, Macmillan, Basingstoke, 1997

Duncan, Peter, J.S., *Russian Foreign Policy from Yeltsin to Putin*, Routledge, London, 2012

Ellison, Herbert J., *Boris Yeltsin and Russia's Democratic Transformation*, University of Washington Press, Seattle, WA, 2007

Ellison, Michael, and Kantorovich, Vladimir (eds), *The Destruction of the Soviet Economic System: An Insider's History*, M.E. Sharpe, Armonk, 1998

Frazer, Graham & Lancelle, George, *Zhirinovsky: The Little Black Book – Making Sense of the Senseless*, Penguin Books, Harmondsworth, 1994

Freeland, Chrystia, *Sale of the Century: the Inside Story of the Second Russian Revolution*, Little, Brown Book Group, London, 2005

Hoffman, David E., *The Oligarchs: Wealth and Power in the New Russia*, Public Affairs, Jackson, TN, 2003

Hough, Jerry, *Democratization and Revolution in Russia, 1985–1991*, Brookings, Washington DC, 1997

Khazanov, A. M., *After the USSR: Ethnicity, Nationalism and Politics in the Commonwealth of Independent States*, University of Wisconsin Press, Madison, WI, 1996

Marples, David R., *The Collapse of the Soviet Union, 1985–1991*, Longman, Harlow, 2004

Miller, John, *Mikhail Gorbachev and the End of Soviet Power*, Macmillan London, 1993

Neumann, Iver B., *Russia and the Idea of Europe*, Routledge, London, 1996

Richards, Susan, *Epics of Everyday Life: Encounters in a Changing Russia*, Penguin Books, Harmondsworth, 1991

Sakwa, Richard, *Russian Politics and Society*, Routledge, London, 2008

Vardis, Vytas S. & Sedaitis, Judith B., *Lithuania: The Rebel Nation*, Westview Press, Boulder, CO, 1997

THE PUTIN ERA

Arutunyan, Anna, *The Putin Mystique: Inside Russia's Power Cult*, Skyscraper Publications, London, 2014

Bacon, Edwin, *Contemporary Russia*, Palgrave Macmillan, Basingstoke, 2014

De Haas, Marcel, *Russia's Foreign Security Policy in the 21st Century: Putin, Medvedev and Beyond*, Routledge, London, 2011

Garrard, John & Carol, *Russian Orthodoxy Resurgent: Faith and Power in the New Russia*, Princeton University Press, Princeton, NJ, 2014

Judah, Ben, *Fragile Empire: How Russia Fell in and Out of Love with Vladimir Putin*, Yale University Press, New Haven, CT, 2013

Laruelle, Marlene (ed), *Russian Nationalism and the Reassertion of Russia*, Routledge, London, 2010

Lucas, Edward, *The New Cold War: Putin's Threat and the West*, Bloomsbury Paperbacks, London, 2014

Roxburgh, Angus, *The Strongman: Vladimir Putin and the Struggle for Russia*, I. B. Tauris, London, 2011

Sakwa, Richard, *Putin: Russia's Choice*, Routledge, London, 2007

Shevtsova, Lilia, *Russia Lost in Transition: The Yeltsin and Putin Legacies*, Carnegie Endowment for International Peace, Washington DC, 2007

Shoemaker, M. Wesley, *Russia and the Commonwealth of Independent States*, Rowman and Littlefield, Oxford, 2014

Sixsmith, Martin, *Putin's Oil: The Yukos Affair and the Struggle for Russia*, Continuum Publishing Corporation, London, 2010

Treisman, Daniel, *The Return: Russia's Journey from Gorbachev to Medvedev*, The Free Press, New York, 2012

Van Herpen, Marcel H., *Putin's Wars: The Rise of Russia's New Imperialism*, Rowman and Littlefield, Oxford, 2014

Vymyatina, Yulia & Antonova, Dana, *Creating a Eurasian Union: Economic Integration of the Former Soviet Republics*, Palgrave Macmillan, Basingstoke, 2014

White, Stephen, *Understanding Russian Politics*, Cambridge University Press, Cambridge, 2011

Nationhood in the Caucasus, New York University Press, New York, NY, 2007

SUCCESSOR STATES AND REPUBLICS

Gammer, Moshe, *The Lone Wolf and the Bear: Three Centuries of Chechen Defiance of Russian Rule*, C. Hurst, London, 2006

Hill, William H., *Russia, the Near Abroad: Lessons from the Moldova-Transdniestra Conflict*, Johns Hopkins University Press, Baltimore, MD, 2012

Hunter, Shireen, *Islam in Russia: the Politics of Identity and Security*, M. E. Sharpe, London, 2004

Kalter, Johannes & Pavaloi, Margareta, *Uzbekistan*, Thames & Hudson, London, 1997

Kasekamp, Andres, *A History of the Baltic States*, Palgrave Macmillan, Basingstoke, 2010

Lieven, Anatol, *Chechnya: Tombstone of Russian Power*, Yale University Press, New Haven, CT, 1998

Payasian, Simon, *The History of Armenia*, Palgrave Macmillan, Basingstoke, 2008

Rayfield, Donald, *Edge of Empires: A History of Georgia*, Reaktion Books, London, 2012

Saparov, Arsène, *From Conflict to Autonomy in the Caucasus: The Soviet Union and the Making of Abhkazia, South Ossetia, and Nagorno-Karabakh*, Routledge, London, 2014

Smith, Jeremy, *Red Nations: the Nationalities Experience in and After the USSR*, Cambridge University Press, Cambridge, 2012

Smith, Sebastian, *Allah's Mountains: The Battle for Chechnya*, I. B. Tauris, London, 2005

Taagepera, Rein, *The Finno-Ugric Republics and the Russian State*, Hurst and Co., London, 1999

Tsutsiev, Arthur & Favorov, Nora Seligman, *Atlas of the Ethno-political History of the Caucasus*, Yale University Press, New Haven, CT. 2014

Wilson, Andrew, *Belarus. The Last European Dictatorship*, Yale University Press, London, 2011

Wilson, Andrew, *Ukraine Crisis: What it Means for the West*, Yale University Press, New Haven, CT, 2014

Wilson, Andrew, *Ukraine's Orange Revolution*, Yale University Press, London, 2005

Zürcher, Christopher, *The Post-Soviet Wars: Rebellion, Ethnic Conflicts, and Nationhood in the Caucasus*, New York University Press, New York, NY, 2007

ACKNOWLEDGMENTS

The publishers would like to thank the following picture libraries for their kind permission to use their pictures and illustrations:

RLPPMA Ltd   36, 58, 146
Getty Archive   8, 22, 28, 38, 50, 54, 70, 82, 84, 96, 104,106, 108, 116, 146, 172, 192, 200

For Historia Publishing Limited:
Cartography: Jeanne Radford, Alexander Swanston, Malcolm Swanston and Jonathan Young
Typesetting: Jeanne Radford
Picture Research: Malcolm Swanston
Editor: Elizabeth Wyse
Additional contribution by Professor Dominic Lieven

INDEX

MAP LIST